Debating Federalism

Debating Federalism

From the Founding to Today

Edited and Introduced by
Aaron N. Coleman and Christopher S. Leskiw

LEXINGTON BOOKS
Lanham • Boulder • New York • London

Published by Lexington Books
An imprint of The Rowman & Littlefield Publishing Group, Inc.
4501 Forbes Boulevard, Suite 200, Lanham, Maryland 20706
www.rowman.com

6 Tinworth Street, London SE11 5AL, United Kingdom

British Library Cataloguing in Publication Information Available

Library of Congress Cataloging-in-Publication Data

ISBN 978-1-4985-4287-6 (cloth : alk. paper)
ISBN 978-1-4985-4289-0 (pbk. : alk. paper)
ISBN 978-1-4985-4288-3 (electronic)

♾™ The paper used in this publication meets the minimum requirements of American National Standard for Information Sciences—Permanence of Paper for Printed Library Materials, ANSI/NISO Z39.48-1992.

Printed in the United States of America

Aaron: To my parents, Jerry and Sue. For instilling in me a love of learning, the value of hard work, the importance and necessity of sacrifice, and for showing me, through example, how to be a loving and devoted parent, I dedicate this work to you.

Chris: To my family, my students, and to the Lord Almighty.

Contents

Acknowledgments

This project developed quickly and soon became one of love. But like most who seek to turn a project into a publication, we needed our fair share of assistance. Those who aided us in completing this edition share in its successes, but are absolved from any potential oversights we might have made. In particular, we must thank our two tireless assistants, Ms. Esmerelda Garcia and Ms. Sara Donahue. Ms. Garcia may be one of the most joyful people we have known. As an undergraduate student, her tireless energy, unflagging happiness, and incredible work ethic made the tracking down, typing, and formatting of a large number of the documents in the collection possible. Simply put, without her, this project would not have seen the light of day. We are honored to know her and be her teachers. We look forward to the bright future that she has. Ms. Donahue, the History and Political Science Department's administrative assistant, not only typed a number of documents, aided us in formatting them, and setting the table of contents, but she did all of this while also juggling the other responsibilities of running a department full of forgetful professors. For that alone, we are amazed. Considering how she did all this while keeping a wonderful sense of humor and her ever-present laugh, makes it all the more impressive. A huge thanks and our deepest gratitude to the both of them. In all seriousness, this project would not have been possible without you!

Also, we would like to thank Brian Hill and Eric Kuntzman, our acquisitions editors at Lexington. From the initial email where we broached the idea of a federalism reader, both Brian and Eric have been supportive—and intensely patient—of this project. Knowing we had their enthusiastic backing made us even more determined to see this work in print. Thank you both!

Finally, we would like to thank the teachers who attended our "Federalism: From the Founding to Today" Professional Development training in late 2015. It was from this event and our excellent discussions that lead us to consider publishing a document collection on federalism. Thank you!

AARON

First, I must thank my coeditor, Chris Leskiw. This project was a team effort, and I could not have had a better teammate. Although the academic life can sometimes lead to jading and cynicism, Chris remains bereft of these traits. I consider myself very blessed to call him my Vice President for Academic Affairs, colleague, coeditor, and, more importantly, friend.

Additional thanks to my great friends David Hollingsworth and Adam Tate who encouraged the development of this work and offered suggestions for documents. Also deserving of thanks is Josh DeBorde. Our Appleby's conversations about history, politics, and the differences and similarities of teaching High School and College courses are always a bright spot for me. Thank you for what you do in the classroom and for your enthusiasm for this project!

Thanks to my parents, Jerry and Sue, who gave the kind of encouragement that only excellent parents can. I love you both dearly and my appreciation for all you've done for me is more profound than you realize.

Finally, to my wife, Emily, and our two kids, Alex and Lorelei, go my deepest thanks and love. Without the three of them, none of this would be worth it. Thank you for your patience, faith in me, and, greatest of all, your love.

CHRIS

I too open with a word of thanks for my coeditor and friend, Aaron Coleman. The idea of this project is really one that developed out of Coleman's notable text, *The American Revolution, State Sovereignty, and the American Constitutional Settlement, 1765–1800.* His text exemplifies the importance of primary source research. As educators, it is our desire to equip our students with the ability to make well-informed arguments and decisions. Primary source materials play a key role in this process.

I am grateful for the students whom I taught over the last decade and a half. It never gets old to see them captivated by the richness and complexity only a primary source document can provide.

A Note on Documents and Editing

The documents included in this collection range from treatises, pamphlets, letters, speeches, presidential actions, and court cases. Many have never been published in any modern collection. The book is divided into four themes: sovereignty/reserved powers, civil rights, commerce clause, and incorporation. We selected these themes partially because of the quantity of sources on these topics, but, more importantly, because they are the key themes debates over federalism have historically revolved. Although thematically organized, the documents are arranged chronologically. Doing so allows readers to trace the historical development of that particular theme. Many of the documents could be put in various categories, of course, but we elected to place them in the most relevant theme. For example, President Johnson's veto of the 1866 Civil Rights Act addressed the fundamental question of sovereignty and reserved powers, but it did so because of the context of civil rights. Thus, we placed it under the Civil Rights section.

A note on the editing method needs mentioning. The quantity and size of some of the sources demanded editing, but we took every effort to preserve as much of the documents as possible. Doing so, we believe, allows the sources to speak for themselves as much as possible. This, in turn, gives readers a greater understanding of author's arguments. In editing the documents, we used ellipses to signify breaks inside of sentences and within paragraphs as well as at the start of a paragraph that was not the original next paragraph in the document. If a paragraph continued but we edited it out, we did not use ellipses to signify that the paragraph continued. We stopped the paragraph with the last relevant word. We felt that too many ellipses would be too confusing to readers (and some documents, court cases especially, already have numerous ellipses). In the court cases, we edited out most of the citations to other cases. Also, we elected to not include any description or background to

xvi A Note on Documents and Editing

the individual documents. Doing so would have not only consumed valuable space, thus leading to fewer documents, but since we hope this book will be used in various history and political science courses, we do not want to provide any undue influence to students and other readers. We want readers to develop their own interpretations rather than be influenced by ours. Instead, each document segment has its own broad introduction that ties into the introductory essay. Finally, we did not include the Declaration of Independence nor the Constitution in our collection. The absence of these two foundational documents may appear odd in a collection on federalism but given the ease of access to these documents, we did not believe it necessary to include them.

Aaron N. Coleman and Christopher S. Leskiw,
May 17, 2018

Introductory Essay

Aaron N. Coleman and Christopher Leskiw

"SPLITTING THE ATOM OF SOVEREIGNTY?": FEDERALISM IN AMERICAN HISTORY

Federalism represents one of the most important American contributions to constitutionalism. Most Americans today, however, have very little understanding of what federalism means and its importance throughout American history. While Americans recognize the value of their state governments, the natural assumption today is that the federal government can exercise nearly any power it wants over any issue. This belief manifested itself during the contentious debate over the Affordable Care Act when a constituent questioned California representative, Pete Stark, on the constitutionality of the then-proposed bill. A constituent asked that since the Constitution "specifically enumerates certain powers to the federal government and leaves the other authority to the states . . . or the people. . . . And if they [the federal government] can do this, what can't they do?" Representative Stark's answer was reflexive, blunt, and perhaps more honest than he realized. "The federal government, yes, can do most anything in this country."[1] Although Stark's reply epitomizes modern assumptions on federal power, it nevertheless represents a recent, and radical, departure from American history. For most of American history, the federal government remained relatively confined in its power, with most authority resting with the states. This division of authority between the states and the federal government is known as federalism.

This essay provides an overview of federalism from the time of the American founding to today but leaves the details of those arguments and developments to the documents and the classroom.[2] Quite often, scholars and textbooks describe federalism using the metaphors of either a layered, or marbled, cake. In the layered metaphor, each level of government contains its own separate powers, static and unchanging. A marble cake federalism, by contrast, offers a blending of governmental powers. Rather than being separate and defined, they are mixed so thoroughly as to not know where one element ends and the other begins. These examples are unsatisfactory. The more accurate metaphor is "separate spheres." Not only was the term used at the time of the founding, but it better represents the division between the states and the general government. Even during the founding, however, explaining the nature and comparative sizes of these spheres proved controversial. What this collection reveals, and this essay helps explain, is that defining the size and boundaries of those separate spheres *is* the debate over federalism. This makes a federalism an attempt, often bitter and fiercely contended, to find an equilibrium within constant political, legal, social, and economic, and constitutional change.

The history of American federalism is not one of a process of a gradual evolution. Rather, crises have shaped federalism. A punctuated equilibrium model captures the contentious debate rather well. In this model, the extant system functions almost without notice to most, providing a perception of stability. This perception persists until an event occurs which brings with it the potential for sudden and possibly radical change. These shocks to the system range anywhere from long-simmering issues such as civil liberties or commerce between the states to the rather mundane, or even historically obscure issues. Any number of forces or players, such as federal and state bureaucracies, individual leaders in elected office, judges and justices, or individual citizens or corporations can upset the balance and force a recalibration of the system.

At the same time, and even with these punctuated moments, there can be no doubt that throughout the twentieth and twenty-first centuries American federalism has declined erratically, but persistently. The moments of crisis that often punctuate federalism have almost always resulted in the growth and power of the federal government. As the federal sphere has grown, the states' has atrophied, thus establishing an equilibrium that much more difficult. This decline, however, should not be viewed as a rout, at least not yet. The growth of centralization, while undeniable, has not gone unchallenged. They have been met, stymied, and sometimes defeated by those advancing a greater parity of the spheres. Excavating the history of federalism in America, therefore, uncovers a contentious constitutional concept whose influence has waxed and waned over the course of two centuries.

Sovereignty and Reserved Powers

The most important element of federalism is sovereignty. Since the writings of Jean Bodin and Thomas Hobbes of the sixteenth and seventeenth centuries, sovereignty has been defined as the supreme, unappealable power or authority in a governmental system. This belief in its indivisibility explains why sovereignty underlies practically every moment of punctuation; the core of those conflicts hinge on the question of sovereignty's location in a system of federalism. For the first century of the American experience, most Americans accepted the idea that sovereignty rested with the states, with the federal government's powers being a grant of particular powers voluntarily surrendered to the federal government. Since the Civil War, and especially during the twentieth century, that notion has flipped. Sovereignty now rests with the federal government, with the states exercising only those powers the federal government does not want.

While this dichotomy of state or federal sovereignty provides the axis of American belief on sovereignty, opposition to each side has always existed. This opposition, and their calls for sovereignty residing with the nondominant side, often provide those moments of punctuation and crisis. It is what led to the American Revolution, the writing and adoption of the Constitution, the battles between Federalists and Jeffersonians, and drove the conflict of the Civil War and Reconstruction Amendments. It provided a key source of conflict with the Progressives, the New Deal, the Great Society, and Civil Rights Movement while being a major element of Ronald Regan's political success. In more recent times, questions of sovereignty underpin major issues such as education, homosexual marriage, drug legalization, and even euthanasia.

The American Revolution represents the first of these crises over sovereignty's location. Both sides, interestingly, agreed that sovereignty remained undivided. Where they differed widely and irreconcilably was over whether that sovereignty rested with the Parliament or with the Colonial Assemblies. Parliament argued that it resided exclusively with them. By claiming an indivisible sovereignty over the whole empire, Parliament argued it could govern the colonies "in all cases, whatsoever." The American argument, of course, rejected Parliament's claim. The colonial argument drew upon a traditional imperial arrangement rooted in decentralization. This tradition led colonial Americans to consider sovereignty as being located in the Colonial Assembly, meaning that the actions of the individual colonies, which received monarchial approval, was the supreme power over each colony. Hence, instead of colonies living under a unified sovereignty in Parliament, it was thirteen separate sovereigns united only in their mutual acceptance and loyalty to the British crown.

The colonial argument against Parliamentary sovereignty established four primary ideas behind American federalism. With some modifications, these elements provide the basic refrain which has guided American understanding of federalism's importance ever since. First, they argued that sovereignty resting in the individual assemblies allowed for actual self-government.

Since colonial (and later, state) legislatures come from the same environs, possess the same concerns, wants, and desires as their neighbors, Americans believed these governments responded better to the will of the people and became harder to succumb to tyranny. A neighbor, rather than a Member of Parliament, was far less likely to enact oppressive legislation that applied to him just as much as it did his neighbor. Second, and building directly from the first point, federalism allowed diversity to flourish. It acknowledged and respected the distinct varieties of climates, geographies, economies, cultures, and religious beliefs, yet still allowed the pursuit of the common good of the collective group. Third, embracing federalism reflected the traditional Anglo-American fear of centralized, or consolidated, government. Americans considered consolidated government the opposite of self-governing; it epitomized empire and tyranny. It transformed local self-government into empire and empire brought with it a flattening—not a social leveling, necessarily, but a flattening of liberty. Under empire, the distinctions that federalism respected succumbed to a one-size-fits-all universal legislation, no matter how ungainly, counterproductive, or oppressive it might be to a particular area. In short, empire meant slavery, not chattel slavery, but political slavery, of being subjected to the arbitrary will of far-distant rulers in charge of peoples they knew little about, cared even less, and whose only concern was the glory and power of the empire. Finally, these three lessons culminated into federalism's fourth, and most important, influence on American constitutionalism, namely that federalism protected liberty. By protecting self-government, respecting the diversity of people and places, and preventing the tyranny of consolidated empire, a federalism that divided sovereignty safeguarded liberty. And since liberty required constant vigilance, a federalism allowed for the sentinels of liberty to stand guard and thwart the growth of consolidation and political slavery.

These four elements of federalism, rooted in the sovereignty of the states, became the foundational constitutional points during the American founding. Americans first constitutionalized the idea in the Article II of the Articles of Confederation. That Article, arguably the greatest expression of the American understanding of federalism and sovereignty, confirmed that "Each state retains its sovereignty, freedom, and independence, and every power, jurisdiction, and right, which is not by this Confederation expressly delegated to the United States, in Congress assembled." By noting that the states retained all authority not expressly delegated the Confederation Congress, Article II maintained an indivisible sovereignty located in the states but granted the Confederation only those powers necessary to promote the general welfare of the United States.

Not all Americans believed the states should maintain their sovereignty. A distinct minority believed, like Alexander Hamilton did, that "a want of power in Congress" represented the primary "defect" in the Articles. These nationalist Americans believed that, by 1787, the United States was in a constitutional crisis that threatened the Revolution. Hence, they sought a national government lodged with full sovereign powers. Although the Constitution that emerged from the Philadelphia Convention addressed some of their concerns, the persistent American belief in an indivisible sovereignty residing in their states defeated most of their objectives. Nevertheless, and in an attempt to win acceptance of the Constitution, supporters of the new Constitution argued that the proposed government established a "partly national, partly federal" scheme that divided sovereignty into separate spheres, with overlapping kept to a minimum and confined to issues of taxation and the militia.

Most Americans, however, initially opposed the adoption of the Constitution. They considered the Nationalists' cries of crisis little more than hyperbole with the idea of dividing sovereignty into separate spheres a "solecism." Employing the same arguments used against English during the Revolution, the Constitution's opponents believed the proposed government offered little more than a chimera of protection since no government could "suit so extensive a country, embracing so many climates and containing inhabitants so very different in manners, habits, and customs." With decision making "into the hands of a set of men who live one thousand miles distant," the taxing power; the Federal Judiciary; the Necessary and Proper Clause; the General Welfare Clause; the Times, Place, and Manner Clause of Article I, Section 4, promised to sink federalism the into an abyss of "consolidation."

Not until the Constitution's supporters agreed to amend the Constitution to include a bill of rights, and a provision acknowledging that all powers not granted to the Constitution remained reserved to the states did opponents acquiesce. By securing this amendment—what ultimately became the Tenth Amendment—and different language from Article II of the Articles of Confederation, many of the Constitution's opponents believed they secured the continuation of sovereignty resting indivisibility in the states and the new federal government only receiving the powers voluntarily surrendered by the states. In essence, they considered the amendment an acknowledgment that the Constitution represented a compact of the several states and provide an interpretative guide on the powers of the federal government.

The ratification of the Constitution and the Tenth Amendment did not end the debate. The entire decade of the 1790s was one of crisis as proponents of federal sovereignty made repeated attempts to achieve their goal. The first, and most important, punctuation came from Alexander Hamilton and his "Report on the Constitutionality of the Bank of the United States." In his report, Hamilton advanced the idea of separate spheres of sovereignty, noting how "the powers of sovereignty are in this country divided between the National and State governments." More importantly, he offered for a robust defense of what that sovereignty meant at the national level. To Hamilton, "it is unquestionably incident to sovereign power to erect corporations, and consequently to that of the United States, in relation to the objects intrusted to the management of the government."

Sovereignty, as Hamilton understood it, therefore, rejected the idea that the states still retained an indivisible sovereignty, with the Constitution containing powers surrendered by the states. His understanding of separate spheres meant that, in those areas where the federal government possessed power, the federal government wielded an indisputable sovereignty. This sovereignty, moreover, provided wide latitude in how the federal government chose to carry out its responsibilities. The Tenth Amendment, he argued, in what would become the standard interpretation of the amendment in the twentieth century, acknowledged this separate sphere claiming it "nothing more than a consequence of this republican maxim." The Constitution's enumerated powers provided only the categories of the sovereign power, rather than the actual powers, possessed by the national government. Instead of being confined by those powers, Hamilton insisted that, since the powers were categorical, the federal government, and the federal government only, could decide on how to discharge those powers. Thus, they could execute those powers as widely or narrowly as it so pleased. If those powers happened to breach powers possessed by the states, the states must yield. Since the Constitution was sovereign, it "conceded that implied powers are to be considered as delegated equally with express ones . . . because it is incident to a general sovereign or legislative power to regulate a thing, to employ all the means which relate to its regulation to the best and greatest advantage." Thus, to Hamilton and future advocates of federal power ever since, the Constitution provided the broad means in which to fulfill the sovereign ends of the national government.

Hamilton's argument remains the single most important and influential argument made in defense of national sovereignty and provided intellectual foundations to those defending expansive federal powers. John Marshall and Joseph Story in the early nineteenth century, and Abraham Lincoln and Charles Sumner later that century, and, in the twentieth and twenty-first centuries, Theodore and Franklin Roosevelt, Lyndon Johnson and George W. Bush and Barack Obama have all echoed its primary arguments. At its core, Hamilton's argument allowed the federal government to achieve broad sweeping goals and objectives, often when no clear or obvious Constitutional proscription existed. It provided the justification for the federal intervention in an issue the federal government deemed necessary. While his advocacy of separate spheres acknowledged the sovereignty of the states, his argument made it clear that the federal sphere should be the largest.

Hamilton's argument directly challenged that of his colleague, Secretary of State, Thomas Jefferson. Like Hamilton's opinion, Jefferson's emerged as an authority for those maintaining a sovereignty resting with the states. Defending the traditional American position of sovereignty resting with the states, Jefferson argued for the powers of the federal government as limited, finite, and confined strictly to the Constitution's enumerations. Should the government "take a single step beyond the boundaries thus specially drawn around the powers of Congress," meant it could claim "possession of a boundless field of power, no longer susceptible of any definition." Acquiring this unbridled power completely contradicted the language of the Tenth Amendment, which Jefferson, echoing most American's thoughts, considered the "foundation of the Constitution."

Hamilton's argument punctured state sovereignty-based federalism. While it swam upstream from the majority of American thought, it nevertheless established the groundwork for the future shift in sovereignty location to the federal government. From Hamilton's opinion onward, Americans could no longer assume or take for granted the notion of a state sovereignty-based federalism. It had to compete with repeated attempts to rupture the system and replace it with federal sovereignty.

The second great episode of punctuation in the decade occurred in 1798. In that year, the Federalist Party-controlled Congress, working from Hamilton's argument for a broad sphere of federal sovereignty, enacted the infamous Alien and Sedition Acts. The measures violated the clear language of the First and Tenth Amendments. In response, Thomas Jefferson and James Madison anonymously authored the Kentucky and Virginia Resolutions. Passed by those states respective legislatures, the Resolutions restated the principle that, when adopting the Constitution, "the several states composing the United States of America, are not united on the principle of unlimited submission to their General Government." Rather than being a separate sovereign, both Jefferson and Madison argued that the Constitution represented a compact between the several states. When states, acting through their separate ratification conventions, created the Constitution to aid in the pursuit of the more perfect union, the states retained all the powers not delegated to the federal government. The powers of the Constitution were not categorical, but confined the federal government to only those exact powers. Since the Constitution did not grant the federal government the power to limit the freedom of speech and press as well as limit the immigration of people into a state, it could not exercise that power.

As a compact between the states, Jefferson maintained "that whensoever the General Government assumes undelegated powers, its acts are unauthoritative, void, and of no force; that to this compact each state acceded as a state, and is an integral party; that the Government created by this compact was not made the exclusive or final judge of the extent of the powers delegated to itself; since that would have made its discretion, and not the Constitution, the measure of its powers; but that, as in all other cases of compact among powers having no common judge, each party has an equal right to judge for itself, as well of infractions as of the mode and measure of redress." In other words, the nature of the compact meant that the only states, not the federal government, could determine whether the federal government violated the Constitution. Madison added that whenever the federal government threatened the liberty of the people, "states who are parties thereto, have the right, and are in duty bound, to interpose for arresting the progress of the evil, and for maintaining within their respective limits, the authorities, rights and liberties appertaining to them."

Jefferson and Madison's argument represents perhaps the most aggressive defense in American history of a federal system based upon the sovereignty of the states. Not only were the states clearly sovereign and the federal government limited to only those powers the states decided to give it, but, through the exercise of their sovereignty via interposition, the states checked centralized power. At the same time, however, the idea of interposition did not emerge from Jefferson or Madison. Instead, those ideas drew from previous arguments. Merriweather Smith, for example, in his 1783 pamphlet against provisions in the Treaty of Paris, maintained that states needed to intervene to protect the liberties of their citizens. Madison himself made an argument for interposition in his contributions as "Publius" in the Federalist papers. Perhaps most ironic of all, Hamilton echoed his coauthor's argument in Federalist 26, arguing that "the State legislatures, who will always be not only vigilant but suspicious and jealous guardians of the rights of the citizens against encroachments from the federal government, will constantly have their attention awake to the conduct of the national rulers, and will be ready enough, if any thing improper appears, to sound the alarm to the people, and not only to be the VOICE, but, if necessary, the ARM of their discontent."

The arguments of Hamilton, Jefferson, and Madison became the poles of American constitutionalism. During this time, and with the election of Jefferson in 1800, the idea that the sovereignty rested with the states and the Constitution was a compact of the states dominated constitutional thinking. Moments of intense controversy certainly occurred. Two, in particular, are worth noting. The first came in 1819 with Chief Justice John Marshall's *McCulloch v. Maryland* decision. In this case, Marshall drew upon Hamilton's "Bank Opinion" and the broad definition of sovereignty it contained to defend the Second Bank of the United States. The decision proved a considerable puncturing of state sovereignty federalism. Prior to Marshall's decision, only state sovereignty received constitutional recognition through the Tenth Amendment. Hamilton's argument, while a major punctuation to that idea, remained confined to political debate only; it lacked Constitutional sanctioning. By using Hamilton's opinion and reasoning to defend the Court's opinion, the *McCulloch* decision converted the idea of broad federal sovereignty into a constitutional reality.

The Nullification Crisis of the 1830s represents the greatest moment of constitutional crisis between Jefferson's election and the Civil War. The controversy surrounded whether a state possessed the power to nullify—to make void and unenforceable in their borders—a law passed by the federal government. South Carolina's effort to nullify the Tariff of 1828, which they called the Tariff of Abominations due to its disastrous economic effect to the state, became the first real attempt to put the arguments of the Kentucky and Virginia Resolutions into practice. President Andrew Jackson, despite being an advocate of limited government and state sovereignty, rejected South Carolina's argument. Calling nullification a "strange position," that gave states the "power of resisting all laws," he noted that, "by the theory, there is no appeal, the reasons alleged by the State, good or bad, must prevail." What makes Jackson's proclamation interesting is how it straddled the Hamilton/Jefferson axis. While Jackson acknowledged the traditional Jeffersonian position that, in cases when measures are "too oppressive to be endured," the states could interpose to protect liberty. Yet, taking the more Hamiltonian position, Jackson maintained that the Constitution "forms a government, not a league and whether it be formed by compact between the States, or in any other manner, its character is the same." In those areas where the federal government had clear constitutional authority, its power was supreme. The 1828 Tariff, enacted with clear constitutional authority, meant that the states had to obey.

These two moments of punctuation, the *McCulloch* decision and the Nullification crisis, prepared the ground floor for the fundamental shift away from a federalism of sovereignty states to one of the federal government. That shift began in earnest with the greatest crisis in American history, the Civil War. When the southern states seceded in 1860–1861, they invoked the compact theory of the union as part of their justification. President Lincoln, however, rejected those arguments. He maintained, much like Daniel Webster in his famous debate with Senator Hayne in 1830, the perpetuity and indissolubility of the union. Lincoln even argued, against historical evidence, that the Union predated the states, thereby making the states the creature of the national government. This argument flipped on its head the traditional notion that sovereignty resting with the states. Complete sovereignty, in this line of thinking, rested with the federal government with the states exercising only those power the Constitution did not seek to exercise. This explains why Lincoln, in the Gettysburg Address, made the subtle, but immensely important, rhetorical shift from "union" to "nation." Union signified compact, a gathering of separate peoples into a unit while still maintaining their distinctiveness. Nation, however, meant one whole and indistinguishable body.

In other words, Lincoln's argument refuted the many of the core arguments behind federalism. This belief in a perpetual, indissoluble nation, he maintained, necessitated the need for military force. The Northern victory in the Civil War transformed Lincoln's argument into an American creed.

The theoretical transformation of the federal system emerged more prominently with other members of Lincoln's party, the Republicans. Massachusetts Senator, Charles Sumner, advanced the radical idea that when the southern states attempted to leave the union, they committed suicide and reverted to territorial status. As territories, they lacked the sovereignty possessed by the states and became subjected wholesale to the sovereignty of the federal government. This "state suicide theory" drove some of the more aggressive reconstruction policies and helped secure the idea of complete federal sovereignty. But, the domination of the radical notion of state suicide did not last. In the 1877 case of *Texas v. White*, Chief Justice, Salmon P. Chase, a Lincoln appointee, constitutionalized the slain president's general theme on the perpetuity of American federalism. In the case, Chase maintained that the "Constitution, in all its provisions, looks to an indestructible Union, composed of indestructible States."

The most important constitutional development that emerged from Civil War was the Fourteenth Amendment. Nothing has done more to alter the nature of American federalism. It recalibrated the location of sovereignty within the federal system by dramatically increasing the federal sphere while shrinking that of the states. Whether or not the drafters of the amendment intended for this alteration remains a subject of serious academic debate, but it is indisputable that the 150-year history of the amendment has accomplished this transformation. Through the amendment's provision prohibiting "State's from depriving any person of life, liberty, or property, without due process of law" the federal government, federal courts more specifically, can intervene in state actions over practically any issue, including provisions contained within the states' constitutions. As will be seen in the separate sections of this essay, the Supreme Court's interpretation of the Fourteenth Amendment as incorporating the Bill of Rights against the states sweeps across an array of issues traditionally reserved to the states. With the shift from state to federal sovereignty via the Fourteenth Amendment, the result has been the increasing elimination of the diversity that federalism preserves and the ensconcement of that one-size-fits all mentality that federalism resists. In many ways, the Fourteenth Amendment accomplishes what Virginia Plan at the Constitutional Convention failed to do, give the national government a veto over state laws.

While Civil War and Reconstruction era punctuated the traditional arrangement of federalism by initiating the transformation to federal sovereignty, the revolution was not immediate or total. The full ramifications of the Fourteenth Amendment's effect upon federalism would not occur until the twentieth century. Thus, for the first few decades after the Civil War, the traditional arrangement of federalism remained, although significantly weaker. The pace of the transformation begun by the Civil War accelerated with the two most important moments of the first half of the twentieth-century, the Progressive Movement and the New Deal.

The Progressive Movement emerged in response to the dramatic economic growth of the United States in the last decades of nineteenth century. Deeply influenced by the German political system that removed democratic processes into bureaucratic control, and believing gross inequalities and exploitation existed in America's economic expansion, self-proclaimed Progressive's sought an unelected administrative apparatus to cure these woes. This administrative state, Progressives maintained, would cure the social and economic ills they believe existed by moving the political and democratic process into the hands of unelected experts. Progress toward this utopia, therefore, required a robust, active, and indisputably supreme federal government. Federalism, however, hampered those efforts and thus became a target of progressive reform.

This desire for an expanded sphere of federal power explains why the Progressives attacked the federalism and Constitution and an outdated and obsolete obstacle. They argued instead for a "living constitution." Rather than being confined to the limits of federalism and enumerated powers as constructed by the American founders and even modified by the Civil War, Progressives, such as Albert Beveridge and Woodrow Wilson, argued that the Founders realized "the necessities of the people for all time could not possibly have been foreseen by the men who wrote the Constitution, it follows that they could not have intended to confine the purposes of the Constitution and the powers it confers to the necessities of the people of 1789; that they so wrote it that it might meet the requirements of the people for all time. . . . If that is so, it follows that the Constitution must steadily grow, because the requirements of the people steadily grow." In other words, the Founders drafted a Constitution detached from historical fetters with the flexibility necessary to address Progressive concerns.

Federalism became a casualty of the Progressive argument for a living constitution. As Progressives advanced federal policies of economic regulation, all under the guise that the new industrial age provided constitutional sanctioning of this expansion of federal sovereignty, the authority of the states became increasingly less important. Perhaps the most direct Progressive attack on federalism came from the Seventeenth Amendment. Ratified in 1913, the amendment ended the practice of state legislatures selecting Senators. Instead, Senators became elected directly through popular vote. Although Progressives asserted the Amendment was a response to the corruption of state legislatures, by removing the state legislatures from the selection process, the Amendment detached the states completely from having any role in federal policymaking. As a result, as the power of the federal government expanded, states became less able to halt invasions into their sovereignty and those powers traditionally reserved to them.

The deep puncturing to the separate spheres of federalism during the Progressive era set the stage for what remains as the greatest expansion of federal sovereignty in American history, President Franklin Roosevelt's "New Deal." Containing large elements of the earlier Progressive agenda, the New Deal sought "national planning for and supervision of all forms of transportation and of communications and other utilities which have a definitely public character." The New Deal was a complicated scheme of nationalization of large portions of the economy and a myriad of federal programs such as Social Security. Roosevelt defended the New Deal through the progressive idea of the living constitution, that "Our Constitution is so simple and practical that it is possible always to meet extraordinary needs by changes in emphasis and arrangement without loss of essential form."

Rooted in the living constitution, the Hamiltonian understanding of expansive federal sovereignty, and aided by a Supreme Court that dismissed the Tenth Amendment's stipulation for reserved powers as nothing more than a "truism" that had no interpretive power, the New Deal attacked the foundations of federalism. With its centralized program of economic recovery all rooted in bureaucratic executive agencies administered, distant and unelected rulers made decisions for people and places they knew little about. Federalism's purpose of stopping one-size-fits-all legislation ill-suited for distinct geographies and peoples died as the New Deal came alive. The broad sweeping powers and intervention of the New Deal left little room for the states to act in ways that they believed best for their state. In other words, the federal government, and only the federal government, provided the ways and means economic recovery. Although Roosevelt claimed that his actions would not alter the "essential form" of the Constitution, nevertheless, a fundamental alteration did occur. The New Deal moved sovereignty away from the separate spheres into a single sphere of federal power.

The half-century following the New Deal witnessed the near uninterrupted growth of federal sovereignty. In areas of Housing and Urban Development and Education, to President Lyndon Johnson's Great Society and War on Poverty, the federal government increasingly nationalized areas historically and constitutionally reserved to the states. The result was the final and complete puncturing of federalism as understood at the time of the founding. Sanctioned by nearly six decades of uninterrupted Supreme Court decisions that upheld the expansive use of federal power, sovereignty was now located in the federal government. What was left to the states were only those powers the federal government chose not to exercise. Attempts to explain this new extant system often used the term "corporative federalism." Under this reasoning, the federal government worked with the states to provide grants for the state governments to administer federal programs. Proponents asserted that this "marbled cake" approach, the other name for corporative federalism, allowed for a shared governance and responsibility. Instead of sovereignty flowing from the states, or even the Hamiltonian idea of sovereignty being divided into two separate spheres, corporative federalism turned the states into administrative agencies of the federal government. When corporative federalism was combined with the Fourteenth Amendment and the incorporation doctrine (discussed below), the authority of the states became negligible as they answered to the federal government on practically every area of governance, even in areas, such as criminal law.

Yet, federal dominance did not, and has not, go unchallenged. As with the federal system based upon state sovereignty, punctuations to federal sovereignty emerged. Beginning with the election of Ronald Reagan in 1980, signs that corporative federalism might be weakening appeared. In his inaugural address in 1981 and throughout his presidency, Reagan singled his "intention to curb the size and influence of the Federal establishment and to demand recognition of the distinction between the powers granted to the Federal Government and those reserved to the States or to the people. All of us need to be reminded that the Federal Government did not create the States; the States created the Federal Government." The first major politician in decades to speak of federalism in this traditional sense, Reagan's policies, which he styled "New Federalism," sought to weaken the administrative state and return decision making back to the states. In areas of judicial appointments, Reagan nominated jurists who advocated a return to the "original intent" of the founders.

While not completely successful in living up to its lofty goals, Reagan's New Federalism not only helped somewhat revive a federalism that seeks equilibrium, but it had one major, and often overlooked, consequence. It saved the idea of a federalism of state sovereignty from it mid-twentieth-century association with racism. During the Civil Rights movements of the 1950s and 1960s, opponents of desegregation and other federal civil rights actions used the language of state sovereignty to defend objectively racist and discriminatory practices and legislation. While these arguments ignored the obvious intent and language of the Fourteenth Amendment, a consequence of their rhetoric was to attach federalism to white supremacy. Reagan's administration, however, reassured that federalism and state sovereignty was not inherently racist nor discriminatory. His administration followed the traditional idea that linked federalism to self-government and liberty.

For all its shortcomings, Reagan's administration did begin a resurgence in the understanding of a federalism rooted in state sovereignty. Nowhere was this resurgence more noticeable than in the Supreme Court. Starting with the 1793 case of *Chisholm v. Georgia*, the Supreme Court has served as a bastion of centralization. Under the Chief Justiceship of William Rehnquist, however, the Court reasserted a federalism of divided sovereignty. In cases such as *New York v. United States* and *Printz v. United States, United States v. Lopez*, the Court moved away from its long practice of upholding federal actions against the states. Instead, the Court recognized that a "residual state sovereignty was also implicit, of course, in the Constitution's conferral upon Congress of not all governmental powers, but only discrete, enumerated ones, Art. I, § 8, which implication was rendered express by the Tenth [Amendment]." When compared to the judicial reasoning of the previous half-century, Rehnquist Court of the 1990s returned, at least to some degree, a federalism of separate spheres.

Although much of this early resurgence of federalism seemed confined to the Supreme Court, it remains unclear how vibrant or enduring it may be. Over the past two decades, several moments of particular—and contentious—punctuations reveal that the resurgence might not be lasting. Take for instance the issue of homosexual marriage. For most of American history, this issue never presented itself on any political agenda. What has transpired with this issue over just the last decade is truly remarkable. When homosexual marriage rose to national discussion in the 1980s and 1990s, the overwhelming majority of State and National political leaders staunchly opposed it. In fact, the Defense of Marriage Act (DOMA) which the federal government enacted in 1996 and defined marriage as the union of one man and one woman, received support from a Democratic President and bipartisan supermajorities from the House (342) and the Senate (85). Additionally, in a ten-year period started in 1998, roughly thirty states drafted constitutional amendments to ban same-sex marriage. During the same time, only a handful of states moved in the other direction. All these actions indicated that the issue remained one reserved to the sovereignty of the states with the federal government, beyond establishing its own definition of federal law, having practically no interference.

All of these limitations on same-sex marriage abruptly changed in 2013 with the Supreme Court case of *United States v. Windsor,* which declared key elements of DOMA as unconstitutional. Following just two years later, the *Obergefell v Hodges* case invoked the Fourteenth Amendment to declare that same-sex couples possessed a fundamental right to marry that the states nor federal government could impair. Fueled by interested parties and the echo chambers of a 24-hour news cycle and social media, federal protection of same-sex marriage is arguably one of the fastest and abrupt changes not only in our constitutional history, but for our culture as well. While the full explanation of this sudden change is far beyond the scope of this essay, suffice it to say the case points to the complete sovereignty of the federal government. The Federal government, the Supreme Court more specifically, pushed back against the majority of states in effectively overruling their constitutional prohibitions against homosexual marriage.

Another current example, however, reveals that the return of state sovereignty might have teeth after all. That issue is the legality of certain recreational drugs, primarily marijuana. Like many nations, the United States has an interesting history with the degree to which mind-altering substances were given various levels of legalization and restriction. The federal government declared its sovereignty over the topic by determining which drugs had legitimate medical uses, and which were strictly prohibited for their lack of medical purpose. With the passage of the Controlled Substances Act in 1970, the federal government initiated its modern "war on drugs" campaign. The Reagan administration renewed emphasis on the war in the 1980s, but in a time line that is the mirror image of the same-sex marriage debate, the situation is primed for a radical change. Since the mid-1990s, efforts at the state levels to legalize marijuana for certain uses grew. At the same time as thirty states were banning same-sex marriage, a similar number of were legalizing marijuana in either medical usage or, more recently, as a purely recreational drug. The federal government exerted its sovereignty over the issue in the 2005 case of the *Gonzales v. Raich*. Even with this decision that allows the Federal government to maintain its control and ban of marijuana, states continue to venture forth by passing laws in contradiction to this outcome. With the growth of the state recognized the legal sale of this drug into the billions of dollars in sales, it seems inevitable that another confrontation between the federal and state governments will occur.

At the same time, in the early twenty-first century, states began a more concerted effort at reaffirming their sovereignty. Starting around 2008, a number of states enacted "Tenth Amendment Resolutions." Designed as responses to the War on Terror and legislation such as the Patriot Act, federal intervention into health care, and deepening involvement in education, the Resolutions reminded the federal government that limits to its powers existed. Although it is too early to know what the effect of these resolutions may have in preserving at least some semblance of federalism, what is clear that the notion of federalism has not completely disappeared from the constitutional and political landscape.

Civil Liberties

Freedoms or rights guaranteed to citizens by the government are typically known as civil liberties. That is, those rights that are given or delineated as a condition of entering the social contract. The government acknowledges these rights and often provides a procedure or guiding principles for their interpretation or for their boundaries to be maintained. The right of a trial by an impartial jury in a criminal case is an example of a civil liberty granted to citizens via the Sixth Amendment of the U.S. Constitution. In the selected documents that follow, it will be evident that there is a give and take the type of relationship between the Federal government and the State governments on this issue.

Starting in the mid-1950s, the Supreme Court grew increasingly concerned with civil liberty issues. Most of these cases were in response to the growing demands of the Civil Rights movement which sought to promote equality of opportunity. In *Brown v. Board of Education*, the differences in how equality was perceived by the federal government and those of state governments became readily apparent. This case ushered in several more in which the sovereignty of the federal government eclipsed that of the states. These substantive issues changed over time, from segregation to same-sex marriage and abortion, but the general tone remained. The federal government has its thumb on the scale of federalism. The Supreme Court consistently overruled state laws and governmental actions as violations of civil rights. If the federalism can be seen as separate spheres, clearly the federal sphere is the largest in issues of civil rights.

Commerce Clause

The modern era of Commerce Clause cases is not easily parsed into a winning or losing camp. First, it is important to recognize that the Commerce Clause is indeed an explicit power given to the National government via Article I, Section 8 of the U.S. Constitution. The clause, however, suggests more than just a means of conveying the sovereignty of the federal government. In many ways, the Commerce Clause provides a mindset or even a culture of power. That is, Supreme Court has used the clause to justify federal power and action into areas that seem far removed from commerce or the enumeration of powers in the Constitution. The Court employed the clause during the Civil Rights movement to combat segregation. As the commerce cases herein reveal, the economic dimension of an issue is often not the Court's first consideration, but is the means by which the government is spurred into action. For instance, in the case of *Katzenbach v. McClung*, the Court relied upon commerce powers in establishing the need to seek rest and nourishment as a part of interstate travel. This line of reasoning allowed the federal government to legally force desegregation on individual business owners. In recent times, the Supreme Court has applied the Commerce Clause into novel areas like women's rights, gun laws, and recreational drug use.

Incorporation

When asked in national surveys, the average American consistently demonstrates a cursory knowledge of the exact substance of the Amendments. More worrying, however, is the fact that they also lose sight of the purpose of the Amendments, their intended targets, and the requisite historical events that gave rise to them. Do the Amendments only apply to the National government or are they relevant to the States as well? The notion of incorporation touches upon all these facets of the Amendments.

The procedure of actually amending the Constitution is relatively straightforward as is provided in Article V of the Constitution itself. The procedure is effectively where the easy to understand part of the Amendments end. The philosophical discussions surrounding the notion of amendments, and the Bill of Rights in particular, is far beyond the scope of this current work. What needs to be stated though, is that the first ten Amendments do not create new rights. Not when they were first proposed, nor do we find new rights in them today. Rather, the Bill of Rights sets limits. Far too often, the Amendments are thought of as the enumerated rights given by the government to its citizens. Nothing could be farther from the truth. How can a government that operates on a social contract whereby its citizens enter voluntarily give its people something that is not it's own to give? In other words, the Amendments themselves do not establish rights but set the government on notice of the boundaries of those possessed by the people. Much of the discussion of the Amendments focuses on what those rights actually mean, however, an equally prescient question is determining the target of those boundaries or limitations.

On its face, the Constitution is the very document that creates the National government. Thus, as the preamble to the Bill of Rights asserted, the amendments were "to prevent misconstruction or abuse of its powers." Thus, the Bill of Rights could reasonably be assumed to provide limitations and boundaries that were intended to constrain the National government. A relatively early Supreme Court case, *Barron v. Baltimore* (1833), reinforced this notion. This case, however, settled until the ratification of the Fourteenth Amendment. That amendment covers a lot of ground, but, as the section on sovereignty revealed, it placed prohibitions on State governments. Which prohibitions and their degree of restraint have been the subject of debate over the last 150 years.

The *Gitlow v. New York* (1925) case ushered in the modern area of the incorporation doctrine. Incorporation means that the rights are not just applicable to the National government, but to the states as well. Instead of settling this issue of law, the case added a new wrinkle. The *Gitlow* case introduced the doctrine of selective incorporation. Selective incorporation works just as a simple reading of the phrase leads one to believe. It provides for rights supported in the Bill of Rights to be applied to State governments in a step-wise fashion. That is, the protections of the Bill of Rights are not automatically applied to States. Consequently, the tension between an individual's rights and protections from the Federal government can very much be at odds with those afforded by State governments.

For a selective incorporation to proceed, there first needs to be some sort of perceived rights-based infringement at the state level that provides the ripeness needed for the Supreme Court to act. The Court then narrowly considers whether and how that right constrains a state's actions. As explored in this text, the progression of selective incorporation fits with the punctuated equilibrium model of change. These applications of rights emerge as a response to sudden swings in public opinion or after a particular case of a gross violation of what is believed to be a fundamental right. The most recent incorporation case was *McDonald v. City of Chicago* (2010) and its net effect was to apply an individual's Second Amendment rights and protections against state prohibition of such rights.

NOTES

1. Pete Stark, "The Federal Government, yes, can do almost anything" at https://www.youtube.com/watch?v=W1-eBz8hyoE accessed on July 21, 2018.

2. We intend this essay as an overview of federalism's development in American history. The intricacies and complexities of the debates surrounding federalism throughout American history forced us to simplify and compress many events and issues. Thus, in no way are we claiming this essay as a comprehensive or that it represents the only interpretation available from the documents in this collection. We want this interpretative essay to provide readers with a way to understand arguments contained within these documents. Additionally, we have not included notes to the quotations mentioned throughout. Except for the previous note, all quotations originate from documents within this collection. Citations to those documents are provided throughout the collection.

Part I

Sovereignty and Reserved Powers

Editors' Note: The location of sovereignty is the most critical element of American federalism. The documents in this section cover how Americans have addressed that question throughout their history. They draw attention to those contrasting visions, first explained in the introductory essay, between state versus federal sovereignty. Readers should note the arguments each side employed in defending their respected positions. While examining the differences between both sides, also consider what, if anything, these documents may reveal about possible internal differences within each camp. Did those defending state sovereignty emphasize one element over another over two centuries? Have arguments for federal sovereignty always concentrated on the same points? If different times lead to different emphasis, consider how the role of historical contexts and the importance of crisis, in particular, shaped the historical understanding and arguments behind sovereignty and federalism.

The structure of this section follows the general chronology established in the introductory essay. It opens with the intellectual arguments on nature of sovereignty, the quality of large republics, and the idea of confederations. These ideas represent the received wisdom on the subject by the time of the mid-eighteenth century. The crisis that became the American Revolution required Americans to either accept or challenge this wisdom. The documents reveal how Americans, although certainly not all, accepted the idea of state sovereignty federalism at the time of the founding and early republic. It is in this section that the notion of "separate spheres" first takes hold. The shift from state to federal sovereignty, which began as a result of the Civil War but accelerated in the late nineteenth-century, is characterized by two elements. First, the degree to which the documents attacked the notion of state sovereignty, or "states' rights," as an antiquated limitation to addressing national concerns and achieving national greatness. Secondly, how, in the midst of attacking state sovereignty, they appealed to the idea of undivided federal sovereignty. When the section moves into the 20th century, the concept of state sovereignty all but disappears. Supplanting it was the notion that sovereignty in the federal government can address and cure practically any concern and social ill and serve as a caretaker of the people. State sovereignty federalism declines, even more, when the racial segregationists of the mid-twentieth century appeal to state sovereignty in their attempts to perpetuate the violation of civil rights of African Americans. The section concludes with the recovery of the importance of state sovereignty federalism. The re-emphasis on state sovereignty began with Reagan administration of the 1980s and its somewhat sputtering invocation in the decades since. In particular, readers should notice that much of the return to the idea of state sovereignty emerged, not from the states themselves, but from the United States Supreme Court. Consider what it means to have federal courts, rather than state governments, defend or explain the nature of state sovereignty. How does this affect the efforts of the states in their recent appeals to the Tenth Amendment?

JEAN BODIN *ON SOVEREIGNTY*[1]

Sovereignty is the absolute and perpetual power vested in a commonwealth which in Latin is termed *majestas*.

. . . A perpetual authority therefore must be understood to mean one that lasts for the lifetime of him who exercises it. If a sovereign magistrate is given office for one year, or for any other predetermined period, and continues to exercise the authority bestowed on him after the conclusion of his term, he does so either by consent or by force and violence. If he does so by force, it is manifest tyranny. The tyrant is a true sovereign for all that. The robber's possession by violence is true and natural possession although contrary to the law, for those who were formerly in possession have been disseized. But if the magistrate continues in office by consent, he is not a sovereign prince, seeing that he only exercises power on sufferance. Still less is he a sovereign if the term of his office is not fixed, for in that case he has no more than a precarious commission.

. . . Let us now turn to the other term of our definition and consider the force of the word *absolute*. The people or the magnates of a commonwealth can bestow simply and unconditionally upon someone of their choice a sovereign and perpetual power to dispose of their property and persons, to govern the state as he thinks fit, and to order the succession, in the same way that any proprietor, out of his liberality, can freely and unconditionally make a gift of his property to another. Such a form of gift, not being mad qualified in any way, is the only true gift, being at once unconditional and irrevocable. Gifts burdened with obligations and hedged with conditions are not true gifts. Similarly sovereign power given to a prince charged with conditions is neither properly sovereign, nor absolute, unless the conditions of appointment are only such as are inherent in the laws of God and of nature . . .

. . . On the other hand it is the distinguishing mark of the sovereign that he cannot in any way be subject to the commands of another, for it is he who makes law for the subject, abrogates law already made, and amends obsolete law. No one who is subject either to the law or to some other person can do this. That is why it is laid down in the civil law that the prince is above the law, for the word *law* in Latin implies the command of him who is invested with sovereign power. Therefore we find in all statutes the phrase "notwithstanding all edicts and ordinances to the contrary that we have infringed, or do infringe by these present." This clause applies both to former acts of the prince himself, and to those of his predecessors. For all laws, ordinances, letters patent, privileges, and grants whatsoever issued by the prince, have force only during his own lifetime, and must be expressly, or at least tacitly, confirmed by the reigning prince who was cognizance of them . . . In proof of which, it is the custom of this realm for all corporations and corporate bodies to ask for the confirmation of their privileges, rights, and jurisdictions, on the accession of a new king. Even Parliaments and high courts do this, as well as individual officers of the crown.

. . . It is far otherwise with divine and natural laws. All the princes of the earth are subject to them, and cannot contravene them without treason and rebellion against God. His yoke is upon them, and they must bow their heads in fear and reverence before His divine majesty. The absolute power of princes and sovereign lords does not extend to the laws of God and of nature. He who best understood the meaning of absolute power, and made kings and emperors submit to his will, defined his sovereignty as a power to override positive law; he did not claim power to set aside divine and natural law.

. . . From all this it is clear that the principal mark of sovereign majesty and absolute power is the right to impose laws generally on all subjects regardless of their consent. . . And if it is expedient that if he is to govern his state well, a sovereign prince must be above the law, it is even more expedient that the ruling class in an aristocracy should be so, and inevitable in a popular state. A monarch in a kingdom is set apart from his subjects, and the ruling class from the people in an aristocracy. There are therefore in each case two parties, those that rule on the one hand, and those that are ruled on the other. This is the cause of the disputes about sovereignty that arise in them, but cannot in a popular state . . . There the people, rulers and ruled, form a single body and cannot bind themselves by their own laws.

. . . A distinction must therefore be made between right and the law, for one implies what is equitable and the other what is commanded. Law is nothing else than the command of the sovereign in the exercise of his sovereign power. A sovereign prince is not the subject to the laws of the Greeks, or any other alien power, or even those of the Romans, much less to his own laws, except in so far as they embody the law of nature which, according to Pindar, is the law to which all kings and princes are subject. Neither Pope nor Emperor is exempt from this law, though certain flatters say they can take the goods of their subjects at will. But both civilians and canonists have repudiated this opinion as contrary to the law of God. They err who assert that in virtue of their sovereign power princes can do this. It is rather the law of the jungle, an act of force and violence. For as we have shown above, absolute power implies freedom in relation to positive laws, and not in relation to the law of God. God has declared explicitly in His Law that it is not just to take, or even to cover, the goods of another. Those who defend such opinions are even more dangerous than those who act on them. They show the lion his claws, and arm princes under a cover of just claims. The evil will of a tyrant, drunk with such flatteries, urges him to an abuse of absolute power and excites his violent passions to the pitch where avarice issues in confiscations, desire in adultery, and anger in murder . . .

Since then the prince has no power to exceed the laws of nature which God Himself, whose image he is, has decreed, he cannot take his subject's property without just and reasonable cause, that is to say by purchase, exchange, legitimate confiscation, or to secure peace with the enemy when it cannot be otherwise achieved. Natural reason instructs us that the public good must be preferred to the particular, and that subjects should give up not only their mutual antagonisms and animosities, but also their possessions, for the safety of the commonwealth . . .

. . . If justice is the end of the law, the law the work of the prince, and the prince the image of God, it follows of necessity that the law of the prince should be modelled on the law of God.

THOMAS HOBBES, *LEVIATHAN*[2]

The final Cause, End, or Desire of men, (who naturally love Liberty, and Dominion over others,) in the introduction of that restraint upon themselves, (in which we see them live in Commonwealths) is the foresight of their own preservation, and of a more contended life thereby; that is to say, of getting themselves out from that miserable condition of War, which is necessarily consequent (as has been shown) to the natural Passions of men, when there is no visible Power to keep them in awe, and tie them by fear of punishment to the performance of their Covenants, and observation of those Laws of Nature.

For the Laws of Nature (as *Justice, Equity, Modesty, Mercy*, and (in sum) *doing to others, as we would be done to*,) of themselves, without the terror of some Power to cause them to be observed, are contrary to our natural Passions, that carry us to Partiality, Pride, Revenge, and the like. And Covenants, without the Sword, are but Words, and of no strength to secure a man at all. Therefore notwithstanding the Laws of Nature, (which every one has then kept, when he has the will to keep them, when he can do it safely,) if there be no Power erected, or not great enough for our security; every man will, and may lawfully rely on his own strength and art, for caution against all other men. And in all places, where men have lived by small Families, to rob and spoil one another, has been a Trade, and so far from being reputed against the Law of Nature, that the greater spoils they gained, the greater was their honor; and men observed no other Laws therein, but the Laws of Honor; that is, to abstain from cruelty, leaving to men their lives, and instruments of husbandry. And as small Families did then; so now do Cities and Kingdoms which are but greater Families (for their own security) enlarge their Dominions, upon all pretenses of danger, and fear of Invasion, or assistance that may be given to Invaders, endeavor as much as they can, to subdue, or weaken their neighbors, by open force, and secret arts, for want of other Caution, justly; and are remembered for it in after ages with honor.

Nor is it the joining together of a final number of men, that gives them this security; because in small numbers, small additions on the one side or the other, make the advantage of strength so great, as is sufficient to carry the Victory; and therefore gives encouragement to an Invasion. The Multitude sufficient to confide in for our Security, not determined by any certain number, but by comparison with the Enemy we fear; and is then sufficient, when the odds of the Enemy is not of so visible and conspicuous moment, to determine the event of war, as to move him to attempt.

And be there never so great a Multitude; yet if their actions be directed according to their particular judgements, and particular appetites, they can expect thereby no defense, nor protection, neither against a Common enemy, nor against the injuries of one another. For being distracted in opinions concerning the best use and application of their strength, they do not help, but hinder one another; and reduce their strength by mutual opposition to nothing: whereby they are easily, not only subdued by a very few that agree together; but also when there is no common enemy, they make war upon each other, for their particular interests. For if we could suppose a great Multitude of men to consent in the observation of Justice, and other Laws of Nature, without a common Power to keep them all in awe; we might as well suppose all Man-kind to do the same; and then there neither would be, nor need to be any Civil Government, or Common-wealth at all; because there would be Peace without subjection.

Nor is it enough for the security, which men desire should last all the time of their life, that they be governed, and directed by one judgment, for a limited time; as in one Battle, or one War. For though they obtain a Victory by their unanimous endeavor against a foreign enemy; yet afterwards, when either they have no common enemy, or he that by one part is held for an enemy, is by another part held for a friend, they must needs by the difference of their interests dissolve, and fall again into a War amongst themselves.

It is true, that certain living creatures, as Bees, and Ants, live sociably one with another, (which are therefore by *Aristotle* numbered amongst Political creatures;) and yet have no other direction, than their particular judgements and appetites; nor speech, whereby one of them can signify to another, what he thinks expedient for the common benefit: and therefore some man may perhaps desire to know, why Man-kind cannot do the same. To which I answer,

First, that men are continually in competition for Honor and Dignity, which these creatures are not; and consequently amongst men there arises on that ground, Envy and Hatred, and finally War; but amongst these not so.

Secondly, that amongst these creatures, the Common good differed not from the Private; and being by nature inclined to their private, they procure thereby the common benefit. But man, whose Joy consisted in comparing himself with other men, can relish nothing but what is eminent.

Thirdly, that these creatures, having not (as man) the use of reason, do not see, nor think they see any fault, in the administration of their common business: whereas amongst men, there are very many, that think themselves wiser, and abler to govern the Public, better than the rest; and these strive to reform and innovate, one this way, another that way; and thereby bring it into Distraction and Civil war.

Fourthly, that these creatures, though they have some use of voice, in making known to one another their desires, and other affections; yet they want that art of words, by which some men can represent to others, that which is Good, in the likenesses of Evil; and Evil, in the likenesses of Good; and augment, or diminish the apparent greatness of Good and Evil; discontenting men, and rumbling their Peace at their pleasure.

Fifthly, Irrational creatures cannot distinguish between *Injury*, and *Damage*; and therefore as long as they be at ease, they are not offended with their fellows: whereas Man is then most troublesome, when he is most at ease: for then it is that he loves to show his Wisdom, and control the Actions of them that govern the Common-wealth.

Lastly, the agreement of these creatures is Natural; that of men, is by Covenant only, which is Artificial: and therefore it is no wonder if there be somewhat else required (besides Covenant) to make their Agreement constant and lasting; which is a Common Power, to keep them in awe, and to direct their actions to the Common Benefit.

The only way to erect such a Common Power, as may be able to defend them from the invasion of Foreigners, and the injuries of one another, and thereby to secure them in such sort, as that by their own industry, and by the fruits of the Earth, they may nourish themselves and live contentedly; is, to confrere all their power and strength upon one Man, or upon one Assembly of men, to bear their Person; and every one to own, and acknowledge himself to be Author of whatsoever he that so bear their Person, shall Act, or cause to be Acted, in those things which concern the Common Peace and Safety; and therein to submit their Wills, every one to his Will, and their Judgements, to his Judgment. This is more than Consent, or Concord; it is a real Unity of them all, in one and the same Person, made by Covenant of every man with every man, in such manner, as if every man should say to every man, *I Authorize and give up my Right of Governing myself, to this Man, or to this Assembly of men, on this condition, that thou give up thy Right to him, and Authorize all his Actions in lie manner.* This done, the Multitude so united in one Person, is called a COMMON-WEALTH, in latin CIVITAS. This is the Generation of that great LEVIATHAN, or rather (to speak more reverently) of that *Mortal God*, to which we owe under the *Immortal God*, our peace and defense. For by this Authority, given him by every particular man in the Common-Wealth, he hath the use of so much Power and Strength conferred on him, that by terror thereof, he is enabled to conform the wills of them all, to Peace at home, and mutual aid against their enemies abroad. And in him consisted the Essence of the Commonwealth; which (to define it,) is *One Person, of whose Acts a great Multitude, by mutual covenants one with another, have made themselves every one the Author, to the end he may use the strength and means of them all, as he shall think expedient, for their Peace and Common Defense.*

And he that carried this Person, is called SOVEREIGN, and said to have *Sovereign Power*: and every one besides, his SUBJECT.

The attaining to this Sovereign Power, is by two ways. One, by Natural force; as when a man make his children, to submit themselves, and their children to his government, as being able to destroy them if they refuse; or by War subdue his enemies to his will giving them their lives on that condition. The other, is when men agree amongst themselves, to submit to some Man, or Assembly of men, voluntarily, on confidence to be protected by him against all others. This letter, may be called a Political Commonwealth by *Acquisition*.

MONTESQUIEU, *SPIRIT OF LAWS*[3]

. . . It is natural for a republic to have only a small territory; otherwise it cannot long subsist. In an extensive republic there are men of large fortunes, and consequently of less moderation; there are trusts too considerable to be placed in any single subject; he has interests of his own; he soon begins to think that he may be happy and glorious, by oppressing his fellow-citizens; and that he may raise himself to grandeur on the ruins of his country.

In an extensive republic the public good is sacrificed to a thousand private views; it is subordinate to exceptions, and depends on accidents. In a small one, the interest of the public is more obvious, better understood, and more within the reach of every citizen; abuses have less extent, and, of course, are less protected.

. . . A large empire supposes a despotic authority in the person who governs. It is necessary that the quickness of the prince's resolutions should supply the distance of the places they are sent to; that fear should prevent the remissness of the distant governor or magistrate; that the law should be derived from a single person, and should shift continually, according to the accidents which incessantly multiply in a state in proportion to its extent.

VATTEL, *LAW OF NATIONS*[4]

A nation or a state is, as has been said at the beginning of this work, a body politic, or a society of men united together for the purpose of promoting their mutual safety and advantage by their combined strength.

From the very design that induces a number of men to form a society which has its common interests, and which is to act in concert, it is necessary that there should be established a *Public Authority*, to order and direct what is to be done by each in relation to the end of the association. This political authority is the *Sovereignty*; and he or they who are invested with it are the *Sovereign.*

It is evident, that, by the very act of the civil or political association, each citizen subjects himself to the authority of the entire body, in everything that relates to the common welfare. The authority of all over each member, therefore, essentially belongs to the body politic, or state; but the exercise of that authority may be placed in different hands, according as the society may have ordained.

. . . Every nation that governs itself, under what form so ever, without dependence on any foreign power, is a *Sovereign State*. Its rights are naturally the same as those of any other state. Such are the moral persons who live together in a natural society, subject to the law of the nations. To give a nation a right to make an immediate figure in this grand society, it is sufficient that it be really sovereign and independent, that is, that it govern itself by its own authority and laws.

. . . Finally, several sovereign and independent states may unite themselves together by a perpetual confederacy, without ceasing to be, each individually, a perfect state. They will together constitute a federal republic: their joint deliberations will not impair the sovereignty of each member, though they may, in certain respects, put some restraint on the exercise of it, in virtue of voluntary engagements. A person does not cease to be free and independent, when he is obliged to fulfil engagements which he has voluntarily contracted.

BLACKSTONE'S *COMMENTARIES*[5]

. . . There is and must be . . . a supreme, irresistible, absolute, uncontrolled authority, in which the *jura summi imperii*, or the rights of sovereignty, reside. And this authority is placed in those hands, wherein (according to the opinion of the founders of such respective states, either expressly given, or collected from their tacit approbation) the qualities requisite for supremacy, wisdom, goodness, and power, are not the most likely to be found.

. . . By the sovereign power, as was before observed, is meant the making of laws; for wherever that power resides, all others must conform to, and be directed by it, whatever appearance the outward form and administration of the government may put on. For it is at any time in the option of the legislature to alter that form and administration by a new edict or rule, and to put the execution of the laws into whatever hands it pleases; by constituting one, or a few, or many executive magistrates: and all the other powers of the state must obey the legislature power in the discharge of their several functions, or else the constitution is at an end.

. . . But, happily for us of this island, the British constitution has long remained . . . . For, as with us the executive power of the laws is lodged in a single person, they have all the advantages of strength and dispatch, that are to be found in the most absolute monarchy: and as the legislature of the kingdom is entrusted to three distinct powers, entirely independent of each other; first, the king; secondly, the lords spiritual and temporal, which is an aristocratical assembly of persons selected for their piety, their birth, their wisdom, their valor, or their property; and, thirdly, the house of the commons, freely chosen by the people form among themselves, which makes it a kind of democracy; as this aggregate body, actuated by different springs, and attentive to different interests, composes the British parliament, and has the supreme disposal of everything; there can no inconvenience be attempted by either of the three branches, but will be withstood by one of the other two;

each branch being armed with a negative power, sufficient to repel any innovation which it shall think inexpedient or dangerous.

Here then is lodged the sovereignty of the British constitution; and lodged as beneficially as is possible for society. For in no other shape could we be so certain of finding the three great qualities of government so well and so happily united. If the supreme power were lodged in any one of the three branches separately, we must be exposed to the inconveniences of either absolute monarchy, aristocracy, or democracy; and so want two of the three principal ingredients of good polity, either virtue, wisdom, or power. If it were lodged in any two of the branches; for instance, in the king and house of lords; our laws might be providently made, and well executed, but they might not always have the good of the people in view: if lodged in the king and commons, we should want that circumspection and mediatory caution, which the wisdom of the peers is to afford: if the supreme rights of legislature were lodged in the two houses only, and the king had no negative upon their proceedings, they might be tempted to encroach upon the royal prerogative, or perhaps to abolish the kingly office, and thereby weaken (if not totally destroy) the strength of the executive power. But the constitutional government of this island is so admirably tempered and compounded, that nothing can endanger or hurt it, but destroying the equilibrium of power between one branch of the legislature and the rest. For if ever it should happen that the independence of any one of the three should be lost, or that it should become subservient to the views of either of the other two, there would soon be an end of our constitution. The legislature would be changed from that, which (upon the supposition of an original contract, either actual or implied) is presumed to have been originally set up by the general consent of the bands of government; and the people are thereby reduced to a state of anarchy, with liberty to constitute to themselves a new legislature power.

Having thus curiously considered the three usual species of government, and our own singular constitution, selected and compounded from them all, I proceed to observe, that, as the power of making laws constitutes the supreme authority, so wherever the supreme authority in any state resides, it is the right of that authority to make laws; that is, in the words of our definition, *to prescribe the rule of civil action*. And this may be discovered from the very end and institution of civil states. For a state is a collective body, composed of a multitude of individuals, united for their safety and convenience, and intending to act together as one man. If it therefore is to act as one man, it ought to act by one uniform will. But, inasmuch as political communities are made up of many natural persons, each of whom has his particular will and inclination, these several wills cannot by any *natural* union be joined together, or tempered and disposed into a lasting harmony, so as to constitute and produce that one uniform will of the whole. It can therefore be no otherwise produced than by a *political* union; by the consent of all persons to submit their own private wills to the will of one man, or of one or more assemblies of men, to whom the supreme authority is entrusted: and this will of that one man, or assemblage of men, is in different states, according to their different constitutions, understood to be law.

Thus far as to the *right* of the supreme power to make laws; but farther, it is its *duty* likewise. For since the respective members are bound to conform themselves to the will of the state, it is expedient that they receive directions from the state declaratory of that its will. But, as it is impossible, in so great a multitude, to give injunctions to every particular man, relative to each particular action, it is therefore incumbent on the state to establish general rules, for the perpetual information and direction of all persons in all points, whether of positive or negative duty. And this, in order that every man may know what to look upon as his own, what as another's; what absolute and what relative duties are required at his hands; what is to be esteemed honest, dishonest, or indifferent; what degree every man retains of his natural liberty; what he has given up as the price of the benefits of society; and after what manner each person is to moderate the use and exercise of those rights which the state assigns him, in order to promote and secure the public tranquility.

DECLARATORY ACT[6]

An act for the better securing the dependency of his majesty's dominions in America upon the crown and parliament of Great Britain.

Whereas several of the houses of representatives in his Majesty's colonies and plantations in America, have of late against law, claimed to themselves, or to the general assemblies of the same, the sole and exclusive right of imposing duties and taxes upon his majesty's subjects in the said colonies and plantations; and have in pursuance of such claim, passed certain votes, resolutions, and orders derogatory to the legislative authority of parliament, and inconsistent with the dependency of the said colonies and plantations upon the crown of Great Britain: may it therefore please your most excellent Majesty, that it may be declared; and be it declared by the King's most excellent majesty, by and with the advice and consent of the lords spiritual and temporal, and commons, in this present parliament assembled, and by the authority of the same, That the said colonies and plantations in America have been, are, and of right ought to be, subordinate unto, and dependent upon the imperial crown and parliament of Great Britain; and that the King's majesty, by and with the advice and consent of the lords spiritual and temporal, and commons of Great Britain, in parliament assembled, had hath, and of right ought to have, full power and authority to make laws and statutes of sufficient force and validity to bind the colonies and people of America, subjects of the crown of Great Britain, in all cases whatsoever,

And be it further declared and enacted by the authority aforesaid, That all resolutions, votes, orders, and proceedings, in any of the said colonies or plantations, whereby the power and authority of the parliament of Great Britain, to make laws and statutes as aforesaid, is denied, or drawn into question, arc, and are hereby declared to be, utterly null and void to all in purposes whatsoever.

RICHARD BLAND, *INQUIRY INTO THE RIGHTS OF THE BRITISH COLONIES*[7]

. . . From this Detail of the Charters, and other Acts of the Crown, under which the first Colony in North America was established, it is evident that "the Colonists were not a few unhappy Fugitives who had wandered into a distant Part of the World to enjoy their civil and religious Liberties, which they were deprived of at home," but had a regular Government long before the first Act of Navigation, and were respected as a distinct State, independent, as to their *internal* Government, of the original Kingdom, but united with her, as to their *external* Polity, in the closest and most intimate LEAGUE AND AMITY, under the same Allegiance, and enjoying the Benefits of a reciprocal Intercourse.

STEPHEN HOPKINS, *THE RIGHTS OF THE COLONIES EXAMINED*[8]

We are not insensible that when liberty is in danger, the liberty of complaining is dangerous . . . And we believe no good reason can be given why the colonies should not modestly and soberly inquire what right the Parliament of Great Britain have to tax them . . . . If the British House of Commons are rightfully possessed of a power to tax the colonies in America, this power must be vested in them by the British constitution, as they are one branch of the great legislative body of the nation. As they are the representatives of all the people in Britain, they have beyond doubt all the power such a representation can possibly give; yet great as this power is, surely it cannot exceed that of their constituents. And can it possibly be shown that the people in Britain have a sovereign authority over their fellow subjects in America? Yet such is the authority that must be exercised in taking people's estates from them by taxes, or otherwise without their consent. In all aids granted to the crown by the Parliament, it is said with the greatest propriety, "We freely give unto Your Majesty"; for they give their own money and the money of those who have entrusted them with a proper power for that purpose. But can they with the same propriety give away the money of the Americans, who have never given any such power? Before a thing can be justly given away, the giver must certainly have acquired a property in it; and have the people in Britain justly acquired such a property in the goods and estates of the people in these colonies that they may give them away at pleasure?

In an imperial state, which consists of many separate governments each of which hath peculiar privileges and of which kind it is evident the empire of Great Britain is, no single part, though greater than another part, is by that superiority entitled to make laws for or to tax such lesser part; but all laws and all taxations which bind the whole must be made by the whole. . . . Indeed, it must be absurd to suppose that the common people of Great Britain have a sovereign and absolute authority over their fellow subjects in America, or even any sort of power whatsoever over them; but it will be still more absurd to suppose they can give a power to their representatives which they have not themselves. If the House of Commons do not receive this authority from their constituents it will be difficult to tell by what means they obtained it, except it be vested in them by mere superiority and power.

ALEXANDER HAMILTON, *THE FARMER REFUTED*[9]

There seems to be a necessity for vesting the regulation of our trade there, because in time our commercial interests might otherwise interfere with hers. But with respect to making laws for us, there is not the least necessity, or even propriety, in it. Our Legislatures are confined to ourselves, and cannot interfere with Great Britain. We are best acquainted with our own circumstances, and therefore best qualified to make suitable regulations. It is of no force to object that no particular colony has power to enact general laws for all the colonies. There is no need of such general laws. Let every colony attend to its own internal police, and all will be well. How have we managed heretofore? The Parliament has made no general laws for our good, and yet our affairs have been conducted much to our ease and satisfaction. If any discord has sprung up among us, it is wholly imputable to the incursions of Great Britain. We should be peaceable and happy, if unmolested by her. We are not so destitute of wisdom as to be in want of her assistance to devise proper and salutary laws for us.

ARTICLES OF CONFEDERATION

Article II

Each state retains its sovereignty, freedom, and independence, and every Power, Jurisdiction and right, which is not by this confederation expressly delegated to the United States, in Congress assembled.

Article III

The said states hereby severally enter into a firm league of friendship with each other, for their common defence, the security of their Liberties, and their mutual and general welfare, binding themselves to assist each other, against all force offered to, or attacks made upon them, or any of them, on account of religion, sovereignty, trade, or any other pretense whatever.

Article IX

The united states in congress assembled, shall have the sole and exclusive right and power of determining on peace and war, except in the cases mentioned in the sixth article—of sending and receiving ambassadors—entering into treaties and alliances, provided that no treaty of commerce shall be made whereby the legislative power of the respective states shall be restrained from imposing such imposts and duties on foreigners as their own people are subjected to, or from prohibiting the exportation or importation of any species of goods or commodities, whatsoever—of establishing rules for deciding in all cases, what captures on land or water shall be legal, and in what manner prizes taken by land or naval forces in the service of the united states shall be divided or appropriated—of granting letters of marque and reprisal in times of peace—appointing courts for the trial of piracies and felonies committed on the high seas and establishing courts for receiving and determining finally appeals in all cases of captures, provided that no member of congress shall be appointed a judge of any of the said courts.

ALEXANDER HAMILTON, "THE CONTINENTALIST NO. 1"[10]

It would be the extreme of vanity in us not to be sensible, that we began this revolution with very vague and confined notions of the practical business of government. To the greater part of us it was a novelty: Of those, who under the former constitution had had opportunities of acquiring experience, a large proportion adhered to the opposite side, and the remainder can only be supposed to have possessed ideas adapted to the narrow colonial sphere, in which they had been accustomed to move, not of that enlarged kind suited to the government of an INDEPENDENT NATION.

There were no doubt exceptions to these observations—men in all respects qualified for conducting the public affairs, with skill and advantage; but their number was small; they were not always brought forward in our councils; and when they were, their influence was too commonly borne down by the prevailing torrent of ignorance and prejudice.

On a retrospect however, of our transactions, under the disadvantages with which we commenced, it is perhaps more to be wondered at, that we have done so well, than that we have not done better. There are indeed some traits in our conduct, as conspicuous for sound policy, as others for magnanimity. But, on the other hand, it must also be confessed, there have been many false steps, many chimerical projects and utopian speculations, in the management of our civil as well as of our military affairs. A part of these were the natural effects of the spirit of the times dictated by our situation. An extreme jealousy of power is the attendant on all popular revolutions, and has seldom been without its evils. It is to this source we are to trace many of the fatal mistakes, which have so deeply endangered the common cause; particularly that defect, which will be the object of these remarks, A WANT OF POWER IN CONGRESS.

The present Congress, respectable for abilities and integrity, by experience convinced of the necessity of a change, are preparing several important articles to be submitted to the respective states, for augmenting the powers of the Confederation. But though there is hardly at this time a man of information in America, who will not acknowledge, as a general proposition, that in its present form, it is unequal, either to a vigorous prosecution of the war, or to the preservation of the union in peace; yet when the principle comes to be applied to practice, there seems not to be the same agreement in the modes of remedying the defect; and it is to be feared, from a disposition which appeared in some of the states on a late occasion, that the salutary intentions of Congress may meet with more delay and opposition, than the critical posture of the states will justify.

It will be attempted to show in a course of papers what ought to be done, and the mischiefs of a contrary policy.

In the first stages of the controversy it was excusable to err. Good intentions, rather than great skill, were to have been expected from us. But we have now had sufficient time for reflection and experience, as ample as unfortunate, to rectify our errors. To persist in them, becomes disgraceful and even criminal, and belies that character of good sense and a quick discernment of our interests, which, in spite of our mistakes, we have been hitherto allowed.

It will prove, that our sagacity is limited to interests of inferior moment; and that we are incapable of those enlightened and liberal views, necessary to make us a great and a flourishing people.

History is full of examples, where in contests for liberty, a jealousy of power has either defeated the attempts to recover or preserve it in the first instance, or has afterwards subverted it by clogging government with too great precautions for its felicity, or by leaving too wide a door for sedition and popular licentiousness. In a government framed for durable liberty, not less regard must be paid to giving the magistrate a proper degree of authority, to make and execute the laws with rigor, than to guarding against encroachments upon the rights of the community. As too much power leads to despotism, too little leads to anarchy, and both eventually to the ruin of the people. These are maxims well known, but never sufficiently attended to, in adjusting the frames of governments. Some momentary interest or passion is sure to give a wrong bias, and pervert the most favorable opportunities.

No friend to order or to rational liberty, can read without pain and disgust the history of the commonwealth of Greece. Generally speaking, they were a constant scene of the alternate tyranny of one part of the people over the other, or of a few usurping demagogues over the whole. Most of them had been originally governed by kings, whose despotism (the natural disease of monarchy) had obliged their subjects to murder, expel, depose, or reduce them to a nominal existence, and institute popular governments. In these governments, that of Sparta excepted, the jealousy of power hindered the people from trusting out of their own hands a competent authority, to maintain the repose and stability of the commonwealth; whence originated the frequent revolutions and civil broils with which they were distracted. This, and the want of a solid federal union to restrain the ambition and rivalship of the different cities, after a rapid succession of bloody wars, ended in their total loss of liberty and subjugation to foreign powers.

In comparison of our governments with those of the ancient republics, we must, without hesitation, give the preference to our own; because, every power with us is exercised by representation, not in tumultuary assemblies of the collective body of the people, where the art or impudence of the ORATOR or TRIBUNE, rather than the utility or justice of the measure could seldom fail to govern. Yet whatever may be the advantage on our side, in such a comparison, men who estimate the value of institutions, not from prejudices of the moment, but from experience and reason, must be persuaded, that the same JEALOUSY of POWER has prevented our reaping all the advantages, from the examples of other nations, which we ought to have done, and has rendered our constitutions in many respects feeble and imperfect.

Perhaps the evil is not very great in respect to our constitutions; for notwithstanding their imperfections, they may, for some time, be made to operate in such a manner, as to answer the purposes of the common defense and the maintenance of order; and they seem to have, in themselves, and in the progress of society among us, the seeds of improvement.

But this is not the case with respect to the FEDERAL GOVERNMENT; if it is too weak at first, it will continually grow weaker. The ambition and local interests of the respective members, will be constantly undermining and usurping upon its prerogatives, till it comes to a dissolution; if a partial combination of some of the more powerful ones does not bring it to a more SPEEDY and VIOLENT END.

1783 TREATY OF PEACE

Article 1

His Brittanic Majesty acknowledges the said United States, viz., New Hampshire, Massachusetts Bay, Rhode Island and Providence Plantations, Connecticut, New York, New Jersey, Pennsylvania, Maryland, Virginia, North Carolina, South Carolina and Georgia, to be free sovereign and independent states, that he treats with them as such, and for himself, his heirs, and successors, relinquishes all claims to the government, propriety, and territorial rights of the same and every part thereof.

Article 4

It is agreed that creditors on either side shall meet with no lawful impediment to the recovery of the full value in sterling money of all bona fide debts heretofore contracted.

Article 5

It is agreed that Congress shall earnestly recommend it to the legislatures of the respective states to provide for the restitution of all estates, rights, and properties, which have been confiscated belonging to real British subjects; and also of the estates, rights, and properties of persons resident in districts in the possession on his Majesty's arms and who have not borne arms against the said United States. And that persons of any other description shall have free liberty to go to any part or parts of any of the thirteen United States and therein to remain twelve months unmolested in their endeavors to obtain the restitution of such of their estates, rights, and properties as may have been confiscated; and that Congress shall also earnestly recommend to the several states a reconsideration and revision of all acts or laws regarding the premises, so as to render the said laws or acts perfectly consistent not only with justice and equity but with that spirit of conciliation which on the return of the blessings of peace should universally prevail. And that Congress shall also earnestly recommend to the several states that the estates, rights, and properties, of such last mentioned persons shall be restored to them, they refunding to any persons who may be now in possession the bona fide price (where any has been given) which such persons may have paid on purchasing any of the said lands, rights, or properties since the confiscation.

And it is agreed that all persons who have any interest in confiscated lands, either by debts, marriage settlements, or otherwise, shall meet with no lawful impediment in the prosecution of their just rights.

Article 6

That there shall be no future confiscations made nor any prosecutions commenced against any person or persons for, or by reason of, the part which he or they may have taken in the present war, and that no person shall on that account suffer any future loss or damage, either in his person, liberty, or property; and that those who may be in confinement on such charges at the time of the ratification of the treaty in America shall be immediately set at liberty, and the prosecutions so commenced be discontinued.

MERIWETHER SMITH, "OBSERVATIONS ON THE FOURTH AND FIFTH ARTICLES OF THE PRELIMINARIES"[11]

Sensible that, by the laws of nations upon the principal of revolution, where the people, changing their political capacity, cease to be the *same people*, everything not expressly received in the new social compact, and which was dependent on the old government, was abrogated, dissolved, and become void; it has been judged necessary to renew the claims of individuals by the fourth article. How far this stipulation [i.e., Article 4 of the Treaty of Peace] on the parts of the *ministers* of *congress* is consistent with the *sovereignty* and rights of *legislation* of an individual state is worthy of consideration, and perhaps it will be found, that being *contrary to the laws of the state*, and to the rights of the citizens *derived from the resolution and the positive law of the state, that the ministers of congress* had no right to stipulate in the *manner* they have agreed as to the 4th article, and consequently that there is no authority to carry it into execution but that which arises from the *consent* of the *legislature* of the *state* and of the individuals inscribed herein. The individuals have a positive law of this state in their favor which leaves them not at the unity of British creditors, and the authority of congress extends to no individual in any state. For, the ministers of congress to say then, that there shall be no lawful impeachment to the recovery of the full value of their debts in storing money, is affirming the right of legislation here,—it is subjecting the citizens within the state to their authority, and directing a repeal of such laws as they disapprove—in fine, it is depriving the state of its sovereignty and independence received by the confederation. If congress found it necessary for the sake of peace, it might have stipulated to make good the losses of British creditors of British subjects in any point of view, and the equivalent might have been paid out of the vast conquests of the unites states or such other funds as they had a power over, but congress has no right to contradict the act of the legislature of this state, to compel us to receive British subjects or others whom we disapprove, or to subject the citizens of this state, to the mercy of British subjects, within the same.

2d. When the 4th and 5th articles are compared, it will be difficult to reconcile the principals on which they have been agreed. The 5th article discovers a partially in favor of the *state and of the individuals in possession of confiscated property*;—it does not bind the state to restore the confiscated property even to *risk British subjects* (as they are called) which certainly comprehends all those who did not enter into the new social compact; and it is *recommended* that *traitors* shall be reported *on paying a compensation*. Here is *tenderness* with respect to the *sovereignty* of the individual states and to the *authority of their laws*. Here is at least a tactic acknowledgement of the authority of the *state* to confiscate the property *even of British subjects* without any power in *congress* to compel restitution; and in this case, the *right* and the *interest* of the *state*, that is, of the *majority of the citizens within a state* have been considered; and the *states* may, if it be their interest, retain the benefit arising from confiscated property, and this they will probably do where it is considerable, and where the present possessors are not disposed to give it up.

But the *interest* of some states differ from that of others, inasmuch as some have great of confiscated property, and but few debts; others, were greatly indebted, and have but little confiscated property. In the letter case the individuals, who have risked their lives, their liberty and their property to assist their *fellow citizens* in establishing and securing *their* rights and *property*, are to be given up to the *mercy of British creditors* and sacrificed to the *interest of British subjects* their enemies, and of those who support their cause among us, without any compensation for their various losses, during this unequal war. They are to be left to answer the debts due, *before this revolution*, to the very persons who by various means have been contributing to plunder and ruin them, contrary to every principal of the usage of nations.

Here the right of the state and of the citizens is exactly the same herein the case of confiscation; for the principal of revolution applies equally; and congress have no more authority in the one case than in the other. It is the duty of the individuals to defend themselves, and it is the duty of the state to preserve its authority and the dignity of its laws, and to save its citizens from the ruin which threatens them. *Wisdom* and *firmness* in the *legislature* will be a sure state guard to the people.

. . . Every individual who was indebted to British subjects, and entered into a new community, laid the community under obligation to him, not only for his *personal services* but also for the *use of property which* he was *possessed* of. Every *individual* of the community also was under obligations to him, because he shared the same *common danger* and the same *common expense.* Had he withdrawn himself and his property, he would have risked nothing, and he would have weakened their case: He is therefore entitled to justice and to the protection of his fellow-citizens.

By entering into the new social compact, the *individual* indebted to British subjects, risked his *life*, his *liberty* and not only that where withal he might have discharged the debt, but also the *remaining part of his property.* If he was indebted a *fourth* part, and hath lost *three fourths* of his property, by the 4th article of the preliminaries, he is to lose the *other* part also. Here the *British subject* who is an *enemy*, risks *nothing* the *citizen* of the state, risks *all*; and having risked all, must give up to an enemy that which he hath saved. The terms are unequal and unjust with respect to the citizen;—they are disgraceful to the state.

VIRGINIA PLAN[12]

6. Resolved that each branch ought to possess the right of originating Acts; that the National Legislature ought to be impowered to enjoy the Legislative Rights vested in Congress bar the Confederation & moreover to legislate in all cases to which the separate States are incompetent, or in which the harmony of the United States may be interrupted by the exercise of individual Legislation; to negative all laws passed by the several States, contravening in the opinion of the National Legislature the articles of Union; and to call forth the force of the Union agst any member of the Union failing to fulfill its duty under the articles thereof.

8. Res^d that the Executive and a convenient number of the National Judiciary, ought to compose a Council of revision with authority to examine every act of the National Legislature before it shall operate, & every act of a particular Legislature before a Negative thereon shall be final; and that the

dissent of the said Council shall amount to a rejection, unless the Act of the National Legislature be again passed, or that of a particular Legislature be again negatived by of the members of each branch.

NEW JERSEY PLAN[13]

1. Resd. that the articles of Confederation ought to be so revised, corrected & enlarged, as to render the federal Constitution adequate to the exigencies of Government, & the preservation of the Union.

2. Resd. that in addition to the powers vested in the U. States in Congress, by the present existing articles of Confederation, they be authorized to pass acts for raising a revenue, by levying a duty or duties on all goods or merchandizes of foreign growth or manufacture, imported into any part of the U. States, by Stamps on paper, vellum or parchment, and by a postage on all letters or packages passing through the general post-office, to be applied to such federal purposes as they shall deem proper & expedient; to make rules & regulations for the collection thereof; and the same from time to time, to alter & amend in such manner as they shall think proper: to pass Acts for the regulation of trade & commerce as well with foreign nations as with each other: provided that all punishments, fines, forfeitures & penalties to be incurred for contravening such acts rules and regulations shall be adjudged by the Common law Judiciaries of the State in which any offence contrary to the true intent & meaning of such Acts rules & regulations shall have been committed or perpetrated, with liberty of commencing in the first instance all suits & prosecutions for that purpose in the superior common law Judiciary in such State, subject nevertheless, for the correction of all errors, both in law & fact in rendering Judgment, to an appeal to the Judiciary of the U. States.

6. Resd. that all Acts of the U. States in Congs. made by virtue & in pursuance of the powers hereby & by the articles of Confederation vested in them, and all Treaties made & ratified under the authority of the U. States shall be the supreme law of the respective States so far forth as those Acts or Treaties shall relate to the said States or their Citizens, and that the Judiciary of the several States shall be bound thereby in their decisions, any thing in the respective laws of the Individual States to the contrary notwithstanding; and that if any State, or any body of men in any State shall oppose or prevent yd. carrying into execution such acts or treaties, the federal Executive shall be authorized to call forth ye. power of the Confederated States, or so much thereof as may be necessary to enforce and compel an obedience to such Acts, or an observance of such Treaties.

JAMES WILSON, "STATE HOUSE SPEECH"[14]

When the people established the powers of legislation under their separate governments, they invested their representatives with every right and authority which they did not in explicit terms reserve; and therefore upon every question respecting the jurisdiction of the House of Assembly, if the frame of government is silent, the jurisdiction is efficient and complete. But in delegating federal powers, another criterion was necessarily introduced, and the congressional power is to be collected, not from tacit implication, but from the positive grant expressed in the instrument of the union. Hence, it is evident, that in the former case everything which is not reserved is given; but in the latter the reverse of the proposition prevails, and everything which is not given is reserved.

This distinction being recognized, will furnish an answer to those who think the omission of a bill of rights a defect in the proposed constitution; for it would have been superfluous and absurd to have stipulated with a federal body of our own creation, that we should enjoy those privileges of which we are not divested, either by the intention or the act that has brought the body into existence. For instance, the liberty of the press, which has been a copious source of declamation and opposition—what control can proceed from the Federal government to shackle or destroy that sacred palladium of national freedom? If, indeed, a power similar to that which has been granted for the regulation of commerce had been granted to regulate literary publications, it would have been as necessary to stipulate that the liberty of the press should be preserved inviolate, as that the impost should be general in its operation.

Another objection that has been fabricated against the new constitution, is expressed in this disingenuous form—"The trial by jury is abolished in civil cases." I must be excused, my fellow citizens, if upon this point I take advantage of my professional experience to detect the futility of the assertion. Let it be remembered then, that the business of the Federal Convention was not local, but general—not limited to the views and establishments of a single State, but co-extensive with the continent, and comprehending the views and establishments of thirteen independent sovereignties. When, therefore, this subject was in discussion, we were involved in difficulties which pressed on all sides, and no precedent could be discovered to direct our course. The cases open to a trial by jury differed in the different States. It was therefore impracticable, on that ground, to have made a general rule. The want of uniformity would have rendered any reference to the practice of the States idle and useless; and it could not with any propriety be said that, "The trial by jury shall be as heretofore," since there has never existed any federal system of jurisprudence, to which the declaration could relate. Besides, it is not in all cases that the trial by jury is adopted in civil questions; for cases depending in courts of admiralty, such as relate to maritime captures, and such as are agitated in courts of equity, do not require the intervention of that tribunal. How, then was the line of discrimination to be drawn? The Convention found the task too difficult for them, and they left the business as it stands, in the fullest confidence that no danger could possibly ensue, since the proceedings of the Supreme Court are to be regulated by the Congress, which is a faithful representation of the people; and the oppression of government is effectually barred, by declaring that in all criminal cases the trial by jury shall be preserved.

. . . The next accusation I shall consider is that which represents the federal constitution, as not only calculated, but designedly framed, to reduce the State governments to mere corporations and eventually to annihilate them. Those who have employed the term corporation upon this occasion are not perhaps aware of its extent. In common parlance, indeed, it is generally applied to petty associations for the ease and convenience of a few individuals; but in its enlarged sense, it will comprehend the government of Pennsylvania, the existing union of the States, and even this projected system is nothing more than a formal act of incorporation. But upon what presence can it be alleged that it was designed to annihilate the State governments? For I will undertake to prove that upon their existence depends the existence of the Federal plan. For this purpose, permit me to call your attention to the manner in which the President, Senate and House of Representatives are proposed to be appointed. The President is to be chosen by electors, nominated in such manner as the legislature of each State may direct; so that if there is no legislature there can be no electors, and consequently the office of President cannot be supplied.

The Senate is to be composed of two Senators from each State, chosen by the Legislature; and, therefore, if there is no Legislature, there can be no Senate. The House of Representatives is to be composed of members chosen every second year by the people of the several States, and the electors in each State shall have the qualifications requisite for electors of the most numerous branch of the State Legislature; unless, therefore, there is a State Legislature, that qualification cannot be ascertained, and the popular branch of the federal constitution must be extinct. From this view, then, it is evidently absurd to suppose that the annihilation of the separate governments will result from their union; or, that having that intention, the authors of the new system would have bound their connection with such indissoluble ties. Let me here advert to an arrangement highly advantageous, for you will perceive, without prejudice to the powers of the Legislature in the election of Senators, the people at large will acquire an additional privilege in returning members to the House of Representatives; whereas, by the present confederation, it is the Legislature alone that appoints the delegates to Congress.

FEDERALIST NO. 10[15]

Among the numerous advantages promised by a well-constructed Union, none deserves to be more accurately developed than its tendency to break and control the violence of faction.

By a faction, I understand a number of citizens, whether amounting to a majority or a minority of the whole, who are united and actuated by some common impulse of passion, or of interest, adverse to the rights of other citizens, or to the permanent and aggregate interests of the community.

. . . Liberty is to faction what air is to fire, an aliment without which it instantly expires. But it could not be less folly to abolish liberty, which is essential to political life, because it nourishes faction, than it would be to wish the annihilation of air, which is essential to animal life, because it imparts to fire its destructive agency.

. . . The latent causes of faction are thus sown in the nature of man; and we see them everywhere brought into different degrees of activity, according to the different circumstances of civil society.

. . . The two great points of difference between a democracy and a republic are: first, the delegation of the government, in the latter, to a small number of citizens elected by the rest; secondly, the greater number of citizens, and greater sphere of country, over which the latter may be extended.

The effect of the first difference is, on the one hand, to refine and enlarge the public views, by passing them through the medium of a chosen body of citizens, whose wisdom may best discern the true interest of their country, and whose patriotism and love of justice will be least likely to sacrifice it to temporary or partial considerations. Under such a regulation, it may well happen that the public voice, pronounced by the representatives of the people, will be more consonant to the public good than if pronounced by the people themselves, convened for the purpose. On the other hand, the effect may be inverted. Men of factious tempers, of local prejudices, or of sinister designs, may, by intrigue, by corruption, or by other means, first obtain the suffrages, and then betray the interests, of the people. The question resulting is, whether small or extensive republics are more favorable to the election of proper guardians of the public weal; and it is clearly decided in favor of the latter by two obvious considerations:

In the first place, it is to be remarked that, however small the republic may be, the representatives must be raised to a certain number, in order to guard against the cabals of a few; and that, however large it may be, they must be limited to a certain number, in order to guard against the confusion of a multitude. Hence, the number of representatives in the two cases not being in proportion to that of the two constituents, and being proportionally greater in the small republic, it follows that, if the proportion of fit characters be not less in the large than in the small republic, the former will present a greater option, and consequently a greater probability of a fit choice.

In the next place, as each representative will be chosen by a greater number of citizens in the large than in the small republic, it will be more difficult for unworthy candidates to practice with success the vicious arts by which elections are too often carried; and the suffrages of the people being more free, will be more likely to center in men who possess the most attractive merit and the most diffusive and established characters.

It must be confessed that in this, as in most other cases, there is a mean, on both sides of which inconveniences will be found to lie. By enlarging too much the number of electors, you render the representatives too little acquainted with all their local circumstances and lesser interests; as by reducing it too much, you render him unduly attached to these, and too little fit to comprehend and pursue great and national objects. The federal Constitution forms a happy combination in this respect; the great and aggregate interests being referred to the national, the local and particular to the State legislatures.

The other point of difference is, the greater number of citizens and extent of territory which may be brought within the compass of republican than of democratic government; and it is this circumstance principally which renders factious combinations less to be dreaded in the former than in the latter. The smaller the society, the fewer probably will be the distinct parties and interests composing it; the fewer the distinct parties and interests, the more frequently will a majority be found of the same party; and the smaller the number of individuals composing a majority, and the smaller the compass within which they are placed, the more easily will they concert and execute their plans of oppression. Extend the sphere, and you take in a greater variety of parties and interests; you make it less probable that a majority of the whole will have a common motive to invade the rights of other citizens; or if such a common motive exists, it will be more difficult for all who feel it to discover their own strength, and to act in unison with each other. Besides other impediments, it may be remarked that, where there is a consciousness of unjust or dishonorable purposes, communication is always checked by distrust in proportion to the number whose concurrence is necessary.

Hence, it clearly appears, that the same advantage which a republic has over a democracy, in controlling the effects of faction, is enjoyed by a large over a small republic,—is enjoyed by the Union over the States composing it. Does the advantage consist in the substitution of representatives whose enlightened views and virtuous sentiments render them superior to local prejudices and schemes of injustice? It will not be denied that the representation of the Union will be most likely to possess these requisite endowments. Does it consist in the greater security afforded by a greater variety of parties, against the event of any one party being able to outnumber and oppress the rest? In an equal degree does the increased variety of parties comprised within the Union, increase this security. Does it, in fine, consist in the greater obstacles opposed to the concert and accomplishment of the secret wishes of an unjust and interested majority? Here, again, the extent of the Union gives it the most palpable advantage.

The influence of factious leaders may kindle a flame within their particular States, but will be unable to spread a general conflagration through the other States. A religious sect may degenerate into a political faction in a part of the Confederacy; but the variety of sects dispersed over the entire face of it must secure the national councils against any danger from that source. A rage for paper money, for an abolition of debts, for an equal division of property, or for any other improper or wicked project, will be less apt to pervade the whole body of the Union than a particular member of it; in the same proportion as such a malady is more likely to taint a particular county or district, than an entire State.

In the extent and proper structure of the Union, therefore, we behold a republican remedy for the diseases most incident to republican government. And according to the degree of pleasure and pride we feel in being republicans, ought to be our zeal in cherishing the spirit and supporting the character of Federalists.

FEDERALIST NO. 26[16]

. . . the State legislatures, who will always be not only vigilant but suspicious and jealous guardians of the rights of the citizens against encroachments from the federal government, will constantly have their attention awake to the conduct of the national rulers, and will be ready enough, if any thing improper appears, to sound the alarm to the people, and not only to be the VOICE, but, if necessary, the ARM of their discontent.

FEDERALIST NO. 39[17]

. . . If we resort for a criterion to the different principles on which different forms of government are established, we may define a republic to be, or at least may bestow that name on, a government which derives all its powers directly or indirectly from the great body of the people, and is administered by persons holding their offices during pleasure, for a limited period, or during good behavior. It is ESSENTIAL to such a government that it be derived from the great body of the society, not from an inconsiderable proportion, or a favored class of it; otherwise a handful of tyrannical nobles, exercising their oppressions by a delegation of their powers, might aspire to the rank of republicans, and claim for their government the honorable title of republic. It is SUFFICIENT for such a government that the persons administering it be appointed, either directly or indirectly, by the people; and that they hold their appointments by either of the tenures just specified; otherwise every government in the United States, as well as every other popular government that has been or can be well organized or well executed, would be degraded from the republican character.

. . . "But it was not sufficient," say the adversaries of the proposed Constitution, "for the convention to adhere to the republican form. They ought, with equal care, to have preserved the FEDERAL form, which regards the Union as a CONFEDERACY of sovereign states; instead of which, they have framed a NATIONAL government, which regards the Union as a CONSOLIDATION of the States." And it is asked by what authority this bold and radical innovation was undertaken? The handle which has been made of this objection requires that it should be examined with some precision.

. . . In order to ascertain the real character of the government, it may be considered in relation to the foundation on which it is to be established; to the sources from which its ordinary powers are to be drawn; to the operation of those powers; to the extent of them; and to the authority by which future changes in the government are to be introduced.

On examining the first relation, it appears, on one hand, that the Constitution is to be founded on the assent and ratification of the people of America, given by deputies elected for the special purpose; but, on the other, that this assent and ratification is to be given by the people, not as individuals composing one entire nation, but as composing the distinct and independent States to which they respectively belong. It is to be the assent and ratification of the several States, derived from the supreme authority in each State, the authority of the people themselves. The act, therefore, establishing the Constitution, will not be a NATIONAL, but a FEDERAL act.

That it will be a federal and not a national act, as these terms are understood by the objectors; the act of the people, as forming so many independent States, not as forming one aggregate nation, is obvious from this single consideration, that it is to result neither from the decision of a MAJORITY of the people of the Union, nor from that of a MAJORITY of the States. It must result from the UNANIMOUS assent of the several States that are parties to it, differing no otherwise from their ordinary assent than in its being expressed, not by the legislative authority, but by that of the people themselves. Were the people regarded in this transaction as forming one nation, the will of the majority of the whole people of the United States would bind the minority, in the same manner as the majority in each State must bind the minority; and the will of the majority must be determined either by a comparison of the individual votes, or by considering the will of the majority of the States as evidence of the will of a majority of the people of the United States. Neither of these rules have been adopted. Each State, in ratifying the Constitution, is considered as a sovereign body, independent of all others, and only to be bound by its own voluntary act. In this relation, then, the new Constitution will, if established, be a FEDERAL, and not a NATIONAL constitution.

The next relation is, to the sources from which the ordinary powers of government are to be derived. The House of Representatives will derive its powers from the people of America; and the people will be represented in the same proportion, and on the same principle, as they are in the legislature of a particular State. So far the government is NATIONAL, not FEDERAL. The Senate, on the other hand, will derive its powers from the States, as political and coequal societies; and these will be represented on the principle of equality in the Senate, as they now are in the existing Congress. So far the government is FEDERAL, not NATIONAL. The executive power will be derived from a very compound source. The immediate election of the President is to be made by the States in their political characters. The votes allotted to them are in a compound ratio, which considers them partly as distinct and coequal societies, partly as unequal members of the same society. The eventual election, again, is to be made by that branch of the legislature which consists of the national representatives; but in this particular act they are to be thrown into the form of individual delegations, from so many distinct and coequal bodies politic. From this aspect of the government it appears to be of a mixed character, presenting at least as many FEDERAL as NATIONAL features.

The difference between a federal and national government, as it relates to the OPERATION OF THE GOVERNMENT, is supposed to consist in this, that in the former the powers operate on the political bodies composing the Confederacy, in their political capacities; in the latter, on the individual citizens composing the nation, in their individual capacities. On trying the Constitution by this criterion, it falls under the NATIONAL, not the FEDERAL character; though perhaps not so completely as has been understood. In several cases, and particularly in the trial of controversies to which States may be parties, they must be viewed and proceeded against in their collective and political capacities only. So far the national countenance of the government on this side seems to be disfigured by a few federal features. But this blemish is perhaps unavoidable in any plan; and the operation of the government on the people, in their individual capacities, in its ordinary and most essential proceedings, may, on the whole, designate it, in this relation, a NATIONAL government.

But if the government be national with regard to the OPERATION of its powers, it changes its aspect again when we contemplate it in relation to the

EXTENT of its powers. The idea of a national government involves in it, not only an authority over the individual citizens, but an indefinite supremacy over all persons and things, so far as they are objects of lawful government. Among a people consolidated into one nation, this supremacy is completely vested in the national legislature. Among communities united for particular purposes, it is vested partly in the general and partly in the municipal legislatures. In the former case, all local authorities are subordinate to the supreme; and may be controlled, directed, or abolished by it at pleasure. In the latter, the local or municipal authorities form distinct and independent portions of the supremacy, no more subject, within their respective spheres, to the general authority, than the general authority is subject to them, within its own sphere. In this relation, then, the proposed government cannot be deemed a NATIONAL one; since its jurisdiction extends to certain enumerated objects only, and leaves to the several States a residuary and inviolable sovereignty over all other objects. It is true that in controversies relating to the boundary between the two jurisdictions, the tribunal which is ultimately to decide, is to be established under the general government. But this does not change the principle of the case. The decision is to be impartially made, according to the rules of the Constitution; and all the usual and most effectual precautions are taken to secure this impartiality. Some such tribunal is clearly essential to prevent an appeal to the sword and a dissolution of the compact; and that it ought to be established under the general rather than under the local governments, or, to speak more properly, that it could be safely established under the first alone, is a position not likely to be combated.

If we try the Constitution by its last relation to the authority by which amendments are to be made, we find it neither wholly NATIONAL nor wholly FEDERAL. Were it wholly national, the supreme and ultimate authority would reside in the MAJORITY of the people of the Union; and this authority would be competent at all times, like that of a majority of every national society, to alter or abolish its established government. Were it wholly federal, on the other hand, the concurrence of each State in the Union would be essential to every alteration that would be binding on all. The mode provided by the plan of the convention is not founded on either of these principles. In requiring more than a majority, and principles. In requiring more than a majority, and particularly in computing the proportion by STATES, not by CITIZENS, it departs from the NATIONAL and advances towards the FEDERAL character; in rendering the concurrence of less than the whole number of States sufficient, it loses again the FEDERAL and partakes of the NATIONAL character.

The proposed Constitution, therefore, is, in strictness, neither a national nor a federal Constitution, but a composition of both. In its foundation it is federal, not national; in the sources from which the ordinary powers of the government are drawn, it is partly federal and partly national; in the operation of these powers, it is national, not federal; in the extent of them, again, it is federal, not national; and, finally, in the authoritative mode of introducing amendments, it is neither wholly federal nor wholly national.

FEDERALIST NO. 44[18]

. . . "power to make all laws which shall be necessary and proper for carrying into execution the foregoing powers, and all other powers vested by this Constitution in the government of the United States, or in any department or officer thereof." Few parts of the Constitution have been assailed with more intemperance than this; yet on a fair investigation of it, no part can appear more completely invulnerable. Without the SUBSTANCE of this power, the whole Constitution would be a dead letter. Those who object to the article, therefore, as a part of the Constitution, can only mean that the FORM of the provision is improper. But have they considered whether a better form could have been substituted? There are four other possible methods which the Constitution might have taken on this subject. They might have copied the second article of the existing Confederation, which would have prohibited the exercise of any power not EXPRESSLY delegated; they might have attempted a positive enumeration of the powers comprehended under the general terms "necessary and proper"; they might have attempted a negative enumeration of them, by specifying the powers excepted from the general definition; they might have been altogether silent on the subject, leaving these necessary and proper powers to construction and inference. Had the convention taken the first method of adopting the second article of Confederation, it is evident that the new Congress would be continually exposed, as their predecessors have been, to the alternative of construing the term "EXPRESSLY" with so much rigor, as to disarm the government of all real authority whatever, or with so much latitude as to destroy altogether the force of the restriction.

. . . If it be asked what is to be the consequence, in case the Congress shall misconstrue this part of the Constitution, and exercise powers not warranted by its true meaning, I answer, the same as if they should misconstrue or enlarge any other power vested in them; as if the general power had been reduced to particulars, and any one of these were to be violated; the same, in short, as if the State legislatures should violate the irrespective constitutional authorities. In the first instance, the success of the usurpation will depend on the executive and judiciary departments, which are to expound and give effect to the legislative acts; and in the last resort a remedy must be obtained from the people who can, by the election of more faithful representatives, annul the acts of the usurpers. The truth is, that this ultimate redress may be more confided in against unconstitutional acts of the federal than of the State legislatures, for this plain reason, that as every such act of the former will be an invasion of the rights of the latter, these will be ever ready to mark the innovation, to sound the alarm to the people, and to exert their local influence in effecting a change of federal representatives.

BRUTUS 1[19]

. . . The first question that presents itself on the subject is, whether a confederated government be the best for the United States or not? Or in other words, whether the thirteen United States should be reduced to one great republic, governed by one legislature, and under the direction of one executive and judicial; or whether they should continue thirteen confederated republics, under the direction and control of a supreme federal head for certain defined national purposes only?

This enquiry is important, because, although the government reported by the convention does not go to a perfect and entire consolidation, yet it approaches so near to it, that it must, if executed, certainly and infallibly terminate in it.

This government is to possess absolute and uncontrollable power, legislative, executive and judicial, with respect to every object to which it extends for by, the last clause of section 8th, article 1st, it is declared "that the Congress shall have power to make all laws which shall be necessary and proper for carrying into execution the foregoing powers, and all other powers vested by this constitution, in the government of the United States; or in any department or office thereof" And by the 6th article, it is declared "that this constitution, and the laws of the United States, which shall be made in pursuance thereof and the treaties made, or which shall be made, under the authority of the United States, shall be the supreme law of the land; and the judges in every state shall be bound thereby, anything in the constitution, or law of any state to the contrary notwithstanding." It appears from these articles that there is no need of any intervention of the state governments, between the Congress and the people, to execute any one power vested in the general government, and that the constitution and laws of every state are nullified and declared void, so far as they are or shall be inconsistent with this constitution, or the laws made in pursuance of it, or with treaties made under the authority of the United States.—The government then, so far as it extends, is a complete one, and not a confederation. It is as much one complete government as that of New-York or Massachusetts, has as absolute and perfect powers to make and execute all laws, to appoint officers, institute courts, declare offences, and annex penalties, with respect to every object to which it extends, as any other in the world. So far therefore as its powers reach, all ideas of confederation are given up and lost. It is true this government is limited to certain objects, or to speak more properly, some small degree of power is still left to the states, but a little attention to the powers vested in the general government, will convince every candid man, that if it is capable of being executed, all that is reserved for the individual states must very soon be annihilated, except so far as they are barely necessary to the organization of the general government. The powers of the general legislature extend to every case that is of the least importance—there is nothing valuable to human nature, nothing dear to freemen, but what is within its power. It has authority to make laws which will affect the lives, the liberty, and property of everyman in the United States; nor can the constitution or laws of any state, in anyway prevent or impede the full and complete execution of every power given.

. . . Let us now proceed to enquire, as I at first proposed, whether it be best the thirteen United States should be reduced to one great republic, or not? It is here taken for granted, that all agree in this, that whatever government we adopt, it ought to be a free one; that it should be so framed as to secure the liberty of the citizens of America, and such an one as to admit of a full, fair, and equal representation of the people. The question then will be, whether a government thus constituted, and founded on such principles, is practicable, and can be exercised over the whole United States, reduced into one state?

If respect is to be paid to the opinion of the greatest and wisest men who have ever thought or wrote on the science of government, we shall be constrained to conclude, that a free republic cannot succeed over a country of such immense extent, containing such a number of inhabitants, and these increasing in such rapid progression as that of the whole United States. Among the many illustrious authorities which might be produced to this point, I shall content myself with quoting only two. The one is the baron de Montesquieu, spirit of laws, chap. xvi. vol. 1. "It is natural to a republic to have only a small territory, otherwise it cannot long subsist. In a large republic there are men of large fortunes, and consequently less moderation; there are trusts too great to be placed in any single subject; he has interest of his own; he soon begins to think that he may be happy, great and glorious, by oppressing his fellow citizens; and that he may raise himself to grandeur on the ruins of his country. In a large republic, the public good is sacrificed to a thousand views; it is subordinate to exceptions, and depends on accidents. In a small one, the interest of the public is easier perceived, better understood, and more within the reach of every citizen; abuses are of less extent, and of course are less protected."

History furnishes no example of a free republic, any thing like the extent of the United States. The Grecian republics were of small extent; so also was that of the Romans. Both of these, it is true, in process of time, extended their conquests over large territories of country; and the consequence was, that their governments were changed from that of free governments to those of the most tyrannical that ever existed in the world.

Not only the opinion of the greatest men, and the experience of mankind, are against the idea of an extensive republic, but a variety of reasons may be drawn from the reason and nature of things, against it. In every government, the will of the sovereign is the law.

. . . In a free republic, although all laws are derived from the consent of the people, yet the people do not declare their consent by themselves in person, but representatives, chosen by them, who are supposed to know the minds of their constituents, and to be possessed of integrity to declare this mind.

In every free government, the people must give their assent to the laws by which they are governed. This is the true criterion between a free government and an arbitrary one. The former are ruled by the will of the whole, expressed in any manner they may agree upon; the latter by the will of one, or a few. If the people are to give their assent to the laws, by persons chosen and appointed by them, the manner of the choice and the number chosen, must be such, as to possess, be disposed, and consequently qualified to declare the sentiments of the people; for if they do not know, or are not disposed to speak the sentiments of the people, the people do not govern, but the sovereignty is in a few. Now, in a large extended country, it is impossible to have a representation, possessing the sentiments, and of integrity, to declare the minds of the people, without having it so numerous and unwieldy, as to be subject in great measure to the inconveniency a democratic government.

The territory of the United States is of vast extent; it now contains near three millions of souls, and is capable of containing much more than ten times that number. Is it practicable for a country, so large and so numerous as they will soon become, to elect a representation, that will speak their sentiments, without their becoming so numerous as to be incapable of transacting public business? It certainly is not.

In a republic, the manners, sentiments, and interests of the people should be similar. If this be not the case, there will be a constant clashing of opinions; and the representatives of one part will be continually striving against those of the other. This will retard the operations of government, and prevent such conclusions as will promote the public good. If we apply this remark to the condition of the United States, we shall be convinced that it forbids that we should be one government. The United States includes a variety of climates. The productions of the different parts of the union are very variant, and their interests, of consequence, diverse. Their manners and habits differ as much as their climates and productions; and their sentiments are by no means coincident. The laws and customs of the several states are, in many respects, very diverse, and in some opposite; each would be in favor of its own interests and customs, and, of consequence, a legislature, formed of representatives from the respective parts, would not only be too numerous to act with any care or decision, but would be composed of such heterogenous and discordant principles, as would constantly be contending with each other.

The laws cannot be executed in a republic, of an extent equal to that of the United States, with promptitude.

The magistrates in every government must be supported in the execution of the laws, either by an armed force, maintained the public expense for that purpose; or by the people turning out to aid the magistrate upon his command, in case of resistance.

In despotic governments, as well as in all the monarchies of Europe, standing armies are kept up to execute the commands of the prince or the magistrate, and are employed for this purpose when occasion requires: But they have always proved the destruction of liberty, and is abhorrent to the spirit of a free republic. In England, where they depend upon the parliament for their annual support, they have always been complained of as oppressive and unconstitutional, and are seldom employed in executing of the laws; never except on extraordinary occasions, and then under the direction of a civil magistrate.

A free republic will never keep a standing army to execute its laws. It must depend upon the support of its citizens. But when a government is to receive its support from the aid of the citizens, it must be so constructed as to have the confidence, respect, and affection of the people. Men who, upon the call of the magistrate, offer themselves to execute the laws, are influenced to do it either by affection to the government, or from fear; where a standing army is at hand to punish offenders, every man is actuated by the latter principle, and therefore, when the magistrate calls, will obey: but, where this is not the case, the government must rest for its support upon the confidence and respect which the people have for their government and laws. The body of the people being attached, the government will always be sufficient to support and execute its laws, and to operate upon the fears of any faction which maybe opposed to it, not only to prevent an opposition to the execution of the laws themselves, but also to compel the most of them to aid the magistrate; but the people will not be likely to have such confidence in their rulers, in a republic so extensive as the United States, as necessary for these purposes. The confidence which the people have in their rulers, in a free republic, arises from their knowing them, from their being responsible to them for their conduct, and from the power they have of displacing them when they misbehave: but in a republic of the extent of this continent, the people in general would be acquainted with very few of their rulers: the people at large would know little of their proceedings, and it would be extremely difficult to change them. The people in Georgia and New-Hampshire would not know one another's mind, and therefore could not act in concert to enable them to effect a general change representatives. The different parts of so extensive a country could not possibly be made acquainted with the conduct of their representatives, nor be informed of the reasons upon which measures were founded. The consequence will be, they will have no confidence in their legislature, suspect them of ambitious views, be jealous of every measure they adopt, and will not support the laws they pass. Hence the government will be nerveless and inefficient, and no way will be left to render it otherwise, but by establishing an armed force to execute the laws at the point of the bayonet—a government of all others the most to be dreaded.

In a republic of such vast extent as the United-States, the legislature cannot attend to the various concerns and wants of its different parts. It cannot be sufficiently numerous to be acquainted with the local condition and wants of the different districts, and if it could, it is impossible it should have sufficient time to attend to and provide for all the variety of cases of this nature, that would be continually arising.

In so extensive a republic, the great officers of government would soon become above the control of the people, and abuse their power to the purpose aggrandizing themselves, and oppressing them. The trust committed to the executive offices, in a country of the extent of the United-States, must be various and of magnitude. The command of all the troops and navy of the republic, the appointment of officers, the power of pardoning offences, the collecting of all the public revenues, and the power of expending them, with a number of other powers, must be lodged and exercised in every state, in the hands of a few. When these are attended with great honor and emolument, as they always will be in large states, so as greatly to interest men to pursue them, and to be proper objects for ambitious and designing men, such men will be ever restless in their pursuit after them. They will use the power, when they have acquired it, to the purposes of gratifying their own interest and ambition, and it is scarcely possible, in a very large republic, to call them to account for their misconduct, or to prevent their abuse of power.

These are some of the reasons by which it appears, that a free republic cannot long subsist over a country of the great extent of these states. If then this new constitution is calculated to consolidate the thirteen states into one, as it evidently is, it ought not to be adopted.

BRUTUS 6[20]

. . . The question therefore between us, this being admitted, is, whether or not this system is so formed as either directly to annihilate the state governments, or that in its operation it will certainly effect it. If this is answered in the affirmative, then the system ought not to be adopted, without such amendments as will avoid this consequence. If on the contrary it can be show, that the state governments are secured in their rights to manage the internal police of the respective states, we must confine ourselves in our enquiries to the organization of the government and the guards and provisions it contains to prevent a misuse or abuse of power . . .

The general government is to be vested with authority to levy and collect taxes, duties, and excises; the separate states have also power to impose taxes, duties, and excises, except that they cannot lay duties on exports and imports without the consent of Congress. Here then the two governments have concurrent jurisdiction; both may lay impositions of this kind. But then the general government have supperadded to this power, authority to make all laws which shall be necessary and proper for carrying the foregoing power into execution. Suppose then that both governments should lay taxes, duties, and excises, and it should fall so heavy on the people that they would be unable, or be so burdensome that they would refuse to pay them both—would it not be necessary that the general legislature should suspend the collection of the state tax? It certainly would. For, if the people could not, or would not pay both, they must be discharged from the tax to the state, or the tax to the general government could not be collected.—The conclusion therefore is inevitable, that the respective state governments will not have the power to raise one shilling in any way, but by the permission of the Congress. I presume no one will pretend, that the states can exercise legislative authority, or administer justice among their citizens for any length of time, without being able to raise a sufficiency to pay those who administer their governments.

If this be true, and if the states can raise money only by permission of the general government, it follows that the state governments will be dependent on the will of the general government for their existence.

What will render this power in Congress effectual and sure in its operation is, that the government will have complete judicial and executive authority to carry all their laws into effect, which will be paramount to the judicial and executive authority of the individual states: in vain therefore will be all interference of the legislatures, courts, or magistrates of any of the states on the subject; for they will be subordinate to the general government, and engaged by oath to support it, and will be constitutionally bound to submit to their decisions.

The general legislature will be empowered to lay any tax they chose, to annex any penalties they please to the breach of their revenue laws; and to appoint as many officers as they may think proper to collect the taxes. They will have authority to farm the revenues and to vest the farmer general, with his subalterns, with plenary powers to collect them, in anyway which to them may appear eligible. And the courts of law, which they will be authorized to institute, will have cognizance of every case arising under the revenue laws, the conduct of all the officers employed in collecting them; and the officers of these courts will execute their judgments. There is no way, therefore, of avoiding the destruction of the state governments, whenever the Congress please to do it, unless the people rise up, and, with a strong hand, resist and prevent the execution constitutional laws. The fear of this, will, it is presumed, restrain the general government, for some time, within proper bounds; but it will not be many years before they will have a revenue, and force, at their command, which will place them above any apprehensions on that score.

How far the power to lay and collect duties and excises, may operate to dissolve the state governments, and oppress the people, it is impossible to say. It would assist us much in forming just opinion on this head, to consider the various objects to which this kind of taxes extend, in European nations, and the infinity of laws they have passed respecting them. Perhaps, if leisure will permit, this may be essayed in some future paper.

. . . This power, exercised without limitation, will introduce itself into every corner of the city, and country-It will wait upon the ladies at their toilet, and will not leave them in any of their domestic concerns; it will accompany them to the ball, the play, and the assembly; it will go with them when they visit, and will, on all occasions, sit beside them in their carriages, nor will it desert them even at church; it will enter the house of every gentleman, watch over his cellar, wait upon his cook in the kitchen, follow the servants into the parlor, preside over the table, and note down all he eats or drinks; it will attend him to his bed-chamber, and watch him while he sleeps; it will take cognizance of the professional man in his office, or his study; it will watch the merchant in the counting-house, or in his store; it will follow the mechanic to his shop, and in his work, and will haunt him in his family, and in his bed; it will be a constant companion of the industrious farmer in all his labor, it will be with him in the house, and in the field, observe the toil of his hands, arid the sweat of his brow; it will penetrate into the most obscure cottage; and finally, it will light upon the head of every person in the United States. To all these different classes of people, and in all these circumstances, in which it will attend them, the language in which it will address them, will be GIVE! GIVE!

A power that has such latitude, which reaches every person in the community in every conceivable circumstance, and lays hold of every species of property they possess, and which has no bounds set to it, but the discretion of those who exercise it. I say, such a power must necessarily, from its very nature, swallow up all the power of the state governments.

SAMUEL ADAMS TO RICHARD HENRY
LEE, DECEMBER 3, 1787[21]

I confess, as I enter the Building I stumble at the Threshold. I meet with a National Government, instead of a Federal Union of Sovereign States. I am not able to conceive why the Wisdom of the Convention led them to give the Preference to the former before the latter. If the several States in the Union are to become one entire Nation, under one Legislature, the Powers of which shall extend to every Subject of Legislation, and its Laws be supreme & control the whole, the Idea of Sovereignty in these States must be lost. Indeed I think, upon such a Supposition, those Sovereignties ought to be eradicated from the Mind; for they would be *Imperia in Imperio* justly deemed a Solecism in Politics, & they would be highly dangerous, and destructive of the Peace Union and Safety of the Nation. And can this National Legislature be competent to make Laws for the free internal Government of one People, living in Climates so remote and whose "Habits & particular Interests" are and probably always will be so different. Is it to be expected that General Laws can be adapted to the Feelings of the more Eastern and the more Southern Parts of so extensive a Nation? It appears to me difficult if practicable. Hence then may we not look for Discontent, Mistrust, Disaffection to Government and frequent Insurrections, which will require standing Armies to suppress them in one Place & another where they may happen to arise. Or if Laws could be made, adapted to the local Habits, Feelings, Views & Interests of those distant Parts, would they not cause Jealousies of Partiality in Government which would excite Envy and other malignant Passions productive of Wars and fighting. But should we continue distinct sovereign States, confederated for the Purposes of mutual Safety and Happiness, each contributing to the federal Head such a Part of its Sovereignty as would render the Government fully adequate to those Purposes and no more, the People would govern themselves more easily, the Laws of each State being well adapted to its own Genius & Circumstances, and the Liberties of the United States would be more secure than they can be, as I humbly conceive, under the proposed new Constitution. You are sensible, Sir, that the Seeds of Aristocracy began to spring even before the Conclusion of our Struggle for the natural Rights of Men, Seeds which like a Canker Worm lie at the Root of free Governments. So great is the Wickedness of some Men, & the stupid Servility of others, that one would be almost inclined to conclude that Communities cannot be free. The few haughty Families, think They must govern. The Body of the People tamely consent & submit to be their Slaves. This unravels the Mystery of Millions being enslaved by the few!

AN OLD WHIG II[22]

The first principle which the gentleman [James Wilson] endeavors to establish in his speech is a very important one, if true; and lays a sure foundation to reason upon, in answer to the objection which is made to the new constitution, from the want of a bill of rights. The principle is this: that "in delegating federal powers, the congressional authority is to be collected, not from tacit implication, but from the positive grant expressed in the instrument of union," "that every thing which is not given is reserved." If this be a just representation of the matter, the authority of the several states will be sufficient to protect our liberties from the encroachments of Congress, without any continental bill of rights; unless the powers which are expressly given to Congress are too large.

Without examining particularly present, whether the powers expressly given to Congress are too large or too small, I shall beg leave to consider, whether the author of this speech is sufficiently accurate in his statement of the proposition above referred to- To strip it of unnecessary words, the position may be reduced to this short sentence, "that every thing which is not expressly given to Congress is reserved;" or in other words "that Congress cannot exercise any power or authority that is not in express words delegated to them." This certainly is the case under the first articles confederation which hitherto have been the rule and standard of the powers of Congress; for in the second of those articles "each state retains its sovereignty freedom and independence and every power, jurisdiction and right which is not by this confederation expressly delegated to the United States in Congress assembled." It was the misfortune of these articles of confederation that they did not by express words give to Congress power sufficient for the purposes of the union; for Congress could not go beyond those powers so expressly given. The position of the speech, therefore is strictly true if applied to the first articles confederation; "that everything which is not expressly given is reserved." We are not however to suppose that the speaker meant insidiously to argue from an article in the old confederation in favor of the new constitution, unless the same thing was also in the new constitution. Let us then fairly examine whether in the proposed new constitution there be any thing from which the gentleman can be justified in his opinion, "that every thing which is not expressly given to Congress is reserved."

In the first place then it is most certain that we find no such clause or article in the new constitution. There is nothing in the new constitution which either in form or substance bears the least resemblance to the second article of the confederation. It might nevertheless be a fair argument to insist upon from the nature of delegated powers, that no more power is given in such cases than is expressly given. Whether or not this ground of argument would be such as we might safely rest our liberties upon; or whether it would be more prudent to stipulate expressly as is done in the present confederation for the reservation of all such powers as are not expressly given, it is hardly necessary to determine at present. It strikes me that by the proposed constitution, so far from the reservation of all powers that are not expressly given, the future Congress will be fully authorized to assume all such powers as they in their wisdom or wickedness, according as the one or the other may happen to prevail, shall from time to time think proper to assume.

Let us weigh this matter carefully; for it is certainly of the utmost importance, and, if I am right in my opinion, the new constitution vests Congress with such unlimited powers as ought never to be entrusted to any men or body of men. It is justly observed that the possession of sovereign power is a temptation too great for human nature to resist; and although we have read in history of one or two illustrious characters who have refused to enslave their country when it was in their power;-although have seen one illustrious character in our own times resisting the possession of power when set in competition with his duty to his country, yet these instances are so very rare, that it would be worse than madness to trust to the chance of their being often repeated.

To proceed then with the enquiry, whether the future Congress will be restricted to those powers which are expressly given to them. I would observe that in the opinion of Montesquieu, and of most other writers, ancient as well as modern, the legislature is the sovereign power . . . Let us then see what are the powers expressly given to the legislature of Congress, and what checks are interposed in the way of the continental legislature's assuming what further power they shall think proper to assume.

To this end let us look to the first article of the proposed new constitution, which treats of the legislative powers of Congress; and to the eighth section which pretends to define those powers. We find here that the congress, in its legislative capacity, shall have the power "to lay and collect taxes, duties and excises; to borrow money; to regulate commerce; to fix the rule for naturalization and the laws of bankruptcy; to coin money; to punish counterfeiters; establish post offices and post roads; to secure copyrights to authors; to constitute tribunals; to define and punish piracies; to declare war; to raise and support armies; to provide and support a navy; to make rules for the army and navy; to call forth the militia; to organize, arm and discipline the militia; to exercise absolute power over a district of ten miles square, independent of all the state legislatures, and to be alike absolute over all forts, magazines, arsenals, dockyards and other needful buildings thereunto belonging." This is a short abstract of the powers expressly given to Congress. These powers are very extensive, but I shall not stay at present to inquire whether these express powers were necessary to be given to Congress? whether they are too great or too small? My object is to consider that undefined, unbounded and immense power which is comprised in the following clause; "And, to make all laws which shall be necessary and proper for carrying into execution the foregoing powers and all other powers vested by this constitution in the government of the United States; or in any department or offices thereof." Under such a clause as this can any thing be said to be reserved and kept back from Congress? Can it be said that the Congress have no power but what is expressed? "To make all laws which shall be necessary and proper" is in other words to make all such laws which the Congress shall think necessary and proper, for who shall judge for the legislature what is necessary and proper-Who shall set themselves above the sovereign? What inferior legislature shall set itself above the supreme legislature?—To me it appears that no other power on earth can dictate to them or control them, unless by force; and force either internal or external is one of those calamities which every good man would wish his country at all times to be delivered from. -This generation in America have seen enough of war and its usual concomitants to prevent all of us from wishing to see anymore of it; -all except those who make a trade of war. But to the question; -without force what can restrain the Congress from making such laws as they please? What limits are there to their authority? I fear none at all; for surely it cannot justly be said that they have no power but what is expressly given to them, whereby the very terms of their creation they are vested with the powers of making laws in all cases necessary and proper; when from the nature of their power they must necessarily be the judges, what laws are necessary and proper. The British act of Parliament, declaring the power of Parliament to make laws to bind America in all cases whatsoever, was not more extensive; for it is as true as a maxim, that even the British Parliament neither could nor would pass any law in any case in which they did not either deem it necessary and proper to make such law or pretend to deem it so. And in such cases it is not of a farthing consequence whether they really are of opinion that the law is necessary and proper, or only pretend to think so; for who can overrule their pretensions?-No one, unless we had a bill of rights to which we might appeal, and under which we might contend against any assumption of undue power and appeal to the judicial branch of the government to protect us by their judgements. This reasoning I fear Mr. Printer is but too just; and yet, if any man should doubt the truth of it; let me ask him one other question, what is the meaning of the latter part of the clause which vests the Congress with the authority of making all laws which shall be necessary and proper for carrying into execution ALL OTHER POWERS;—besides the foregoing powers vested, &c. &c. Was it thought that the foregoing powers might perhaps admit of some restraint in their construction as to what was necessary and proper to carry them into execution? Or was it deemed right to add still further that they should not be restrained to the powers already named? -besides the powers already mentioned, other powers may be assumed hereafter as contained by implication in this constitution. The Congress shall judge of what is necessary and proper in all these cases and in all other cases;—in short in all cases whatsoever.

Where then is the restraint? How are Congress bound down to the powers expressly given? what is reserved or can be reserved?

Yet even this is not all—as if it were determined that no doubt should remain, by the sixth article of the constitution it is declared that, "this constitution, and the laws of the United States which shall be made in pursuance thereof; and all treaties made, or which shall be made, under the authority of the United States, shall be the supreme law of the land, and the judges in every state shall be bound thereby, any thing in the constitutions or laws of any state to the contrary notwithstanding." The Congress are therefore vested with the supreme legislative power, without control. In giving such immense, such unlimited powers, was there no necessity of a bill of rights to secure to the people their liberties? Is it not evident that we are left wholly dependent on the wisdom and virtue of the men who shall from time to time be the members of Congress? and who shall be able to say seven years hence, the members of Congress will be wise and good men, or of the contrary character.

PATRICK HENRY, VIRGINIA
RATIFYING CONVENTION[23]

I am not free from suspicion: I am apt to entertain doubts: I rose yesterday to ask a question, which arose in my own mind. When I asked the question, I thought the meaning of my interrogation was obvious: The fate of this question and America may depend on this: Have they said, we the States? Have they made a proposal of a compact between States? If they had, this would be a confederation: It is otherwise most clearly a consolidated government. The question turns, Sir, on that poor little thing—the expression, We, the people, instead of the States of America. I need not take much pains to show, that the principles of this system, are extremely pernicious, impolitic, and dangerous. Is this a Monarchy, like England—a compact between Prince and people; with checks on the former, to secure the liberty of the latter? Is this a Confederacy, like Holland—an association of a number of independent States, each of which retain its individual sovereignty? It is not a democracy, wherein the people retain all their rights securely. Had these principles been adhered to, we should not have been brought to this alarming transition, from a Confederacy to a consolidated Government. We have no detail of those great considerations which, in my opinion, ought to have abounded before we should recur to a government of this kind. Here is a revolution as radical as that which separated us from Great Britain. It is as radical, if in this transition our rights and privileges are endangered, and the sovereignty of the States be relinquished: And cannot we plainly see, that this is actually the case? The rights of conscience, trial by jury, liberty of the press, all your immunities and franchises, all pretensions to human rights and privileges, are rendered insecure, if not lost, by this change so loudly talked of by some, and inconsiderately by others. Is this same relinquishment of rights worthy of freemen? Is it worthy of that manly fortitude that ought to characterize republicans: It is said eight States have adopted this plan. I declare that if twelve States and an half had adopted it, I would with manly firmness, and in spite of an erring world, reject it. You are not to inquire how your trade may be increased, nor how you are to become a great and powerful people, but how your liberties can be secured; for liberty ought to be the direct end of your Government.

. . . The distinction between a National Government and a Confederacy is not sufficiently discerned. Had the delegates who were sent to Philadelphia a power to propose a Consolidated Government instead of a Confederacy? Were they not deputed by States, and not by the people? The assent of the people in their collective capacity is not necessary to the formation of a Federal Government. The people have no right to enter into leagues, alliances, or confederations: They are not the proper agents for this purpose: States and sovereign powers are the only proper agents for this kind of Government: Show me an instance where the people have exercised this business: Has it not always gone through the Legislatures? I refer you to the treaties with France, Holland, and other nations: How were they made? Were they not made by the States? Are the people therefore in their aggregate capacity, the proper persons to form a Confederacy? This, therefore, ought to depend on the consent of the Legislatures; the people having never sent delegates to make any proposition of changing the Government. Yet I must say, at the same time, that it was made on grounds the most pure, and perhaps I might have been brought to consent to it so far as to the change of Government; but there is one thing in it which I never would acquiesce in. I mean the changing it into a Consolidated Government; which is so abhorrent to my mind. The Honorable Gentleman then went on to the figure we make with foreign nations; the contemptible one we make in France and Holland; which, according to the system of my notes, he attributes to the present feeble Government. An opinion has gone forth, we find, that we are a contemptible people: The time has been when we were thought otherwise: Under this same despised Government, we commanded the respect of all Europe: Wherefore are we now reckoned otherwise? The American spirit has fled from hence: It has gone to regions, where it has never been expected: It has gone to the people of France in search of a splendid Government—a strong energetic Government. Shall we imitate the example of those nations who have gone from a simple to a splendid Government. Are those nations more worthy of our imitation? What can make an adequate satisfaction to them for the loss they suffered in attaining such a Government for the loss of their liberty? If we admit this Consolidated Government it will be because we like a great splendid one. Some way or other we must be a great and mighty empire; we must have an army, and a navy, and a number of things: When the American spirit was in its youth, the language of America was different: Liberty, Sir, was then the primary object. We are descended from a people whose Government was founded on liberty: Our glorious forefathers of Great-Britain, made liberty the foundation of every thing. That country is become a great, mighty, and splendid nation; not because their Government is strong and energetic; but, Sir, because liberty is its direct end and foundation: We drew the spirit of liberty from our British ancestors; by that spirit we have triumphed over every difficulty: But now, Sir, the American spirit, assisted by the ropes and chains of consolidation, is about to convert this country to a powerful and mighty empire: If you make the citizens of this country agree to become the subjects of one great consolidated empire of America, your Government will not have sufficient energy to keep them together: Such a Government is incompatible with the genius of republicanism: There will be no checks, no real balances, in this Government: What can avail your specious imaginary balances, your rope-dancing, chain-rattling, ridiculous ideal checks and contrivances? But, Sir, we are not feared by foreigners: we do not make nations tremble: Would this, Sir, constitute happiness, or secure liberty? I trust, Sir, our political hemisphere will ever direct their operations to the security of those objects. Consider our situation, Sir: Go to the poor man, ask him what he does; he will inform you, that he enjoys the fruits of his labor, under his own fig-tree, with his wife and children around him, in peace and security. Go to every other member of the society, you will find the same tranquil ease and content; you will find no alarms or disturbances: Why then tell us of dangers to terrify us into an adoption of this new Government? and yet who knows the dangers that this new system may produce; they are out of the sight of the common people: They cannot foresee latent consequences: I dread the operation of it on the middling and lower class of people: It is for them I fear the adoption of this system.

TENTH AMENDMENT (RATIFIED DECEMBER 15, 1791)

The powers not delegated to the United States by the Constitution, nor prohibited by it to the States, are reserved to the States respectively, or to the people.

THOMAS JEFFERSON OPINION ON THE
CONSTITUTIONALITY OF A NATIONAL BANK[24]

. . . I consider the foundation of the Constitution as laid on this ground: That " all powers not delegated to the United States, by the Constitution, nor prohibited by it to the States, are reserved to the States or to the people." [10th amendment.] To take a single step beyond the boundaries thus specially drawn around the powers of Congress, is to take possession of a boundless field of power, no longer susceptible of any definition.

. . . II. Nor are they within either of the general phrases, which are the two following:

1. To lay taxes to provide for the general welfare of the United States, that is to say, "to lay taxes for *the purpose of* providing for the general welfare." For the laying of taxes is the *power*, and the general welfare the *purpose* for which the power is to be exercised. They are not to lay taxes *ad libitum for any purpose they please*; but only *to pay the debts or provide for the welfare of the Union*. In like manner, they are not *to do anything they please* to provide for the general welfare, but only to *lay taxes* for that purpose. To consider the latter phrase, not as describing the purpose of the first, but as giving a distinct and independent power to do any act they please, which might be for the good of the Union, would render all the preceding and subsequent enumerations of power completely useless.

It would reduce the whole instrument to a single phrase, that of instituting a Congress with power to do whatever would be for the good of the United States; and, as they would be the sole judges of the good or evil, it would be also a power to do whatever evil they please.

. . . 2. The second general phrase is, "to make all laws *necessary* and proper for carrying into execution the enumerated powers." But they can all be carried into execution without a bank. A bank therefore is not *necessary*, and consequently not authorized by this phrase.

If has been urged that a bank will give great facility or convenience in the collection of taxes, Suppose this were true: yet the Constitution allows only the means which are "*necessary*," not those which are merely "convenient" for effecting the enumerated powers. If such a latitude of construction be allowed to this phrase as to give any non-enumerated power, it will go to everyone, for there is not one which ingenuity may not torture into a *convenience* in some instance *or other*, to *some one* of so long a list of enumerated powers. It would swallow up all the delegated powers, and reduce the whole to one power, as before observed. Therefore it was that the Constitution restrained them to the *necessary* means, that is to say, to those means without which the grant of power would be nugatory.

ALEXANDER HAMILTON OPINION ON THE
CONSTITUTIONALITY OF A NATIONAL BANK[25]

Now it appears to the Secretary of the Treasury that this general principle is inherent in the very definition of government, and essential to every step of progress to be made by that of the United States, namely: That every power vested in a government is in its nature sovereign, and includes, by force of the term, a right to employ all the means requisite and fairly applicable to the attainment of the ends of such power, and which are not precluded by restrictions and exceptions specified in the Constitution, or not immoral, or not contrary to the essential ends of political society.

This principle, in its application to government in general, would be admitted as an axiom; and it will be incumbent upon those who may incline to deny it, to prove a distinction, and to show that a rule which, in the general system of things, is essential to the preservation of the social order, is inapplicable to the United States.

The circumstance that the powers of sovereignty are in this country divided between the National and State governments, does not afford the distinction required. It does not follow from this, that each of the portion of powers delegated to the one or to the other, is not sovereign with regard to its proper objects. It will only follow from it, that each has sovereign power as to certain things, and not as to other things. To deny that the government of the United States has sovereign power, as to its declared purposes and trusts, because its power does not extend to all cases would be equally to deny that the State governments have sovereign power in any case, because their power does not extend to every case. The tenth section of the first article of the Constitution exhibits a long list of very important things which they may not do. And thus the United States would furnish the singular spectacle of a political society without sovereignty, or of a people governed, without government.

If it would be necessary to bring proof to a proposition so clear, as that which affirms that the powers of the federal government, as to its objects, were sovereign, there is a clause of its Constitution which would be decisive. It is that which declares that the Constitution, and the laws of the United States made in pursuance of it, and all treaties made, or which shall be made, under their authority, shall be the serene law of the land. The power which can create the supreme law of the land in any case, is doubtless sovereign as to such case.

. . . The first of these arguments is, that the foundation of the Constitution is laid on this ground: "That all powers not delegated to the United States by the Constitution, nor prohibited to it by the States, are reserved for the States, or to the people." Whence it is meant to be inferred, that Congress can in no case exercise any power not Included in those not enumerated in the Constitution.

And it is affirmed, that the power of erecting a corporation is not included in any of the enumerated powers.

The main proposition here laid down, in its true signification is not to be questioned. It is nothing more than a consequence of this republican maxim, that all government is a delegation of power. But how much is delegated in each case, is a question of fact, to be made out by fair reasoning and construction, upon the particular provisions of the Constitution, taking as guides the general principles and general ends of governments.

It is not denied that there are implied well as express powers, and that the former are as effectually delegated as the tatter. And for the sake of accuracy it shall be mentioned, that there is another class of powers, which may be properly denominated resting powers. It will not be doubted, that if the United States should make a conquest of any of the territories of its neighbors, they would possess sovereign jurisdiction over the conquered territory. This would be rather a result, from the whole mass of the powers of the government, and from the nature of political society, than a consequence of either of the powers specially enumerated.

. . . To return: . . . The only question must be in this, as in every other case, whether the mean to be employed or in this instance, the corporation to be erected, has a natural relation to any of the acknowledged objects or lawful ends of the government.

. . . It is certain that neither the grammatical nor popular sense of the term requires that construction. According to both, necessary often means no more than needful, requisite, incidental, useful, or conducive to. It is a common mode of expression to say, that it is necessary for a government or a person to do this or that thing, when nothing more is intended or understood, than that the interests of the government or person require, or will be promoted by, the doing of this or that thing. The imagination can be at no loss for exemplifications of the use of the word in this sense. And it is the true one in which it is to be understood as used in the Constitution. The whole turn of the clause containing it indicates, that it was the intent of the Convention, by that clause, to give a liberal latitude to the exercise of the specified powers. The expressions have peculiar comprehensiveness. They are thought to make all laws necessary and proper for carrying into execution the foregoing powers, and all other powers vested by the Constitution in the government of the United States, or in any department or officer thereof."

. . . It may be truly said of every government, as well as of that of the United States, that it has only a right to pass such laws as are necessary and proper to accomplish the objects intrusted to it. For no government has a right to do merely what it pleases. . . .

The degree in which a measure is necessary, can never be a test of the legal right to adopt it; that must be a matter of opinion, and can only be a test of expediency. The relation between the measure and the end; between the nature of the mean employed toward the execution of a power, and the object of that power must be the criterion of constitutionality, not the more or less of necessity or utility.

. . . The truth is, that difficulties on this point are inherent in the nature of the Federal Constitution; they result inevitably from a division of the legislative power. The consequence of this division is, that there will be cases clearly within the power of the national government; others, clearly without its powers; and a third class, which will leave room for controversy and difference of opinion, and concerning which a reasonable latitude of judgment must be allowed.

But the doctrine which is contended for is not chargeable with the consequences imputed to it. It does not affirm that the national government is sovereign in all respects, but that it is sovereign to a certain extent; that is, to the extent of the objects of its specified powers.

It leaves, therefore, a criterion of what is constitutional, and of what is not so. This criterion is the end, to which the measure relates as a mean. If the end be clearly comprehended within any of the specified powers, and if the measure have an obvious relation to that end, and is not forbidden by any particular provision of the Constitution, it may safely be deemed to come within the compass of the national authority. There is also this further criterion, which may materially assist the decision: Does the proposed measure abridge a pre-existing right of any State or of any individual? If it does not, there is a strong presumption in favor of its constitutionality, and slighter relations to any declared object of the Constitution may be permitted to turn the scale.

CHISHOLM v. GEORGIA[26]

[Justice Wilson:] This is a case of uncommon magnitude. One of the parties to it is a State—certainly respectable, claiming to be sovereign. The question to be determined is whether this State, so respectable, and whose claim soars so high, is amenable to the jurisdiction of the Supreme Court of the United States? This question, important in itself, will depend on others more important still, and, may, perhaps, be ultimately resolved into one no less radical than this: "do the people of the United States form a Nation?"

. . . To the Constitution of the United States, the term SOVEREIGN, is totally unknown. There is but one place where it could have been used with propriety. But even in that place, it would not, perhaps, have comported with the delicacy of those who ordained and established that Constitution. They might have announced themselves "SOVEREIGN" people of the United States. But serenely conscious of the fact, they avoided the ostentatious declaration.

. . . In one sense, the term "sovereign" has for its correlative "subject." In this sense, the term can receive no application, for it has no object in the Constitution of the United states. Under that Constitution, there are citizens, but no subjects. "Citizen of the United states." "Citizens of another state." "Citizens of different states." "A state or citizen thereof." The term, subject, occurs, indeed, once in the instrument; but to mark the contrast strongly, the epithet "foreign" is prefixed. In this sense, I presume the state of Georgia has no claim upon her own citizens. In this sense, I am certain, she can have no claim upon the citizens of another state.

In another sense, according to some writers, state, which governs itself without any dependence on another power is a sovereign state. Whether, with regard to her own citizens, this is the case of the state of Georgia; whether those citizens have done, as the individuals of England are said by their late instructors to have done, surrendered the supreme power to the state or government, and reserved nothing to themselves; or whether, like the people of other states, and of the United states, the citizens of Georgia have reserved the supreme power in their own hands, and on that supreme power have made the state dependent, instead of being sovereign—these are questions to which, as a judge in this cause, I can neither know nor suggest the proper answers, though, as a citizen of the Union, I know, and am interested to know that the most satisfactory answers can be given. As a citizen, I know the government of that state to be republican; and my short definition of such a government is one constructed on this principle—that the supreme power resides in the body of the people. As a judge of this court, I know, and can decide upon the knowledge that the citizens of Georgia, when they acted upon the large scale of the Union, as a part of the "People of the United states," did not surrender the supreme or sovereign power to that state, but, as to the purposes of the Union, retained it to themselves. As to the purposes of the Union, therefore, Georgia is NOT a sovereign state. If the judicial decision of this case forms one of those purposes, the allegation that Georgia is a sovereign state is unsupported by the fact. Whether the judicial decision of this cause is or is not one of those purposes is a question which will be examined particularly in a subsequent part of my argument.

There is a third sense, in which the term "sovereign" is frequently used, and which it is very material to trace and explain, as it furnishes a basis for what I presume to be one of the principal objections against the jurisdiction of this court over the State of Georgia. In this sense, sovereignty is derived from a feudal source, and, like many other parts of that system so degrading to man, still retains its influence over our sentiments and conduct, though the cause by which that influence was produced never extended to the American states.

. . . The principle is that all human law must be prescribed by a superior. This principle I mean not now to examine. Suffice it at present to say that another principle, very different in its nature and operations, forms, in my judgment, the basis of sound and genuine jurisprudence; laws derived from the pure source of equality and justice must be founded on the CONSENT of those whose obedience they require. The sovereign, when traced to his source, must be found in the man.

. . . I find nothing which tends to evince an exemption of the state of Georgia from the jurisdiction of the court. I find everything to have a contrary tendency.

. . . I am, thirdly, and chiefly, to examine the important question now before us by the Constitution of the United states, and the legitimate result of that valuable instrument. Under this view, the question is naturally subdivided into two others. 1. Could the Constitution of the United states vest a jurisdiction over the State of Georgia? 2. Has that Constitution vested such jurisdiction in this Court? I have already remarked that, in the practice, and even in the science, of politics, there has been frequently a strong current against the natural order of things, and an inconsiderate or an interested disposition to sacrifice the end to the means. This remark deserves a more particular illustration. Even in almost every nation which has been denominated free, the state has assumed a supercilious preeminence above the people who have formed it. Hence the haughty notions of state independence, state sovereignty and state supremacy

. . . In the United states, and in the several states, which compose the Union, we go not so far, but still we go one step farther than we ought to go in this unnatural and inverted order of things. The states, rather than the people, for whose sakes the states exist, are frequently the objects which attract and arrest our principal attention. This, I believe, has produced much of the confusion and perplexity which have appeared in several proceedings and several publications on state politics, and on the politics, too, of the United states. Sentiments and expressions of this inaccurate kind prevail in our common, even in our convivial, language. Is a toast asked? "The United states," instead of the "People of the United states," is the toast given. This is not politically correct. The toast is meant to present to view the first great object in the Union: it presents only the second. It presents only the artificial person, instead of the natural persons who spoke it into existence. A state I cheerfully fully admit, is the noblest work of Man. But, Man himself, free and honest, is, I speak as to this world, the noblest work of God.

Concerning . . . the sovereignty of states, much has been said and written; but little has been said and written concerning a subject much more dignified and important, the majesty of the people. The mode of expression, which I would substitute in the place of that generally used, is not only politically, but also (for between true liberty and true taste there is a close alliance) classically more correct. . . . With the strictest propriety, therefore, classical and political, our national scene opens with the most magnificent object which the nation could present. "The PEOPLE of the United states" are the first personages introduced. Who were those people? They were the citizens of thirteen states, each of which had a separate constitution and government, and all of which were connected together by Articles of Confederation. To the purposes of public strength and felicity, that Confederacy was totally inadequate. A requisition on the several states terminated its legislative authority. Executive or judicial authority it had none. In order therefore to form a more perfect union, to establish justice, to ensure domestic tranquility, to provide for common defense, and to secure the blessings of liberty, those people, among whom were the people of Georgia, ordained and established the present Constitution. By that Constitution legislative power is vested, executive power is vested, judicial power is vested.

The question now opens fairly to our view, could the people of those states, among whom were those of Georgia, bind those states, and Georgia among the others, by the legislative, executive, and judicial power so vested? If the principles on which I have founded myself are just and true, this question must unavoidably receive an affirmative answer. If those states were the work of those people, those people, and that I may apply the case closely, the people of Georgia, in particular, could alter as they pleased their former work. To any given degree, they could diminish as well as enlarge it. Any or all of the former state powers, they could extinguish or transfer. The inference which necessarily results is that the Constitution ordained and established by those people, and, still closely to apply the case, in particular by the people of Georgia, could vest jurisdiction or judicial power over those states and over the State of Georgia in particular.

The next question under this head, is has the Constitution done so? Did those people mean to exercise this, their undoubted power? These questions may be resolved either by fair and conclusive deductions or by direct and explicit declarations. In order ultimately to discover whether the people of the United states intended to bind those states by the judicial power vested by the national Constitution, a previous enquiry will naturally be: did those people intend to bind those states by the legislative power vested by that Constitution? The Articles of Confederation, it is well known, did not operate upon individual citizens, but operated only upon states. This defect was remedied by the national Constitution, which, as all allow, has an operation on individual citizens. But if an opinion which some seem to entertain be just, the defect remedied on one side was balanced by a defect introduced on the other. For they seem to think that the present Constitution operates only on individual citizens, and not on states. This opinion, however, appears to be altogether unfounded. When certain laws of the states are declared to be "subject to the revision and control of the Congress," it cannot, surely, be contended that the legislative power of the national government was meant to have no operation on the several states. The fact, uncontrovertibly established in one instance, proves the principle in all other instances to which the facts will be found to apply. We may then infer that the people of the United states intended to bind the several states by the legislative power of the national government.

In order to make the discovery at which we ultimately aim, a second previous enquiry will naturally be: did the people of the United states intend to bind the several states by the executive power of the national government? The affirmative answer to the former question directs, unavoidably, an affirmative answer to this. . . . Fair and conclusive deduction, then, evinces that the people of the United states did vest this court with jurisdiction over the State of Georgia. The same truth may be deduced from the declared objects and the general texture of the Constitution of the United states. One of its declared objects is to form an Union more perfect than, before that time, had been formed. Before that time, the Union possessed legislative, but unenforced legislative power over the states. Nothing could be more natural than to intend that this legislative power should be enforced by powers executive and judicial. Another declared object is, "to establish justice." This points, in a particular manner, to the judicial authority. And when we view this object in conjunction with the declaration, "that no state shall pass a law impairing the obligation of contracts," we shall probably think that this object points, in a particular manner, to the jurisdiction of the court over the several states. What good purpose could this constitutional provision secure if a state might pass a law impairing the obligation of its own contracts, and be amenable, for such a violation of right to no controlling judiciary power? We have seen that on the principles of general jurisprudence, a state, for the breach of a contract, may be liable for damages. A third declared object is "to ensure domestic tranquility." This tranquility is most likely to be disturbed by controversies between states. These consequences will be most peaceably and effectually decided by the establishment and by the exercise of a superintending judicial authority. By such exercise and establishment, the law of nations, the rule between contending states, will be enforced among the several states in the same manner as municipal law.

Whoever considers, in a combined and comprehensive view, the general texture of the Constitution will be satisfied that the people of the United states intended to form themselves into a nation for national purposes. They instituted for such purposes a national government, complete in all its parts, with powers legislative, executive and judicial, and in all those powers extending over the whole nation.

ELEVENTH AMENDMENT (RATIFIED FEBRUARY 7, 1798)

The Judicial power of the United States shall not be construed to extend to any suit in law or equity, commenced or prosecuted against one of the United States by Citizens of another State, or by Citizens or Subjects of any Foreign State.

THE KENTUCKY RESOLUTION[27]

Resolved, That the several States composing the United States of America, are not united on the principle of unlimited submission to their General Government; but that, by a compact under the style and title of a Constitution for the United States, and of amendments thereto, they constituted a General Government for special purposes,—delegated to that government certain definite powers, reserving, each State to itself, the residuary mass of right to their own self-government; and that whensoever the General Government assumes undelegated powers, its acts are unauthoritative, void, and of no force; that to this compact each State acceded as a State, and is an integral party, its co-States forming, as to itself, the other party: that the government created by this compact was not made the exclusive or final judge of the extent of the powers delegated to itself; since that would have made its discretion, and not the Constitution, the measure of its powers; but that, as in all other cases of compact among powers having no common judge, each party has an equal right to judge for itself, as well of infractions as of the mode and measure of redress.

Resolved, That the Constitution of the United States, having delegated to Congress a power to punish treason, counterfeiting the securities and current coin of the United States, piracies, and felonies committed on the high seas, and offences against the law of nations, and no other crimes whatsoever; and it being true as a general principle, and one of the amendments to the Constitution having also declared, that "the powers not delegated to the United States by the Constitution, nor prohibited by it to the States, are reserved to the States respectively, or to the people," therefore the act of Congress, passed on the 14th day of July, 1798, and entitled "An Act in addition to the act entitled An Act for the punishment of certain crimes against the United States," as also the act passed by them on the—day of June, 1798, entitled "An Act to punish frauds committed on the bank of the United States," (and all their other acts which assume to create, define, or punish crimes, other than those so enumerated in the Constitution,) are altogether void, and of no force; and that the power to create, define, and punish such other crimes is reserved, and, of right, appertains solely and exclusively to the respective States, each within its own territory.

Resolved That it is true as a general principle, and is also expressly declared by one of the amendments to the Constitution, that "the powers not delegated to the United States by the Constitution, nor prohibited by it to the States, are reserved to the States respectively, or to the people;" and that no power over the freedom of religion, freedom of speech, or freedom of the press being delegated to the United States by the Constitution, nor prohibited by it to the States, all lawful powers respecting the same did of right remain, and were reserved to the States or the people: that thus was manifested their determination to retain to themselves the right of judging how far the licentiousness of speech and of the press may be abridged without lessening their useful freedom, and how far those abuses which cannot be separated from their use should be tolerated, rather than the use be destroyed. And thus also they guarded against all abridgment by the United States of the freedom of religious opinions and exercises, and retained to themselves the right of protecting the same, as this State, by a law passed on the general demand of its citizens, had already protected them from all human restraint or interference. And that in addition to this general principle and express declaration, another and more special provision has been made by one of the amendments to the Constitution, which expressly declares, that "Congress shall make no law respecting an establishment of religion, or prohibiting the free exercise thereof, or abridging the freedom of speech or of the press:" thereby guarding in the same sentence, and under the same words, the freedom of religion, of speech, and of the press: insomuch, that whatever violated either, throws down the sanctuary which covers the others, and that libels, falsehood, and defamation, equally with heresy and false religion, are withheld from the cognizance of federal tribunals. That, therefore, the act of Congress of the United States, passed on the 14th day of July, 1798, entitled "An Act in addition to the act entitled An Act for the punishment of certain crimes against the United States," which does abridge the freedom of the press, is not law, but is altogether void, and of no force.

Resolved, That alien friends are under the jurisdiction and protection of the laws of the State wherein they are: that no power over them has been delegated to the United States, nor prohibited to the individual States, distinct from their power over citizens. And it being true as a general principle, and one of the amendments to the Constitution having also declared, that "the powers not delegated to the United States by the Constitution, nor prohibited by it to the States, are reserved to the States respectively, or to the people," the act of the Congress of the United States, passed on the—day of July, 1798, entitled "An Act concerning aliens," which assumes powers over alien friends, not delegated by the Constitution, is not law, but is altogether void, and of no force.

Resolved, That in addition to the general principle, as well as the express declaration, that powers not delegated are reserved, another and more special provision, inserted in the Constitution from abundant caution, has declared that "the migration or importation of such persons as any of the States now existing shall think proper to admit, shall not be prohibited by the Congress prior to the year 1808;" that this commonwealth does admit the migration of alien friends, described as the subject of the said act concerning aliens: that a provision against prohibiting their migration, is a provision against all acts equivalent thereto, or it would be nugatory: that to remove them when migrated, is equivalent to a prohibition of their migration, and is, therefore, contrary to the said provision of the Constitution, and void.

Resolved, That a committee of conference and correspondence be appointed, who shall have in charge to communicate the preceding resolutions to the legislatures of the several States; to assure them that this com-monwealth continues in the same esteem of their friendship and union which it has manifested from that moment at which a common danger first suggested a common union: that it considers union, for specified national purposes, and particularly to those specified in their late federal compact, to be friendly to the peace, happiness and prosperity of all the States: that faithful to that compact, according to the plain intent and meaning in which it was understood and acceded to by the several parties, it is sincerely anxious for its preservation: that it does also believe, that to take from the States all the powers of self-government and transfer them to a general and consolidated government, without regard to the special delegations and reservations solemnly agreed to in that compact, is not for the peace, happiness or prosperity of these States; and that therefore this commonwealth is determined, as it doubts not its co-States are, to submit to undelegated, and consequently unlimited powers in no man, or body of men on earth: that in cases of an abuse of the delegated powers, the members of the General Government, being chosen by the people, a change by the people would be the constitutional remedy; but, where powers are assumed which have not been delegated, a nullification of the act is the rightful remedy: that every State has a natural right in cases not within the compact, (*casus non foederis*,) to nullify of their own authority all assumptions of power by others within their limits: that without this right, they would be under the dominion, absolute and unlimited, of whosoever might exercise this right of judgment for them: that nevertheless, this commonwealth, from motives of regard and respect for its co-States, has wished to communicate with them on the subject: that with them alone it is proper to communicate, they alone being parties to the compact, and solely authorized to judge in the last resort of the powers exercised under it, Congress being not a party, but merely the creature of the compact, and subject as to its assumptions of power to the final judgment of those by whom, and for whose use itself and its powers were all created and modified: that if the acts before specified should stand, these conclusions would flow from them; that the General Government may place any act they think proper on the list of crimes, and punish it themselves whether enumerated or not enumerated by the Constitution as cognizable by them: that they may transfer its cognizance to the President, or any other person, who may himself be the accuser, counsel, judge and jury, whose *suspicions* may be the evidence, his *order* the sentence, his *officer* the executioner, and his breast the sole record of the transaction: that a very numerous and valuable description of the inhabitants of these States being, by this precedent, reduced, as outlaws, to the absolute dominion of one man, and the barrier of the Constitution thus swept away from us all, no rampart now remains against the passions and the powers of a majority in Congress to protect from a like exportation, or other more grievous punishment, the minority of the same body, the legislatures, judges, governors, and counsellors of the States, nor their other peaceable inhabitants, who may venture to reclaim the constitutional rights and liberties of the States and people, or who for other causes, good or bad, may be obnoxious to the views, or marked by the suspicions of the President, or be thought dangerous to his or their election, or other interests, public or personal: that the friendless alien has indeed been selected as the safest subject of a first experiment; but the citizen will soon follow, or rather, has already followed, for already has a sedition act marked him as its prey: that these and successive acts of the same character, unless arrested at the threshold, necessarily drive these States into revolution and blood, and will furnish new calumnies against republican government, and new pretexts for those who wish it to be believed that man cannot be governed but by a rod of iron: that it would be a dangerous delusion were a confidence in the men of our choice to silence our fears for the safety of our rights: that confidence is everywhere the parent of despotism—free government is founded in jealousy, and not in confidence; it is jealousy and not confidence which prescribes limited constitutions, to bind down those whom we are obliged to trust with power: that our Constitution has accordingly fixed the limits to which, and no further, our confidence may go; and let the honest advocate of confidence read the alien and sedition acts, and say if the Constitution has not been wise in fixing limits to the government it created, and whether we should be wise in destroying those limits. Let him say what the government is, if it be not a tyranny, which the men of our choice have conferred on our President, and the President of our choice has assented to, and accepted over the friendly strangers to whom the mild spirit of our country and its laws have pledged hospitality and protection: that the men of our choice have more respected the bare *suspicions* of the President, than the solid right of innocence, the claims of justification, the sacred force of truth, and the forms and substance of law and justice.

In questions of power, then, let no more be heard of confidence in man, but bind him down from mischief by the chains of the Constitution. That this commonwealth does therefore call on its co-States for an expression of their sentiments on the acts concerning aliens, and for the punishment of certain crimes herein before specified, plainly declaring whether these acts are or are not authorized by the federal compact. And it doubts not that their sense will be so announced as to prove their attachment unaltered to limited government, whether general or particular. And that the rights and liberties of their co-States will be exposed to no dangers by remaining embarked in a common bottom with their own. That they will concur with this commonwealth in considering the said acts as so palpably against the Constitution as to amount to an undisguised declaration that that compact is not meant to be the measure of the powers of the General Government, but that it will proceed in the exercise over these States, of all powers whatsoever: that they will view this as seizing the rights of the States, and consolidating them in the hands of the General Government, with a power assumed to bind the States, not merely as the cases made federal, (*casus foederis,*) but in all cases whatsoever, by laws made, not with their consent, but by others against their consent: that this would be to surrender the form of government we have chosen, and live under one deriving its powers from its own will, and not from our authority; and that the co-States, recurring to their natural right in cases not made federal, will concur in declaring these acts void, and of no force, and will each take measures of its own for providing that neither these acts, nor any others of the General Government not plainly and intentionally authorized by the Constitution, shall be exercised within their respective territories.

VIRGINIA RESOLUTION[28]

. . . That this assembly most solemnly declares a warm attachment to the Union of the States, to maintain which it pledges all its powers; and that for this end, it is their duty to watch over and oppose every infraction of those principles which constitute the only basis of that Union, because a faithful observance of them, can alone secure its existence and the public happiness.

That this Assembly does explicitly and peremptorily declare, that it views the powers of the federal government, as resulting from the compact, to which the states are parties; as limited by the plain sense and intention of the instrument constituting the compact; as no further valid that they are authorized by the grants enumerated in that compact; and that in case of a deliberate, palpable, and dangerous exercise of other powers, not granted by the said compact, the states who are parties thereto, have the right, and are in duty bound, to interpose for arresting the progress of the evil, and for maintaining within their respective limits, the authorities, rights and liberties appertaining to them.

That the General Assembly does also express its deep regret, that a spirit has in sundry instances, been manifested by the federal government, to enlarge its powers by forced constructions of the constitutional charter which defines them; and that implications have appeared of a design to expound certain general phrases (which having been copied from the very limited grant of power, in the former articles of confederation were the less liable to be misconstrued) so as to destroy the meaning and effect, of the particular enumeration which necessarily explains and limits the general phrases; and so as to consolidate the states by degrees, into one sovereignty, the obvious tendency and inevitable consequence of which would be, to transform the present republican system of the United States, into an absolute, or at best a mixed monarchy.

That the General Assembly doth particularly protest against the palpable and alarming infractions of the Constitution, in the two late cases of the "Alien and Sedition Acts" passed at the last session of Congress; the first of which exercises a power no where delegated to the federal government, and which by uniting legislative and judicial powers to those of executive, subverts the general principles of free government; as well as the particular organization, and positive provisions of the federal constitution; and the other of which acts, exercises in like manner, a power not delegated by the constitution, but on the contrary, expressly and positively forbidden by one of the amendments thereto; a power, which more than any other, ought to produce universal alarm, because it is levelled against that right of freely examining public characters and measures, and of free communication among the people thereon, which has ever been justly deemed, the only effectual guardian of every other right.

That this state having by its Convention, which ratified the federal Constitution, expressly declared, that among other essential rights, "the Liberty of Conscience and of the Press cannot be cancelled, abridged, restrained, or modified by any authority of the United States," and from its extreme anxiety to guard these rights from every possible attack of sophistry or ambition, having with other states, recommended an amendment for that purpose, which amendment was, in due time, annexed to the Constitution; it would mark a reproachable inconsistency, and criminal degeneracy, if an indifference were now show, to the most palpable violation of one of the Rights, thus declared and secured; and to the establishment of a precedent which may be fatal to the other.

That the good people of this commonwealth, having ever felt, and continuing to feel, the most sincere affection for their brethren of the other states; the truest anxiety for establishing and perpetuating the union of all; and the most scrupulous fidelity to that constitution, which is the pledge of mutual friendship, and the instrument of mutual happiness; the General Assembly doth solemnly appeal to the like dispositions of the other states, in confidence that they will concur with this commonwealth in declaring, as it does hereby declare, that the acts aforesaid, are unconstitutional; and that the necessary and proper measures will be taken by each, for co-operating with this state, in maintaining the Authorities, Rights, and Liberties, referred to the States respectively, or to the people.

JAMES MADISON, REPORT OF 1800[29]

"Resolved, That the General Assembly of Virginia doth unequivocally express a firm resolution to maintain and defend the Constitution of the United States, and the Constitution of this state, against every aggression, either foreign or domestic; and that they will support the government of the United States in all measures warranted by the former."

No unfavorable comment can have been made on the sentiments here expressed. To maintain and defend the Constitution of the United States, and of their own state, against every aggression, both foreign and domestic, and to support the government of the United States in all measures warranted by their Constitution, are duties which the General Assembly ought always to feel, and to which, on such an occasion, it was evidently proper to express their sincere and firm adherence.

In their next resolution—"The General Assembly most solemnly declares a warm attachment to the union of the states, to maintain which it pledges all its powers; and that, for this end, it is their duty to watch over and oppose every infraction of those principles which constitute the only basis of that Union, because a faithful observance of them can alone secure its existence and the public happiness."

The observation just made is equally applicable to this solemn declaration of warm attachment to the Union, and this solemn pledge to maintain it; nor can any question arise among enlightened friends of the Union, as to the duty of watching over and opposing every infraction of those principles which constitute its basis, and a faithful observance of which can alone secure its existence, and the public happiness thereon depending.

The third resolution is in the words following:— "That this Assembly doth explicitly and peremptorily declare, that it views the powers of the federal government, as resulting from the compact to which the states are parties, as limited by the plain sense and intention of the instrument constituting that compact—as no further valid than they are authorized by the grants enumerated in that compact; and that, in case of a deliberate, palpable, and dangerous exercise of other powers, not granted by the said compact, the states who are parties thereto have the right, and are in duty bound, to interpose, for arresting the progress of the evil and for maintaining, within their respective limits, the authorities, rights, and liberties, appertaining to them."

. . . The resolution declares, first, that "it views the powers of the federal government as resulting from the compact to which the states are parties"; in other words, that the federal powers are derived from the Constitution; and that the Constitution is a compact to which the states are parties.

Clear as the position must seem, that the federal powers are derived from the Constitution, and from that alone, the committee are not unapprised of a late doctrine which opens another source of federal powers, not less extensive and important than it is new and unexpected. The examination of this doctrine will be most conveniently connected with a review of a succeeding resolution. The committee satisfy themselves here with briefly remarking that, in all the contemporary discussions and comments which the Constitution underwent, it was constantly justified and recommended on the ground that the powers not given to the government were withheld from it; and that, if any doubt could have existed on this subject, under the original text of the Constitution, it is removed, as far as words could remove it, by the 12th amendment, now a part of the Constitution, which expressly declares, "that the powers not delegated to the United States by the Constitution, nor prohibited by it to the states, are reserved to the states respectively, or to the people."

The other position involved in this branch of the resolution, namely, "that the states are parties to the Constitution," or compact, is, in the judgment of the committee, equally free from objection. It is indeed true that the term "states" is sometimes used in a vague sense, and sometimes in different senses, according to the subject to which it is applied. Thus it sometimes means the separate sections of territory occupied by the political societies within each; sometimes the particular governments established by those societies; sometimes those societies as organized into those particular governments; and lastly, it means the people composing those political societies, in their highest sovereign capacity. Although it might be wished that the perfection of language admitted less diversity in the signification of the same words, yet little inconvenience is produced by it, where the true sense can be collected with certainty from the different applications. In the present instance, whatever different construction of the term "states," in the resolution, may have been entertained, all will at least concur in that last mentioned; because in that sense the Constitution was submitted to the "states;" in that sense the "states" ratified it; and in that sense of the term "states," they are consequently parties to the compact from which the powers of the federal government result.

The next position is, that the General Assembly views the powers of the federal government "as limited by the plain sense and intention of the instrument constituting that compact," and "as no further valid than they are authorized by the grants therein enumerated." It does not seem possible that any just objection can lie against either of these clauses. The first amounts merely to a declaration that the compact ought to have the interpretation plainly intended by the parties to it; the other, to a declaration that it ought to have the execution and effect intended by them. If the powers granted be valid, it is solely because they are granted; and if the granted powers are valid because granted, all other powers not granted must not be valid.

The resolution, having taken this view of the federal compact, proceeds to infer, "That, in case of a deliberate, palpable, and dangerous exercise of other powers, not granted by the said compact, the states, who are parties thereto, have the right, and are in duty bound, to interpose for arresting the progress of the evil, and for maintaining, within their respective limits, the authorities, rights, and liberties, appertaining to them."

It appears to your committee to be a plain principle, founded in common sense, illustrated by common practice, and essential to the nature of compacts, that, where resort can be had to no tribunal superior to the authority of the parties, the parties themselves must be the rightful judges, in the last resort, whether the bargain made has been pursued or violated. The Constitution of the United States was formed by the sanction of the states, given by each in its sovereign capacity. It adds to the stability and dignity, as well as to the authority, of the Constitution, that it rests on this legitimate and solid foundation. The states, then, being the parties to the constitutional compact, and in their sovereign capacity, it follows of necessity that there can be no tribunal, above their authority, to decide, in the last resort, whether the compact made by them be violated; and consequently, that, as the parties to it, they must themselves decide, in the last resort, such questions as may be of sufficient magnitude to require their interposition.

It does not follow, however, because the states, as sovereign parties to their constitutional compact, must ultimately decide whether it has been violated, that such a decision ought to be interposed either in a hasty manner or on doubtful and inferior occasions. Even in the case of ordinary conventions between different nations, where, by the strict rule of interpretation, a breach of a part may be deemed a breach of the whole,—every part being deemed a condition of every other part, and of the whole,—it is always laid down that the breach must be both willful and material, to justify an application of the rule. But in the case of an intimate and constitutional union, like that of the United States, it is evident that the interposition of the parties, in their sovereign capacity, can be called for by occasions only deeply and essentially affecting the vital principles of their political system.

The resolution has, accordingly guarded against any misapprehension of its object, by expressly requiring, for such an interposition, "the case of a deliberate, palpable, and dangerous breach of the Constitution, by the exercise of powers not granted by it." It must be a case not of a light and transient nature, but of a nature dangerous to the great purposes for which the Constitution was established. It must be a case, moreover, not obscure or doubtful in its construction, but plain and palpable. Lastly, it must be a case not resulting from a partial consideration or hasty determination, but a case stamped with a final consideration and deliberate adherence. It is not necessary, because the resolution does not require, that the question should be discussed, how far the exercise of any particular power, ungranted by the Constitution, would justify the interposition of the parties to it. As cases might easily be stated, which none would contend ought to fall within that description,—cases, on the other hand, might, with equal ease, be stated, so flagrant and so fatal as to unite every opinion in placing them within the description.

But the resolution has done more than guard against misconstruction, by expressly referring to cases of a deliberate, palpable, and dangerous nature. It specifies the object of the interposition, which it contemplates to be solely that of arresting the progress of the evil of usurpation, and of maintaining the authorities, rights, and liberties, appertaining to the states as parties to the Constitution.

From this view of the resolution, it would seem inconceivable that it can incur any just disapprobation from those who, laying aside all momentary impressions, and recollecting the genuine source and object of the Federal Constitution, shall candidly and accurately interpret the meaning of the General Assembly. If the deliberate exercise of dangerous powers, palpably withheld by the Constitution, could not justify the parties to it in interposing even so far as to arrest the progress of the evil, and thereby to preserve the Constitution itself, as well as to provide for the safety of the parties to it, there would be an end to all relief from usurped power, and a direct subversion of the rights specified or recognized under all the state constitutions, as well as a plain denial of the fundamental principle on which our independence itself was declared.

But it is objected, that the judicial authority is to be regarded as the sole expositor of the Constitution in the last resort; and it may be asked for what reason the declaration by the General Assembly, supposing it to be theoretically true, could be required at the present day, and in so solemn a manner.

On this objection it might be observed, first, that there may be instances of usurped power, which the forms of the Constitution would never draw within the control of the judicial department; secondly, that, if the decision of the judiciary be raised above the authority of the sovereign parties to the Constitution, the decisions of the other departments, not carried by the forms of the Constitution before the judiciary, must be equally authoritative and final with the decisions of that department. But the proper answer to the objection is, that the resolution of the General Assembly relates to those great and extraordinary cases, in which all the forms of the Constitution may prove ineffectual against infractions dangerous to the essential rights of the parties to it. The resolution supposes that dangerous powers, not delegated, may not only be usurped and executed by the other departments, but that the judicial department, also, may exercise or sanction dangerous powers beyond the grant of the Constitution; and, consequently, that the ultimate right of the parties to the Constitution, to judge whether the compact has been dangerously violated, must extend to violations by one delegated authority as well as by another—by the judiciary as well as by the executive, or the legislature.

However true, therefore, it may be, that the judicial department is, in all questions submitted to it by the forms of the Constitution, to decide in the last resort, this resort must necessarily be deemed the last in relation to the authorities of the other departments of the government; not in relation to the rights of the parties to the constitutional compact, from which the judicial, as well as the other departments, hold their delegated trusts. On any other hypothesis, the delegation of judicial power would annul the authority delegating it; and the concurrence of this department with the others in usurped powers, might subvert forever, and beyond the possible reach of any rightful remedy, the very Constitution which all were instituted to preserve.

The truth declared in the resolution being established, the expediency of making the declaration at the present day may safely be left to the temperate consideration and candid judgment of the American public. It will be remembered, that a frequent recurrence to fundamental principles is solemnly enjoined by most of the state constitutions, and particularly by our own, as a necessary safeguard against the danger of degeneracy, to which republics are liable, as well as other governments, though in a less degree than others. And a fair comparison of the political doctrines not infrequent at the present day, with those which characterized the epoch of our revolution, and which form the basis of our republican constitutions, will best determine whether the declaratory recurrence here made to those principles ought to be viewed as unseasonable and improper, or as a vigilant discharge of an important duty. The authority of constitutions over governments, and of the sovereignty of the people over constitutions, are truths which are at all times necessary to be kept in mind; and at no time, perhaps, more necessary than at present.

. . . These observations appear to form a satisfactory reply to every objection which is not founded on a misconception of the terms employed in the resolutions. There is one other, however, which may be of too much importance not to be added. It cannot be forgotten that, among the arguments addressed to those who apprehended danger to liberty from the establishment of the general government over so great a country, the appeal was emphatically made to the intermediate existence of the state governments between the people and that government, to the vigilance with which they would descry the first symptoms of usurpation, and to the promptitude with which they would sound the alarm to the public. This argument was probably not without its effect; and if it was a proper one then to recommend the establishment of a constitution, it must be a proper one now to assist in its interpretation.

McCULLOCH v. MARYLAND[30]

The first question made in the cause is—has congress power to incorporate a bank? It has been truly said, that this can scarcely be considered as an open question, entirely unprejudiced by the former proceedings of the nation respecting it. The principle now contested was introduces at a very early period of our history, has been recognized by many successive legislatures, and has been acted upon by the judicial department, in cases of peculiar delicacy, as the law undoubted obligation . . .

In discussing this question, the counsel for the state of Maryland have deemed it of some importance, in the construction of the constitution, to consider that instrument, not as emanating from the people, but as the act of sovereign and independent states. The powers of the general government, it has been said, are delegated by the states, who alone are truly sovereign; and must be exercised in subordination to the states, who alone possesses supreme dominion. It would be difficult to sustain this proposition. The convention which framed the constitution was indeed elected by the state legislatures. But the instrument, when it came from their hands, was a mere proposal, without obligation, or pretentions to it. It was reported to the then existing congress of the United States, with a request that it might "be submitted" to a convention of delegates, chosen in each state by the people thereof, under the recommendation of its legislature, for their assent and ratification." This mode of processing was adopted: and by the convention, by congress, and by the state legislatures, the instrument was submitted was submitted to the *people*. They acted upon it in the only manner in which they can act safely, effectively and wisely, on such a subject, by assembling in convention. It is true, they assembled in their several states—and where else should they has assembled? No political dreamer was ever wild enough to think of breaking down the lines which separate the states, and of compounding the American people into one common mass. Of consequence, when they act, they act in their states. But the measures they adopt do not, on that account, cease to be the measures of the people themselves, or become the measures of the state governments.

From these conventions, the constitution derives its whole authority. The government proceeds directly from the people; is "ordained and established," in the name of the people; and is declared to be ordained, "in order to from a more perfect union, establish justice, insure domestic tranquility, and secure the blessings of liberty to themselves and to their posterity." The assent of the states, in their sovereign capacity, is implied, in calling a convention, and thus submitting that instrument to the people. But the people were at perfect liberty to accept or reject it; and their act was final. It required not the affirmance, and could not be negatived, by the state governments. The constitution, when thus adopted, was of complete obligation, and bound the state sovereignties . . .

The government of the Union, then (whatever may be the influence of this fact on the case), is emphatically and truly, a government of the people. In form, and in substance, it emanates from them. Its powers are granted by them, and are to be exercised directly on them, and for their benefit.

This government is acknowledged by all, to be one of enumerated powers. The principle, that it can exercise only the powers granted to it, would seem to be apparent, to have required to be enforced by all those arguments, which its enlightened friends, while it was depending before the people, found it necessary to urge; that principle is now universally admitted. But the question respecting the extent of the powers actually granted, is perpetually arising, and will probably continue to arise, so long as our system shall exist. In discussing these questions, the conflicting powers of the general and state governments must be brought into view, and the supremacy of their respective laws, when they are in opposition, must be settled.

If any one proposition could command the universal assent of mankind, we might expect it would be this—that the government of the Union, though limited in its powers, is supreme within its sphere of action. This would seem to result, necessarily, from its nature. It is the government of all; its powers are delegated by all; it represents all, and acts for all. Though any one state may be willing to control its operations, no state is willing to allow others to control them. The nation, on those subjects on which it can act, must necessarily bind its component parts. But this question is not left to mere reason: the people have, in express terms decided it, by saying, "this constitution, and the laws of the United States, which 'shall be made in pursuance thereof,' shall be the supreme law of the land," and by requiring that the members of the state legislatures, and the officers of the executive and judicial departments of the states, shall take the oath of fidelity to it. The government of the United States, then, though limited in its powers, is supreme; and its laws, when made in pursuance of the constitution, form the supreme law of the land, "anything in the constitution or laws of any state to the contrary notwithstanding."

Among the enumerated powers, we do not find that of establishing a bank or creating a corporation. But there is no phrase in the instrument which, like the articles of confederation, excludes incidental or implied powers; and which requires that everything granted shall be expressly and minutely described. Even the 10th amendment, which was framed for the purpose of quieting the excessive jealousies which had been excited, omits the word "expressly," and declares only, that the powers "not delegated to the United States, nor prohibited to the states, are reserved to the states or to the people"; thus leaving the question, whether the particular power which may become the subject of the contest, has been delegated to the one government, or prohibited to the other, to depend on a fair construction of the whole instrument. The men who drew and adopted this amendment had experienced the embarrassments resulting from the insertion of this world in the articles of confederation, and probably omitted it to avoid those embarrassments. A constitution, to contain an accurate detail of all the subdivisions of which its great powers will admit, and of all the means by which they may be carried into execution, would partake of the prolixity of a legal code, and could scarcely be embraced by the human mind. It would, probably, never be understood by the public. Its nature, therefore, requires, that only its great outlines should be marked, its important objects designated, and the minor ingredients which compose those objects, be deduced from the mature of the objects themselves. That this idea was entertained by the framers of the American constitution is not only to be inferred from the nature of the instrument, but from the language. Why else were some of the limitations, found in the 9th section of the 1st article introduced? It is also, in some degree, warranted, by their having omitted to use any restrictive term which might prevent its receiving a fair and just interpretation. In considering this question, then, we must never forget that it is a *constitution* we are expounding.

. . . The government which has a right to do an act, and has imposed on it, the duty of performing the act, must, according to the dictates of reason, be allowed to select the means; and those who contend that is may not select any appropriate means, that one particular mode of effecting the objects is excepted, take upon themselves the burden of establishing that exception.

The creation of a corporation, it is said, appertains to sovereignty. This is admitted. But to what portion of sovereignty does it appertain? Does it belong to one more than to another? In America, the powers of sovereignty are divided between the government of the Union, and those of the states. They are each sovereign, with respect to the objects committed to it, and neither sovereign, with respect to the objects committed to the other. We cannot comprehend that train of reasoning, which would maintain, that the extent of power granted by the people is to be ascertained, not by the nature and terms of the grant, but by its date. Some state constitutions were formed before, some since that of the United States. We cannot believe, that their relation to each other is in any degree dependent on upon this circumstance. Their respective powers must, we think, be precisely the same, as if they had been formed at the same time. Had they been formed at the same time, and had the people conferred on the general government the power contained in the constitution, and on the states the whole residuum of power, would it have been asserted, that the government of the Union was not sovereign, with respect to those objects which were entrusted to it, in relation to which its laws were declared to be supreme? If this could not have been asserted, we cannot well comprehend the process of reasoning which maintains, that a power appertaining to sovereignty cannot be connected with that vast portion of it which is granted to the general government, so far as it is calculated to subserve the legitimate objects of that government. The power of creating a corporation, though appertaining to sovereignty, is not, like the power of making war, or levying taxes, or of regulating commerce, a great substantive and independent power, which cannot be implied as incidental to other powers, or used as a means of executing them. It is never the end for which other powers are exercised, but a means by which other objects are accomplished. No contributions are made to charity, for the sake of an incorporation, but a corporation is created to administer the charity; no seminary of learning is instituted, in order to be incorporated, but the corporate character is conferred to subserve the purpose of education.

. . . We admit, as all must admit, that the powers of the government are limited, and that its limits are not to be transcended. But we think the sound construction of the constitution must allow to the national legislature that discretion, with respect to the means by which the powers it confers are to be carried into execution, which will enable that body to perform the high duties assigned to it, in the manner most beneficial to the people. Let the end be legitimate, let it be within the scope of the constitution, and all means which are appropriate, which are plainly adapted to that end, which are not prohibited, but consist with the letter and spirit of the constitution, are constitutional.

. . . That the power to tax involves the power to destroy; that the power to destroy may defeat and render useless the power to create; that there is a plain repugnance is conferring on one government a power to control the constitutional measures of another, which other, with respect to those very measures, is declared to be supreme over that which exerts the control, are propositions not to be denied. But all inconsistencies are to be reconciled by the magic of the word confidence.

. . . If we apply the principle for which the state of Maryland contends, to the constitution, generally, we shall find it capable of changing totally the character of measures of the government, and of prostrating it at the foot of the states. The American people have declared their constitution and the laws made in pursuance thereof, to be supreme; but this principle would transfer the supremacy, in fact, to the states. If the states may tax one instrument, employed by the government in the execution of its powers, they may tax any and every other instrument. They may tax the mail; they may tax the mint; they may tax patent—rights; they may tax all the means employed by the government, to an excess which would defeat all the ends of government. This was not intended by the American people. They did not design to make their government dependent on the states . . .

The question is, in truth, a question of supremacy; and if the right of the states to tax the means employed by the general governmental be conceded, the declaration that the constitution, and the laws made in pursuance thereof, shall be the supreme law of the land, is empty and unmeaning declamation . . .

It has also been insisted, that, as the power of taxation in the general and state governments is acknowledged to be concurrent, every argument which would sustain the right of the general government to tax banks chartered by the general government. But the two cases are not on the same reason. The people of all the states have created the general government, and have conferred upon in the general power of taxation. The people of all the states, and the states themselves, are represented in congress, and, by their representatives, exercise this power. When they tax the chartered institutions of the states, they tax their constituents; and these taxes must be uniform.

But when a state taxes the operations of the government of the United States, it acts upon institutions created, not by their own constituents, but by people over whom they claim no control. It acts upon the measures of a government created by others as well as themselves, for the benefit of others in common with themselves. The difference is that which always exists, and always must exist, between the action of the whole on a part, and the action of a part on the whole—between the laws of a government declared to be supreme, and those of a government which, when in opposition to those laws, is not supreme . . .

The court has bestowed on this subject its most deliberate consideration. The result is a conviction that the states have no power, by taxation or otherwise, to retard, impede, burden, or in any manner control, the operations of the constitutional laws enacted by congress to carry into execution the powers vested in the general government. This is, we think, the unavoidable consequence of that supremacy which the constitution has declared. We are unanimously of opinion, that the law passed by the legislature of Maryland, imposing a tax on the Bank of the United States, is unconstitutional and void . . .

JOHN TAYLOR OF CAROLINE, *NEW VIEWS OF THE CONSTITUTION OF THE UNITED STATES*[31]

The reader has perceived that the question concerning state powers, is condensed in the word sovereignty, and therefore any new ideas upon the subject, if to be found, would not be unedifying. A will to enact, and a power to execute, constitute its essence. Take away either, and it expires. The state government and the federal government, are the monuments by which state sovereignty, attended with these attributes, is demonstrated. But as the consolidating school will not see it, I will endeavor further to establish its existence, in order to prevent these beautiful examples of political science from falling into ruin.

The constitution, like the declaration of independence, was framed by deputies from the "states of New-Hampshire," &c. and at the threshold of the transaction, we discern a positive admission of the existence of separate states invested with separate sovereignties. This admission expounds the phrase "We, the people of the United States," which co-operates with the separate powers given to their deputies in the convention, and is distinctly repeated by the words "do ordain and establish this constitution for *the United States of America*." Had the sovereignty of each state been wholly abandoned, and the people of all been considered as constituting one nation, the idea would have been expressed in different language . . . The appellation adopted by the declaration of independence, was, "The United States of America." The first confederation declares, that the style of this confederacy shall be, "The United States of America." And the union of 1787, ordains and establishes the constitution for "The United States of America." The three instruments, by adhering to the same style, coextensively affirmed the separate sovereignties of these states. It was a style proper to describe a confederacy of independent states, and improper for describing a consolidated nation. If neither the declaration of independence nor the confederation of 1777, created an American nation, or a concentrated sovereignty, by this style, the conclusion is inevitable, that the constitution was not intended to produce such consequences by the same style. The word America is used to designate the quarter of the globe in which the recited states were established, and not to designate a nation of Americans . . . If the word state does not intrinsically imply sovereign power, there was no word which we could use better calculated for that purpose.

This construction bestows the same meaning upon the same words in our three constituent or elemental instruments, and exhibits the reason why the whole language of the constitution is affianced to the idea of a league between sovereign states, and hostile to that of a consolidated nation. There are many states in America, but no state of America, nor any people of an American state. A constitution for America or Americans, would therefore have been similar to a constitution for Utopia or Utopians.

Hence the constitution is declared to be made for the "United States of America," that is, for certain states enumerated by their names, established upon that portion of the earth's surface, called America. Though no people or nation of America existed, considering these words as defining a political association, states did exist in America, each constituted by a people. By these political individual entities, called states, the constitution was framed; by these individual entities it was ratified; and by these entities it can only be altered. It was made by them and for them, and not by or for a nation of Americans. The people of each state, or each state as constituted by a people, conveyed to a federal authority, organized by states, a portion of state sovereign powers, and retained another portion. In this division, all the details of the constitution are comprised, one dividend consisting of the special powers conferred upon a federal government, and the other, of the powers reserved by the states which conferred these special powers. The deputation and reservation are both bottomed upon the sovereignty of the states, and must both fall or both stand with that principle. If each state, or the people of each state, did not possess a separate sovereignty, they had no right to convey or retain powers. If they had a right both to convey and to retain powers, it could only be in virtue of state sovereignty. Admitting the utmost which can be asked, and more than ought to be conceded, by supposing that these sovereignties, in conveying limited powers to the federal government, conveyed also a portion of sovereignty, it must also be allowed, that by retaining powers, they retained also a portion of sovereignty. If sovereignty was attached to the ceded powers, it was also attached to the powers not ceded, because all or none of the powers of the states must have proceeded from this principle. In this observation, not use is made of the power reserved to the states to amend the federal form of government, by which a positive sovereignty is retained to the states over that government, subversive of the doctrine, that the constitution bestows a sovereignty upon it over the states. But a delegation of limited powers, being an act of sovereignty, could be a renunciation of the sovereignty attached to the powers not delegated. A power to resume the limited delegation, was the strongest expression of sovereignty, and rejects the idea, that the delegated authority may positively or constructively subject the sovereign power to its own will; that no sovereignty may destroy an actual sovereignty. By this power of amendment, the states may re-establish the confederation of 1777, and thus unquestionably revive their separate sovereignties said to be extinct; because they are positively asserted by that confederation. If it is not absurd, it is yet a new idea, that a dead sovereignty contains an inherent power to revive itself whenever it pleases.

The mode of making amendments to the constitution, expresses its true construction, and rejects the doctrine, that an American people created a federal government. Their ratification is to be the act of states. It is the same with that of the confederation, which asserted the sovereignties of the states, in concomitancy with this mode of ratification, with only two differences. By the first confederation, the ratification was to be the act of state legislatures, and unanimous; by the constitution, the ratification of alterations is to be the act of "state conventions, or legislatures by three-fourths." The last differences extended the power of the states, by removing the obstacle of unanimity, and was not intended to diminish it. State legislatures and conventions are united, as equivalent state organs. Thus the constitution construes the phrase, "We, the people of the United States," and refutes the doctrine of an American people, as the sources of federal powers; because, had these powers been derived from that source, it would have referred to the same source for their modification, and not to state legislatures. It declares that both state legislatures and state conventions, are representations of state sovereignties, equally competent to express their will. The same opinion is expressed by declaring that "ratification of the conventions of nine states, shall be sufficient for its establishment between the ratifying states." Of the two equivalent modes of ratification, it selects one for that special occasion, not because it substantially differed from the other, and was not an expression of state will, but because it was apprehended that a considerable transfer of powers from the state governments to a federal government, might produce an opposition from men in the exercise of these powers, although when experience should have ascertained the benefits of the innovation, and time should have cured the wounds of individual ambition, a further adherence to one equivalent mode in preference to the other, might be unnecessary and inconvenient to the states. The equivalency of the modes is obvious, as state legislatures are empowered to revoke the act of state conventions, by which the residence of state sovereignties in these legislatures is considered as the same as its residence in state conventions, upon no other ground, than that both constituted a representation of the state, and not a representation of an unassociated people.

An adherence to our original principle of state sovereignty is demonstrated both by the confederation and constitution. Unanimity was necessary to put the first, and a concurrence of nine states to put the second, "to the states ratifying only." Both consequences are deduced from state sovereignty, by which one state could defeat a union predicted upon unanimity, and four states might have refused to unite with nine. The latter circumstance displays the peculiar propriety or ordaining and establishing the constitution "for the United States of America." The refusing states, though states of America, did not constitute a portion of an American nation; and their right of refusal resulted from their acknowledged sovereignty and independence.

"The United States of America" would have consisted of nine states only, had four refused to accede to the union; and therefore thirteen states could not have been contemplated by the constitution, as having been consolidated into one people. Hence it adheres to the idea of a league, by a style able to describe "the United States of America," had they consisted but of nine, and avoids a style applicable only to one nation or people consisting of thirteen states. By acknowledging the sovereignty of the refusing, it admits equally an evidence of it. The limitation of federal powers by assent, establishes the principle from which the assent flowed. There could be no sound assent, nor any sound limitation, unless one was given, and the other imposed, by a competent authority; and no authority is competent to the establishment of a government, except it is sovereign. The same authority could only possess the right of rejecting the constitution. Had it been the act of an American nation or people, a state would have possessed no such right. The judicial sages have allowed the federal to be a limited government, but how can it be limited if the state sovereignties by which it was limited, do not exist, and if the state powers reserved, which define the limitation, are subject to its control?

Having proved that state sovereignties were established by the declaration of independence; that their existence was asserted by the confederation of 1777; that they are recognized by the constitution of 1787, in the modes of its formation, ratification, and amendment; that this constitution employs the same words to describe the United States, used by the two preceding instruments; that the word state implies a sovereign community; that each state contained an associated people; that an American people never existed; that the constitution was ordained and established, for such states situated in America, as might accede to a union; that its limited powers was a partial and voluntary endowment of state sovereignties, to be exercised by a Congress of the states which should unite; that the word Congress implies a deputation from sovereignties, and was so expounded by the confederation; and that a reservation of sovereign powers cannot be executed without sovereignty; the reader will consider, whether all these principles, essential for the preservation both of the federal and state governments, were intended to be destroyed by the details of the constitution. The attempt to lose twenty-four states, in order to find a consolidated nation, or a judicial sovereignty, reverses the mode of reasoning hitherto admitted to be correct, by deducing principles from effects, and not effects from principles. But in construing the constitution, we shall never come at truth, if we suffer its details, intended to be subservient to established political principles, to deny their allegiance, and rebel against their sovereigns. A will to act, and a power to execute, constitutes sovereignty. The state governments, says the Federalist, are no more dependent on the federal government is on them, in the exercise of its delegated powers.

The treaty between his Britannick majesty and the *United States of America*, acknowledges "the said United States, viz. New-Hampshire, Massachusetts-Bay, Rhode-Island and Providence Plantations, Connecticut, New-York, New-Jersey, Pennsylvania, Delaware, Maryland, Virginia, North-Carolina, South-Carolina, and Georgia, to be free, *sovereign*, and independent states; as such he treats with them, and relinquishes all claim to their government and territorial rights." This king acknowledges, individually, the sovereignty of the states; he relinquishes to them, individually, his territorial rights; three eminent envoys demanded this acknowledgment and relinquishment, as appertaining, individually, to the states; a Congress of the United States ratified the act and the doctrine; the treaty was then unanimously hailed, and is still generally considered, as a consummation of right, justice, and liberty; but now it is said that the states are corporations, subordinate bodies politick, and not sovereign. By the admirers of royal sovereignty, the treat ought to be considered as valid; by those who confide in authority, it ought to be considered as authentic; by such as respect our revolutionary patriots, it ought to be venerated; and by honest expositors of the constitution, it will be allowed to afford conclusive proof, that the phrase "United States of America," used both in the treaty and the constitution, implied the existence, and not the abrogation, of state sovereignty. Consolidators, suprematists, and conquerors, however, will all equally disregard any instrument, however solemn and explicit, by which ambition and avarice will be restrained, and the happiness of mankind improved.

THE WEBSTER-HAYNE DEBATE[32]

Hayne: . . . Sir, I am one of those who believe that the very life of our system is the independence of the States, and that there is no evil more to be deprecated than the consolidation of this Government. It is only by a strict adherence to the limitations imposed by the constitution on the Federal Government, that this system works well, and can answer the great ends for which it was instituted. I am opposed, therefore, in any shape, to all unnecessary extension of the powers, or the influence of the Legislature or Executive of the Union over the States, or the people of the States, and most of all, I am opposed to those partial distributions of favors, whether by appropriation, which has a direct and powerful tendency to spread corruption through the land; to create an abject spirit of dependence; to sow the seeds of dissolution; to produce jealousy among the different portions of the Union, and finally to sap the very foundations of the Government itself.

Webster: . . . Consolidation!—that perpetual cry, both of terror and delusion—consolidation! Sir, when gentleman speak of the effects of a common fund, belonging to all States, as having a tendency to consolidation, what do they mean? Do they mean, or can they mean, anything more than that the Union of all States will be strengthened, by whatever continues or furnishes inducements to the people of the States to hold together? If they mean merely this, then, no doubt, the public lands as well as every thing else in which we have a common interest, tends to consolidation; and to this species of consolidation every true American ought to be attacked; it is neither more nor less than strengthening the Union itself. This is the sense in which the framers of the constitution use the word consolidation; and in which sense I adopt and cherish it. They tell us, in the letter submitting the constitution to the consideration of the country, that, "in all our deliberations on this subject, we kept steadily in our view that which appears to us the greatest interest of every true American—the consolidation of our Union—in which is involved our prosperity, felicity, safety; perhaps our national existence. This is important consideration, seriously and deeply impressed on our minds, led each State in the Convention to be less rigid, on points of inferior magnitude, than might have been otherwise expected."

Hayne: . . . I am proud of having belonged from the very commencement of my political life to the present day, were the democrats of '98. Anarchists, anti-federalist, revolutionists, I think they were sometimes called. They assumed the name of democratic republicans in 1812, and have retained their name and their principles up to the present hour. True to their political faith, they have always, as a party, been in favor of limitations of power; they have insisted that all powers not delegated to the Federal Government as reserved, and have been constantly struggling, as they are now struggling, to preserve the rights of the States, and prevent them from being drawn into the vortex, and swallowed up by one great consolidated Government.

Who then, Mr. President, are the true friends of the Union? Those who would confine the federal government strictly within the limits prescribed by the constitution—who would preserve to the States and the people all powers not expressly delegated—who would make this a federal and not a national Union—and who, administering the government in a spirit of equal justice, would make it a blessing and not a curse. And who are its enemies? Those who are in favor of consolidation; who are constantly stealing power from the States and adding strength to the federal government; who, assuming an unwarrantable jurisdiction over the States and the people, undertake to regulate the whole industry and capital of the country. But, Sir, of all descriptions of men, I consider those as the worst enemies of the Union, who sacrifice the equal rights which belong to every member of the confederacy, to combinations of interested majorities for personal or political objects. But the gentleman apprehends no evil from the dependence of the States on the federal Government; he can see no danger of corruption from the influence of money or of patronage.

The Senator from Massachusetts, in denouncing what he is pleased to call the *Carolina doctrine*, has attempted to throw ridicule upon the idea that the State had any constitutional remedy by the exercise of its sovereign authority against "a gross, palpable, and deliberate violation of the Constitution." He called it an "an idle" or "a ridiculous notion," or something to that effect; and added, that it would make the Union "a mere rope of sand." Now, Sir, as the gentleman has not condescended to enter into an examination of the question, and has been satisfied with throwing the weight of his authority into the scale, I do not deem it necessary to do more than to throw into the opposite scale, the authority on which South Carolina relies; and there, for the present, I am perfectly willing to leave the controversy. The South Carolina doctrines, that is to say, the doctrine contained in the exposition reported by a committee of the legislature in December, 1828, and published by their authority, is the good old Republican doctrine of '98, the doctrine of the Celebrated "Virginia Resolutions," of that year, and of "Madison's Report" of '00.

Webster: . . . What he contends for, is, that it is constitutional to interrupt the administration of the Constitution itself, in the hands of in the hands of those who are chosen and sworn to administer it, by the direct interference, in from of law, of the States, in virtue of their sovereign capacity. The inherent right in the People to reform their government, I do not deny; and they have another right, and that is, to resist unconstitutional laws, without overturning the Government. It is no doctrine of mine, that unconstitutional laws bind the People. The great question is, whose prerogative is it to decide on the unconstitutionality of the laws? On that, the main debate hinges. The proposition, that, in case of a supposed violation of the Constitution by Congress, the Sates have a constitutional right to interfere, and annul the law of Congress, is the proposition of the gentleman: I do not admit it. If the gentleman had intended no more than to assert the right of revolution, for justifiable cause, he would have said only what all agree to. But I cannot conceive that there can be a middle course, between submission to the laws, when regularly pronounced constitutional, on the one hand, and open resistance, which is revolution, or rebellion, on the other. I say, the right of a Sate to annul a law of Congress, cannot be maintained, but on the ground of the unalienable right of man to resist oppression; that is to say, upon the ground of revolution. I admit that there is an ultimate violent remedy, above the Constitution, and in defiance of the Constitution, which may be resorted to, when a revolution is to be justified. But I do not admit that, under the Constitution, and in conformity with it, there is any mode in which a State Government, as a member of the Union, can interfere and stop the progress of the General Government, by force of her own laws, under any circumstances what so ever. This leads us to inquire into the origin of this Government, and the source of its power. Whose agent is it? Is it the creature of the State Legislature, or the creature of the People?

If the Government of the United States be the agent of the State Government, then they may control it, provided they can agree in the manner of controlling it; if it be the agent of the People, then the People alone can control it, restrain it, modify, or reform it. It is observable enough, that the doctrine for which the honorable gentleman contends, leads him to the necessity of maintaining, not only that this General Government is the creature of the States, but that it is the creature of each of the States severally; so that each may assert the power, for itself, of determining whether its acts within the limits of its authority. It is the servant of four-and-twenty masters, of different wills and different purposes, and yet bound to obey all. This absurdity (for it seems no less) arises form a misconception as to the origin of this Government and its true character. It is, sir, the People's Constitution, the People's Government; made for the People; made by the People; and answerable to the People. The People of the United States have declared that this Constitution shall be the Supreme Law. We must either admit the proposition, or dispute their authority. The States are, unquestionably, sovereign, so far as their sovereignty is not affected by this supreme law. But the State Legislatures, as political bodies, however sovereign, are yet not sovereign over the People. So far as the People have given power to the General Government, so far the grant is unquestionably good, and the Government holds of the People, and not of the State Governments. We are all agents of the same supreme power, the People. The General Government and the State Governments derive their authority form the same source. Neither can, in relation to the other, be called primary, though one is definite and restricted, and the other general and residuary. The National Government possesses those powers which it can be shown the People have conferred on it, and no more. All the rest belongs to the State Governments or to the People themselves.

    . . . If there be no power to settle such questions, independent of either of the States, is not the whole Union a rope of sand? Are we not thrown back again, precisely, upon the old Confederation?

    . . . I must now beg to ask, sir, whence is this supposed right [Interposition] of the States derived?—where do they find the power to interfere with the laws of the Union? Sir, the opinion which the honorable gentleman maintains, is a notion, founded in a total misapprehension, in my judgement, of the origin of this Government, and of the foundation on which it stands. I hold it to be a popular Government, erected by the People; those who administer it reasonable to the People; and itself being capable of being amended and modified, just as the People may choose it to be. It is popular, just as truly emanating from the People, as the State Governments. It is created for one purpose; the State Governments for one another. It has its own powers; they have theirs. There is no more authority with them to arrest the operation of a law of Congress, than with Congress to arrest the operation of their laws.

We are here to administer a Constitution emanating immediately from the People, and trusted, by them, to our administration. It is not the creature of the State Governments. It is of no moment to the argument, that certain acts of the State Legislatures are necessary to fill our seats in this body. That is not one of their original Sate powers, a part of the sovereignty of the State. It is a duty which the People, by the Constitution itself, have imposed on the State Legislatures; and which they might have left to be performed elsewhere, if they had seen fit. So they have left the choice of President with electors; but all this does not affect the proposition, that this whole Government, President, Senate, and House of Representatives, is popular Government. It leaves it still all its popular character. The governor of a State, (in some of the States) is chosen, not directly by the People, but by those who are chosen by the People, for the purpose of performing, among other duties, that of electing a Governor. Is the Government of the State, on that account, not a popular Government? This Government, sir, is the independent offspring of the popular will. It is not the creature of State Legislatures; nay, more, if the whole truth must be told, the People brought it into existence, established it, and have hitherto supported it, for the very purpose, amongst others, of imposing certain salutary restraints on State sovereignties. The States can not now make war; they cannot contract alliances; they cannot make, each for itself, separate regulations of commerce; they cannot lay imposts; they cannot coin money. If this Constitution, sir, be the creature of the State Legislatures, it must be admitted that it has obtained a strange control over the violations of its creators.

The People, then, sir, erected this Government. They gave it a Constitution, and in that Constitution they have enumerated the powers which they bestow on it. They have made it a limited Government. They have defined its authority. They have restrained it to the exercise of such powers as are granted; and all others, they declare, are reserved to the States or the People. But, sir, they have not stopped here. If they had, they would have accomplished but half their work. No definition can be so clear, as to avoid possibility of doubt; no limitation so precise, as to exclude all uncertainty. Who, then, shall construe this giant of the People? Who shall interpret their will, where it may be supposed they have left it doubtful? With whom do they repose this ultimate right of deciding on the powers of the Government? Sir, they have settled all this in the fullest manner. They have left it, with the Government itself, in its appropriate branches. Sir, the very chief end, the main design, for which the whole Constitution was framed and adopted, was to establish a Government that should not be obliged to act through State agency, or depend on State opinion and State discretion. The People had had quite enough of that kind of Government, under the Confederacy. Under that system, the legal action— the application of law to individuals, belonged exclusively to the States. Congress could only recommend—their acts were not of binding force, till

the Stated had adopted and sanctioned them. Are we in that condition still?
Are we yet at the mercy of State discretion, and the State construction? Sir,
if we are, then vain will be our attempt to maintain the Constitution under
which we sit.

But, sir, the People have wisely provided, in the Constitution itself, a
proper, suitable mode and tribunal for settling questions of constitutional law.
There are, in the Constitution, grants of powers to Congress; and restrictions
on these powers. There are, also, prohibitions on the States. Some authority
must, therefore, necessarily exist, having the ultimate jurisdiction to fix and
ascertain the interpretation of these grants, restrictions, and prohibitions.
The Constitution has itself pointed out, ordained, and established that authority. How has it accomplished this great and essential end? By declaring, sir,
that *"the Constitution and the laws of the United States, made in pursuance
thereof, shall be the supreme law of the land, any thing in the Constitution or
the laws of any State to the contrary notwithstanding."*

. . . Sir, I deny this power of State Legislature altogether. It cannot stand
the test of examination. Gentleman may say, that in an extreme case, a State
Government might protect the People from intolerable oppression. Sir, in
such a case, the People might protect themselves, without the aid of the State
Governments. Such a case warrants revolution. It must make, when it comes,
a law for itself. A nullifying act of a State Legislature cannot alter the case,
nor make resistance any more lawful. In maintaining these sentiments, sir,
I am but asserting the rights of the People. I state what they have declared,
and insist on their right to declare it. They have chosen to repose this power
to the General Government, and I think it my duty to support it, like other
constitutional powers.

. . . If, sir, the People, in these respects, had done otherwise than they have
done, their Constitution could neither have been preserved, nor would it have
been worth preserving. And, if its plain provisions shall now be disregarded,
and these new doctrines interpolated in it, it will become as feeble and help-
less a being as its enemies, whether early or more recent, could possibly
desire. It will exist in every State, but as a poor dependent on State permission. It must borrow leave to be; and will be, no longer than State pleasure,
or State discretion, sees fit to grant the indulgence, and to prolong its poor
existence.

. . . Mr. President, I have thus stated the reason of my dissent to the doctrines which have been advanced and maintained. I am conscious of having
detained you and the Senate much too long. I was drawn into the debate, with
no previous deliberation such as is suited to the discussion of so grave and
important a subject. But it is a subject of which my heart is full, and I have
not been willing to suppress the utterance of its spontaneous sentiments.
I cannot, even now, persuade myself to relinquish it, without expressing,

once more, my deep conviction, that, since it respects nothing less than the Union of the States, it is of most vital and essential importance to the public happiness. I profess, sir, in my career, hitherto, to have kept steadily in view the prosperity and honor of the whole country, and the preservation of our Federal Union. It is to that Union we owe our safety at home, and our consideration and dignity abroad. It is to that Union that we are chiefly indebted for whatever makes us most proud of our country. That Union we reached only by the discipline of our virtues in the severe school of adversity. It had its origin in the necessities of disordered finance, prostrate commerce, and ruined credit. Under its benign influences, these great interests immediately awoke, as from the dead, and sprang forth with newness of life. Every year of its duration has teemed with fresh proofs of its utility and its blessings; and, although our territory has stretched out wider and wider, and our population spread farther and farther, they have not outrun its protection or its benefits. It has been to us all a copious fountain of a national, social, and personal happiness. I have not allowed myself, sir, to look beyond the Union, to see what might lie hidden in the dark recess behind. I have not coolly weighed the chances of preserving liberty, when the bonds that unite us together shall be broken asunder. I have not accustomed myself to hang over the principle of disunion, to see whether, with my short sight, I can fathom the depth of the abyss below; nor could I regard him as a safe counsellor in the affairs of this Government, whose thoughts should be mainly bent on considering, not how the Union should be best preserved, but how tolerable might be the condition of the People when it shall be broken up and destroyed. While the Union lasts, we have high, exciting, gratifying prospects spread out before us, for us and our children. Beyond that I seek not to penetrate the veil. God grant that, in my day, at least, that curtain may not rise. God grant that on my vision never may be opened what lies behind. When my eyes shall be turned to behold, for the last time, the sun in Heaven, may I not see him shining on the broken and dishonored fragments of a once glorious Union; on the States dissevered, discordant, belligerent; on the land rent with civil feuds, or drenched, it may be, in fraternal blood! Let their last feeble and lingering glance, rather behold the gorgeous Ensign of the Republic, now known and honored throughout the earth, still full high advanced, its arms and trophies streaming in their original lustre, not a stripe erased or polluted, nor a single star obscured—bearing for its motto, no such miserable interrogatory as, *What is all this worth?* Nor those other words of delusion and folly, *Liberty first, and Union afterwards*—but everywhere, spread all over in characters of living light, blazing on all its ample folds, as they float over the sea and over the land, and in every wind under the whole Heavens, that other sentiment, dear to every true American heart—Liberty *and* Union, now and forever, one and inseparable!

JOHN C. CALHOUN "THE FORT HILL ADDRESS"[33]

The question of the relation which the States and General Government bear to each other is not one of recent origin. From the commencement of our system, it has divided public sentiment. Even in the Convention, while the Constitution was struggling into existence, there were two parties as to what this relation should be, whose different sentiments constituted no small impediment in forming that instrument. After the General Government went into operation, experience soon proved that the question had not terminated with the labors of the Convention. The great struggle that preceded the political revolution of 1801, which brought Mr. Jefferson into power, turned essentially on it; and the doctrines and arguments on both sides were embodied and ably sustained—on the one, in the Virginia and Kentucky Resolutions, and the Report to the Virginia Legislature—and on the other, in the replies of the Legislature of Massachusetts and some of the other States.

The great and leading principle is, that the General Government emanated from the people of the several States, forming distinct political communities, and acting in their separate and sovereign capacity, and not from all of the people forming one aggregate political community; that the Constitution of the United States is, in fact, a compact, to which each State is a party, in the character already described; and that the several States, or parties, have a right to judge of its infractions; and in case of a deliberate, palpable, and dangerous exercise of power not delegated, they have the right, in the last resort, to use the language of the Virginia Resolutions, "to interpose for arresting the progress of the evil, and for maintaining, within their respective limits, the authorities, rights, and liberties appertaining to them." This right of interposition, thus solemnly asserted by the State of Virginia, be it called what it may—State-right, veto, nullification, or by any other name—I conceive to be the fundamental principle of our system, resting on facts historically as certain as our revolution itself, and deductions as simple and demonstrative as that of any political, or moral truth whatever; and I firmly believe that on its recognition depend the stability and safety of our political institutions.

I am not ignorant, that those opposed to the doctrine have always, now and formerly, regarded it in a very different light, as anarchical and revolutionary. Could I believe such, in fact, to be its tendency, to me it would be no recommendation. I yield to none, I trust, in a deep and sincere attachment to our political institutions and the union of these States. I never breathed an opposite sentiment; but, on the contrary, I have ever considered them the great instruments of preserving our liberty, and promoting the happiness of ourselves and our posterity; and next to these I have ever held them most dear.

. . . So numerous and diversified are the interests of our country, that they could not be fairly represented in a single government, organized so as to give to each great and leading interest, a separate and distinct voice, as in governments to which I have referred. A plan was adopted better suited to our situation, but perfectly novel in its character. The powers of government were divided, not, as heretofore, in reference to classes, but geographically. One General Government was formed for the whole, to which were delegated all the powers supposed to be necessary to regulate the interests common to all the States, leaving others subject to the separate control of the States, being, from their local and peculiar character, such, that they could not be subject to the will of a majority of the whole Union, without the certain hazard of injustice and oppression. It was thus that the interests of the whole were subjected, as they ought to be, to the will of the whole, while the peculiar and local interests were left under the control of the States separately, to whose custody only, they could be safely confided. This distribution of power, settled solemnly by a constitutional compact, to which all the States are parties, constitutes the peculiar character and excellence of our political system. It is truly and emphatically *American, without example or parallel.*

To realize its perfection, we must view the General Government and those of the States as a whole, each in its proper sphere, sovereign and independent; each perfectly adapted to its respective objects; the States acting separately, representing and protecting the local and peculiar interests; and acting jointly through one General Government, with the weight respectively assigned to each by the Constitution, representing and protecting the interest of the whole; and thus perfecting, by an admirable but simple arrangement, the great principle of representation and responsibility, without which no government can be free or just. To preserve this sacred distribution, as originally settled, by coercing each to move in its prescribed orbit, is the great and difficult problem, on the solution of which, the duration of our Constitution, of our Union, and, in all probability, our liberty depends. How is this to be effected? . . .

Whenever separate and dissimilar interests have been separately represented in any government; whenever the sovereign power has been divided in its exercise, the experience and wisdom of ages have devised but one mode by which such political organization can be preserved—the mode adopted in England, and by all governments, ancient and modern, blessed with constitutions deserving to be called free—to give to each co-estate the right to judge of its powers, with a negative or veto on the acts of the others, in order to protect against encroachments, the interests it particularly represents: a principle which all of our constitutions recognize in the distribution of power among their respective departments, as essential to maintain the independence of each; but which, to all who will duly reflect on the subject, must appear far more essential, for the same object, in that great and fundamental distribution of powers between the states and General Government. So essential is the principle, that, to withhold the right from either, where the sovereign power is divided, is, in fact, *to annul the division* itself, and to *consolidate*, in the one left in the exclusive possession of the right, *all* powers of government; for it is not possible to distinguish, practically, between a government having all power, and one having the right to take what powers it pleases. Nor does it in the least vary the principle, whether the distribution of power be between co-estates, as in England, or between distinctly organized, but connected governments, as with us. The reason is the same in both cases, while the necessity is greater in our case, as the danger of conflict is greater where the interests of a society are divided geographically than in any other, as has already been shown. . . .

I do not deny that a power of so high a nature may be abused by a State; but when I reflect that the States unanimously called the General Government into existence with all of its powers, which they freely delegated on their part, under the conviction that their common peace, safety, and prosperity required it; that they are bound together by a common origin, and the recollection of common suffering and common triumph in the great and splendid achievement of their independence; and that the strongest feelings of our nature, and among them the love of national power and distinction, are on the side of the Union; it does seem to me that the fear which would strip the States of their sovereignty, and degrade them, in fact, to mere dependent corporations, lest they should abuse a right indispensable to the peaceable protection of those interests which they reserved under their own peculiar guardianship when they created the General Government, is unnatural and unreasonable. If those who voluntarily created the system cannot be trusted to preserve it, what power can?

So, far from extreme danger, I hold that there never was a free State in which this great conservative principle, indispensable to all, was ever so safely lodged. In others, when the co-estates representing the dissimilar and conflicting interests of the community came into contact, the only alternative was compromise, submission, or force. Not so in ours. Should the General Government and a State come into conflict, we have a higher remedy: the power which called the General Government into existence, which gave it all of its authority, and can enlarge, contract, or abolish its powers at its pleasure, may be invoked. The States themselves may be appealed to—three-fourths of which, in fact, form a power, whose decrees are the Constitution itself, and whose voice can silence all discontent. The utmost extent, then, of the power is, that a State, acting in its sovereign capacity, as one of the parties to the constitutional compact, may compel the Government, created by that compact, to submit a question touching its infraction, to the parties who created it; to avoid the supposed dangers of which, it is proposed to resort to the novel, the hazardous, and, I must add, fatal project of giving to the General

Government the sole and final right of interpreting the Constitution—thereby reversing the whole system, making that instrument the creature of its will, instead of a rule of action impressed on it at its creation, and annihilating, in fact, the authority which imposed it, and from which the Government itself derives its existence. . . .

Against these conclusive arguments, as they seem to me, it is objected, that, if one of the parties has the right to judge of infractions of the Constitution, so has the other; and that, consequently, in cases of contested powers between a State and the General Government, each would have a right to maintain its opinion, as is the case when sovereign powers differ in the construction of treaties or compacts; and that, of course, it would come to be a mere question of force. The error is in the assumption that the General Government is a party to the constitutional compact. The States, as has been shown, formed the compact, acting as Sovereign and independent communities. The General Government is but its creature; and though, in reality, a government, with all the rights and authority which belong to any other government, within the orbit of its powers, it is, nevertheless, a government emanating from a compact between sovereigns, and partaking, in its nature and object, of the character of a joint commission, appointed to superintend and administer the interests in which all are jointly concerned; but having, beyond its proper sphere, no more power than if it did not exist. To deny this would be to deny the most incontestable facts, and the clearest conclusions; while to acknowledge its truth is, to destroy utterly the objection that the appeal would be to force, in the case supposed. For if each party has a right to judge, then, under our system of government, the final cognizance of a question of contested power would be in the States, and not in the General Government. It would be the duty of the latter, as in all similar cases of a contest between one or more of the principals and a joint commission or agency, to refer the contest to the principals themselves. Such are the plain dictates of both reason and analogy.

SOUTH CAROLINA, ORDINANCE OF NULLIFICATION[34]

Whereas the Congress of the United States by various acts, purporting to be acts laying duties and imposts on foreign imports, but in reality intended for the protection of domestic manufactures and the giving of bounties to classes and individuals engaged in particular employments, at the expense and to the injury and oppression of other classes and individuals, and by wholly exempting from taxation certain foreign commodities, such as are not produced or manufactured in the United States, to afford a pretext for imposing higher and excessive duties on articles similar to those intended to be protected, bath exceeded its just powers under the constitution, which confers on it no authority to afford such protection, and bath violated the true meaning and intent of the constitution, which provides for equality in imposing the burdens of taxation upon the several States and portions of the confederacy: And whereas the said Congress, exceeding its just power to impose taxes and collect revenue for the purpose of effecting and accomplishing the specific objects and purposes which the constitution of the United States authorizes it to effect and accomplish, hath raised and collected unnecessary revenue for objects unauthorized by the constitution.

We, therefore, the people of the State of South Carolina, in convention assembled, do declare and ordain and it is hereby declared and ordained, that the several acts and parts of acts of the Congress of the United States, purporting to be laws for the imposing of duties and imposts on the importation of foreign commodities, and now having actual operation and effect within the United States, and, more especially, an act entitled "An act in alteration of the several acts imposing duties on imports," approved on the nineteenth day of May, one thousand eight hundred and twenty-eight and also an act entitled "An act to alter and amend the several acts imposing duties on imports," approved on the fourteenth day of July, one thousand eight hundred and thirty-two, are unauthorized by the constitution of the United States, and violate the true meaning and intent thereof and are null, void, and no law, nor binding upon this State, its officers or citizens; and all promises, contracts, and obligations, made or entered into, or to be made or entered into, with purpose to secure the duties imposed by said acts, and all judicial proceedings which shall be hereafter had in affirmance thereof, are and shall be held utterly null and void.

And it is further ordained, that it shall not be lawful for any of the constituted authorities, whether of this State or of the United States, to enforce the payment of duties imposed by the said acts within the limits of this State; but it shall be the duty of the legislature to adopt such measures and pass such acts as may be necessary to give full effect to this ordinance, and to prevent the enforcement and arrest the operation of the said acts and parts of acts of the Congress of the United States within the limits of this State, from and after the first day of February next, and the duties of all other constituted authorities, and of all persons residing or being within the limits of this State, and they are hereby required and enjoined to obey and give effect to this ordinance, and such acts and measures of the legislature as may be passed or adopted in obedience thereto.

And it is further ordained, that in no case of law or equity, decided in the courts of this State, wherein shall be drawn in question the authority of this ordinance, or the validity of such act or acts of the legislature as may be passed for the purpose of giving effect thereto, or the validity of the aforesaid acts of Congress, imposing duties, shall any appeal be taken or allowed to the Supreme Court of the United States, nor shall any copy of the record be permitted or allowed for that purpose; and if any such appeal shall be attempted to be taken, the courts of this State shall proceed to execute and enforce their judgments according to the laws and usages of the State, without reference to such attempted appeal, and the person or persons attempting to take such appeal may be dealt with as for a contempt of the court.

And it is further ordained, that all persons now holding any office of honor, profit, or trust, civil or military, under this State (members of the legislature excepted), shall, within such time, and in such manner as the legislature shall prescribe, take an oath well and truly to obey, execute, and enforce this ordinance, and such act or acts of the legislature as may be passed in pursuance thereof, according to the true intent and meaning of the same, and on the neglect or omission of any such person or persons so to do, his or their office or offices shall be forthwith vacated, and shall be filled up as if such person or persons were dead or had resigned; and no person hereafter elected to any office of honor, profit, or trust, civil or military (members of the legislature excepted), shall, until the legislature shall otherwise provide and direct, enter on the execution of his office, or be he any respect competent to discharge the duties thereof until he shall, in like manner, have taken a similar oath; and no juror shall be impaneled in any of the courts of this State, in any cause in which shall be in question this ordinance, or any act of the legislature passed in pursuance thereof, unless he shall first, in addition to the usual oath, have taken an oath that he will well and truly obey, execute, and enforce this ordinance, and such act or acts of the legislature as may be passed to carry the same into operation and effect, according to the true intent and meaning thereof.

And we, the people of South Carolina, to the end that it may be fully understood by the government of the United States, and the people of the co-States, that we are determined to maintain this our ordinance and declaration, at every hazard, do further declare that we will not submit to the application of force on the part of the federal government, to reduce this State to obedience, but that we will consider the passage, by Congress, of any act authorizing the employment of a military or naval force against the State of South Carolina, her constitutional authorities or citizens; or any act abolishing or closing the ports of this State, or any of them, or otherwise obstructing the free ingress and egress of vessels to and from the said ports, or any other act on the part of the federal government, to coerce the State, shut up her ports, destroy or harass her commerce or to enforce the acts hereby declared to be null and void, otherwise than through the civil tribunals of the country, as inconsistent with the longer continuance of South Carolina in the Union; and that the people of this State will henceforth hold themselves absolved from all further obligation to maintain or preserve their political connection with the people of the other States; and will forthwith proceed to organize a separate government, and do all other acts and things which sovereign and independent States may of right do.

ANDREW JACKSON, "PROCLAMATION REGARDING NULLIFICATION"[35]

. . . The ordinance is founded, not on the indefeasible right of resisting acts which are plainly unconstitutional, and too oppressive to be endured, but on the strange position that any one State may not only declare an act of Congress void, but prohibit its execution—that they may do this consistently with the Constitution—that the true construction of that instrument permits a State to retain its place in the Union, and yet be bound by no other of its laws than those it may choose to consider as constitutional. It is true they add, that to justify this abrogation of a law, it must be palpably contrary to the Constitution, but it is evident, that to give the right of resisting laws of that description, coupled with the uncontrolled right to decide what laws deserve that character, is to give the power of resisting all laws. For, as by the theory, there is no appeal, the reasons alleged by the State, good or bad, must prevail. If it should be said that public opinion is a sufficient check against the abuse of this power, it may be asked why it is not deemed a sufficient guard against the passage of an unconstitutional act by Congress. There is, however, a restraint in this last case, which makes the assumed power of a State more indefensible, and which does not exist in the other. There are two appeals from an unconstitutional act passed by Congress-one to the judiciary, the other to the people and the States. There is no appeal from the State decision in theory; and the practical illustration shows that the courts are closed against an application to review it, both judges and jurors being sworn to decide in its favor. But reasoning on this subject is superfluous, when our social compact in express terms declares, that the laws of the United States, its Constitution, and treaties made under it, are the supreme law of the land; and for greater caution adds, "that the judges in every State shall be bound thereby, anything in the Constitution or laws of any State to the contrary notwithstanding." And it may be asserted, without fear of refutation, that no federative government could exist without a similar provision.

. . . If the doctrine of a State veto upon the laws of the Union carries with it internal evidence of its impracticable absurdity, our constitutional history will also afford abundant proof that it would have been repudiated with indignation had it been proposed to form a feature in our Government.

In our colonial state, although dependent on another power, we very early considered ourselves as connected by common interest with each other. Leagues were formed for common defense, and before the Declaration of Independence, we were known in our aggregate character as the United Colonies of America. That decisive and important step was taken jointly. We declared ourselves a nation by a joint, not by several acts; and when the terms of our confederation were reduced to form, it was in that of a solemn league of several States, by which they agreed that they would, collectively, form one nation, for the purpose of conducting some certain domestic concerns, and all foreign relations. In the instrument forming that Union, is found an article which declares that "every State shall abide by the determinations of Congress on all questions which by that Confederation should be submitted to them."

Under the Confederation, then, no State could legally annul a decision of the Congress, or refuse to submit to its execution, but no provision was made to enforce these decisions. Congress made requisitions, but they were not complied with. The Government could not operate on individuals. They had no judiciary, no means of collecting revenue.

But the defects of the Confederation need not be detailed. Under its operation we could scarcely be called a nation. We had neither prosperity at home nor consideration abroad. This state of things could not be endured, and our present happy Constitution was formed, but formed in vain, if this fatal doctrine prevails. It was formed for important objects that are announced in the preamble made in the name and by the authority of the people of the United States, whose delegates framed, and whose conventions approved it.

The most important among these objects, that which is placed first in rank, on which all the others rest, is *"to form a more perfect Union."* Now, is it possible that, even if there were no express provision giving supremacy to the Constitution and laws of the United States over those of the States, it can be conceived that an Instrument made for the purpose of *"forming; a more perfect Union"* than that of the confederation, could be so constructed by the assembled wisdom of our country as to substitute for that confederation a form of government, dependent for its existence on the local interest, the party spirit of a State, or of a prevailing faction in a State? Every man, of plain, unsophisticated understanding, who hears the question, will give such an answer as will preserve the Union. Metaphysical subtlety, in pursuit of an impracticable theory, could alone have devised one that is calculated to destroy it.

I consider, then, the power to annul a law of the United States, assumed by one State, *incompatible with the existence of the Union, contradicted expressly by the letter of the Constitution, unauthorized by its spirit, inconsistent with every principle on which It was founded, and destructive of the great object for which it was formed.*

After this general view of the leading principle, we must examine the particular application of it which is made in the ordinance.

The preamble rests its justification on these grounds: It assumes as a fact, that the obnoxious laws, although they purport to be laws for raising revenue, were in reality intended for the protection of manufactures, which purpose it asserts to be unconstitutional; that the operation of these laws is unequal, that the amount raised by them is greater than is required by the wants of the Government; and, finally, that the proceeds are to be applied to objects unauthorized by the Constitution. These are the only causes alleged to justify an open opposition to the laws of the country, and a threat of seceding from the Union, if any attempt should be made to enforce them. The first virtually acknowledges that the law in question was passed under a power expressly given by the Constitution, to lay and collect imposts, but its constitutionality is drawn in question from the motives of those who passed it. However apparent this purpose may be in the present case, nothing can be more dangerous than to admit the position that an unconstitutional purpose, entertained by the members who assent to a law enacted under a constitutional power, shall make that law void; for how is that purpose to be ascertained? Who is to make the scrutiny? How often may bad purposes be falsely imputed? In how many cases are they concealed by false professions? In how many is no declaration of motive made? Admit this doctrine and you give to the States an uncontrolled right to decide, and every law may be annulled under this pretext. If, therefore, the absurd and dangerous doctrine should be admitted, that a State may annul an unconstitutional law, or one that it deems such, it will not apply to the present case.

The next objection is, that the laws in question operate unequally. This objection may be made with truth to every law that has been or can be passed. The wisdom of man never yet contrived a system of taxation that would operate with perfect equality. If the unequal operation of a law makes it unconstitutional and if all laws of that description may be abrogated by any State for that cause, then, indeed, is the federal Constitution unworthy of the slightest effort for its preservation. We have hitherto relied on it as the perpetual bond of our Union. We have received it as the work of the assembled wisdom of the nation We have trusted to it as to the sheet-anchor of our safety, in the stormy times of conflict with a foreign or domestic foe. We have looked to it with sacred awe as the palladium of our liberties, and with all the solemnities of religion have pledged to each other our lives and fortunes here, and our hopes of happiness hereafter, in its defense and support. Were we mistaken, my countrymen, in attaching this importance to the Constitution of our country? Was our devotion paid to the wretched, inefficient, clumsy contrivance, which this new doctrine would make it? Did we pledge ourselves to the support of an airy nothing-a bubble that must be blown away by the first breath of disaffection? Was this self-destroying, visionary theory the work of the profound statesmen, the exalted patriots, to whom the task of constitutional reform was intrusted? Did the name of Washington sanction, did the States deliberately ratify, such an anomaly in the history of fundamental legislation? No. We were not mistaken. The letter of this great instrument is free from this radical fault; its language directly contradicts the imputation, its spirit, its evident intent, contradicts it. No, we did not err. Our Constitution does not contain the absurdity of giving power to make laws, and another power to resist them. The sages, whose memory will always be reverenced, have given us a practical, and, as they hoped, a permanent constitutional compact. The Father of his Country did not affix his revered name to so palpable an absurdity. Nor did the States, when they severally ratified it, do so under the impression that a veto on the laws of the United States was reserved to them, or that they could exercise it by application. Search the debates in all their conventions-examine the speeches of the most zealous opposers of federal authority-look at the amendments that were proposed. They are all silent— not a syllable uttered, not a vote given, not a motion made, to correct the explicit supremacy given to the laws of the Union over those of the States, or to show that implication, as is now contended, could defeat it. No, we have not erred! The Constitution is still the object of our reverence, the bond of our Union, our defense in danger, the source of our prosperity in peace. It shall descend, as we have received it, uncorrupted by sophistical construction to our posterity; and the sacrifices of local interest, of State prejudices, of personal animosities, that were made to bring it into existence, will again be patriotically offered for its support.

. . . In vain have these sages declared that Congress shall have power to lay and collect taxes, duties, imposts, and excises-in vain have they provided that they shall have power to pass laws which shall be necessary and proper to carry those powers into execution, that those laws and that Constitution shall be the "supreme law of the land; that the judges in every State shall be bound thereby, anything in the constitution or laws of any State to the contrary not-withstanding." In vain have the people of the several States solemnly sanctioned these provisions, made them their paramount law, and individually sworn to support them whenever they were called on to execute any office.

Vain provisions! Ineffectual restrictions! Vile profanation of oaths! Miserable mockery of legislation! If a bare majority of the voters in any one State may, on a real or supposed knowledge of the intent with which a law has been passed, declare themselves free from its operation—say here it gives too little, there too much, and operates unequally—here it suffers articles to be free that ought to be taxed, there it taxes those that ought to be free-in this case the proceeds are intended to be applied to purposes which we do not approve, in that the amount raised is more than is wanted. Congress, it is true, are invested by the Constitution with the right of deciding these questions according to their sound discretion. Congress is composed of the representatives of all the States, and of all the people of all the states; but WE, part of the people of one State, to whom the Constitution has given no power on the subject from whom it has expressly taken it away-we, who have solemnly agreed that this Constitution shall be our law-we, most of whom have sworn to support it-we now abrogate this law, and swear, and force others to swear, that it shall not be obeyed-and we do this, not because Congress have no right to pass such laws; this we do not allege; but because they have passed them with improper views. They are unconstitutional from the motives of those who passed them, which we can never with certainty know, from their unequal operation; although it is impossible from the nature of things that they should be equal-and from the disposition which we presume may be made of their proceeds, although that disposition has not been declared. This is the plain meaning of the ordinance in relation to laws which it abrogates for alleged unconstitutionality. But it does not stop here. It repeals, in express terms, an important part of the Constitution itself, and of laws passed to give it effect, which have never been alleged to be unconstitutional. The Constitution declares that the judicial powers of the United States extend to cases arising under the laws of the United States, and that such laws, the Constitution and treaties, shall be paramount to the State constitutions and laws. The judiciary act prescribes the mode by which the case may be brought before a court of the United States, by appeal, when a State tribunal shall decide against this provision of the Constitution. The ordinance declares there shall be no appeal; makes the State law paramount to the Constitution and laws of the United States; forces judges and jurors to swear that they will disregard their provisions; and even makes it penal in a suitor to attempt relief by appeal. It further declares that it shall not be lawful for the authorities of the United States, or of that State, to enforce the payment of duties imposed by the revenue laws within its limits.

. . . This right to secede is deduced from the nature of the Constitution, which they say is a compact between sovereign States who have preserved their whole sovereignty, and therefore are subject to no superior; that because they made the compact, they can break it when in their opinion it has been departed from by the other States. Fallacious as this course of reasoning is, it enlists State pride, and finds advocates in the honest prejudices of those who have not studied the nature of our government sufficiently to see the radical error on which it rests.

The people of the United States formed the Constitution, acting through the State legislatures, in making the compact, to meet and discuss its provisions, and acting in separate conventions when they ratified those provisions; but the terms used in its construction show it to be a government in which the people of all the States collectively are represented. We are ONE PEOPLE in the choice of the President and Vice President. Here the States have no other agency than to direct the mode in which the vote shall be given. The candidates having the majority of all the votes are chosen. The electors of a majority of States may have given their votes for one candidate, and yet another may be chosen. The people, then, and not the States, are represented in the executive branch.

. . . The Constitution of the United States, then, forms a government, not a league, and whether it be formed by compact between the States, or in any other manner, its character is the same. It is a government in which all the people are represented, which operates directly on the people individually, not upon the States; they retained all the power they did not grant. But each State having expressly parted with so many powers as to constitute jointly with the other States a single nation, cannot from that period possess any right to secede, because such secession does not break a league, but destroys the unity of a nation, and any injury to that unity is not only a breach which would result from the contravention of a compact, but it is an offense against the whole Union. To say that any State may at pleasure secede from the Union, is to say that the United States are not a nation because it would be a solecism to contend that any part of a nation might dissolve its connection with the other parts, to their injury or ruin, without committing any offense. Secession, like any other revolutionary act, may be morally justified by the extremity of oppression; but to call it a constitutional right, is confounding the meaning of terms, and can only be done through gross error, or to deceive those who are willing to assert a right, but would pause before they made a revolution, or incur the penalties consequent upon a failure.

Because the Union was formed by compact, it is said the parties to that compact may, when they feel themselves aggrieved, depart from it; but it is precisely because it is a compact that they cannot. A compact is an agreement or binding obligation. It may by its terms have a sanction or penalty for its breach, or it may not. If it contains no sanction, it may be broken with no other consequence than moral guilt; if it have a sanction, then the breach incurs the designated or implied penalty. A league between independent nations, generally, has no sanction other than a moral one; or if it should contain a penalty, as there is no common superior, it cannot be enforced. A government, on the contrary, always has a sanction, express or implied; and, in our case, it is both necessarily implied and expressly given. An attempt by force of arms to destroy a government is an offense, by whatever means the constitutional compact may have been formed; and such government has the right, by the law of self-defense, to pass acts for punishing the offender, unless that right is modified, restrained, or resumed by the constitutional act. In our system, although it is modified in the case of treason, yet authority is expressly given to pass all laws necessary to carry its powers into effect, and under this grant provision has been made for punishing acts which obstruct the due administration of the laws.

. . . The States severally have not retained their entire sovereignty. It has been shown that in becoming parts of a nation, not members of a league, they surrendered many of their essential parts of sovereignty. The right to make treaties, declare war, levy taxes, exercise exclusive judicial and legislative powers, were all functions of sovereign power. The States, then, for all these important purposes, were no longer sovereign. The allegiance of their citizens was transferred in the first instance to the government of the United States; they became American citizens, and owed obedience to the Constitution of the United States, and to laws made in conformity with the powers vested in Congress. This last position has not been, and cannot be, denied. How then, can that State be said to be sovereign and independent whose citizens owe obedience to laws not made by it, and whose magistrates are sworn to disregard those laws, when they come in conflict with those passed by another? What shows conclusively that the States cannot be said to have reserved an undivided sovereignty, is that they expressly ceded the right to punish treason-not treason against their separate power, but treason against the United States. Treason is an offense against sovereignty, and sovereignty must reside with the power to punish it. But the reserved rights of the States are not less sacred because they have for their common interest made the general government the depository of these powers. The unity of our political character (as has been shown for another purpose) commenced with its very existence. Under the royal government we had no separate character; our opposition to its oppression began as UNITED COLONIES. We were the UNITED STATES under the Confederation, and the name was perpetuated and the Union rendered more perfect by the federal Constitution. In none of these stages did we consider ourselves in any other light than as forming one nation. Treaties and alliances were made in the name of all. Troops were raised for the joint defense. How, then, with all these proofs, that under all changes of our position we had, for designated purposes and with defined powers, created national governments-how is it that the most perfect of these several modes of union should now be considered as a mere league that may be dissolved at pleasure ? It is from an abuse of terms. Compact is used as synonymous with league, although the true term is not employed, because it would at once show the fallacy of the reasoning. It would not do to say that our Constitution was only a league, but it is labored to prove it a compact (which, in one sense, it is), and then to argue that as a league is a compact, every compact between nations must, of course, be a league, and that from such an engagement every sovereign power has a right to recede. But it has been shown that in this sense the States are not sovereign, and that even if they were, and the national

Constitution had been formed by compact, there would be no right in any one State to exonerate itself from the obligation.

So obvious are the reasons which forbid this secession, that it is necessary only to allude to them. The Union was formed for the benefit of all. It was produced by mutual sacrifice of interest and opinions. Can those sacrifices be recalled? Can the States, who magnanimously surrendered their title to the territories of the West, recall the grant? Will the inhabitants of the inland States agree to pay the duties that may be imposed without their assent by those on the Atlantic or the Gulf, for their own benefit? Shall there be a free port in one State, and enormous duties in another? No one believes that any right exists in a single State to involve all the others in these and countless other evils, contrary to engagements solemnly made. Everyone must see that the other States, in self-defense, must oppose it at all hazards.

These are the alternatives that are presented by the convention: A repeal of all the acts for raising revenue, leaving the government without the means of support; or an acquiescence in the dissolution of our Union by the secession of one of its members. When the first was proposed, it was known that it could not be listened to for a moment. It was known if force was applied to oppose the execution of the laws, that it must be repelled by force-that Congress could not, without involving itself in disgrace and the country in ruin, accede to the proposition; and yet if this is not done in a given day, or if any attempt is made to execute the laws, the State is, by the ordinance, declared to be out of the Union. The majority of a convention assembled for the purpose have dictated these terms, or rather this rejection of all terms, in the name of the people of South Carolina. It is true that the governor of the State speaks of the submission of their grievances to a convention of all the States; which, he says, they "sincerely and anxiously seek and desire." Yet this obvious and constitutional mode of obtaining the sense of the other States on the construction of the federal compact, and amending it, if necessary, has never been attempted by those who have urged the State on to this destructive measure. The State might have proposed a call for a general convention to the other States, and Congress, if a sufficient number of them concurred, must have called it. But the first magistrate of South Carolina, when he expressed a hope that "on a review by Congress and the functionaries of the general government of the merits of the controversy," such a convention will be accorded to them, must have known that neither Congress, nor any functionary in the general government, has authority to call such a convention, unless it be demanded by two-thirds of the States. This suggestion, then, is another instance of the reckless inattention to the provisions of the Constitution with which this crisis has been madly hurried on; or of the attempt to persuade the people that a constitutional remedy has been sought and refused. If the legislature of South Carolina "anxiously desire" a general convention to consider their complaints, why have they not made application for it in the way the Constitution points out? The assertion that they "earnestly seek" is completely negatived by the omission.

This, then, is the position in which we stand. A small majority of the citizens of one State in the Union have elected delegates to a State convention; that convention has ordained that all the revenue laws of the United States must be repealed, or that they are no longer a member of the Union. The governor of that State has recommended to the legislature the raising of an army to carry the secession into effect, and that he may be empowered to give clearances to vessels in the name of the State. No act of violent opposition to the laws has yet been committed, but such a state of things is hourly apprehended, and it is the intent of this instrument to PROCLAIM, not only that the duty imposed on me by the Constitution, "to take care that the laws be faithfully executed," shall be performed to the extent of the powers already vested in me by law or of such others as the wisdom of Congress shall devise and Entrust to me for that purpose; but to warn the citizens of South Carolina, who have been deluded into an opposition to the laws, of the danger they will incur by obedience to the illegal and disorganizing ordinance of the convention—to exhort those who have refused to support it to persevere in their determination to uphold the Constitution and laws of their country, and to point out to all the perilous situation into which the good people of that State have been led, and that the course they are urged to pursue is one of ruin and disgrace to the very State whose rights they affect to support.

. . . Your pride was aroused by the assertions that a submission to these laws was a state of vassalage, and that resistance to them was equal, in patriotic merit, to the opposition our fathers offered to the oppressive laws of Great Britain. You were told that this opposition might be peaceably—might be constitutionally made—that you might enjoy all the advantages of the Union and bear none of its burdens. Eloquent appeals to your passions, to your State pride, to your native courage, to your sense of real injury, were used to prepare you for the period when the mask which concealed the hideous features of DISUNION should be taken off. It fell, and you were made to look with complacency on objects which not long since you would have regarded with horror. Look back to the arts which have brought you to this state-look forward to the consequences to which it must inevitably lead! Look back to what was first told you as an inducement to enter into this dangerous course. The great political truth was repeated to you that you had the revolutionary right of resisting all laws that were palpably unconstitutional and intolerably oppressive-it was added that the right to nullify a law rested on the same principle, but that it was a peaceable remedy! This character which was given to it, made you receive with too much confidence the assertions that were made of the unconstitutionality of the law and its oppressive effects. Mark, my fellow-citizens, that by the admission of your leaders the unconstitutionality must be *palpable*, or it will not justify either resistance or nullification! What is the meaning of the word *palpable* in the sense in which it is here used? that which is apparent to everyone, that which no man of ordinary intellect will fail to perceive. Is the unconstitutionality of these laws of that description? Let those among your leaders who once approved and advocated the principles of protective duties, answer the question; and let them choose whether they will be considered as incapable, then, of perceiving that which must have been apparent to every man of common understanding, or as imposing upon your confidence and endeavoring to mislead you now. In either case, they are unsafe guides in the perilous path they urge you to tread. Ponder well on this circumstance, and you will know how to appreciate the exaggerated language they address to you. They are not champions of liberty emulating the fame of our Revolutionary fathers, nor are you an oppressed people, contending, as they repeat to you, against worse than colonial vassalage. You are free members of a flourishing and happy Union. There is no settled design to oppress you. You have, indeed, felt the unequal operation of laws which may have been unwisely, not unconstitutionally passed; but that inequality must necessarily be removed. At the very moment when you were madly urged on to the unfortunate course you have begun, a change in public opinion has commenced. The nearly approaching payment of the public debt, and the consequent necessity of a diminution of duties, had already caused a considerable reduction, and that, too, on some articles of general consumption in your State. The importance of this change was underrated, and you were authoritatively told that no further alleviation of your burdens was to be expected, at the very time when the condition of the country imperiously demanded such a modification of the duties as should reduce them to a just and equitable scale. But as apprehensive of the effect of this change in allaying your discontents, you were precipitated into the fearful state in which you now find yourselves.

I have urged you to look back to the means that were used to burly you on to the position you have now assumed, and forward to the consequences they will produce. Something more is necessary. Contemplate the condition of that country of which you still form an important part; consider its government uniting in one bond of common interest and general protection so many different States—giving to all their inhabitants the proud title of AMERICAN CITIZEN—protecting their commerce-securing their literature and arts—facilitating their intercommunication—defending their frontiers—and making their name respected in the remotest parts of the earth! Consider the extent of its territory its increasing and happy population, its advance in arts, which render life agreeable, and the sciences which elevate the mind! See education spreading the lights of religion, morality, and general information into

every cottage in this wide extent of our Territories and States! Behold it as
the asylum where the wretched and the oppressed find a refuge and support!
Look on this picture of happiness and honor, and say, WE TOO, ARE CITI-
ZENS OF AMERICA—Carolina is one of these proud States her arms have
defended-her best blood has cemented this happy Union! And then add, if
you can, without horror and remorse this happy Union we will dissolve—this
picture of peace and prosperity we will deface—this free intercourse we will
interrupt—these fertile fields we will deluge with blood-the protection of that
glorious flag we renounce—the very name of Americans we discard. And for
what, mistaken men! For what do you throw away these inestimable bless-
ings-for what would you exchange your share in the advantages and honor
of the Union? For the dream of a separate independence-a dream interrupted
by bloody conflicts with your neighbors, and a vile dependence on a foreign
power. If your leaders could succeed in establishing a separation, what would
be your situation? Are you united at home—are you free from the apprehen-
sion of civil discord, with all its fearful consequences? Do our neighboring
republics, every day suffering some new revolution or contending with some
new insurrection—do they excite your envy? But the dictates of a high
duty oblige me solemnly to announce that you cannot succeed. The laws of
the United States must be executed. I have no discretionary power on the
subject-my duty is emphatically pronounced in the Constitution. Those who
told you that you might peaceably prevent their execution, deceived you-they
could not have been deceived themselves. They know that a forcible opposition could alone prevent the execution of the laws, and they know that such
opposition must be repelled. Their object is disunion, hut be not deceived
by names; disunion, by armed force, is TREASON. Are you really ready
to incur its guilt? If you are, on the head of the instigators of the act be the
dreadful consequences-on their heads be the dishonor, but on yours may fall
the punishment-on your unhappy State will inevitably fall all the evils of the
conflict you force upon the government of your country. It cannot accede to
the mad project of disunion, of which you would be the first victims-its first
magistrate cannot, if he would, avoid the performance of his duty-the consequence must be fearful for you, distressing to your fellow-citizens here, and
to the friends of good government throughout the world. Its enemies have
beheld our prosperity with a vexation they could not conceal—it was a standing refutation of their slavish doctrines, and they will point to our discord
with the triumph of malignant joy. It is yet in your power to disappoint them.
There is yet time to show that the descendants of the Pinckneys, the Sumpt-
ers, the Rutledges, and of the thousand other names which adorn the pages
of your Revolutionary history, will not abandon that Union to support which
so many of them fought and bled and died. I adjure you, as you honor their
memory—as you love the cause of freedom, to which they dedicated their

lives—as you prize the peace of your country, the lives of its best citizens, and your own fair fame, to retrace your steps. Snatch from the archives of your State the disorganizing edict of its convention—hid its members to re-assemble and promulgate the decided expressions of your will to remain in the path which alone can conduct you to safety, prosperity, and honor—tell them that compared to disunion, all other evils are light, because that brings with it an accumulation of all-declare that you will never take the field unless the star-spangled banner of your country shall float over you—that you will not be stigmatized when dead, and dishonored and scorned while you live, as the authors of the first attack on the Constitution of your country!-its destroy-ers you cannot be. You may disturb its peace-you may interrupt the course of its prosperity-you may cloud its reputation for stability—but its tranquillity will be restored, its prosperity will return, and the stain upon its national char-acter will be transferred and remain an eternal blot on the memory of those who caused the disorder.

Fellow-citizens of the United States! the threat of unhallowed disunion-the names of those, once respected, by whom it is uttered—the array of military force to support it-denote the approach of a crisis in our affairs on which the continuance of our unexampled prosperity, our political existence, and perhaps that of all free governments, may depend. The con-juncture demanded a free, a full, and explicit enunciation, not only of my intentions, but of my principles of action, and as the claim was asserted of a right by a State to annul the laws of the Union, and even to secede from it at pleasure, a frank exposition of my opinions in relation to the origin and form of our government, and the construction I give to the instrument by which it was created, seemed to be proper. Having the fullest confidence in the justness of the legal and constitutional opinion of my duties which has been expressed, I rely with equal confidence on your undivided support in my determination to execute the laws-to preserve the Union by all constitutional means—to arrest, if possible, by moderate but firm measures, the necessity of a recourse to force; and, if it be the will of Heaven that the recurrence of its primeval curse on man for the shedding of a brother's blood should fall upon our land, that it be not called down by any offensive act on the part of the United States.

Fellow-citizens! the momentous case is before you. On your undivided support of your government depends the decision of the great question it involves, whether your sacred Union will be preserved, and the blessing it secures to us as one people shall be perpetuated. No one can doubt that the unanimity with which that decision will be expressed, will he such as to inspire new confidence in republican institutions, and that the prudence, the wisdom, and the courage which it will bring to their defense, will transmit them unimpaired and invigorated to our children.

May the Great Ruler of nations grant that the signal blessings with which he has favored ours may not, by the madness of party or personal ambition, be disregarded and lost, and may His wise providence bring those who have produced this crisis to see the folly, before they feel the misery, of civil strife, and inspire a returning veneration for that Union which, if we may dare to penetrate his designs, he has chosen, as the only means of attaining the high destinies to which we may reasonably aspire.

ANDREW JACKSON, INTERNAL IMPROVEMENTS VETO[36]

The constitutional power of the Federal Government to construct or promote works of internal improvement presents itself in two points of view—the first as bearing upon the sovereignty of the States within whose limits their execution is contemplated, if jurisdiction of the territory which they may occupy be claimed as necessary to their preservation and use; the second as asserting the simple right to appropriate money from the National Treasury in aid of such works when undertaken by State authority, surrendering the claim of jurisdiction. In the first view the question of power is an open one, and can be decided without the embarrassments attending the other, arising from the practice of the Government. Although frequently and strenuously attempted, the power to this extent has never been exercised by the Government in a single instance. It does not, in my opinion, possess it; and no bill, therefore, which admits it can receive my official sanction.

. . . The bill before me does not call for a more definite opinion upon the particular circumstances which will warrant appropriations of money by Congress to aid works of internal improvement, for although the extension of the power to apply money beyond that of carrying into effect the object for which it is appropriated has, as we have seen, been long claimed and exercised by the Federal Government, yet such grants have always been professedly under the control of the general principle that the works which might be thus aided should be "of a general, not local, national, not State," character. A disregard of this distinction would of necessity lead to the subversion of the federal system. That even this is an unsafe one, arbitrary in its nature, and liable, consequently, to great abuses, is too obvious to require the confirmation of experience.

Considering the magnitude and importance of the power, and the embarrassments to which, from the very nature of the thing, its exercise must necessarily be subjected, the real friends of internal improvement ought not to be willing to confide it to accident and chance. What is properly national in its character or otherwise is an inquiry which is often extremely difficult of solution. The appropriations of one year for an object which is considered national may be rendered nugatory by the refusal of a succeeding Congress to continue the work on the ground that it is local. No aid can be derived from the intervention of corporations. The question regards the character of the work, not that of those by whom it is to be accomplished. Notwithstanding the union of the Government with the corporation by whose immediate agency any work of internal improvement is carried on, the inquiry will still remain. Is it national and conducive to the benefit of the whole, or local and operating only to the advantage of a portion of the Union?

. . . Although many of the States, with a laudable zeal and under the influence of an enlightened policy, are successfully applying their separate efforts to works of this character, the desire to enlist the aid of the General Government in the construction of such as from their nature ought to devolve upon it, and to which the means of the individual States are inadequate, is both rational and patriotic, and if that desire is not gratified now it does not follow that it never will be.

ANDREW JACKSON VETO MESSAGE REGARDING THE BANK OF THE UNITED STATES[37]

. . . If the opinion of the Supreme Court covered the whole ground of this act, it ought not to control the coordinate authorities of this Government. The Congress, the Executive, and the Court must each for itself be guided by its own opinion of the Constitution . . . The authority of the Supreme Court must not, therefore, be permitted to control the Congress or the Executive when acting in their legislative capacities, but to have only such influence as the force of their reasoning may deserve.

. . . The several States reserved the power at the formation of the Constitution to regulate and control titles and transfers of real property, and most, if not all, of them have laws disqualifying aliens from acquiring or holding lands within their limits. But this act, in disregard of the undoubted right of the States to prescribe such disqualifications, gives to aliens stockholders in this bank an interest and title, as members of the corporation, to all the real property it may acquire within any of the States of this Union. This privilege granted to aliens is not "necessary" to enable the bank to perform its public duties, nor in any sense "proper," because it is vitally subversive of the rights of the States.

. . . By its silence, considered in connection with the decision of the Supreme Court in the case of McCulloch against the State of Maryland, this act takes from the States the power to tax a portion of the banking business carried on within their limits, in subversion of one of the strongest barriers which secured them against Federal encroachments. Banking, like farming, manufacturing, or any other occupation or profession, is a business, the right to follow which is not originally derived from the laws. Every citizen and every company of citizens in all of our States possessed the right until the State legislatures deemed it good policy to prohibit private banking by law. If the prohibitory State laws were now repealed, every citizen would again possess the right. The State banks are a qualified restoration of the right which has been taken away by the laws against banking, guarded by such provisions and limitations as in the opinion of the State legislatures the public interest requires. These corporations, unless there be an exemption in their charter, are, like private bankers and banking companies, subject to State taxation. The manner in which these taxes shall be laid depends wholly on legislative discretion. It may be upon the bank, upon the stock, upon the profits, or in any other mode which the sovereign power shall will.

Upon the formation of the Constitution the States guarded their taxing power with peculiar jealousy. They surrendered it only as it regards imports and exports. In relation to every other object within their jurisdiction, whether persons, property, business, or professions, it was secured in as ample a manner as it was before possessed. All persons, though United States officers, are liable to a poll tax by the States within which they reside. The lands of the United States are liable to the usual land tax, except in the new States, from whom agreements that they will not tax unsold lands are exacted when they are admitted into the Union. Horses, wagons, any beasts or vehicles, tools, or property belonging to private citizens, though employed in the service of the United States, are subject to State taxation. Every private business, whether carried on by an officer of the General Government or not, whether it be mixed with public concerns or not, even if it be carried on by the Government of the United States itself, separately or in partnership, falls within the scope of the taxing power of the State. Nothing comes more fully within it than banks and the business of banking, by whomsoever instituted and carried on. Over this whole subject-matter it is just as absolute, unlimited, and uncontrollable as if the Constitution had never been adopted, because in the formation of that instrument it was reserved without qualification.

The principle is conceded that the States can not rightfully tax the operations of the General Government. They can not tax the money of the Government deposited in the State banks, nor the agency of those banks in remitting it; but will any man maintain that their mere selection to perform this public service for the General Government would exempt the State banks and their ordinary business from State taxation? Had the United States, instead of establishing a bank at Philadelphia, employed a private banker to keep and transmit their funds, would it have deprived Pennsylvania of the right to tax his bank and his usual banking operations? It will not be pretended. Upon what principal, then, are the banking establishments of the Bank of the United States and their usual banking operations to be exempted from taxation ? It is not their public agency or the deposits of the Government which the States claim a right to tax, but their banks and their banking powers, instituted and exercised within State jurisdiction for their private emolument-those powers and privileges for which they pay a bonus, and which the States tax in their own banks. The exercise of these powers within a State, no matter by whom or under what authority, whether by private citizens in their original right, by corporate bodies created by the States, by foreigners or the agents of foreign governments located within their limits, forms a legitimate object of State taxation. From this and like sources, from the persons, property, and business that are found residing, located, or carried on under their jurisdiction, must the States, since the surrender of their right to raise a revenue from imports and exports, draw all the money necessary for the support of their governments and the maintenance of their independence. There is no more appropriate subject of taxation than banks, banking, and bank stocks, and none to which the States ought more pertinaciously to cling.

It can not be necessary to the character of the bank as a fiscal agent of the Government that its private business should be exempted from that taxation to which all the State banks are liable, nor can I conceive it "proper" that the substantive and most essential powers reserved by the States shall be thus attacked and annihilated as a means of executing the powers delegated to the General Government. It may be safely assumed that none of those sages who had an agency in forming or adopting our Constitution ever imagined that any portion of the taxing power of the States not prohibited to them nor delegated to Congress was to be swept away and annihilated as a means of executing certain powers delegated to Congress.

If our power over means is so absolute that the Supreme Court will not call in question the constitutionality of an act of Congress the subject of which "is not prohibited, and is really calculated to effect any of the objects intrusted to the Government," although, as in the case before me, it takes away powers expressly granted to Congress and rights scrupulously reserved to the States, it becomes us to proceed in our legislation with the utmost caution. Though not directly, our own powers and the rights of the States may be indirectly legislated away in the use of means to execute substantive powers. We may not enact that Congress shall not have the power of exclusive legislation over the District of Columbia, but we may pledge the faith of the United States that as a means of executing other powers it shall not be exercised for twenty years or forever. We may not pass an act prohibiting the States to tax the banking business carried on within their limits, but we may, as a means of executing our powers over other objects, place that business in the hands of our agents and then declare it exempt from State taxation in their hands. Thus may our own powers and the rights of the States, which we can not directly curtail or invade, be frittered away and extinguished in the use of means employed by us to execute other powers. That a bank of the United States, competent to all the duties which may be required by the Government, might be so organized as not to infringe on our own delegated powers or the reserved rights of the States I do not entertain a doubt. Had the Executive been called upon to furnish the project of such an institution, the duty would have been cheerfully performed. In the absence of such a call it was obviously proper that he should confine himself to pointing out those prominent features in the act presented which in his opinion make it incompatible with the Constitution and sound policy. A general discussion will now take place, eliciting new light and settling important principles; and a new Congress, elected in the midst of such discussion, and furnishing an equal representation of the people according to the last census, will bear to the Capitol the verdict of public opinion, and, I doubt not, bring this important question to a satisfactory result.

. . . Nor is our Government to be maintained or our Union preserved by invasions of the rights and powers of the several States. In thus attempting to make our General Government strong we make it weak. Its true strength consists in leaving individuals and States as much as possible to themselves—in making itself felt, not in its power, but in its beneficence; not in its control, but in its protection; not in binding the States more closely to the center, but leaving each to move unobstructed in its proper orbit.

JOHN C. CALHOUN, *A DISCOURSE ON THE CONSTITUTION AND GOVERNMENT OF THE UNITED STATES*[38]

Ours is a system of governments, compounded of the separate governments of the several States composing the Union, and of one common government of all its members, called the Government of the United States. The former preceded the latter, which was created by their agency. Each was framed by written constitutions; those of the several States by the people of each, acting separately, and in their sovereign character; and that of the United States, by the same, acting in the same character—but jointly instead of separately. All were formed on the same model. They all divide the powers of government into legislative, executive, and judicial; and are founded on the great principle of the responsibility of the rulers to the ruled. The entire powers of government are divided between the two; those of a more general character being specifically delegated to the United States; and all others not delegated, being reserved to the several States in their separate character. Each, within its appropriate sphere, possesses all the attributes, and performs all the functions of government. Neither is perfect without the other. The two combined, form one entire and perfect government. With these preliminary remarks, I shall proceed to the consideration of the immediate subject of this discourse.

The Government of the United States was formed by the Constitution of the United States—and ours is a democratic, federal republic.

It is federal, because it is the government of States united in political union, in contradistinction to a government of individuals socially united; that is, by what is usually called, a social compact. To express it more concisely, it is federal and not national, because it is the government of a community of States, and not the government of a single State or nation.

That it is federal and not national, we have the high authority of the convention which framed it. General Washington, as its organ, in his letter submitting the plan to the consideration of the Congress of the then confederacy, calls it, in one place—"the general government of the Union"—and in another—"the federal government of these States." Taken together, the plain meaning is, that the government proposed would be, if adopted, the government of the States adopting it, in their united character as members of a common Union; and, as such, would be a federal government. These expressions were not used without due consideration, and an accurate and full knowledge of their true import. The subject was not a novel one. The convention was familiar with it. It was much agitated in their deliberations. They divided, in reference to it, in the early stages of their proceedings. At first, one party was in favor of a national and the other of a federal government. The former, in the beginning, prevailed; and in the plans which they proposed, the constitution and government are styled "National." But, finally, the latter gained the ascendency, when the term "National" was superseded, and *"United States"* substituted in its place. The constitution was accordingly styled— *"The constitution of the United States of America"*—and the government— *"The government of the United States"* leaving out "America," for the sake of brevity. It cannot admit of a doubt, that the Convention, by the expression "United States," meant the States united in a federal Union; for in no other sense could they, with propriety, call the government, *"the federal government of these States"*—and *"the general government of the Union"*—as they did in the letter referred to. It is thus clear, that the Convention regarded the different expressions—"the federal government of the United States"— "the general government of the Union"—and—"government of the United States"—as meaning the same thing—a federal, in contradistinction to a national government.

The style of the present constitution and government is precisely the style by which the confederacy that existed when it was adopted, and which it superseded, was designated. The instrument that formed the latter was called—"Articles of Confederation and Perpetual Union." Its first article declares that the style of this confederacy shall be, "The United States of America"; and the second, in order to leave no doubt as to the relation in which the States should stand to each other in the confederacy about to be formed, declared—"Each State retains its sovereignty, freedom and independence; and every power, jurisdiction, and right, which is not, by this confederation, expressly delegated to the United States in Congress assembled." If we go one step further back, the style of the confederacy will be found to be the same with that of the revolutionary government, which existed when it was adopted, and which it superseded. It dates its origin with the Declaration of Independence. That act is styled—"The unanimous Declaration of the thirteen United States of America." And here again, that there might be no doubt how these States would stand to each other in the new condition in which they were about to be placed, it concluded by declaring—"that these United Colonies are, and of right ought to be, free and independent States"; "and that, as free and independent States, they have full power to levy war, conclude peace, contract alliances, and to do all other acts and things which independent States may of right do." The "United States" is, then, the baptismal name of these States—received at their birth—by which they have ever since continued to call themselves; by which they have characterized their constitution, government and laws—and by which they are known to the rest of the world.

The retention of the same style, throughout every stage of their existence, affords strong, if not conclusive evidence that the political relation between these States, under their present constitution and government, is substantially the same as under the confederacy and revolutionary government; and what that relation was, we are not left to doubt; as they are declared expressly to be *"free, independent* and *sovereign* States." They, then, are now united, and have been, throughout, simply as confederated States. If it had been intended by the members of the convention which framed the present constitution and government, to make any essential change, either in the relation of the States to each other, or the basis of their union, they would, by retaining the style which designated them under the preceding governments, have practised a deception, utterly unworthy of their character, as sincere and honest men and patriots.

It may, therefore, be fairly inferred, that, retaining the same style, they intended to attach to the expression—"the United States," the same meaning, substantially, which it previously had; and, of course, in calling the present government—"the federal government of these States," they meant by "federal," that they stood in the same relation to each other—that their union rested, without material change, on the same basis—as under the confederacy and the revolutionary government; and that federal, and confederated States, meant substantially the same thing. It follows, also, that the changes made by the present constitution were not in the foundation, but in the superstructure of the system. We accordingly find, in confirmation of this conclusion, that the convention, in their letter to Congress, stating the reasons for the changes that had been made, refer only to the necessity which required a different "*organization*" of the government, without making any allusion whatever to any change in the relations of the States towards each other—or the basis of the system. They state that, "the friends of our country have long seen and desired, that the power of making war, peace, and treaties; that of levying money and regulating commerce, and the correspondent executive and judicial authorities, should be fully and effectually vested in the Government of the Union: but the impropriety of delegating such extensive trusts to one body of men is evident; hence results the necessity of a *different organization.*"

We thus have the authority of the convention itself for asserting that the expression, "United States," has essentially the same meaning, when applied to the present constitution and government, as it had previously; and, of course, that the States have retained their separate existence, as independent and sovereign communities, in all the forms of political existence, through which they have passed. Such, indeed, is the literal import of the expression—"the United States"—and the sense in which it is ever used, when it is applied politically—I say, *politically*—because it is often applied, *geographically*, to designate the portion of this continent occupied by the States composing the Union, including territories belonging to them. This application arose from the fact, that there was no appropriate term for that portion of this continent; and thus, not unnaturally, the name by which these States are politically designated, was employed to designate the region they occupy and possess. The distinction is important, and cannot be overlooked in discussing questions involving the character and nature of the government, without causing great confusion and dangerous misconceptions.

But as conclusive as these reasons are to prove that the government of the United States is federal, in contradistinction to national, it would seem, that they have not been sufficient to prevent the opposite opinion from being entertained. Indeed, this last seems to have become the prevailing one; if we may judge from the general use of the term "national," and the almost entire disuse of that of "federal." National, is now commonly applied to "the general government of the Union"—and "the federal government of these States"—and all that appertains to them or to the Union. It seems to be forgotten that the term was repudiated by the convention, after full consideration; and that it was carefully excluded from the constitution, and the letter laying it before Congress. Even those who know all this—and, of course, how falsely the term is applied—have, for the most part, slided into its use without reflection. But there are not a few who so apply it, because they believe it to be a national government in fact; and among these are men of distinguished talents and standing, who have put forth all their powers of reason and eloquence, in support of the theory. The question involved is one of the first magnitude, and deserves to be investigated thoroughly in all its aspects. With this impression, I deem it proper—clear and conclusive as I regard the reasons already assigned to prove its federal character—to confirm them by historical references; and to repel the arguments adduced to prove it to be a national government. I shall begin with the formation and ratification of the constitution.

That the States, when they formed and ratified the constitution, were distinct, independent, and sovereign communities, has already been established. That the people of the several States, acting in their separate, independent, and sovereign character, adopted their separate State constitutions, is a fact uncontested and incontestable; but it is not more certain than that, acting in the same character, they ratified and adopted the constitution of the United States; with this difference only, that in making and adopting the one, they acted without concert or agreement; but, in the other, with concert in making, and mutual agreement in adopting it. That the delegates who constituted the convention which framed the constitution, were appointed by the several States, each on its own authority; that they voted in the convention by States; and that their votes were counted by States—are recorded and unquestionable facts. So, also, the facts that the constitution, when framed, was submitted to the people of the several States for their respective ratification; that it was ratified by them, each for itself; and that it was binding on each, only in consequence of its being so ratified by it. Until then, it was but the plan of a constitution, without any binding force. It was the act of ratification which established it as a constitution between the States ratifying it; and only between *them*, on the condition that not less than nine of the then thirteen States should concur in the ratification—as is expressly provided by its seventh and last article. It is in the following words: "The ratification of the conventions of nine States shall be sufficient for the establishment of this constitution between the States so ratifying the same." If additional proof be needed to show that it was only binding between the States that ratified it, it may be found in the fact, that two States, North Carolina and Rhode Island, refused, at first, to ratify; and were, in consequence, regarded in the interval as foreign States, without obligation, on their parts, to respect it, or, on the part of their citizens, to obey it. Thus far, there can be no difference of opinion. The facts are too recent and too well established—and the provision of the constitution too explicit, to admit of doubt.

That the States, then, retained, after the ratification of the constitution, the distinct, independent, and sovereign character in which they formed and ratified it, is certain; unless they divested themselves of it by the act of ratification, or by some provision of the constitution. If they have not, the constitution must be federal, and not national; for it would have, in that case, every attribute necessary to constitute it federal, and not one to make it national. On the other hand, if they have divested themselves, then it would necessarily lose its federal character, and become national. Whether, then, the government is federal or national, is reduced to a single question; whether the act of ratification, of itself, or the constitution, by some one, or all of its provisions, did, or did not, divest the several States of their character of separate, independent, and sovereign communities, and merge them all in one great community or nation, called the American people?

. . . Of all the questions which can arise under our system of government, this is by far the most important. It involves many others of great magnitude; and among them, that of the allegiance of the citizen; or, in other words, the question to whom allegiance and obedience are ultimately due. What is the true relation between the two governments—that of the United States and those of the several States? and what is the relation between the individuals respectively composing them? For it is clear, if the States still retain their sovereignty as separate and independent communities, the allegiance and obedience of the citizens of each would be due to their respective States; and that the government of the United States and those of the several States would stand as equals and co-ordinates in their respective spheres; and, instead of being united socially, their citizens would be politically connected through their respective States. On the contrary, if they have, by ratifying the constitution, divested themselves of their individuality and sovereignty, and merged themselves into one great community or nation, it is equally clear, that the sovereignty would reside in the whole—or what is called the American people; and that allegiance and obedience would be due to them. Nor is it less so, that the government of the several States would, in such case, stand to that of the United States, in the relation of inferior and subordinate, to superior and paramount; and that the individuals of the several States, thus fused, as it were, into one general mass, would be united *socially*, and not *politically*. So great a change of condition would have involved a thorough and radical revolution, both socially and politically—a revolution much more radical, indeed, than that which followed the Declaration of Independence.

They who maintain that the ratification of the constitution effected so mighty a change, are bound to establish it by the most demonstrative proof. The presumption is strongly opposed to it. It has already been shown, that the authority of the convention which formed the constitution is clearly against it; and that the history of its ratification, instead of supplying evidence in its favor, furnishes strong testimony in opposition to it. To these, others may be added; and, among them, the presumption drawn from the history of these States, in all the stages of their existence down to the time of the ratification of the constitution. In all, they formed separate, and, as it respects each other, independent communities; and were ever remarkable for the tenacity with which they adhered to their rights as such. It constituted, during the whole period, one of the most striking traits in their character.

 . . . another circumstance of no little weight, drawn from the preliminary steps taken for the ratification of the constitution. The plan was laid, by the convention, before the Congress of the confederacy, for its consideration and action, as has been stated. It was the sole organ and representative of these States in their confederated character. By submitting it, the convention recognized and acknowledged its authority over it, as the organ of distinct, independent, and sovereign States. It had the right to dispose of it as it pleased; and, if it had thought proper, it might have defeated the plan by simply omitting to act on it. But it thought proper to act, and to adopt the course recommended by the convention—which was, to submit it—"to a convention of delegates, chosen in each State, by the people thereof, for their assent and adoption." All this was in strict accord with the federal character of the constitution, but wholly repugnant to the idea of its being national. It received the assent of the States in all the possible modes in which it could be obtained: first—in their confederated character, through its only appropriate organ, the Congress; next, in their individual character, as separate States, through their respective State governments, to which the Congress referred it; and finally, in their high character of independent and sovereign communities, through a convention of the people, called in each State, by the authority of its government. The States acting in these various capacities, might, at every stage, have defeated it or not, at their option, by giving or withholding their consent.

 Nothing more is necessary, in order to show by whom it was ordained and established, than to ascertain who are meant by—"We, the people of the United States"; for, by their authority, it was done. To this there can be but one answer—it meant the people who ratified the instrument; for it was the act of ratification which ordained and established it. Who they were, admits of no doubt. The process preparatory to ratification, and the acts by which it was done, prove, beyond the possibility of a doubt, that it was ratified by the several States, through conventions of delegates, chosen in each State by the people thereof; and acting, each in the name and by the authority of its State: and, as all the States ratified it—"We, the people of the United States"— mean,—We, the people of the several States of the Union. The inference is irresistible. And when it is considered that the States of the Union were then members of the confederacy—and that, by the express provision of one of its articles, "each State retains its sovereignty, freedom, and independence," the proof is demonstrative, that—"We, the people of the United States of America," mean the people of the several States of the Union, acting as free, independent, and sovereign States. This strikingly confirms what has been already stated; to wit, that the convention which formed the constitution, meant the same thing by the terms—"United States"—and, "federal"—when applied to the constitution or government—and that the former, when used politically, always mean—these States united as independent and sovereign communities.

It remains to be shown, *over whom*, it was ordained and established. That it was not over *the several States*, is settled by the seventh article beyond controversy. It declares, that the ratification by nine States shall be sufficient to establish the constitution between the States so ratifying. "Between," necessarily excludes "over"—as that which is *between* States cannot be *over* them. Reason itself, if the constitution had been silent, would have led, with equal certainty, to the same conclusion. For it was the several States, or, what is the same thing, their people, in their sovereign capacity, who ordained and established the constitution. But the authority which ordains and establishes, is higher than that which is ordained and established; and, of course, the latter must be subordinate to the former—and cannot, therefore, be *over* it. "Between," always means more than "over"—and implies in this case, that the authority which ordained and established the constitution, was the joint and united authority of the States ratifying it; and that, among the effects of their ratification, it became a contract between them; and, *as a compact*, binding on them—but only as such. In that sense the term, "between," is appropriately applied. In no other, can it be. It was, doubtless, used in that sense in this instance; but the question still remains, *over whom*, was it ordained and established? After what has been stated, the answer may be readily given. It was *over the government* which it created, and all its functionaries in their official character—and the individuals composing and inhabiting the several States, as far as they might come within the sphere of the powers delegated to the United States.

JOSEPH STORY, *COMMENTARIES ON THE CONSTITUTION OF THE UNITED STATES*[39]

The next and last amendment is: "The powers not delegated to the United States Constitution, nor prohibited by it to the States, are reserved to the States respectively, or to the people.

This amendment is a mere affirmation of what, upon any just reasoning, is a necessary rule of interpreting the Constitution. Being an instrument of limited and enumerated powers, it follows, irresistibly, that what is not conferred is withheld, and belongs to the State authorities if invested by their constitutions of government respectively in them; and if not so invested, it is retained BY THE PEOPLE, as a part of their residuary sovereignty. When this amendment was before Congress, a proposition was moved to insert the world "expressly" before "delegated," so as to read, "the powers not *expressly* delegated to the United States by the Constitution," &c. On that occasion it was remarked, that it is impossible to confine a government to the exercise of express powers. There must necessarily be admitted powers by implication, unless the Constitution descended to the most minute details. It is a general principal that all corporate bodies possess all powers incident to a corporate capacity, without being absolutely expressed. The motion was accordingly negatived. Indeed, one of the great defects of the confederation was (as we have already seen), that it contained a clause prohibiting the exercise of any power, jurisdiction, or right not *expressly delegated.* The consequence was, that Congress were crippled at every step of their progress, and were often compelled, by the very necessities of the times, to usurp powers which they did not constitutionally possess; and thus, in effect, to break down all the great barriers against tyranny and oppression.

It is pain, therefore, that it could not have been the intention of the framers of this amendment to give it effect, as an abridgment of any of the powers granted under the Constitution, whether they are express or implied, direct or incidental. Is sole design is to exclude any interpretation by which other powers should be assumed beyond those which are granted. All that are granted in the original instrument, whether express or implied, whether direct or incidental, are left in their original state. All powers not delegated (not all powers not *expressly* delegated) and not prohibited, are reserved. The attempts then which have been made from time to time to force upon this language an abridging or restrictive influence are utterly unfounded in any just rules of interpreting the words or the sense of the instrument. Stripped of the ingenious disguises in which they are clothed, they are neither more nor less than attempts to foist into the text the word "expressly; " to qualify what is general, and obscure what is clear and defined. They make the sense of the passage bend to the wishes and prejudices of the interpreter, and employ criticism to support a theory, and not to guide it. One should suppose, if the history of the human mind did not furnish abundant proof to the contrary, that no reasonable man would contend for an interpretation founded neither in the letter nor in the spirit of an instrument. Where is controversy to end if we desert both the letter and the spirit? What is to become of constitutions of government if they are to rest, not upon the plain import of their words, but upon conjectural enlargements and restraints, to suit the temporary passions and interests of the day? Let us never forget that our constitutions of government are solemn instruments, addressed to the common sense of the people, and designed to fix and perpetuate their rights and their liberties. They are not to be fritted away to please the demagogues of the day. They are not to be violated to gratify the ambition of political leaders. They are to speak in the same voice now and forever. They are of no man's private interpretation.

They are ordained by the will of the people; and can be changed only by the sovereign command of the people.

It has been justly remarked that the erection of a new government, whatever care or wisdom may distinguish the work, cannot fail to originate questions of intricacy and nicety; and these may, in a particular manner, be expected to flow from the establishment of a constitution founded upon the total or partial incorporation of a number of distinct sovereignties. Time alone can mature and perfect so compound a system; liquidate the meaning of all parts; and adjust them to each other in a harmonious and consistent whole.

ABEL UPSHUR, *A BRIEF ENQUIRY INTO THE TRUE NATURE AND CHARACTER OF OUR FEDERAL GOVERNMENT*[40]

The tenth article of the amendments of the Constitution provides that "The powers not delegated to the United States by the Constitution, nor prohibited by it to the States, are reserved to the States respectively, or to the people." The powers thus reserved, are not only reserved against the federal government in whole, but against each and every department thereof. The judiciary is no more excepted out of the reservation than is the legislature or the executive. Of what nature, then, are those reserved powers? Not the powers, if any such there be, which are possessed by all the States together, for the reservation is to "the States respectively"; that is, to each State separately and distinctly. Now we can form no idea of any power possessed by a State as such, and independent of every other State, which is not, in its nature, a sovereign power. Every power so reserved, therefore, must be of such a character that each State may exercise it, without the least reference or responsibility to any other State whatever.

We have already seen that the Constitution of the United States was formed by States as such, and the reservation above quoted is an admission that, in performing that work, they acted as independent and sovereign States. It is incident to every sovereignty to be alone the judge of its own compacts and agreements. No other State or assemblage of States has the least right to interfere with it, in this respect, and cannot do so without impairing its sovereignty. The Constitution of the United States is but the agreement which each State has made, with each and all the other States, and is not distinguishable, in the principle we are examining, from any other agreement between sovereign States. Each State, therefore, has a right to interpret that agreement for itself, unless it has clearly waived that right in favor of another power. That the right is not waived in the case under consideration, is apparent from the fact already stated, that if the judiciary be the sole judges of the extent of their own powers, their powers are universal, and the enumeration in the Constitution idle and useless. But it is still farther apparent from the following view.

The Federal Government is the creature of the States. It is not a party to the Constitution, but the result of it—the creation of that agreement which was made by the States as parties. It is a mere agent, entrusted with limited powers for certain specific objects; which powers and objects are enumerated in the Constitution. Shall the agent be permitted to judge of the ex-tent of his own powers, without reference to his constituent? To a certain extent he is compelled to do this, in the very act of exercising them, but this is always in subordination to the authority by whom his powers were conferred. If this were not so, the result would be, that the agent would possess every power which the constituent could confer, notwithstanding the plainest and most express terms of the grant. This would be against all principle and all reason. If such a rule should prevail in regard to government, a written constitution would be the idlest thing imaginable. It would afford no barrier against the usurpations of the government, and no security for the rights and liberties of the people. If then the federal government has no I authority to judge, in the last resort, of the extent of its own powers, with what propriety can it be said that a single department of that government may do so? Nay, it is said that this department may not only judge for itself, but for the other department also. This is an absurdity as pernicious as it is gross and palpable. If the judiciary may determine the powers of the federal government, it may pronounce them either less or more than they really are. That government at least would have no right to complain of the decisions of an umpire which it had chosen for itself, and endeavored to force upon the States and the people. Thus a single department might deny to both the others, salutary powers which they really possessed, and which the public interest or the public safety might require them to exercise; or it might confer on them powers never conceded, inconsistent with private right, and dangerous to public liberty.

In construing the powers of a free and equal government, it is enough to disprove the existence of any rule, to show that such consequences as these will result from it. Nothing short of the plainest and most unequivocal language should reconcile us to the adoption of such a rule. No such language can be found in our Constitution. The only clause, from which the rule can be supposed to be derived, is that which confers juris-diction in "all cases arising under the Constitution, and the laws made in pursuance thereof; but this clause is clearly not susceptible of any such construction. Every right may be said to be a constitutional right, because no right exists which the Constitution disallows; and consequently every remedy to enforce those rights presents "a case arising under the Constitution." But a construction so latitudinous will scarcely be con- tended for by any one. The clause under consideration gives jurisdiction only as to those matters, and between those parties, enumerated in the Constitution itself. Whenever such a case arises, the federal courts have cognizance of it; but the right to decide a case arising under the Constitution does not necessarily imply the right to determine in the last resort what that Constitution is. If the federal courts should, in the very teeth of the eleventh amendment, take jurisdiction of cases "commenced or prosecuted against one of the States by citizens of another State," the decision of those courts, that they had jurisdiction, would certainly not settle the Constitution in that particular. The State would be under no obligation to submit to such a decision, and it would resist it by virtue of its sovereign right to decide for itself, whether it had agreed to the exercise of such a jurisdiction or not.

Considering the nature of our system of government, the States ought to be, and I presume always will be, extremely careful not to interpose their sovereign power against the decisions of the supreme court in any case where that court clearly has jurisdiction. Of this character are the cases already cited at the commencement of this inquiry; such, for example, as those between two States, those affecting foreign ministers, those of admiralty and maritime jurisdiction, &c. As to all these subjects the jurisdiction is clear, and no State can have any interest to dispute it. The decisions of the supreme court, therefore, ought to be considered as final and conclusive, and it would be a breach of the contract on the part of any State to refuse submission to them. There are, how-ever, many cases involving questions of the powers of government, State and federal, which cannot assume a proper form for judicial investigation. Most questions of mere political power, are of this sort; and such are all questions between a State and the United States. As to these, the Constitution confers no jurisdiction on the federal courts, and, of course, it provides no common umpire to whose decision they can be referred. In such cases, therefore, the State must of necessity decide for itself. But there are also cases between citizen and citizen, arising under the laws of the United States, and between the United States and the citizen, arising in the same way. So far as the federal tribunals have cognizance of such cases, their decisions are final. If the constitutionality of the law under which the case arises, should come into question, the court has authority to decide it, and there is no relief for the parties, in any other judicial proceeding. If the decision, in a controversy between the United States and a citizen, should be against the United States, it is, of course, final and conclusive. If the decision should be against the citizen, his only relief is by an appeal to his own State. He is under no obligation to submit to federal decisions at all, except so far only as his own State has commanded him to do so; and he has, therefore, a perfect right to ask his State whether her commands extend to the particular case or not. He does not ask whether the federal court has interpreted the law correctly or not, but whether or not she ever consented that congress should pass the law. If congress had such power, he has no relief, for the decision of the highest federal court is final; if congress had not such power, then he is oppressed by the action of a usurped authority, and has a right to look to his own State for redress. His State may interpose in his favor or not, as she may think proper. If she does not, then there is an end of the matter; if she does, then it is no longer a judicial question. The question is then between new parties, who are not bound by the former decision between a sovereign State and its own agent; between a State and the United States. As between these parties the federal tribunals have no jurisdiction, there is no longer a common umpire to whom the controversy can be referred. The State must of necessity judge for itself, by virtue of that inherent, sovereign power and authority, which, as to this matter, it has never surrendered to any other tribunal. Its decision, whatever it may be, is binding upon itself and upon its own people, and no farther.

LUTHER v. BORDEN[41]

[Roger Taney, Chief Justice] The existence and authority of the government under which the defendants acted was called in question, and the plaintiff insists that, before the acts complained of were committed, that government had been displaced and annulled by the people of Rhode Island, and that the plaintiff was engaged in supporting the lawful authority of the State, and the defendants themselves were in arms against it.

This is a new question in this court, and certainly a very grave one, and, at the time when the trespass is alleged to have been committed, it had produced a general and painful excitement in the State, and threatened to end in bloodshed and civil war.

. . . Moreover, the Constitution of the United States, as far as it has provided for an emergency of this kind and authorized the general government to interfere in the domestic concerns of a State, has treated the subject as political in its nature, and placed the power in the hands of that department.

The fourth section of the fourth article of the Constitution of the United States provides that the United States shall guarantee to every State in the Union a republican form of government, and shall protect each of them against invasion, and on the application of the legislature or of the executive (when the legislature cannot be convened) against domestic violence.

Under this article of the Constitution, it rests with Congress to decide what government is the established one in a State. For as the United States guarantee to each State a republican government, Congress must necessarily decide what government is established in the State before it can determine whether it is republican or not. And when the senators and representatives of a State are admitted into the councils of the Union, the authority of the government under which they are appointed, as well as its republican character, is recognized by the proper constitutional authority. And its decision is binding on every other department of the government, and could not be questioned in a judicial tribunal. It is true that the contest in this case did not last long enough to bring the matter to this issue, and, as no senators or representatives were elected under the authority of the government of which Mr. Dorr was the head, Congress was not called upon to decide the controversy. Yet the right to decide is placed there, and not in the courts.

. . . The remaining question is whether the defendants, acting under military orders issued under the authority of the government, were justified in breaking and entering the plaintiff's house. In relation to the act of the legislature declaring martial law, it is not necessary in the case before us to inquire to what extent, nor under what circumstances, that power may be exercised by a State. Unquestionably a military government, established the permanent government of the State, would not be a republican government, and it would be the duty of Congress to overthrow it. But the law of Rhode Island evidently contemplated no such government. It was intended merely for the crisis, and to meet the peril in which the existing government was placed by the armed resistance to its authority. It was so understood and construed by the State authorities. And unquestionably a State may use its military power to put down an armed insurrection too strong to be controlled by the civil authority. The power is essential to the existence of every government, essential to the preservation of order and free institutions, and is as necessary to the States of this Union as to any other government. The State itself must determine what degree of force the crisis demands. And if the government of Rhode Island deemed the armed opposition so formidable and so ramified throughout the State as to require the use of its military force and the declaration of martial law, we see no ground upon which this court can question its authority. It was a state of war, and the established government resorted to the rights and usages of war to maintain itself, and to overcome the unlawful opposition. And in that state of things, the officers engaged in its military service might lawfully arrest anyone who, from the information before them, they had reasonable grounds to believe was engaged in the insurrection, and might order a house to be forcibly entered and searched when there were reasonable grounds for supposing he might be there concealed. Without the power to do this, martial law and the military array of the government would be mere parade, and rather encourage attack than repel it. No more force, however, can be used than is necessary to accomplish the object. And if the power is exercised for the purposes of oppression, or any injury willfully done to person or property, the party by whom, or by whose order, it is committed would undoubtedly be answerable.

. . . Much of the argument on the part of the plaintiff turned upon political rights and political questions, upon which the court has been urged to express an opinion. We decline doing so. The high power has been conferred on this court of passing judgment upon the acts of the State sovereignties, and of the legislative and executive branches of the federal government, and of determining whether they are beyond the limits of power marked out for them respectively by the Constitution of the United States. This tribunal, therefore, should be the last to overstep the boundaries which limit its own jurisdiction. And while it should always be ready to meet any question confided to it by the Constitution, it is equally its duty not to pass beyond its appropriate sphere of action, and to take care not to involve itself in discussions which properly belong to other forums. No one, we believe, has ever doubted the proposition that, according to the institutions of this country, the sovereignty in every State resides in the people of the State, and that they may alter and change their form of government at their own pleasure. But whether they have changed it or not by abolishing an old government and establishing a new one in its place is a question to be settled by the political power. And when that power has decided, the courts are bound to take notice of its decision, and to follow it.

ORDINANCES OF SECESSION[42]

South Carolina

AN ORDINANCE to dissolve the union between the State of South Carolina and other States united with her under the compact entitled "The Constitution of the United States of America."

We, the people of the State of South Carolina, in convention assembled, do declare and ordain, and it is hereby declared and ordained, That the ordinance adopted by us in convention on the twenty-third day of May, in the year of our Lord one thousand seven hundred and eighty-eight, whereby the Constitution of the United States of America was ratified, and also all acts and parts of acts of the General Assembly of this State ratifying amendments of the said Constitution, are hereby repealed; and that the union now subsisting between South Carolina and other States, under the name of the "United States of America," is hereby dissolved.

Mississippi

AN ORDINANCE to dissolve the union between the State of Mississippi and other States united with her under the compact entitled "The Constitution of the United States of America."

The people of the State of Mississippi, in convention assembled, do ordain and declare, and it is hereby ordained and declared, as follows, to wit:

Section 1. That all the laws and ordinances by which the said State of Mississippi became a member of the Federal Union of the United States of America be, and the same are hereby, repealed, and that all obligations on the part of the said State or the people thereof to observe the same be withdrawn, and that the said State doth hereby resume all the rights, functions, and powers which by any of said laws or ordinances were conveyed to the Government of the said United States, and is absolved from all the obligations, restraints, and duties incurred to the said Federal Union, and shall from henceforth be a free, sovereign, and independent State.

Sec. 2. That so much of the first section of the seventh article of the constitution of this State as requires members of the Legislature and all officers, executive and judicial, to take an oath or affirmation to support the Constitution of the United States be, and the same is hereby, abrogated and annulled.

Sec. 3. That all rights acquired and vested under the Constitution of the United States, or under any act of Congress passed, or treaty made, in pursuance thereof, or under any law of this State, and not incompatible with this ordinance, shall remain in force and have the same effect as if this ordinance had not been passed.

Sec. 4. That the people of the State of Mississippi hereby consent to form a federal union with such of the States as may have seceded or may secede from the Union of the United States of America, upon the basis of the present Constitution of the said United States, except such parts thereof as embrace other portions than such seceding States.

Florida

We, the people of the State of Florida, in convention assembled, do solemnly ordain, publish, and declare, That the State of Florida hereby withdraws herself from the confederacy of States existing under the name of the United States of America and from the existing Government of the said States; and that all political connection between her and the Government of said States ought to be, and the same is hereby, totally annulled, and said Union of States dissolved; and the State of Florida is hereby declared a sovereign and independent nation; and that all ordinances heretofore adopted, in so far as they create or recognize said Union, are rescinded; and all laws or parts of laws in force in this State, in so far as they recognize or assent to said Union, be, and they are hereby, repealed.

Alabama

An Ordinance to dissolve the union between the State of Alabama and the other States united under the compact styled "The Constitution of the United States of America"

Whereas, the election of Abraham Lincoln and Hannibal Hamlin to the offices of president and vice-president of the United States of America, by a sectional party, avowedly hostile to the domestic institutions and to the peace and security of the people of the State of Alabama, preceded by many and dangerous infractions of the constitution of the United States by many of the States and people of the Northern section, is a political wrong of so insulting and menacing a character as to justify the people of the State of Alabama in the adoption of prompt and decided measures for their future peace and security, therefore:

Be it declared and ordained by the people of the State of Alabama, in Convention assembled, That the State of Alabama now withdraws, and is hereby withdrawn from the Union known as "the United States of America," and henceforth ceases to be one of said United States, and is, and of right ought to be a Sovereign and Independent State.

Sec 2. Be it further declared and ordained by the people of the State of Alabama in Convention assembled, That all powers over the Territory of said State, and over the people thereof, heretofore delegated to the Government of the United States of America, be and they are hereby withdrawn from said Government, and are hereby resumed and vested in the people of the State of Alabama.

And as it is the desire and purpose of the people of Alabama to meet the slaveholding States of the South, who may approve such purpose, in order to frame a provisional as well as permanent Government upon the principles of the Constitution of the United States,

Georgia

We the people of the State of Georgia in Convention assembled do declare and ordain and it is hereby declared and ordained that the ordinance adopted by the State of Georgia in convention on the 2nd day of January in the year of our Lord seventeen hundred and eighty-eight, whereby the constitution of the United States of America was assented to, ratified and adopted, and also all acts and parts of acts of the general assembly of this State, ratifying and adopting amendments to said constitution, are hereby repealed, rescinded and abrogated.

We do further declare and ordain that the union now existing between the State of Georgia and other States under the name of the United States of

America is hereby dissolved, and that the State of Georgia is in full possession and exercise of all those rights of sovereignty which belong and appertain to a free and independent State.

Louisiana

AN ORDINANCE to dissolve the union between the State of Louisiana and other States united with her under the compact entitled "The Constitution of the United States of America."

We, the people of the State of Louisiana, in convention assembled, do declare and ordain, and it is hereby declared and ordained, That the ordinance passed by us in convention on the 22nd day of November, in the year eighteen hundred and eleven, whereby the Constitution of the United States of America and the amendments of the said Constitution were adopted, and all laws and ordinances by which the State of Louisiana became a member of the Federal Union, be, and the same are hereby, repealed and abrogated; and that the union now subsisting between Louisiana and other States under the name of "The United States of America" is hereby dissolved.

We do further declare and ordain, That the State of Louisiana hereby resumes all rights and powers heretofore delegated to the Government of the United States of America; that her citizens are absolved from all allegiance to said Government; and that she is in full possession and exercise of all those rights of sovereignty which appertain to a free and independent State.

We do further declare and ordain, That all rights acquired and vested under the Constitution of the United States, or any act of Congress, or treaty, or under any law of this State, and not incompatible with this ordinance, shall remain in force and have the same effect as if this ordinance had not been passed.

Texas

AN ORDINANCE To dissolve the Union between the State of Texas and the other States united under the Compact styled "the Constitution of the United States of America."

WHEREAS, The Federal Government has failed to accomplish the purposes of the compact of union between these States, in giving protection either to the persons of our people upon an exposed frontier, or to the property of our citizens, and

WHEREAS, the action of the Northern States of the Union is violative of the compact between the States and the guarantees of the Constitution; and,

WHEREAS, The recent developments in Federal affairs make it evident that the power of the Federal Government is sought to be made a weapon with which to strike down the interests and property of the people of Texas, and her sister slave-holding States, instead of permitting it to be, as was intended, our shield against outrage and aggression; THEREFORE,

SECTION 1.—We, the people of the State of Texas, by delegates in convention assembled, do declare and ordain that the ordinance adopted by our convention of delegates on the 4th day of July, A.D. 1845, and afterwards ratified by us, under which the Republic of Texas was admitted into the Union with other States, and became a party to the compact styled "The Constitution of the United States of America," be, and is hereby, repealed and annulled; that all the powers which, by the said compact, were delegated by Texas to the Federal Government are revoked and resumed; that Texas is of right absolved from all restraints and obligations incurred by said compact, and is a separate sovereign State, and that her citizens and people are absolved from all allegiance to the United States or the government thereof.

SEC. 2. This ordinance shall be submitted to the people of Texas for their ratification or rejection, by the qualified voters, on the 23rd day of February, 1861, and unless rejected by a majority of the votes cast, shall take effect and be in force on and after the 2d day of March, A.D. 1861. PROVIDED, that in the Representative District of El Paso said election may be held on the 18th day of February, 1861.

Virginia

AN ORDINANCE to repeal the ratification of the Constitution of the United State of America by the State of Virginia, and to resume all the rights and powers granted under said Constitution.

The people of Virginia in their ratification of the Constitution of the United States of America, adopted by them in convention on the twenty-fifth day of June, in the year of our Lord one thousand seven hundred and eighty-eight, having declared that the powers granted under said Constitution were derived from the people of the United States and might be resumed whensoever the same should be perverted to their injury and oppression, and the Federal Government having perverted said powers not only to the injury of the people of Virginia, but to the oppression of the Southern slave-holding States:

Now, therefore, we, the people of Virginia, do declare and ordain, That the ordinance adopted by the people of this State in convention on the twenty-fifth day of June, in the year of our Lord one thousand seven hundred and eighty-eight, whereby the Constitution of the United States of America was ratified, and all acts of the General Assembly of this State ratifying and adopting amendments to said Constitution, are hereby repealed and abrogated; that the union between the State of Virginia and the other States under the Constitution aforesaid is hereby dissolved, and that the State of Virginia is in the full possession and exercise of all the rights of sovereignty which belong and appertain to a free and independent State.

And they do further declare, That said Constitution of the United States of America is no longer binding on any of the citizens of this State.

This ordinance shall take effect and be an act of this day, when ratified by a majority of the voter of the people of this State cast at a poll to be taken thereon on the fourth Thursday in May next, in pursuance of a schedule hereafter to be enacted.

Arkansas

AN ORDINANCE to dissolve the union now existing between the State of Arkansas and the other States united with her under the compact entitled "The Constitution of the United States of America."

Whereas, in addition to the well-founded causes of complaint set forth by this convention, in resolutions adopted on the 11th of March, A.D. 1861, against the sectional party now in power in Washington City, headed by Abraham Lincoln, he has, in the face of resolutions passed by this convention pledging the State of Arkansas to resist to the last extremity any attempt on the part of such power to coerce any State that had seceded from the old Union, proclaimed to the world that war should be waged against such States until they should be compelled to submit to their rule, and large forces to accomplish this have by this same power been called out, and are now being marshaled to carry out this inhuman design; and to longer submit to such rule, or remain in the old Union of the United States, would be disgraceful and ruinous to the State of Arkansas:

Therefore we, the people of the State of Arkansas, in convention assembled, do hereby declare and ordain, and it is hereby declared and ordained, That the "ordinance and acceptance of compact" passed and approved by the General Assembly of the State of Arkansas on the 18th day of October, A.D. 1836, whereby it was by said General Assembly ordained that by virtue of the authority vested in said General Assembly by the provisions of the ordinance adopted by the convention of delegates assembled at Little Rock for the purpose of forming a constitution and system of government for said State, the propositions set forth in "An act supplementary to an act entitled 'An act for the admission of the State of Arkansas into the Union, and to provide for the due execution of the laws of the United States within the same, and for other purposes,'" were freely accepted, ratified, and irrevocably confirmed, articles of compact and union between the State of Arkansas and the United States, and all other laws and every other law and ordinance, whereby the State of Arkansas became a member of the Federal Union, be, and the same are hereby, in all respects and for every purpose herewith consistent, repealed, abrogated, and fully set aside; and the union now subsisting between the State of Arkansas and the other States, under the name of the United States of America, is hereby forever dissolved.

And we do further hereby declare and ordain, That the State of Arkansas hereby resumes to herself all rights and powers heretofore delegated to the Government of the United States of America; that her citizens are absolved from all allegiance to said Government of the United States, and that she is in full possession and exercise of all the rights and sovereignty which appertain to a free and independent State.

We do further ordain and declare, That all rights acquired and vested under the Constitution of the United States of America, or of any act or acts of Congress, or treaty, or under any law of this State, and not incompatible with this ordinance, shall remain in full force and effect, in nowise altered or impaired, and have the same effect as if this ordinance had not been passed.

North Carolina

AN ORDINANCE to dissolve the union between the State of North Carolina and the other States united with her, under the compact of government entitled "The Constitution of the United States."

We, the people of the State of North Carolina in convention assembled, do declare and ordain, and it is hereby declared and ordained, That the ordinance adopted by the State of North Carolina in the convention of 1789, whereby the Constitution of the United States was ratified and adopted, and also all acts and parts of acts of the General Assembly ratifying and adopting amendments to the said Constitution, are hereby repealed, rescinded, and abrogated.

We do further declare and ordain, That the union now subsisting between the State of North Carolina and the other States, under the title of the United States of America, is hereby dissolved, and that the State of North Carolina is in full possession and exercise of all those rights of sovereignty which belong and appertain to a free and independent State.

Tennessee

DECLARATION OF INDEPENDENCE AND ORDINANCE dissolving the federal relations between the State of Tennessee and the United States of America.

First. We, the people of the State of Tennessee, waiving any expression of opinion as to the abstract doctrine of secession, but asserting the right, as a free and independent people, to alter, reform, or abolish our form of government in such manner as we think proper, do ordain and declare that all the laws and ordinances by which the State of Tennessee became a member of the Federal Union of the United States of America are hereby abrogated and annulled, and that all the rights, functions, and powers which by any of said laws and ordinances were conveyed to the Government of the United States, and to absolve ourselves from all the obligations, restraints, and duties incurred thereto; and do hereby henceforth become a free, sovereign, and independent State.

Second. We furthermore declare and ordain that article 10, sections 1 and 2, of the constitution of the State of Tennessee, which requires members of the General Assembly and all officers, civil and military, to take an oath to support the Constitution of the United States be, and the same are hereby, abrogated and annulled, and all parts of the constitution of the State of Tennessee making citizenship of the United States a qualification for office and recognizing the Constitution of the United States as the supreme law of this State are in like manner abrogated and annulled.

Third. We furthermore ordain and declare that all rights acquired and vested under the Constitution of the United States, or under any act of Congress passed in pursuance thereof, or under any laws of this State, and not incompatible with this ordinance, shall remain in force and have the same effect as if this ordinance had not been passed.

ABRAHAM LINCOLN, MESSAGE TO CONGRESS IN SPECIAL SESSION[43]

At the beginning of the present Presidential term, four months ago, the functions of the Federal Government were found to be generally suspended within the several States of South Carolina, Georgia, Alabama, Mississippi, Louisiana, and Florida, excepting only those of the Post Office Department.

. . . And this issue embraces more than the fate of these United States. It presents to the whole family of man, the question, whether a constitutional republic, or a democracy—a government of the people, by the same people— can, or cannot, maintain its territorial integrity, against its own domestic foes. It presents the question, whether discontented individuals, too few in numbers to control administration, according to organic law, in any case, can always, upon the pretenses made in this case, or on any other pretenses, or arbitrarily, without any pretense, break up their Government, and thus practically put an end to free government upon the earth. It forces us to ask: "Is there, in all republics, this inherent, and fatal weakness?" "Must a government, of necessity, be too strong for the liberties of its own people, or too weak to maintain its own existence?"

. . . The course taken in Virginia was the most remarkable—perhaps the most important. A convention, elected by the people of that State, to consider this very question of disrupting the Federal Union, was in session at the capital of Virginia when Fort Sumter fell. To this body the people had chosen a large majority of professed Union men. Almost immediately after the fall of Sumter, many members of that majority went over to the original disunion minority, and, with them, adopted an ordinance for withdrawing the State from the Union. Whether this change was wrought by their great approval of the assault upon Sumter, or their great resentment at the government's resistance to that assault, is not definitely known. Although they submitted the ordinance, for ratification, to vote of the people, to be taken on a day then somewhat more than a month distant, the convention, and the Legislature, (Which was also in session at the same time and place) with leading men of the State, not members of either, immediately commenced acting, as if the State were already out of the Union. They pushed military preparations vigorously forward all over the state. They seized the United States Armory at Harper's Ferry, and the Navy-yard at Gosport, near Norfolk. They received—perhaps invited—into their state, large bodies of troops, with their warlike appointments, from the so-called seceded States. They formally entered into a treaty of temporary alliance, and co-operation with the so-called "Confederate States," and sent members to their Congress at Montgomery. And, finally, they permitted the insurrectionary government to be transferred to their capital at Richmond.

The people of Virginia have thus allowed this giant insurrection to make its nest within her borders; and this government has no choice left but to deal with it, where it finds it. And it has the less regret, as the loyal citizens have, in due form, claimed its protection. Those loyal citizens, this government is bound to recognize, and protect, as being Virginia.

In the border States, so called—in fact, the middle states—there are those who favor a policy which they call "armed neutrality"—that is, an arming of those states to prevent the Union forces passing one way, or the disunion, the other, over their soil. This would be disunion completed. Figuratively speaking, it would be the building of an impassable wall along the line of separation. And yet, not quite an impassable one; for, under the guise of neutrality, it would tie the hands of the Union men, and freely pass supplies from among them, to the insurrectionists, which it could not do as an open enemy. At a stroke, it would take all the trouble off the hands of secession, except only what proceeds from the external blockade. It would do for the disunionists that which, of all things, they most desire—feed them well, and give them disunion without a struggle of their own. It recognizes no fidelity to the Constitution, no obligation to maintain the Union; and while (very many who have favored it) are, doubtless, loyal citizens, it is, nevertheless, treason in effect.

. . . It might seem, at first thought, to be of little difference whether the present movement at the South be called "secession" or "rebellion."

The movers, however, well understand the difference. At the beginning, they knew they could never raise their treason to any respectable magnitude, by any name which implies violation of law. They knew their people possessed as much of moral sense, as much of devotion to law and order, and as much pride in, and reverence for, the history, and government, of their common country, as any other civilized, and patriotic people. They knew they could make no advancement directly in the teeth of these strong and noble sentiments. Accordingly they commenced by an insidious debauching of the public mind. They invented an ingenious sophism, which, if conceded, was followed by perfectly logical steps, through all the incidents, to the complete destruction of the Union. The sophism itself is, that any state of the Union may, consistently with the national Constitution, and therefore lawfully, and peacefully, withdraw from the Union, without the consent of the Union, or of any other state. The little disguise that the supposed right is to be exercised only for just cause, themselves to be the sole judge of its justice, is too thin to merit any notice.

. . . This sophism derives much—perhaps the whole—of its currency, from the assumption, that there is some omnipotent, and sacred supremacy, pertaining to a State—to each State of our Federal Union. Our States have neither more, nor less power, than that reserved to them, in the Union, by the Constitution—no one of them ever having been a State out of the Union. The original ones passed into the Union even before they cast off their British colonial dependence; and the new ones each came into the Union directly from a condition of dependence, excepting Texas. And even Texas, in its temporary independence, was never designated a State. The new ones only took the designation of States, on coming into the Union, while that name was first adopted for the old ones, in, and by, the Declaration of Independence. Therein the "United Colonies" were declared to be "Free and Independent States"; but, even then, the object plainly was not to declare their independence of one another, or of the Union; but directly the contrary, as their mutual pledge, and their mutual action, before, at the time, and afterwards, abundantly show. The express plighting of faith, by each and all of the original thirteen, in the Articles of Confederation, two years later, that the Union shall be perpetual, is most conclusive. Having never been States, either in substance, or in name, outside of the Union, whence this magical omnipotence of "State rights," asserting a claim of power to lawfully destroy the Union itself? Much is said about the "sovereignty" of the States; but the word, even, is not in the national Constitution; nor, as is believed, in any of the State constitutions. What is a "sovereignty," in the political sense of the term? Would it be far wrong to define it "A political community, without a political superior"? Tested by this, no one of our States, except Texas, ever was a sovereignty. And even Texas gave up the character on coming into the Union; by which act, she acknowledged the Constitution of the United States, and the laws and treaties of the United States made in pursuance of the Constitution, to be, for her, the supreme law of the land. The States have their status IN the Union, and they have no other legal status. If they break from this, they can only do so against law, and by revolution. The Union, and not themselves separately, procured their independence, and their liberty. By conquest, or purchase, the Union gave each of them, whatever of independence, and liberty, it has. The Union is older than any of the States; and, in fact, it created them as States. Originally, some dependent colonies made the Union; and, in turn, the Union threw off their old dependence, for them, and made them States, such as they are. Not one of them ever had a State constitution, independent of the Union. Of course, it is not forgotten that all the new States framed their constitutions, before they entered the Union; nevertheless, dependent upon, and preparatory to, coming into the Union.

Unquestionably the States have the powers, and rights, reserved to them in, and by the National Constitution; but among these, surely, are not included all conceivable powers, however mischievous, or destructive; but, at most, such only, as were known in the world, at the time, as governmental powers; and certainly, a power to destroy the government itself, had never been known as a governmental—as a merely administrative power. This relative matter of National power, and State rights, as a principle, is no other than the principle of generality, and locality. Whatever concerns the whole, should be confided to the whole—to the general government; while, whatever concerns only the State, should be left exclusively, to the State. This is all there is of original principle about it. Whether the National Constitution, in defining boundaries between the two, has applied the principle with exact accuracy, is not to be questioned. We are all bound by that defining, without question.

. . . The seceders insist that our Constitution admits of secession. They have assumed to make a National Constitution of their own, in which, of necessity, they have either discarded, or retained, the right of secession, as they insist, it exists in ours. If they have discarded it, they thereby admit that, on principle, it ought not to be in ours. If they have retained it, by their own construction of ours they show that to be consistent they must secede from one another, whenever they shall find it the easiest way of settling their debts, or effecting any other selfish, or unjust object. The principle itself is one of disintegration, and upon which no government can possibly endure.

If all the States, save one, should assert the power to drive that one out of the Union, it is presumed the whole class of seceder politicians would at once deny the power, and denounce the act as the greatest outrage upon State rights. But suppose that precisely the same act, instead of being called "driving the one out," should be called "the seceding of the others from that one," it would be exactly what the seceders claim to do; unless, indeed, they make the point, that the one, because it is a minority, may rightfully do, what the others, because they are a majority, may not rightfully do. These politicians are subtle, and profound, on the rights of minorities. They are not partial to that power which made the Constitution, and speaks from the preamble, calling itself "We, the People."

. . . This is essentially a People's contest. On the side of the Union, it is a struggle for maintaining in the world, that form, and substance of government, whose leading object is, to elevate the condition of men—to lift artificial weights from all shoulders—to clear the paths of laudable pursuit for all—to afford all, an unfettered start, and a fair chance, in the race of life. Yielding to partial, and temporary departures, from necessity, this is the leading object of the government for whose existence we contend.

. . . Our popular government has often been called an experiment. Two points in it, our people have already settled—the successful establishing, and the successful administering of it. One still remains—its successful maintenance against a formidable [internal] attempt to overthrow it. It is now for them to demonstrate to the world, that those who can fairly carry an election, can also suppress a rebellion—that ballots are the rightful, and peaceful, successors of bullets; and that when ballots have fairly, and constitutionally, decided, there can be no successful appeal, back to bullets; that there can be no successful appeal, except to ballots themselves, at succeeding elections. Such will be a great lesson of peace; teaching men that what they cannot take by an election, neither can they take it by a war—teaching all, the folly of being the beginners of a war.

. . . The Constitution provides, and all the States have accepted the provision, that "The United States shall guarantee to every State in this Union a republican form of government." But, if a State may lawfully go out of the Union, having done so, it may also discard the republican form of government; so that to prevent its going out, is an indispensable means, to the end, of maintaining the guaranty mentioned; and when an end is lawful and obligatory, the indispensable means to it, are also lawful, and obligatory.

ABRAHAM LINCOLN, GETTYSBURG ADDRESS[44]

Four score and seven years ago our fathers brought forth on this continent, a new nation, conceived in Liberty, and dedicated to the proposition that all men are created equal.

Now we are engaged in a great civil war, testing whether that nation, or any nation so conceived and so dedicated, can long endure. We are met on a great battle-field of that war. We have come to dedicate a portion of that field, as a final resting place for those who here gave their lives that that nation might live. It is altogether fitting and proper that we should do this. But, in a larger sense, we can not dedicate—we can not consecrate—we can not hallow—this ground. The brave men, living and dead, who struggled here, have consecrated it, far above our poor power to add or detract. The world will little note, nor long remember what we say here, but it can never forget what they did here. It is for us the living, rather, to be dedicated here to the unfinished work which they who fought here have thus far so nobly advanced. It is rather for us to be here dedicated to the great task remaining before us—that from these honored dead we take increased devotion to that cause for which they gave the last full measure of devotion—that we here highly resolve that these dead shall not have died in vain—that this nation, under God, shall have a new birth of freedom—and that government of the people, by the people, for the people, shall not perish from the earth.

CHARLES SUMNER, STATE SUICIDE RESOLUTIONS[45]

Resolutions declaratory of the Relations between the United States and the Territory once occupied by certain states, and now usurped by the pretended Governments without Constitutional or Legal Right.

Whereas certain states, rightfully belonging to the Union of the United States, have, through their respective Governments, wickedly undertaken to abjure all those duties by which their connection with the Union was maintained, to renounce all allegiance to the Constitution, to levy war upon the National Government, and, for the consummation of this treason, have unconstitutionally and unlawfully confederated together with the declared purpose of putting an end, by force, to the supremacy of the Constitution within their respective limits.

And whereas this condition of insurrection, organized by pretended Governments, openly exists in North Carolina, South Carolina, Georgia, Florida, Alabama, Mississippi, Louisiana, Texas, Arkansas, Tennessee, and Virginia,—except in Eastern Tennessee and Western Virginia,—and the President of the United States, in a proclamation duly made in conformity with an Act of Congress, has declared the same to exist throughout this territory, with the exceptions already named;

And whereas the extensive territory thus usurped by these pretended Governments and organized into a hostile confederation *belongs to the United States, as an inseparable part thereof, under the sanctions of the Constitution*, to be held in trust for the inhabitants in the present and future generations, and is so completely interlinked with the Union that is forever dependent thereupon.

And whereas the Constitution, which is the supreme law of the land, cannot be displaced within this territory, but must ever continue the supreme law thereof, notwithstanding the doing of any pretended Governments, acting singly or in confederation, hostile to its supremacy: Therefore, -

1. *Resolved*, That any vote of secession, or other act, by a State hostile to the supremacy of the Constitution within its territory, *is inoperative and void against the Constitution*, and, when sustained by *force*, becomes a practical abdication by the State of all rights under the Constitution, while treason in it involves works instant forfeiture of all functions and powers essential to the continued existence of the State as a body politic; so that from such time forward the territory falls under the exclusive jurisdiction of Congress, as other territory, and the State becomes, according to the language of the law, *felo de sc.*
2. That any combination of men assuming to act in the place of such State, and attempting to ensure or coerce its inhabitants into a confederation hostile to the Union, is rebellious, treasonable, and destitute of all moral authority; and such combination is a usurpation incapable of constitutional existence and utterly lawless, *so that everything dependent upon it is without constitutional or legal support.*
3. That the termination of a State under the Constitution necessarily causes the termination of those peculiar local institutes which, having no origin in the Constitution, or in natural right independent of the Constitution, are upheld by the sole and exclusive authority of the State.
4. That Slavery, being a peculiar local institution, derived from local law, *without any origin in the Constitution or in natural right*, is upheld by the sole and exclusive authority of the State, and must therefore cease, legally and constitutionally, when the State on which it depends has lapsed; for the incident must follow the principal.
5. That, in the exercise of exclusive jurisdiction over the territory once occupied by the States, it is the duty of Congress to see that the supremacy of the Constitution is maintained in its essential principles, so that everywhere in this extensive territory Slavery shall cease to exist in fact, as it has already ceased to exist in law or Constitution.
6. That any recognition of Slavery in such territory, or surrender of slaves under pretended laws of such states, by an officer of the United States, civil of military, is a practical recognition of the pretended Governments, to the exclusion of the jurisdiction of Congress under the Constitution, and is in the nature of aid and comfort to the Rebellion that has been organized.
7. That any such recognition of Slavery, or surrender of pretended slaves besides being a practical recognition of the pretended Governments,

giving them aid and comfort, is a denial of the rights of persons who by the action of the States have become free, so that, under the Constitution, they cannot again be enslaved.

8. That allegiance from the inhabitant and protection from the Government are corresponding obligations, dependent upon each other; so that, while the allegiance of every inhabitant of this territory, without distinction of class or color, is due to the United States, and cannot in any way be defeated by the action of any pretended Government, or by any pretence of property or claim to service, the corresponding obligation of protection is at the same time due from the Unites States to every such inhabitant, without distinction of class or color; and it follows that inhabitants held as slaves, whose paramount allegiance is to the United States, may justly look to the National Government for protection.

9. That the duty cast upon Congress by the action of the States is enforced by the positive requirement of the Constitution, that "no State shall enter into any confederation," or "without the consent of Congress, keep troops or ships of war in time of peace," or "enter into any agreement or compact with another State," or "grant letters of marque and reprisal," or "coin money," or "emit bills of credit," or, "without the consent of the Congress, lay any imposts or duties on imports or exports," all of which have been done by these pretended Governments, and also by the positive injunction of the Constitution, addressed to the Nation, that "the United States shall guaranty to every State in this Union a republican form of Government" ; and that, in pursuance of this duty cast upon Congress, and further enjoined by the Constitution, *Congress will assume complete jurisdiction of such vacated territory, where such unconstitutional and illegal things have been attempted, and will proceed to establish therein republican forms of government under the Constitution*, and, in the execution of this trust, will provide carefully for the protection of all the inhabitants thereof, for the security of families, the organization of labor, the encouragement of industry, and the welfare of society, and will in every way discharge the duties of a just, merciful, and paternal Government.

ANDREW JOHNSON, VETO OF THE
FIRST RECONSTRUCTION ACT[46]

. . . The bill places all the people of the ten States therein named under the absolute domination of military rule; and the preamble undertakes to give the reason upon which the measure is based and the ground upon which it is justified. It declares that there exists in those States no legal governments and no adequate protection for life or property, and asserts the necessity of enforcing peace and good order within their limits. This is not true as a matter of fact.

It is not denied that the States in question have each of them an actual government, with all the powers—executive, judicial, and legislative—which properly belong to a free State. They are organized like the other States of the Union, and, like them, they make, administer, and execute the laws which concern their domestic affairs. An existing de facto government, exercising such functions as these, is itself the law of the State upon all matters within its jurisdiction. To pronounce the supreme law making power of an established State illegal is to say that law itself is unlawful.

The provisions which these governments have made for the preservation of order, the suppression of crime, and the redress of private injuries are in substance and principle the same as those which prevail in the Northern States and in other civilized countries. They certainly have not succeeded in preventing the commission of all crime, nor has this been accomplished any where in the world . . . . But that people are maintaining local governments for themselves which habitually defeat the object of all government and render their own lives and property insecure is in itself utterly improbable, and the averment of the bill to that effect is not supported by any evidence which has come to my knowledge.

The bill, however, would seem to show upon its face that the establishment of peace and good order is not its real object. The fifth section declares that the preceding sections shall cease to operate in any State where certain events shall have happened. These events are, first, the selection of delegates to a State convention by an election at which Negroes shall be allowed to vote; second, the formation of a State constitution by the convention so chosen; third, the insertion into the State constitution of a provision which will secure the right of voting at all elections to Negroes and to such white men as may not be disfranchised for rebellion or felony; fourth, the submission of the constitution for ratification by their vote; fifth, the submission of the State constitution to Congress for examination and approval, and the actual approval of it by that body; sixth, the adoption of a certain amendment to the Federal Constitution by a vote of Legislature elected under the new constitution; seventh, the adoption of said amendment by a sufficient number of other States to make it a part of the Constitution of the United States. All these conditions must be fulfilled before the people of any of these States can be relieved from the bondage of military domination; but when they are fulfilled, then immediately the pains and penalties of the bill are to cease, no matter whether there be peace and order or not, and without any reference to the security of life or property.

The excuse given for the bill in the preamble is one of necessity. The military rule which it establishes is plainly to be used, not for any purpose of order or for the prevention of crime, but solely as a means of coercing the people into the adoption of principles and measures to which it is known that they are opposed, and upon which they have an undeniable right to exercise their own judgment.

I submit to Congress whether this measure is not in its whole character, scope, and object without precedent and without authority, in palpable conflict with the plainest provisions of liberty and humanity for which our ancestors on both sides of the Atlantic have shed so much blood, and expended so much treasure.

. . . If, therefore, the Southern States were in truth out of the Union, we could not treat their people in a way which the fundamental law forbids. Some persons assume that the success of our arms in crushing the opposition which was made in some of the States to the execution of the Federal laws reduced those States and all their people—the innocent as well as the guilty—to the condition of vassalage and gave us a power over them which the Constitution does not bestow or define or limit. No fallacy can be more transparent than this. Our victories subjected the insurgents to legal obedience, not to the yoke of an arbitrary despotism. When an absolute sovereign reduces his rebellious subjects, he may deal with them according to his pleasure, because he had that power before. But when a limited monarch puts down an insurrection, he must still govern according to law.

. . . I have always contended that the Government of the United States was sovereign within its constitutional sphere; that it executed its laws like the States themselves, by applying its coercive power directly to individuals; and that it could put down insurrection with the same effect as a State and no other. The opposite doctrine is the worst heresy of those who advocated secession, and can not be agreed to without admitting that heresy to be right.

. . . That the measure proposed by this bill does violate the Constitution in the particulars mentioned and in many other ways which I forbear to enumerate is too clear to admit the least doubt. It only remains to consider whether the injunctions of that instrument ought to be obeyed or not. I think they ought to be obeyed, for reasons which I will proceed to give as briefly as possible. In the first place, it is the only system of free Government which we can hope to have as a Nation. When it ceases to be the rule of our conduct, we may perhaps take our choice between complete anarchy, a consolidated despotism, and a total dissolution of the Union; but national liberty regulated by law will have passed beyond our reach.

It was to punish the gross crime of defying the Constitution and to vindicate its supreme authority that we carried on a bloody war of four years' duration. Shall we now acknowledge that we sacrificed a million of lives and expended billions of treasure to enforce a Constitution which is not worthy of respect and preservation?

TEXAS v. WHITE[47]

The first inquires to which our attention was directed by counsel, arose upon the allegations . . . that the State, having severed her relations with a majority of the States of the Union, and having by her ordinance of secession attempted to throw off her allegiance to the Constitution and government of the United States, has so far changed her status as to be disabled from prosecuting suits in the National courts . . .

If, therefore, it is true that the state of Texas was not at the time of filing this bill, or is not now, one of the United States, we have no jurisdiction of this suit, and it is our duty to dismiss it

. . . In the Constitution the term state most frequently expresses the combined idea just noticed, of people, territory, and government. A state, in the ordinary sense of the Constitution, is a political community of free citizens, occupying a territory of defined boundaries, and organized under a government sanctioned and limited by a written constitution, and established by the consent of the governed. It is the union of such states, under a common constitution, which forms the distinct and greater political unit, which that Constitution designates as the United States, and makes of the people and states which compose it one people and one country . . .

. . . From the date of admission, until 1861, the State was represented in the Congress of the United States by her senators and representatives, and her relations as a member of the Union remained unimpaired. In that year, acting upon the theory that the rights of a State under the Constitution might be renounced, and her obligations thrown off at pleasure, Texas undertook to sever the bond thus formed, and to break up her constitutional relations with the United States.

The position thus assumed could only be maintained by arms, and Texas accordingly took part, with the other Confederate States, in the war of the rebellion, which these events made inevitable. During the whole of that war there was no governor, or judge, or any other State officer in Texas, who recognized the National authority. Nor was any officer of the United States permitted to exercise any authority whatever under the National government within the limits of the State, except under the immediate protection of the National military forces.

Did Texas, in consequence of these acts, cease to be a State? Or, if not, did the State cease to be a member of the Union?

It is needless to discuss, at length, the question whether the right of a State to withdraw from the Union for any cause, regarded by herself as sufficient, is consistent with the Constitution of the United States.

The Union of the States never was a purely artificial and arbitrary relation. It began among the Colonies, and grew out of common origin, mutual sympathies, kindred principles, similar interests, and geographical relations. It was confirmed and strengthened by the necessities of war, and received definite form, and character, and sanction from the Articles of Confederation. By these the Union was solemnly declared to "be perpetual." And when these Articles were found to be inadequate to the exigencies of the country, the Constitution was ordained "to form a more perfect Union." It is difficult to convey the idea of indissoluble unity more clearly than by these words. What can be indissoluble if a perpetual Union, made more perfect, is not?

But the perpetuity and indissolubility of the Union, by no means implies the loss of distinct and individual existence, or of the right of self-government by the States. Under the Articles of Confederation each State retained its sovereignty, freedom, and independence, and every power, jurisdiction, and right not expressly delegated to the United States. Under the Constitution, thought the powers of the States were much restricted, still, all powers not delegated to the United States, nor prohibited to the States, are reserved to the States respectively, or to the people. And we have already had occasion to remark at this term, that "the people of each State compose a State, having its own government, and endowed with all the functions essential to separate and independent existence," and that "without the States in Union, there could be no loss of separate and independent autonomy to the States, through their union under the Constitution, but it may be not unreasonably said that the preservations of the States, and the maintenance of their governments, are as much within the design and care of the Constitution as the preservation of the Union and the maintenance of the National government. The Constitution, in all its provisions, looks to an indestructible Union, composed of indestructible States.

When, therefore, Texas became one of the United States, she entered into an indissoluble relation. All the obligations of perpetual union, and all of the guaranties of republican government in the Union, attached at once to the State. The act which consummated her admission into the Union was something more than a compact; it was the incorporation of a new member into the political body. And it was final. The union between Texas and the other States was as complete, as perpetual, and as indissoluble as the union between the original States. There was no place for reconsideration, or revocation, except through revolution, or through consent of the States.

Considered therefore as transactions under the Constitution, the ordinance of secession, adopted by the convention and ratified by a majority of the citizens of Texas, and all the acts of her legislature intended to give effect to that ordinance, were absolutely null. They were utterly without operation in law. The obligations of the State, as a member of the Union, and of every citizen of the State, as a citizen of the United States, remained perfect and unimpaired. It certainly follows that the State did not cease to be the State, nor her citizens to be citizens to be citizens of the Union. If this were otherwise, the State must have become foreign, and her citizens foreigners. The war must have ceased to become a war for conquest and subjugation.

Our conclusion therefore is, that Texas continued to be a State, and a State of the Union, notwithstanding the transactions to which we have referred. And this conclusion, in our judgement, is not in conflict with any act or declaration of any department of the National government, but entirely in accordance with the whole series of such acts and declarations since the outbreak of the rebellion.

WOODROW WILSON, "THE STATES AND THE FEDERAL GOVERNMENT"[48]

The question of the relation of the States to the Federal Government is the cardinal question of our constitutional system. At every turn of our national development we have been brought face to face with it, and no definition either of statesmen or of judges has ever quieted or decided it. It cannot, indeed, be settled by the opinion of any one generation, because it is a question of growth, and every successive stage of our political and economic development gives it a new aspect, makes it a new question. The general lines of definition which were to run between the powers granted to Congress and the powers reserved to the States the makers of the Constitution were able to draw with their characteristic foresight and lucidity; but the subject-matter of that definition is constantly changing, for it is the life of the nation itself. Our activities change alike their scope and their character with every generation. The old measures of the Constitution are every day to be filled with new grain as the varying crop of circumstances comes to maturity. It is clear enough that the general commercial, financial, economic interests of the country were meant to be brought under the regulation of the Federal Government, which should act for all; and it is equally clear that what are the general commercial, financial, economic interests of the country is a question of fact, to be determined by circumstances which change under our very eyes, and that, case by case, we are inevitably drawn on to include under the established definitions of the law matters new and unforeseen which seem in their magnitude to give to the powers of Congress a sweep and vigor certainly never conceived possible by earlier generations of statesmen, sometimes almost revolutionary even in our own eyes. The subject-matter of this troublesome definition is the living body of affairs.

The principle of the division of powers between State and Federal governments is a very simple one when stated in its most general terms. It is that the Legislatures of the States shall have control of all the general subject-matter of law, of private rights of every kind, of local interests and of everything that directly concerns their people as communities,—free choice with regard to all matters of local regulation and development, and that Congress shall have control only of such matters as concern the peace and the commerce of the country as a whole.

. . . Which parts of the many-sided processes of the nation's economic development shall be left to the regulation of the States, which parts shall be given over to the regulation of the Federal Government? I do not propound this as a mere question of statesmanship, but also as a question, a very fundamental question, of constitutional law. What, reading our Constitution in its true spirit, neither stinking in its letter nor yet forcing it arbitrarily to mean what we wish it to mean, shall be the answer of our generation to the old question of the distribution of powers between Congress and the States? For us, as for previous generations, it is a deeply critical question. The very stuff of all our political principles, of all our political experience, is involved in it. In this all too indistinctly marked field of right choice our statesmanship shall achieve new triumphs or come to eventual shipwreck.

The old theory of the sovereignty of the States, which used so to engage our passions, has lost its vitality. The war between the States established at least this principle, that the Federal Government is, through its courts, the final judge of its own powers. Since that stern arbitrament it would be idle, in any practical argument, to ask by what law of abstract principle the Federal Government is bound and restrained. Its power is "to regulate commerce between the States," and the attempts now made during every session of Congress to carry the implications of that power beyond the utmost boundaries of reasonable and honest inference show that the only limits likely to be observed by politicians are those set by the good sense and conservative temper of the country.

It is important, therefore, to look at the at facts and to understand the real character of the political and economic materials of our own day with a clear and statesmanlike vision, as the makers of the Constitution understood the conditions they dealt with. If the jealousies of the colonies and of the little States which sprang out of them had not obliged the makers of the Constitution to leave the greater part of legal regulation in the hands of the States, it would have been wise, it would have been necessary, to invent such a division of powers as was actually agreed upon. It is not, at bottom, a question of sovereignty or of any other political abstraction; it is a question of vitality. Uniform regulation of the economic conditions of a vast territory and a various people like the United States would be mischievous, if not impossible. The statesmanship which really attempts it is premature and unwise. Undoubtedly the recent economic development of the country, particularly the development of the last two decades, has obliterated many boundaries, made many interests national and common which until our own day were separate and distinct; but the lines of these great changes we have not yet clearly traced or studiously enough considered. To distinguish them and provide for them is the task which is to test the statesmanship of our generation; and it is already plain that, great as they are, these new combinations of interest have not yet gone so far as to make the States mere units of local government. Not our legal conscience merely, but our practical interests as well, call upon us to discriminate and be careful, with the care of men who handle the vital stuff of a great constitutional system.

The United States are not a single, homogeneous community. In spite of a certain superficial sameness which seems to impart to Americans a common type and point of view, they still contain communities at almost every stage of development, illustrating in their social and economic structure almost every modern variety of interest and prejudice, following occupations of every kind, in climates of every sort that the temperate zone affords. This variety of fact and condition, these substantial economic and social contrasts, do not in all cases follow State lines. They are often contrasts between region and region rather than between State and State. But they are none the less real, and are in many instances permanent and ineradicable.

From the first the United States have been socially and economically divided into regions rather than into States.

We are too apt to think that our American political system is distinguished by its central structure, by its President and Congress and courts, which the Constitution of the Union set up. As a matter of fact, it is distinguished by its local structure, by the extreme vitality of its parts. It would be an impossibility without its division of powers. From the first it has been a nation in the making. It has come to maturity by the stimulation of no central force or guidance but by the abounding self-helping, self-sufficing energy of its parts, which severally brought themselves into existence and added themselves to the Union, pleasing first of all themselves in the framing of their laws and constitutions, not asking leave to exist, but existing first and asking leave afterwards, self-originated, self-constituted, self-confident, self-sustaining, veritable communities, demanding only recognition. Communities develop, not by external, but by internal forces. Else they do not live at all. Our commonwealths have not come into existence by invitation, like plants in a tended garden; they have sprung up on themselves, irrepressible, a sturdy, spontaneous product of the nature of men nurtured in a free air.

The division of powers between the States and the Federal Government effected by our Federal Constitution was the normal and natural division for this purpose. Under it the States possess all the ordinary legal choices that shape a people's life. Theirs is the whole of the ordinary field of law: the regulation of domestic relations and of the ordinary field of law: the regulation of domestic relations and of the relations between employer and employee, the determination of property rights and of the validity and enforcement of contracts, the definition of crimes and their punishments, the definition of the many and subtle rights and obligations which lie outside the fields of property and contract, the establishment of the laws of incorporation and of the rules governing the conduct of every kind of business. The presumption insisted upon by the Courts in every argument with regard to the Federal Government is that it has no power not explicitly granted it by the Federal Constitution or reasonably to be inferred as the natural or necessary accompaniment of the powers there conveyed to it; but the presumption with regard to the powers of the States they have always held to be exactly the opposite kind. It is that the States of course possess every power that government has ever anywhere exercised, except only those powers which their own constitutions or the Constitution of the United States explicitly or by plain inference withhold. They are the ordinary governments of the country; the Federal Government is its instrument only for particular purposes.

Congress is, indeed, the immediate government of the people. It does not govern the States, but acts directly upon individuals, as directly as the governments of the States themselves. It does not stand at a distance and look on,—to be ready for an occasional interference,—but is the immediate and familiar instrument of the people in everything that it undertakes, as if there were no States. The States do not stand between it and the people. Bu the field of its action is distinct, restricted, and definite.

Added to this doubt and difficulty of analysis which makes it a constant matter of debate what the powers of Congress are is the growing dissatisfaction with the part the States are playing in the economic life of the day. They either let the pressing problems of the time alone and attempt no regulation at all, however loudly opinion and circumstance itself may call for it, or they try every half-considered remedy, embark upon a thousand experiments, and bring utter confusion upon the industry of the country by contradicting and offsetting each other's measures. No two States act alike. Manufacturers and carriers who serve commerce in many States find it impossible to obey the laws of all, and the enforcement of the laws of the States in all their variety threatens the country with a new war of conflicting regulations as serious as that which made the Philadelphia convention of 1787 necessary and gave us a new Federal Constitution. This conflict of laws in matters which vitally interest the whole country and in which no State or region can wisely stand apart to serve any particular interest of its own constitutes the greatest political danger of our day. It is more apt and powerful than any other cause to bring upon us radical and ill-considered changes. It confuses our thinking up on essential matters and makes us hasty reformers out of mere impatience. We are in danger of acting before we clearly know what we want or comprehend the consequences of what we do,—in danger of altering the character of the government in order to escape a temporary inconvenience.

We are an industrial people. The development of the resources of the country, the command of the markets of the world, is for the time being more important in our eyes than any political theory or lawyer's discrimination of functions. We are intensely "practical," moreover, and insist that every obstacle, whether of law or fact, be swept out of the way. It is not the right temper for constitutional understandings. Too "practical" a purpose may give us a government such as we never should have chosen had we made the choice more thoughtfully and deliberately. We cannot afford to belie our reputation for political sagacity and self-possession by any such hasty processes as those into which such a temper of mere impatience seems likely to hurry us.

. . . There is, however, something else that comes to the surface, and that explains not a little of our present dissatisfaction with State legislation upon matters of vital national importance. Their failure to correct their own processes may prove that there is something radically wrong with the structure and operation of their governments,—that they have ceased to be sensitive and efficient instruments for the creation and realization of opinion,—the real function of constitutional governments.

It is better to learn the true political lesson than merely to improve business. There is something involved which is deeper than the mere question of the distribution of legislative powers within our Federal system. We have come to the test of the intimate and detailed processes of self-government to which it was supposed that our principles and our experience had committed us. There are many evidences that we are losing confidence in our State Legislatures, and yet it is evident that it is through them that we attempt all the more intimate measures of self-government. To lose faith in them is to lose faith in our very system of government, and that is a very serious matter. It is this loss of confidence in our local legislatures that has led our people to give so much heed to the radical suggestions of change made by those who advocate the use of the initiative and the referendum in our processes of legislation, the virtual abandonment of the representative principle and the attempt to put into the hands of the voters themselves the power to initiate and negative laws,— in order to enable them to do for themselves what they have not been able to get satisfactorily done through the representatives they have hitherto chosen to act for them.

The truth is that our State governments are many of them no longer truly representative governments. We are not, in fact, dissatisfied with local representative assemblies and the government which they impose; we are dissatisfied, rather, with regulations imposed by commissions and assemblies which are no longer representative.

. . . The country feels, therefore, that, however selected, they are in some sense more representative, more to be depended on to register its thoughtful judgments, than the members of State Legislatures are.

It is for this reason as much as for any other that the balance of powers between the States and the Federal Government now trembles at an unstable equilibrium and we hesitate into which scale to throw the weight of our purpose and preference with regard to the legislation by which we shall attempt to thread the maze of our present economic needs and perplexities. It may turn out that what our State governments need is not to be sapped of their powers and subordinated to Congress, but to be reorganized along simpler lines which will make them real organs of popular opinion. A government must have organs; it cannot act inorganically, by masses. It must have a law-making body; it can no more make laws through its voters than it can make them through its newspapers.

It would be fatal to our political vitality really to strip the States of their powers and transfer them to the Federal Government. It cannot be too often repeated that it has been the privilege of separate development secured to the several regions of the country by the Constitution, and not the privilege of separate development only, but also that other more fundamental privilege that lies back of it, the privilege of independent local opinion and individual conviction, which has given speed, facility, vigor, and certainty to the processes of our economic and political growth. To buy temporary ease and convenience for the performance of a few great tasks of the hour at the expense of that would be to pay too great a price and to cheat all generations for the sake of one.

Undoubtedly the powers of the Federal Government have grown enormously since the creation of the Government; and they have grown for the most part without amendment of the Constitution. But they have grown in almost every instance by a process which must be regarded as perfectly normal and legitimate. The Constitution cannot be regarded as a mere legal document, to be read as a will or a contract would be. It must of the necessity of the case be a vehicle of life. As the life of the nation changes so much the interpretation of the document which contains it change, by a nice adjustment determined, not by the original intention of those who drew the paper, but by the exigencies and the new aspects of life itself. Changes of fact and alterations of opinion bring in their train actual extensions of community of interest, actual additions to the catalogue of things which must be included under the general terms of the law. The commerce of great systems of railway is of course not the commerce of wagon roads, the only land commerce known in the days when the Constitution was drafted. The common interests of a nation bound together in thought and interest and action by the telegraph and the telephone, as well as by the rushing mails which every express train carries, have a scope and variety, an infinite multiplication and intricate interlacing of which a simpler day can have had no conception. Every general term of the Constitution has come to have a meaning as varied as the actual variety of the things which the country now shares in common.

The character of the process of constitutional adaptation depends first of all upon the wise or unwise choice of statesmen, but ultimately and chiefly upon the opinion and purpose of the courts. The chief instrumentality by which the law of the Constitution has been extended to cover the facts of national development has been judicial interpretation, the decisions of the courts. The process of formal amendment of the Constitution itself that it has seldom been feasible to use it; and the difficulty of formal amendment has undoubt-edly made the courts more liberal, not to say more lax, in their interpretation than they would otherwise have been. The whole business of adaptation was theirs, and they have undertaken it with open minds, sometimes even with boldness and a touch of audacity. But, though they have sometimes been lax, though they have sometimes yielded, it may be, to the pressure of popular agitation and of party interest, they have not often overstepped the bounds of legitimate extension. By legitimate extension I mean extension which does not change the character of the Federal power but only its items,—which does not make new kinds, but only new particulars of power.

The members of courts are necessarily men of their own generation: we would not wish to have them men of another. Constitutional law, as well as statesmanship, must look forward, not backward, and, while we should wish the courts to be conservative, we should certainly be deeply uneasy were they to hold affairs back from their natural alteration. Change as well as stability may be conservative. Conservative change is conservative, not of prejudices, but of principles, of established purposes and conceptions, the only things which in government or in any other field of action can abide. Conservative progress is a process, not of revolution, but of modification. In our own case and in the matter now under discussion it consists in a slowly progressive modification and transfer of functions as between the States and the Federal Government along the lines of actual development, along the lines of actual and substantial alterations of interest and of that national consciousness which is the breath of all true amendment,—and not along lines of party or individual purpose, nor by way of desperate search for remedies for existing evils.

No doubt courts must "make" law for their own day, must have the insight which adapts law to its uses rather than its uses to it, must sometimes ven-ture upon decisions which have a certain touch of statesmanlike initiative in them. We shall often find ourselves looking to them for strong and fearless opinions. But there are two kinds of "strong" opinions, as a distinguished English jurist long ago pointed out. There are those which are strong with the strength of insight and intelligence and those which are strong with the mere strength of will. The latter sort all judges who act with conscience, mindful of their oaths of office, should eschew as they would eschew the actual breaking of law. That the Federal courts should have such a conscience is essential to the integrity of our whole national action. Actual alterations of interest in the make-up of our national life, actual, unmistakable changes in our national consciousness, actual modifications in our national activities such as give a new aspect and significance to the well-known purposes of our fundamental law, should of course be taken up into decisions which add to the number of things in which the national Government must take cognizance and regulative control. That is a function of insight and intelligence. The courage it calls for on the part of the courts is the courage of conviction. But they are, on the other hand, called on to display the more noble courage which defends ancient conviction and established principle against the clamor, the class interest and the changeful moods of parties. They should never permit themselves willfully to seek to find in the phrases of the Constitution remedies for evils which the Federal Government was never intended to deal with.

Moral and social questions originally left to the several States for settlement can be drawn into the field of Federal authority only at the expense of the self-dependence and efficiency of the several communities of which our complex body politic is made up. Paternal morals, morals enforced by the judgment and choices of the central authority at Washington, do not and cannot create vital habits or methods of life unless sustained by local opinion and purpose, local prejudice and convenience,—unless supported by local convenience and interest; and only communities capable of taking care of themselves will, taken together, constitute a nation capable of vital action and control. You cannot atrophy the parts without atrophying the whole. Deliberate adding to the powers of the Federal Government by sheer judicial authority, because the Supreme Court can no longer be withstood or contradicted in the States, both saps the legal morality upon which a sound constitutional system must rest and deprives the Federal structure as a whole of the vitality which has given the Supreme Court itself its increase of power. It is the alchemy of decay.

It would certainly mean that we had acquired a new political temper, never hitherto characteristic of us, that we had utterly lost confidence in what we set out to do, were we now to substitute abolition for reform,—were by degrees to do away with our boasted system of self-government out of mere impatience and disgust, like those who got rid of an instrument they no longer knew how to use. There are some hopeful signs that we may be about to return to the better way of a time when we knew how to restrict government and adapt it to our uses in accordance with principles we did not doubt, but adhered to with an ardent fervor which was the best evidence of youth and virility.

We have long been painfully conscious that we have failed in the matter of city government. It is an age of cities, and if we cannot govern our cities we cannot govern at all. For a little while we acted as if in despair. We began to strip our city governments of their powers and to transfer them to State commissions or back to the Legislatures of the States, very much as we are now stripping the States of their powers and putting them in the hands of Federal commissions. The attempt was made to put the police departments of some of our citifies, for example, in the hands of State officers, and to put the granting of city franchises back into the hands of the central Legislature of the State, in the hope, apparently, that a uniform regulation of such things by the opinion of the whole State might take the place of corrupt control by city politicians. But it did not take us long, fortunately, to see that we were moving in the wrong direction. We have now turned to the better way of reconsidering the whole question of the organization of city governments, and are likely within a generation to purify them by simplifying them, to moralize them by placing their government in the hands of a few persons who can really be selected by popular preference instead of by the private processes of nomination by party managers, and who, because few and conspicuous, can really be watched and held to a responsibility which they will honor because they cannot escape.

It is to be hoped that we shall presently have the same light dawn upon us with regard to our State governments, and, instead of upsetting an ancient system, hallowed by long use and deep devotion, revitalize it by reorganization. And that, not only because it is an old system long beloved, but also because we are certified by all political history of the fact that centralization is not vitalization. Moralization is by life, not by statue, by the interior impulse and experience of communities, not by fostering legislation which is merely the abstraction of an experience which may belong to a nation as a whole or to many parts of it without having yet touched the thought of the rest anywhere to the quick. The object of our Federal system is to bring the understandings of constitutional government home to the people of every part of the nation, to make them part of their consciousness as they go about their daily tasks. If we cannot successfully effect its adjustments by the nice local adaptations of our older practice e, we have failed as constitutional statesmen.

ALBERT BEVERIDGE, "VITALITY OF THE AMERICAN CONSTITUTION"[49]

. . . our Constitution proceeded from "progressive history," and therefore is capable of future growth, just as it is the result of past growth. The Constitution was not a contract between thirteen allies called states, and so to be construed as a contract is to be construed; it was and is an ordinance of nationality springing from the necessities of the people and established directly by the people themselves. And as the Constitution gradually grew out of the necessities of the people in the past and was formulated out of the necessities of the people at the time of its adoption, so it embraces the necessities of the people for all time. But as the necessities of the people for all time could not possibly have been foreseen by the men who wrote the Constitution, it follows that they could not have intended to confine the purposes of the Constitution and the powers it confers to the necessities of the people of 1789; that they so wrote it that it might meet the requirements of the people for all time.

If that is so, it follows that the Constitution must steadily grow, because the requirements of the people steadily grow. . . . So, the vitality of the American Constitution and all constitutions must reside in their power to grow as the people grow, and furnish scope for the people's power and the Nation's necessities in exact proportion as the people's power and the Nation's necessities enlarge.

. . . The Golden Rule of constitutional interpretation is this: *The Constitution exists for the people, not the people for the Constitution.* But how can a written Constitution grow? Its words are there not to be changed. But the people change; conditions change; new problems arise; the happiness and welfare of the Nation constantly demand new methods, enlarging powers, activities in directions hitherto unknown. And if the Constitution cannot keep pace with the needs of the people, it ceases to be useful to the people and becomes oppressive to them.

. . . If the Constitution had locked up the people's energies and prevented the recognition of their ever-increasing necessities and paralyzed their ever-enlarging powers, the people would have made short work of the Constitution. They would have over-thrown it by revolution, if necessary, just as the people will overthrow anything which stands in the way of the prosperity of their homes, the happiness of their firesides. The march of nationality is not to be withstood; and so the salvation of the Constitution is in its capacity for growth; and he is the enemy, no matter how much he may think himself the friend, of our fundamental law, who does not recognize its capacity for self-enlargement, determined by the enlarging necessities of the people. He is the enemy of the American Constitution who binds the American people to the letter of that instrument; for if that were done, the people's expanding necessities would overthrow a constitution which retarded and op-pressed them.

. . . So it follows that whatever may be essential to the development of the people's nationality lies latent in the Constitution's general terms, awaiting the necessity of events to call it into action. . . . [We are] a Nation of the people, deriving its powers directly from them and not from the states. If that is so, if nationality is the great purpose of the Constitution, if the people directly are the source of its power and the object of its beneficence, then unexpressed powers and duties in the National Government were called into being, which upon any other theory could not possibly exist.

... This aspiration of the common people toward nationality has expressed itself through every branch of the Government, legislative as well as judicial, executive as well as legislative. Indeed, the Constitution may be said to have been construed, as it was created, by the people's common instinct of nationality. The doctrinaires declared that internal improvements by the National Government were unconstitutional. Three of our Presidents were sure of it. Jefferson so believed. Madison vetoed the first internal-improvement bill on the ground of its unconstitutionality. Monroe made it the subject of a message to Congress.

But the common people knew better than the theorists. No matter what refined logic, spun from mere words and names, might conclude, the farmer and the trader, the feller of forests, the tiller of fields. the builder of homes, the makers, one and all of the Nation, knew that they were fellow-citizens of the American Republic, and not mere members of friendly localities, and so they said: "It is the business of our common Nation to build canals, construct the national highways; clear the rivers, dredge the harbors of our common country; it is absurd to leave to each neighborhood its portion of the work, which if undone impairs and possibly destroys the whole;" and so internal improvements have become an unquestioned practice of the National Government.

... The exercise of the doctrine of implied powers has surrounded the written Constitution with a body of judicial decisions and legislative and executive practices which have grown to be as firm a part of our fundamental law as the written word of the instrument itself; and so it is that the Constitution has grown steadily and will grow steadily just as long and just as fast as the people themselves make progress. If this had not been so, the Constitution would have been a curse instead of a blessing. It would have been an iron band pressed around a young and growing tree, checking its growth and finally strangling it to death, instead of the bark which surrounds the trunk and expands as the great and substantial body within makes progress toward maturity. For the people are the real tree; the Nation is the real trunk; the Constitution is the vital encasement which sur-rounds and protects it, but which keeps progress with the growth of the tree itself.

... These inherent powers exist in the nature of government. They are a part of the thing called sovereignty, without which government could not exist. The government is a real and not a fictitious thing. It lives. It is not an automaton operated through written instruments alone. Whatever is necessary to its continued life and to its beneficent operation exists by virtue of the existence of the government itself. If you name government, you imply powers needful for that government's operation; and therefore when government is established that very act creates those powers which sleep till necessity awakens them.

. . . Whether you agree to this or not, all must concede that, *as a matter of fact*, both Congress and the Executive are almost daily exercising powers not mentioned in the Constitution. And it is certain that the only two theories upon which this exercise of power may be justified are either, first, that these powers are inherent in sovereignty, or else, second, that they are powers reserved to the people and exercised by the people through their agents.

. . . But the future of the American people is heavy with difficulties; so is all opportunity for great and splendid work. Increasing population; the knitting together by railway, telegraph and telephone of places most remote until the Republic is a single and consolidated community; the combination of capital and labor, which this development makes necessary; the shrinking of the very globe itself by these same agencies, until nations are neighbors and alien peoples are at elbow touch: the new problems and novel responsibilities, which all this brings: the still undreamed of emergencies of a yet undreamed of future—all these will demand of the American people all their resourcefulness, purity and power.

And the American people will solve and overcome them all if their hands are not fettered. The hands of the American people were not fettered, but armed with strength, when the Constitution was adopted. That free hand was not paralyzed, but connected with the mind and heart of the Nation . . . So is our Constitution a source of life and power—the spirit and soul of a mighty people's progress. And so God defend and God preserve the American Constitution—a living spirit and not a dead and fading parchment!

THEODORE ROOSEVELT, "NEW NATIONALISM"[50]

I stand for the square deal. But when I say that I am for the square deal, I mean not merely that I stand for fair play under the present rules of the game, but that I stand for having those rules changed so as to work for a more substantial equality of opportunity and of reward for equally good service.

. . . Now, this means that our government, national and state, must be freed from the sinister influence or control of special interests. Exactly as the special interests of cotton and slavery threatened our political integrity before the Civil War, so now the great special business interests too often control and corrupt the men and methods of government for their own profit. We must drive the special interests out of politics. That is one of our tasks to-day. Every special interest is entitled to justice—full, fair, and complete—and, now, mind you, if there were any attempt by mob-violence to plunder and work harm to the special interest, whatever it may be, that I most dislike, and the wealthy man, whomsoever he may be, for whom I have the greatest contempt, I would fight for him, and you would if you were worth your salt. He should have justice. For every special interest is entitled to justice, but not one is entitled to a vote in Congress, to a voice on the bench, or to representation in any public office. The Constitution guarantees protection to property, and we must make that promise good. But it does not give the right of suffrage to any corporation.

The true friend of property, the true conservative, is he who insists that property shall be the servant and not the master of the commonwealth; who insists that the creature of man's making shall be the servant and not the master of the man who made it. The citizens of the United States must effectively control the mighty commercial forces which they have called into being.

There can be no effective control of corporations while their political activity remains. To put an end to it will be neither a short nor an easy task, but it can be done.

We must have complete and effective publicity of corporate affairs, so that the people may know beyond peradventure whether the corporations obey the law and whether their management entitles them to the confidence of the public. It is necessary that laws should be passed to prohibit the use of corporate funds directly or indirectly for political purposes; it is still more necessary that such laws should be thoroughly enforced. Corporate expenditures for political purposes, and especially such expenditures by public service corporations, have supplied one of the principal sources of corruption in our political affairs.

It has become entirely clear that we must have government supervision of the capitalization, not only of public service corporations, including, particularly, railways, but of all corporations doing an interstate business. I do not wish to see the nation forced into the ownership of the railways if it can possibly be avoided, and the only alternative is thoroughgoing and effective legislation, which shall be based on a full knowledge of all the facts, including a physical valuation of property.

. . . The absence of effective State, and, especially, national, restraint upon unfair money-getting has tended to create a small class of enormously wealthy and economically powerful men, whose chief object is to hold and increase their power. The prime need to is to change the conditions which enable these men to accumulate power which it is not for the general welfare that they should hold or exercise. We grudge no man a fortune which represents his own power and sagacity, when exercised with entire regard to the welfare of his fellows.

. . . This, I know, implies a policy of a far more active governmental interference with social and economic conditions in this country than we have yet had, but I think we have got to face the fact that such an increase in governmental control is now necessary.

. . . Nothing is more true than that excess of every kind is followed by reaction; a fact which should be pondered by reformer and reactionary alike. We are face to face with new conceptions of the relations of property to human welfare, chiefly because certain advocates of the rights of property as against the rights of men have been pushing their claims too far. The man who wrongly holds that every human right is secondary to his profit must now give way to the advocate of human welfare, who rightly maintains that every man holds his property subject to the general right of the community to regulate its use to whatever degree the public welfare may require it.

But I think we may go still further. The right to regulate the use of wealth in the public interest is universally admitted. Let us admit also the right to regulate the terms and conditions of labor, which is the chief element of wealth, directly in the interest of the common good. The fundamental thing to do for every man is to give him a chance to reach a place in which he will make the greatest possible contribution to the public welfare. Understand what I say there. Give him a chance, not push him up if he will not be pushed. Help any man who stumbles; if he lies down, it is a poor job to try to carry him; but if he is a worthy man, try your best to see that he gets a chance to show the worth that is in him. No man can be a good citizen unless he has a wage more than sufficient to cover the bare cost of living, and hours of labor short enough so after his day's work is done he will have time and energy to bear his share in the management of the community, to help in carrying the general load. We keep countless men from being good citizens by the conditions of life by which we surround them. We need comprehensive workman's compensation acts, both State and national laws to regulate child labor and work for women, and, especially, we need in our common schools not merely education in book-learning, but also practical training for daily life and work. We need to enforce better sanitary conditions for our workers and to extend the use of safety appliances for workers in industry and commerce, both within and between the States. Also, friends, in the interest of the working man himself, we need to set our faces like flint against mob-violence just as against corporate greed; against violence and injustice and lawlessness by wage-workers just as much as against lawless cunning and greed and selfish arrogance of employers.

National efficiency has many factors. It is a necessary result of the principle of conservation widely applied. In the end, it will determine our failure or success as a nation. National efficiency has to do, not only with natural resources and with men, but it is equally concerned with institutions. The State must be made efficient for the work which concerns only the people of the State; and the nation for that which concerns all the people. There must remain no neutral ground to serve as a refuge for lawbreakers, and especially for lawbreakers of great wealth, who can hire the vulpine legal cunning which will teach them how to avoid both jurisdictions. It is a misfortune when the national legislature fails to do its duty in providing a national remedy, so that the only national activity is the purely negative activity of the judiciary forbidding the State to exercise power in the premises.

I do not ask for the over centralization; but I do ask that we work in a spirit of broad and far-reaching nationalism where we work for what concerns our people as a whole. We are all Americans. Our common interests are as broad as the continent. I speak to you here in Kansas exactly as I would speak in New York or Georgia, for the most vital problems are those which affect us all alike. The National Government belongs to the whole American people, and where the whole American people are interested, that interest can be guarded effectively only by the National Government. The betterment which we seek must be accomplished, I believe, mainly through the National Government.

The American people are right in demanding that New Nationalism, without which we cannot hope to deal with new problems. The New Nationalism puts the national need before sectional or personal advantage. It is impatient of the utter confusion that results from local legislatures attempting to treat national issues as local issues. It is still more impatient of the impotence which springs from over division of governmental powers, the impotence which makes it possible for local selfishness or for legal cunning, hired by wealthy special interests, to bring national activities to a deadlock. This New Nationalism regards the executive power as the steward of the public welfare. It demands of the judiciary that it shall be interested primarily in human welfare rather than in property, just as it demands that the representative body shall represent all the people rather than any one class or section of the people.

I believe in shaping the ends of government to protect property as well as human welfare. Normally, and in the long run, the ends are the same; but whenever the alternative must be faced, I am for men and not for property, as you were in the Civil War. I am far from underestimating the importance of dividends; but I rank dividends below human character. Again, I do not have any sympathy with the reformer who says he does not care for dividends. Of course, economic welfare is necessary, for a man must pull his own weight and be able to support his family. I know well that the reformers must not bring upon the people economic ruin, or the reforms themselves will go down in the ruin. But we must be ready to face temporary disaster, whether or not brought on by those who will war against us to the knife. Those who oppose reform will do well to remember that ruin in its worst form is inevitable if our national life brings us nothing better than swollen fortunes for the few and the triumph in both politics and business of a sordid and selfish materialism.

. . . The object of government is the welfare of the people. The material progress and prosperity of a nation are desirable chiefly so long as they lead to the moral and material welfare of all good citizens. Just in proportion as the average man and woman are honest, capable of sound judgment and high ideals, active in public affairs,—but, first of all, sound in their home, and the father and mother of healthy children whom they bring up well,—just so far, and no farther, we may count our civilization a success. We must have—I believe we have already—a genuine and permanent moral awakening, without which no wisdom of legislation or administration really means anything; and, on the other hand, we must try to secure the social and economic legislation without which any improvement due to purely moral agitation is necessarily evanescent. . . . No matter how honest and decent we are in our private lives, if we do not have the right kind of law and the right kind of administration of the law, we cannot go forward as a nation. That is imperative; but it must be an addition to, and not a substitute for, the qualities that make us good citizens. In the last analysis, the most important elements in any man's career must be the sum of those qualities which, in the aggregate, we speak of as character. If he has not got it, then no law that the wit of man can devise, no administration of the law by the boldest and strongest executive, will avail to help him. We must have the right kind of character—character that makes a man, first of all, a good man in the home, a good father, and a good husband—that makes a man a good neighbor. You must have that, and, then, in addition, you must have the kind of law and the kind of administration of the law which will give to those qualities in the private citizen the best possible chance for development. The prime problem of our nation is to get the right type of good citizenship, and, to get it, we must have progress, and our public men must be genuinely progressive.

DEMOCRATIC PARTY PLATFORM 1912[51]

Rights of the States

We believe in the preservation and maintenance in their full strength and integrity of the three co-ordinate branches of the Federal government—the executive, the legislative, and the judicial—each keeping within its own bounds and not encroaching upon the just powers of either of the others.

Believing that the most efficient results under our system of government are to be attained by the full exercise by the States of their reserved sovereign powers, we denounce as usurpation the efforts of our opponents to deprive the States of any of the rights reserved to them, and to enlarge and magnify by indirection the powers of the Federal government.

We insist upon the full exercise of all the powers of the Government, both State and national, to protect the people from injustice at the hands of those who seek to make the government a private asset in business. There is no twilight zone between the nation and the State in which exploiting interests can take refuge from both. It is as necessary that the Federal government shall exercise the powers delegated to it as it is that the States shall exercise the powers reserved to them, but we insist that Federal remedies for the regulation of interstate commerce and for the prevention of private monopoly, shall be added to, and not substituted for State remedies.

PROGRESSIVE PARTY PLATFORM 1912[52]

The conscience of the people, in a time of grave national problems, has called into being a new party, born of the nation's sense of justice. We of the Progressive party here dedicate ourselves to the fulfillment of the duty laid upon us by our fathers to maintain the government of the people, by the people and for the people whose foundations they laid.

We hold with Thomas Jefferson and Abraham Lincoln that the people are the masters of their Constitution, to fulfill its purposes and to safeguard it from those who, by perversion of its intent, would convert it into an instrument of injustice. In accordance with the needs of each generation the people must use their sovereign powers to establish and maintain equal opportunity and industrial justice, to secure which this Government was founded and without which no republic can endure.

This country belongs to the people who inhabit it. Its resources, its business, its institutions and its laws should be utilized, maintained or altered in whatever manner will best promote the general interest.

It is time to set the public welfare in the first place.

Amendment of Constitution

The Progressive party, believing that a free people should have the power from time to time to amend their fundamental law so as to adapt it progressively to the changing needs of the people, pledges itself to provide a more easy and expeditious method of amending the Federal Constitution.

Nation and State

Up to the limit of the Constitution, and later by amendment of the Constitution, if found necessary, we advocate bringing under effective national jurisdiction those problems which have expanded beyond reach of the individual States.

It is as grotesque as it is intolerable that the several States should by unequal laws in matter of common concern become competing commercial agencies, barter the lives of their children, the health of their women and the safety and well being of their working people for the benefit of their financial interests.

The extreme insistence on States' rights by the Democratic party in the Baltimore platform demonstrates anew its inability to understand the world into which it has survived or to administer the affairs of a union of States which have in all essential respects become one people.

HERBERT CROLY, *THE PROMISE OF AMERICAN LIFE*[53]

[The Constitution's] success has been due to the fact that its makers [i.e. The Framers], with all their apprehensions about democracy, were possessed of a wise and positive political faith. They believed in liberty. They believed that the essential condition of fruitful liberty was an efficient central government. They knew that no government could be efficient unless its powers equaled its responsibilities. They were willing to trust to such a government the security and the welfare of the American people. The Constitution has proved capable of development chiefly as the instrument of these positive political ideas. Thanks to the theory of implied powers, to the liberal construction of the Supreme Court during the first forty years of its existence, and to the results of the Civil War the Federal government has, on the whole, become more rather than less efficient as the national political organ of the American people. Almost from the start American life has grown more and more national in substance, in such wise that a rigid constitution which could not have been developed in a national direction would have been an increasing source of irritation and protest. But this reinforcement of the substance of American national life has, until recently, found an adequate expression in the increasing scope and efficiency of the Federal government. The Federalists had the insight to anticipate the kind of government which their country needed; and this was a great and a rare achievement—all the more so because they were obliged in a measure to impose it on their fellow-countrymen.

. . . There is, however, another face to the shield. The Constitution was the expression not only of a political faith, but also of political fears. It was wrought both as the organ of the national interest and as the bulwark of certain individual and local rights. The Federalists sought to surround private property, freedom of contract, and personal liberty with an impregnable legal fortress; and they were forced by their opponents to amend the original draft of the Constitution in order to include a still more stringent bill of individual and state rights. Now I am far from pretending that these legal restrictions have not had their value in American national history, and were not the expression of an essential element in the composition and the ideal of the American nation. The security of private property and personal liberty, and a proper distribution of activity between the local and the central governments, demanded at that time, and within limits still demand, adequate legal guarantees. It remains none the less true, however, that every popular government should in the end, and after a necessarily prolonged deliberation, possess the power of taking any action, which, in the opinion of a decisive majority of the people, is demanded by the public welfare. Such is not the case with the government organized under the Federal Constitution. In respect to certain fundamental provisions, which necessarily receive the most rigid interpretation on the part of the courts, it is practically unmodifiable. A very small percentage of the American people can in this respect permanently thwart the will of an enormous majority, and there can be no justification for such a condition on any possible theory of popular Sovereignty. This defect has not hitherto had very many practical inconveniences, but it is an absolute violation of the theory and the spirit of American democratic institutions. The time may come when the fulfillment of a justifiable democratic purpose may demand the limitation of certain rights, to which the Constitution affords such absolute guarantees; and in that case the American democracy might be forced to seek by revolutionary means the accomplishment of a result which should be attainable under the law.

. . . The transformation of the old sense of a glorious national destiny into the sense of a serious national purpose will inevitably tend to make the popular realization of the Promise of American life both more explicit and more serious. As long as Americans believed they were able to fulfill a noble national Promise merely by virtue of maintaining intact a set of political institutions and by the vigorous individual pursuit of private ends, their allegiance to their national fulfillment remained more a matter of words than of deeds; but now that they are being aroused from their patriotic slumber, the effect is inevitably to disentangle the national idea and to give it more dignity. The redemption of the national Promise has become a cause for which the good American must fight, and the cause for which a man fights is a cause which he more than ever values. The American idea is no longer to be propagated merely by multiplying the children of the West and by granting ignorant aliens permission to vote. Like all sacred causes, it must be propagated by the Word and by that right arm of the Word, which is the Sword.

The more enlightened reformers are conscious of the additional dignity and value which the popularity of reform has bestowed upon the American idea, but they still fail to realize the deeper implications of their own program.

In abandoning the older conception of an automatic fulfillment of our national destiny, they have abandoned more of the traditional American point of view than they are aware. The traditional American optimistic fatalism was not of accidental origin, and it cannot be abandoned without involving in its fall some other important ingredients in the accepted American tradition. Not only was it dependent on economic conditions which prevailed until comparatively recent times, but it has been associated with certain erroneous but highly cherished political theories. It has been wrought into the fabric of our popular economic and political ideas to such an extent that its overthrow necessitates a partial revision of some of the most important articles in the traditional American creed.

The extent and the character of this revision may be inferred from a brief consideration of the effect upon the substance of our national Promise of an alteration in its proposed method of fulfillment. The substance of our national Promise has consisted, as we have seen, of an improving popular economic condition, guaranteed by democratic political institutions, and resulting in moral and social amelioration. These manifold benefits were to be obtained merely by liberating the enlightened self-interest of the American people. The beneficent result followed inevitably from the action of wholly selfish motives—provided, of course, the democratic political system of equal rights was maintained in its integrity. The fulfillment of the American Promise was considered inevitable because it was based upon a combination of self-interest and the natural goodness of human nature. On the other hand, if the fulfillment of our national Promise can no longer be considered inevitable, if it must be considered as equivalent to a conscious national purpose instead of an inexorable national destiny, the implication necessarily is that the trust reposed in individual self-interest has been in some measure betrayed. No pre-established harmony can then exist between the free and abundant satisfaction of private needs and the accomplishment of a morally and socially desirable result. The Promise of American life is to be fulfilled—not merely by a maximum amount of economic freedom, but by a certain measure of discipline; not merely by the abundant satisfaction of individual desires, but by a large measure of individual subordination and self-denial. And this necessity of subordinating the satisfaction of individual desires to the fulfillment of a national purpose is attached particularly to the absorbing occupation of the American people,—the occupation, viz.: of accumulating wealth. The automatic fulfillment of the American national Promise is to be abandoned, if at all, precisely because the traditional American confidence in individual freedom has resulted in a morally and socially undesirable distribution of wealth.

. . . The consequences, then, of converting our American national destiny into a national purpose are beginning to be revolutionary. When the Promise of American life is conceived as a national ideal, whose fulfillment is a matter of artful and laborious work, the effect thereof is substantially to identify the national purpose with the social problem. What the American people of the present and the future have really been promised by our patriotic prophecies is an attempt to solve that problem. They have been promised on American soil comfort, prosperity, and the opportunity for self-improvement; and the lesson of the existing crisis is that such a Promise can never be redeemed by an indiscriminate individual scramble for wealth. The individual competition, even when it starts under fair conditions and rules, results, not only, as it should, in the triumph of the strongest, but in the attempt to perpetuate the victory; and it is this attempt which must be recognized and forestalled in the interest of the American national purpose. The way to realize a purpose is, not to leave it to chance, but to keep it loyally in mind, and adopt means proper to the importance and the difficulty of the task. No voluntary association of individuals, resourceful and disinterested though they be, is competent to assume the responsibility. The problem belongs to the American national democracy, and its solution must be attempted chiefly by means of official national action.

MISSOURI v. HOLLAND[54]

. . . The Treaty of August 16, 1916, 39 Stat. 1702, with Great Britain, providing for the protection, by close seasons and in other ways, of migratory birds in the United States and Canada, and . . . as a necessary and proper means of effectuating the treaty, and the treaty and statute, by bringing such birds within the paramount protection and regulation of the Government do not infringe property rights or sovereign powers respecting such birds reserved to the States by the Tenth Amendment.

This is a bill in equity brought by the State of Missouri to prevent a game warden of the United States from attempting to enforce the Migratory Bird Treaty Act of July 3, 1918 . . . The ground of the bill is that the statute is an unconstitutional interference with the rights reserved to the States by the Tenth Amendment, and that the acts of the defendant done and threatened under that authority invade the sovereign right of the State and contravene its will manifested in statutes. The State also alleges a pecuniary interest, as owner of the wild birds within its borders and otherwise, admitted by the Government to be sufficient, but it is enough that the bill is a reasonable and proper means to assert the alleged *quasi* sovereign rights of a State . . .

On December 8, 1916, a treaty between the United States and Great Britain . . . recited that many species of birds in their annual migrations traversed certain parts of the United States and of Canada, that they were of great value . . . [and] provided for specified close seasons and protection in other forms.

[I]t is not enough to refer to the Tenth Amendment, reserving the powers not delegated to the United States, because, by Article II, § 2, the power to make treaties is delegated expressly, and by Article VI treaties . . . are declared the supreme law of the land. . . .

It is said that a treaty cannot be valid if it infringes the Constitution, that there are limits, therefore, to the treaty-making power, and that one such limit is that what an act of Congress could not do unaided, in derogation of the powers reserved to the States, a treaty cannot do . . . What was said in that case with regard to the powers of the States applies with equal force to the powers of the nation in cases where the States individually are incompetent to act. . . .

The State, as we have intimated, founds its claim of exclusive authority upon an assertion of title to migratory birds, an assertion that is embodied in statute. No doubt it is true that, as between a State and its inhabitants, the State may regulate the killing and sale of such birds, but it does not follow that its authority is exclusive of paramount powers. . . . Wild birds are not in the possession of anyone, and possession is the beginning of ownership. . . . we cannot put the case of the State upon higher ground than that the treaty deals with creatures that, for the moment are within the state borders, that it must be carried out by officers of the United States within the same territory, and that, but for the treaty, the State would be free to regulate this subject itself.

. . . Here, a national interest of very nearly the first magnitude is involved. It can be protected only by national action in concert with that of another power. The subject matter is only transitorily within the State, and has no permanent habitat therein. But for the treaty and the statute, there soon might be no birds for any powers to deal with. We see nothing in the Constitution that compels the Government to sit by while a food supply is cut off and the protectors of our forests and our crops are destroyed. It is not sufficient to rely upon the States. The reliance is vain, and were it otherwise, the question is whether the United States is forbidden to act. We are of opinion that the treaty and statute must be upheld.

FRANKLIN ROOSEVELT, FIRST INAUGURAL ADDRESS[55]

I am certain that my fellow Americans expect that on my induction into the Presidency I will address them with a candor and a decision which the present situation of our Nation impels. This is preeminently the time to speak the truth, the whole truth, frankly and boldly. Nor need we shrink from honestly facing conditions in our country today. This great Nation will endure as it has endured, will revive and will prosper. So, first of all, let me assert my firm belief that the only thing we have to fear is fear itself—nameless, unreasoning, unjustified terror which paralyzes needed efforts to convert retreat into advance. In every dark hour of our national life a leadership of frankness and vigor has met with that understanding and support of the people themselves which is essential to victory. I am convinced that you will again give that support to leadership in these critical days.

. . . This Nation asks for action, and action now.

. . . Hand in hand with this we must frankly recognize the overbalance of population in our industrial centers and, by engaging on a national scale in a redistribution, endeavor to provide a better use of the land for those best fitted for the land. The task can be helped by definite efforts to raise the values of agricultural products and with this the power to purchase the output of our cities. It can be helped by preventing realistically the tragedy of the growing loss through foreclosure of our small homes and our farms. It can be helped by insistence that the Federal, State, and local governments act forthwith on the demand that their cost be drastically reduced. It can be helped by the unifying of relief activities which today are often scattered, uneconomical, and unequal. It can be helped by national planning for and supervision of all forms of transportation and of communications and other utilities which have a definitely public character. There are many ways in which it can be helped, but it can never be helped merely by talking about it. We must act and act quickly.

. . . If I read the temper of our people correctly, we now realize as we have never realized before our interdependence on each other; that we can not merely take but we must give as well; that if we are to go forward, we must move as a trained and loyal army willing to sacrifice for the good of a common discipline, because without such discipline no progress is made, no leadership becomes effective. We are, I know, ready and willing to submit our lives and property to such discipline, because it makes possible a leadership which aims at a larger good. This I propose to offer, pledging that the larger purposes will bind upon us all as a sacred obligation with a unity of duty hitherto evoked only in time of armed strife.

With this pledge taken, I assume unhesitatingly the leadership of this great army of our people dedicated to a disciplined attack upon our common problems.

Action in this image and to this end is feasible under the form of government which we have inherited from our ancestors. Our Constitution is so simple and practical that it is possible always to meet extraordinary needs by changes in emphasis and arrangement without loss of essential form. That is why our constitutional system has proved itself the most superbly enduring political mechanism the modern world has produced. It has met every stress of vast expansion of territory, of foreign wars, of bitter internal strife, of world relations.

It is to be hoped that the normal balance of executive and legislative authority may be wholly adequate to meet the unprecedented task before us. But it may be that an unprecedented demand and need for undelayed action may call for temporary departure from that normal balance of public procedure.

I am prepared under my constitutional duty to recommend the measures that a stricken nation in the midst of a stricken world may require. These measures, or such other measures as the Congress may build out of its experience and wisdom, I shall seek, within my constitutional authority, to bring to speedy adoption.

But in the event that the Congress shall fail to take one of these two courses, and in the event that the national emergency is still critical, I shall not evade the clear course of duty that will then confront me. I shall ask the Congress for the one remaining instrument to meet the crisis—broad Executive power to wage a war against the emergency, as great as the power that would be given to me if we were in fact invaded by a foreign foe.

For the trust reposed in me I will return the courage and the devotion that befit the time. I can do no less.

We face the arduous days that lie before us in the warm courage of the national unity; with the clear consciousness of seeking old and precious moral values; with the clean satisfaction that comes from the stem performance of duty by old and young alike. We aim at the assurance of a rounded and permanent national life.

FRANKLIN D. ROOSEVELT, MESSAGE TO THE FIFTH ANNUAL WOMEN'S CONFERENCE[56]

. . . If we limit government to the functions of merely punishing the criminal after crimes have been committed, of gathering up the wreckage of society after the devastation of an economic collapse, or of fighting a war that reason might have prevented, then government fails to satisfy those urgent human purposes, which, in essence, gave it its beginning and provide its present justification.

Modern government has become an instrument through which citizens may apply their reasoned methods of prevention in addition to methods of correction. Government has become one of the most important instruments for the prevention and cure of these evils of society which I have mentioned. Its concern at the moment is unabated. It conceives of itself as an instrument. through which social justice may prevail more greatly among men. In the determination of the standards that make up social justice, the widest discussion is necessary. In the last analysis, government can be no more than the collective wisdom of its citizens. The duty of citizens is to increase this collective wisdom by common counsel, by the discovery and consideration of facts relating to the common life, and by the discouragement of those who for selfish ends or through careless speech distort facts and disseminate untruth.

LYNDON B. JOHNSON, "GREAT SOCIETY SPEECH"[57]

. . . The purpose of protecting the life of our Nation and preserving the liberty of our citizens is to pursue the happiness of our people. Our success in that pursuit is the test of our success as a Nation.

. . . The Great Society rests on abundance and liberty for all. It demands an end to poverty and racial injustice, to which we are totally committed in our time. But that is just the beginning. The Great Society is a place where every child can find knowledge to enrich his mind and to enlarge his talents. It is a place where leisure is a welcome chance to build and reflect, not a feared cause of boredom and restlessness. It is a place where the city of man serves not only the needs of the body and the demands of commerce but the desire for beauty and the hunger for community.

It is a place where man can renew contact with nature. It is a place which honors creation for its own sake and for what it adds to the understanding of the race. It is a place where men are more concerned with the quality of their goals than the quantity of their goods.

But most of all, the Great Society is not a safe harbor, a resting place, a final objective, a finished work. It is a challenge constantly renewed, beckoning us toward a destiny where the meaning of our lives matches the marvelous products of our labor.

So I want to talk to you today about three places where we begin to build the Great Society—in our cities, in our countryside, and in our classrooms.

Many of you will live to see the day, perhaps 50 years from now, when there will be 400 million Americans—four-fifths of them in urban areas. In the remainder of this century urban population will double, city land will double, and we will have to build homes, highways, and facilities equal to all those built since this country was first settled. So in the next 40 years we must re-build the entire urban United States.

. . . A second place where we begin to build the Great Society is in our countryside. We have always prided ourselves on being not only America the strong and America the free, but America the beautiful. Today that beauty is in danger. The water we drink, the food we eat, the very air that we breathe, are threatened with pollution. Our parks are overcrowded, our seashores over-burdened. Green fields and dense forests are disappearing.

. . . For once the battle is lost, once our natural splendor is destroyed, it can never be recaptured. And once man can no longer walk with beauty or wonder at nature his spirit will wither and his sustenance be wasted.

A third place to build the Great Society is in the classrooms of America. There your children's lives will be shaped. Our society will not be great until every young mind is set free to scan the farthest reaches of thought and imagination. We are still far from that goal.

Today, 8 million adult Americans, more than the entire population of Michigan, have not finished 5 years of school. Nearly 20 million have not finished 8 years of school. Nearly 54 million—more than one quarter of all America—have not even finished high school.

Each year more than 100,000 high school graduates, with proved ability, do not enter college because they cannot afford it. And if we cannot educate today's youth, what will we do in 1970 when elementary school enrollment will be 5 million greater than 1960? And high school enrollment will rise by 5 million. College enrollment will increase by more than 3 million.

In many places, classrooms are overcrowded and curricula are outdated. Most of our qualified teachers are underpaid, and many of our paid teachers are unqualified. So we must give every child a place to sit and a teacher to learn from. Poverty must not be a bar to learning, and learning must offer an escape from poverty.

But more classrooms and more teachers are not enough. We must seek an educational system which grows in excellence as it grows in size. This means better training for our teachers. It means preparing youth to enjoy their hours of leisure as well as their hours of labor. It means exploring new techniques of teaching, to find new ways to stimulate the love of learning and the capacity for creation.

These are three of the central issues of the Great Society. While our Government has many programs directed at those issues, I do not pretend that we have the full answer to those problems.

But I do promise this: We are going to assemble the best thought and the broadest knowledge from all over the world to find those answers for America. I intend to establish working groups to prepare a series of White House conferences and meetings—on the cities, on natural beauty, on the quality of education, and on other emerging challenges. And from these meetings and from this inspiration and from these studies we will begin to set our course toward the Great Society.

The solution to these problems does not rest on a massive program in Washington, nor can it rely solely on the strained resources of local authority.

They require us to create new concepts of cooperation, a creative federalism, between the National Capital and the leaders of local communities.

. . . For better or for worse, your generation has been appointed by history to deal with those problems and to lead America toward a new age. You have the chance never before afforded to any people in any age. You can help build a society where the demands of morality, and the needs of the spirit, can be realized in the life of the Nation.

So, will you join in the battle to give every citizen the full equality which God enjoins and the law requires, whatever his belief, or race, or the color of his skin?

Will you join in the battle to give every citizen an escape from the crushing weight of poverty?

Will you join in the battle to make it possible for all nations to live in enduring peace—as neighbors and not as mortal enemies?

Will you join in the battle to build the Great Society, to prove that our material progress is only the foundation on which we will build a richer life of mind and spirit?

There are those timid souls who say this battle cannot be won; that we are condemned to a soulless wealth. I do not agree. We have the power to shape the civilization that we want. But we need your will, your labor, your hearts, if we are to build that kind of society.

RICHARD NIXON, "ADDRESS TO THE NATION ON DOMESTIC PROGRAMS"[58]

Every time I return to the United States after such a trip, I realize how fortunate we are to live in this rich land. We have the world's most advanced industrial economy, the greatest wealth ever known to man, the fullest measure of freedom ever enjoyed by any people, anywhere.

Yet we, too, have an urgent need to modernize our institutions—and our need is no less than theirs.

We face an urban crisis, a social crisis-and at the same time, a crisis of confidence in the capacity of government to do its job.

A third of a century of centralizing power and responsibility in Washington has produced a bureaucratic monstrosity, cumbersome, unresponsive, ineffective.

A third of a century of social experiment has left us a legacy of entrenched programs that have outlived their time or outgrown their purposes.

A third of a century of unprecedented growth and change has strained our institutions, and raised serious questions about whether they are still adequate to the times.

It is no accident, therefore, that we find increasing skepticism—and not only among our young people, but among citizens everywhere—about the continuing capacity of government to master the challenges we face.

Nowhere has the failure of government been more tragically apparent than in its efforts to help the poor and especially in its system of public welfare.

... My purpose tonight, however, is not to review the past record, but to present a new set of reforms—a new set of proposals—a new and drastically different approach to the way in which government cares for those in need, and to the way the responsibilities are shared between the State and the Federal Government.

I have chosen to do so in a direct report to the people because these proposals call for public decisions of the first importance; because they represent a fundamental change in the Nation's approach to one of its most pressing social problems; and because, quite deliberately, they also represent the first major reversal of the trend toward ever more centralization of government in Washington, D.C. After a third of a century of power flowing from the people and the States to Washington it is time for a New Federalism in which power, funds, and responsibility will flow from Washington to the States and to the people.

Welfare

Whether measured by the anguish of the poor themselves, or by the drastically mounting burden on the taxpayer, the present welfare system has to be judged a colossal failure.

Our States and cities find themselves sinking in a welfare quagmire, as caseloads increase, as costs escalate, and as the welfare system stagnates enterprise and perpetuates dependency.

What began on a small scale in the depression 30's has become a huge monster in the prosperous 60's. And the tragedy is not only that it is bringing States and cities to the brink of financial disaster, but also that it is failing to meet the elementary human, social, and financial needs of the poor.

It breaks up homes. It often penalizes work. It robs recipients of dignity. And it grows.

... What I am proposing is that the Federal Government build a foundation under the income of every American family with dependent children that cannot care for itself—and wherever in America that family may live.

Manpower Training

Therefore, I am also sending a message to Congress calling for a complete overhaul of the Nation's manpower training services.

The Federal Government's job training programs have been a terrible tangle of confusion and waste.

To remedy the confusion, arbitrariness, and rigidity of the present system, the new Manpower Training Act would basically do three things.

- It would pull together the jumble of programs that presently exist, and equalize standards of eligibility.
- It would provide flexible funding-so that Federal money would follow the demands of labor and industry, and flow into those programs that people most want and most need.
- It would decentralize administration, gradually moving it away from the Washington bureaucracy and turning it over to States and localities.

In terms of its symbolic importance, I can hardly overemphasize this last point. For the first time, applying the principles of the New Federalism, administration of a major established Federal program would be turned over to the States and local governments, recognizing that they are in a position to do the job better.

For years, thoughtful Americans have talked of the need to decentralize Government. The time has come to begin.

Revenue Sharing

We come now to a proposal which I consider profoundly important to the future of our Federal system of shared responsibilities. When we speak of poverty or jobs or opportunity or making government more effective or getting it closer to the people, it brings us directly to the financial plight of our States and cities.

We can no longer have effective government at any level unless we have it at all levels. There is too much to be done for the cities to do it alone, for Washington to do it alone, or for the States to do it alone.

For a third of a century, power and responsibility have flowed toward Washington, and Washington has taken for its own the best sources of revenue.

We intend to reverse this tide, and to turn back to the States a greater measure of responsibility—not as a way of avoiding problems, but as a better way of solving problems.

Along with this would go a share of Federal revenues. I shall propose to the Congress next week that a set portion of the revenues from Federal income taxes be remitted directly to the States, with a minimum of Federal restrictions on how those dollars are to be used, and with a requirement that a percentage of them be channeled through for the use of local governments.

The funds provided under this program will not be great in the first year. But the principle will have been established, and the amounts will increase as our budgetary situation improves.

This start on revenue sharing is a step toward what I call the New Federalism. It is a gesture of faith in America's State and local governments and in the principle of democratic self-government.

RONALD REAGAN, FIRST INAUGURAL ADDRESS[59]

The business of our nation goes forward. These United States are confronted with an economic affliction of great proportions. We suffer from the longest and one of the worst sustained inflations in our national history. It distorts our economic decisions, penalizes thrift, and crushes the struggling young and the fixed-income elderly alike. It threatens to shatter the lives of millions of our people.

. . . In this present crisis, government is not the solution to our problem; government is the problem.

From time to time, we have been tempted to believe that society has become too complex to be managed by self-rule, that government by an elite group is superior to government for, by, and of the people. But if no one among us is capable of governing himself, then who among us has the capacity to govern someone else? All of us together, in and out of government, must bear the burden. The solutions we seek must be equitable, with no one group singled out to pay a higher price.

. . . It is my intention to curb the size and influence of the Federal establishment and to demand recognition of the distinction between the powers granted to the Federal Government and those reserved to the States or to the people. All of us need to be reminded that the Federal Government did not create the States; the States created the Federal Government.

Now, so there will be no misunderstanding, it is not my intention to do away with government. It is, rather, to make it work-work with us, not over us; to stand by our side, not ride on our back. Government can and must provide opportunity, not smother it; foster productivity, not stifle it.

If we look to the answer as to why, for so many years, we achieved so much, prospered as no other people on Earth, it was because here, in this land, we unleashed the energy and individual genius of man to a greater extent than has ever been done before. Freedom and the dignity of the individual have been more available and assured here than in any other place on Earth. The price for this freedom at times has been high, but we have never been unwilling to pay that price.

It is no coincidence that our present troubles parallel and are proportionate to the intervention and intrusion in our lives that result from unnecessary and excessive growth of government. It is time for us to realize that we are too great a nation to limit ourselves to small dreams. We are not, as some would have us believe, loomed to an inevitable decline. I do not believe in a fate that will all on us no matter what we do. I do believe in a fate that will fall on us if we do nothing. So, with all the creative energy at our command, let us begin an era of national renewal. Let us renew our determination, our courage, and our strength. And let us renew; our faith and our hope.

RONALD REAGAN, "REMARKS IN ATLANTA, GEORGIA, AT THE ANNUAL CONVENTION OF THE NATIONAL CONFERENCE OF STATE LEGISLATURES"[60]

. . . I believe our campaign to give the government back to the people hit a nerve deeper and quicker than anyone first realized. The government in Washington has finally heard what the people have been saying for years: "We need relief from oppression of big government. We don't want to wait any longer. We want tax relief and we want it now."

The people of this country are saying that we've been on a road that they don't want to stay on. Now we're on a road that leads to growth and opportunity, to increasing productivity and an increasing standard of living for anyone. It was a road once that led to the driveway of a home that could be afforded by all kinds of Americans, not just the affluent.

. . . With the help of these same Americans and with the help of the States, one of our next goals is to renew the concept of federalism. The changes here will be as exciting and even more profound in the long run than the changes produced in the economic package.

This Nation has never fully debated the fact that over the past 40 years, federalism—one of the underlying principles of our Constitution—has nearly disappeared as a guiding force in American politics and government. My administration intends to initiate such a debate, and no more appropriate forum can be found than before the National Conference of State Legislatures.

My administration is committed heart and soul to the broad principles of American federalism which are outlined in the Federalist Papers of Hamilton, Madison, and Jay and, as your President told you, they're in that tenth article of the Bill of Rights.

The designers of our Constitution realized that in federalism there's diversity. The Founding Fathers saw the federal system as constructed something like a masonry wall: The States are the bricks, the National Government is the mortar. For the structure to stand plumb with the Constitution, there must be a proper mix of that brick and mortar. Unfortunately, over the years, many people have come increasingly to believe that Washington is the whole wall—a wall that, incidentally, leans, sags, and bulges under its own weight.

The traumatic experience of the Great Depression provided the impetus and the rationale for a government that was more centralized than America had previously known. You had to have lived then, during those depression years, to understand the drabness of that period.

FDR brought the colors of hope and confidence to the era and I, like millions of others, became an enthusiastic New Dealer. We followed FDR because he offered a mix of ideas and movement. A former Governor himself, I believe that FDR would today be amazed and appalled at the growth of the Federal Government's power. Too many in government in recent years have invoked his name to justify what they were doing, forgetting that it was FDR who said, "In the conduct of public utilities, of banks, of insurance, of agriculture, of education, of social welfare—Washington must be discouraged from interfering."

Well, today the Federal Government takes too much taxes from the people, too much authority from the States, and too much liberty with the Constitution.

Americans have at last begun to realize that the steady flow of power and tax dollars to Washington has something to do with the fact that things don't seem to work anymore. The Federal Government is overloaded, musclebound, if you will, having assumed more responsibilities than it can properly manage. There's been a loss of accountability as the distinction between the duties of the Federal and State governments have blurred, and the Federal Government is so far removed from the people that Members of Congress spend less time legislating than cutting through bureaucratic red tape for their constituents.

Block grants are designed to eliminate burdensome reporting requirements and regulations, unnecessary administrative costs, and program duplication. Block grants are not a mere strategy in our budget as some have suggested; they stand on their own as a federalist tool for transferring power back to the State and to the local level.

In normal times, what we've managed to get through the Congress concerning block grants would be a victory. Yet, we did not provide the States with the degree of freedom in dealing with the budget cuts that we had ardently hoped we could get. We got some categorical grants into block grants, but many of our block grant proposals are still up on the Hill, and that doesn't mean the end of the dream. Together, you and I will be going back and back and back until we obtain the flexibility that you need and deserve.

The ultimate objective, as I have told some of you in meetings in Washington, is to use block grants, however, as only a bridge, leading to the day when you'll have not only the responsibility for the programs that properly belong at the State level, but you will have the tax sources now usurped by

Washington returned to you, ending that round-trip of the peoples' money to Washington, where a carrying charge is deducted, and then back to you.

Now, we also are reviving the cause of federalism by cutting back on unnecessary regulations. The Federal Register is the road atlas of new Federal regulations, and for the past 10 years, all roads have led to Washington . . . Accepting a government grant with its accompanying rules is like marrying a girl and finding out her entire family is moving in with you before the honeymoon.

. . . Now, one of their goals will be recommending allowing States to fulfill the creative role they once played as laboratories of economic and social development. North Dakota enacted one of the country's first child labor laws. Wyoming gave the vote to women decades before it was adopted nationally. And California, during the term of a Governor Reagan—I wonder whatever became of him—[laughter]—we enacted a clear air act that was tougher than the Federal measure that followed years later.

And, incidentally, while it's true that I do not believe in the equal rights amendment as the best way to end discrimination against women, I believe such discrimination must be eliminated. And in California, we found 14 State statutes that did so discriminate. We wiped those statutes off the books. Now, if you won't think me presumptuous, may I suggest that when you go back to your statehouses you might take a look at the statutes and regulations in your respective States.

The constitutional concept of federalism recognizes and protects diversity. Today, federalism is one check that is out of balance as the diversity of the States has given way to the uniformity of Washington. And our task is to restore the constitutional symmetry between the central Government and the States and to reestablish the freedom and variety of federalism. In the process, we'll return the citizen to his rightful place in the scheme of our democracy, and that place is close to his government. We must never forget it. It is not the Federal Government or the States who retain the power—the people retain the power. And I hope that you'll join me in strengthening the fabric of federalism. If the Federal Government is more responsive to the States, the States will be more responsive to the people, and that's the reason that you, as State legislators, and I, as President, are in office—not to retain power but to serve the people.

NEW YORK v. US[61]

[JUSTICE Sandra O'CONNOR] Congress exercises its conferred powers subject to the limitations contained in the Constitution. Thus, for example, under the Commerce Clause Congress may regulate publishers engaged in

interstate commerce, but Congress is constrained in the exercise of that power
by the First Amendment. The Tenth Amendment likewise restrains the power
of Congress, but this limit is not derived from the text of the Tenth Amendment itself, which, as we have discussed is essentially a tautology. Instead,
the Tenth Amendment confirms that the power of the Federal Government is
subject to limits that may, in a given instance, reserve power to the States.
The Tenth Amendment thus directs us to determine, as in this case, whether
an incident of state sovereignty is protected by a limitation on an Article
I power.

. . . This framework has been sufficiently flexible over the past two centuries to allow for enormous changes in the nature of government. The Federal
Government undertakes activities today that would have been unimaginable
to the Framers in two senses; first, because the Framers would not have
conceived that *any* government would conduct such activities; and second,
because the Framers would not have believed that the *Federal* Government,
rather than the States, would assume such responsibilities. Yet the powers
conferred upon the Federal Government by the Constitution were phrased
in language broad enough to allow for the expansion of the Federal Government's role. Among the provisions of the Constitution that have been particularly important in this regard, three concern us here.

. . . In the end, the Convention opted for a Constitution in which Congress
would exercise its legislative authority directly over individuals rather than
over States; for a variety of reasons, it rejected the New Jersey Plan in favor
of the Virginia Plan.

In providing for a stronger central government, therefore, the Framers
explicitly chose a Constitution that confers upon Congress the power to regulate individuals, not States. . . .

This is not to say that Congress lacks the ability to encourage a State to
regulate in a particular way, or that Congress may not hold out incentives to
the States as a method of influencing a State's policy choices.

By contrast, where the Federal Government compels States to regulate, the
accountability of both state and federal officials is diminished. If the citizens
of New York, for example, do not consider that making provision for the
disposal of radioactive waste is in their best interest, they may elect state
officials who share their view. That view can always be pre-empted under the
Supremacy Clause if it is contrary to the national view, but in such a case it
is the Federal Government that makes the decision in full view of the public,
and it will be federal officials that suffer the consequences if the decision
turns out to be detrimental or unpopular.

. . . But where the Federal Government directs the States to regulate, it may
be state officials who will bear the brunt of public disapproval, while the federal officials who devised the regulatory program may remain insulated from

the electoral ramifications of their decision. Accountability is thus diminished when, due to federal coercion, elected state officials cannot regulate in accordance with the views of the local electorate in matters not pre-empted by federal regulation.

. . . The Act's first set of incentives, in which Congress has conditioned grants to the States upon the States' attainment of a series of milestones, is thus well within the authority of Congress under the Commerce and Spending Clauses. Because the first set of incentives is supported by affirmative constitutional grants of power to Congress, it is not inconsistent with the Tenth Amendment.

. . . In the second set of incentives, Congress has authorized States and regional compacts with disposal sites gradually to increase the cost of access to the sites, and then to deny access altogether, to radioactive waste generated in States that do not meet federal deadlines.

. . . The Act's second set of incentives thus represents a conditional exercise of Congress' commerce power, along the lines of those we have held to be within Congress' authority. As a result, the second set of incentives does not intrude on the sovereignty reserved to the States by the Tenth Amendment.

. . . The take title provision is of a different character. This third so-called "incentive" offers States, as an alternative to regulating pursuant to Congress' direction, the option of taking title to and possession of the low level radioactive waste generated within their borders and becoming liable for all damages waste generators suffer as a result of the States' failure to do so promptly. In this provision, Congress has crossed the line distinguishing encouragement from coercion.

. . . The take title provision offers state governments a "choice" of either accepting ownership of waste or regulating according to the instructions of Congress. Respondents do not claim that the Constitution would authorize Congress to impose either option as a freestanding requirement. On one hand, the Constitution would not permit Congress simply to transfer radioactive waste from generators to state governments. Such a forced transfer, standing alone, would in principle be no different than a congressionally compelled subsidy from state governments to radioactive waste producers. The same is true of the provision requiring the States to become liable for the generators' damages. Standing alone, this provision would be indistinguishable from an Act of Congress directing the States to assume the liabilities of certain state residents. Either type of federal action would "commandeer" state governments into the service of federal regulatory purposes, and would for this reason be inconsistent with the Constitution's division of authority between federal and state governments. On the other hand, the second alternative held out to state governments-regulating pursuant to Congress' direction—would, standing alone, present a simple command to state governments to implement legislation enacted by Congress. As we have seen, the Constitution does not empower Congress to subject state governments to this type of instruction.

Because an instruction to state governments to take title to waste, standing alone, would be beyond the authority of Congress, and because a direct order to regulate, standing alone, would also be beyond the authority of Congress, it follows that Congress lacks the power to offer the States a choice between the two.

. . . While the Framers no doubt endowed Congress with the power to regulate interstate commerce in order to avoid further instances of the inter-state trade disputes that were common under the Articles of Confederation, the Framers did *not* intend that Congress should exercise that power through the mechanism of mandating state regulation. The Constitution established Congress as "a superintending authority over the reciprocal trade" among the States, by empowering Congress to regulate that trade directly, not by autho-rizing Congress to issue trade-related orders to state governments. As Madi-son and Hamilton explained, "a sovereignty over sovereigns, a government over governments, a legislation for communities, as contradistinguished from individuals, as it is a solecism in theory, so in practice it is subversive of the order and ends of civil polity."

. . . How can a federal statute be found an unconstitutional infringement of state sovereignty when state officials consented to the statute's enactment?

The answer follows from an understanding of the fundamental purpose served by our Government's federal structure. The Constitution does not protect the sovereignty of States for the benefit of the States or state govern-ments as abstract political entities, or even for the benefit of the public offi-cials governing the States. To the contrary, the Constitution divides authority between federal and state governments for the protection of individuals. State sovereignty is not just an end in itself: "Rather, federalism secures to citizens the liberties that derive from the diffusion of sovereign power."

. . . Where Congress exceeds its authority relative to the States, therefore, the departure from the constitutional plan cannot be ratified by the "consent" of state officials . . . Where state officials purport to submit to the direction of Congress in this manner, federalism is hardly being advanced.

. . . Petitioners also contend that the Act is inconsistent with the Constitu-tion's Guarantee Clause, which directs the United States to "guarantee to every State in this Union a Republican Form of Government." U. S. Const., Art. IV; § 4.

. . . Even if we assume that petitioners' claim is justiciable, neither the monetary incentives provided by the Act nor the possibility that a State's waste producers may find themselves excluded from the disposal sites of another State can reasonably be said to deny any State a republican form of government. As we have seen, these two incentives represent permissible conditional exercises of Congress' authority under the Spending and Commerce Clauses respectively, in forms that have now grown commonplace. Under each, Congress offers the States a legitimate choice rather than issuing an unavoidable command. The States thereby retain the ability to set their legislative agendas; state government officials remain accountable to the local electorate. The twin threats imposed by the first two challenged provisions of the Act hat New York may miss out on a share of federal spending or that those generating radioactive waste within New York may lose out-of-state disposal outlets-do not pose any realistic risk of altering the form or the method of functioning of New York's government. Thus even indulging the assumption that the Guarantee Clause provides a basis upon which a State or its subdivisions may sue to enjoin the enforcement of a federal statute, petitioners have not made out such a claim in these cases.

PRINTZ, SHERIFF/CORONER, RAVALLI COUNTY, MONTANA v. UNITED STATES[62]

[JUSTICE Antonin SCALIA] The question presented in these cases is whether certain interim provisions of the Brady Handgun Violence Prevention Act commanding state and local law enforcement officers to conduct background checks on prospective handgun purchasers and to perform certain related tasks, violate the Constitution.

. . . it is apparent that the Brady Act purports to direct state law enforcement officers to participate, albeit only temporarily, in the administration of a federally enacted regulatory scheme.

. . . Petitioners contend that compelled enlistment of state executive officers for the administration of federal programs is, until very recent years at least, unprecedented. The Government contends, to the contrary, that "the earliest Congresses enacted statutes that required the participation of state officials in the implementation of federal laws," . . . Conversely if, as petitioners contend, earlier Congresses avoided use of this highly attractive power, we would have reason to believe that the power was thought not to exist.

. . . we do not think the early statutes imposing obligations on state courts imply a power of Congress to impress the state executive into its service.

. . . Although the States surrendered many of their powers to the new Federal Government, they retained "a residuary and inviolable sovereignty," This is reflected throughout the Constitution's text, including (to mention only a few examples) the prohibition on any involuntary reduction or combination of a State's territory, Art. IV, § 3; the Judicial Power Clause, Art. III, § 2, and the Privileges and Immunities Clause, Art. IV, § 2, which speak of the "Citizens" of the States; the amendment provision, Article V, which requires the votes of three-fourths of the States to amend the Constitution; and the Guarantee Clause, Art. IV, § 4, which "presupposes the continued existence of the states and . . . those means and instrumentalities which are the creation of their sovereign and reserved rights," Residual state sovereignty was also implicit, of course, in the Constitution's conferral upon Congress of not all governmental powers, but only discrete, enumerated ones, Art. I, § 8, which implication was rendered express by the Tenth Amendment's assertion that "[t]he powers not delegated to the United States by the Constitution, nor prohibited by it to the States, are reserved to the States respectively, or to the people."

. . . the question discussed earlier, whether laws conscripting state officers violate state sovereignty and are thus not in accord with the Constitution. . . . Even assuming, moreover, that the Brady Act leaves no "policymaking" discretion with the States, we fail to see how that improves rather than worsens the intrusion upon state sovereignty. Preservation of the States as independent and autonomous political entities is arguably less undermined by requiring them to make policy in certain fields than by "reduc[ing] [them] to puppets of a ventriloquist Congress," It is an essential attribute of the States' retained sovereignty that they remain independent and autonomous within their proper sphere of authority. It is no more compatible with this independence and autonomy that their officers be "dragooned" into administering federal law, than it would be compatible with the independence and autonomy of the United States that its officers be impressed into service for the execution of state laws.

WILLIAM J. CLINTON, EXECUTIVE ORDER 13132[63]

Federalism

By the authority vested in me as President by the Constitution and the laws of the United States of America, and in order to guarantee the division of governmental responsibilities between the national government and the States that was intended by the Framers of the Constitution, to ensure that the principles of federalism established by the Framers guide the executive departments and agencies in the formulation and implementation of policies, and to further the policies of the Unfunded Mandates Reform Act, it is hereby ordered as follows:

. . . Sec. 2. Fundamental Federalism Principles. In formulating and implementing policies that have federalism implications, agencies shall be guided by the following fundamental federalism principles:

a. Federalism is rooted in the belief that issues that are not national in scope or significance are most appropriately addressed by the level of government closest to the people.

b. The people of the States created the national government and delegated to it enumerated governmental powers. All other sovereign powers, save those expressly prohibited the States by the Constitution, are reserved to the States or to the people.

c. The constitutional relationship among sovereign governments, State and national, is inherent in the very structure of the Constitution and is formalized in and protected by the Tenth Amendment to the Constitution.

d. The people of the States are free, subject only to restrictions in the Constitution itself or in constitutionally authorized Acts of Congress, to define the moral, political, and legal character of their lives.

e. The Framers recognized that the States possess unique authorities, qualities, and abilities to meet the needs of the people and should function as laboratories of democracy.

f. The nature of our constitutional system encourages a healthy diversity in the public policies adopted by the people of the several States according to their own conditions, needs, and desires. In the search for enlightened public policy, individual States and communities are free to experiment with a variety of approaches to public issues. One-size-fits-all approaches to public policy problems can inhibit the creation of effective solutions to those problems.

g. Acts of the national government—whether legislative, executive, or judicial in nature—that exceed the enumerated powers of that government under the Constitution violate the principle of federalism established by the Framers.

h. Policies of the national government should recognize the responsibility of—and should encourage opportunities for—individuals, families, neighborhoods, local governments, and private associations to achieve their personal, social, and economic objectives through cooperative effort.

i. The national government should be deferential to the States when taking action that affects the policymaking discretion of the States and should act only with the greatest caution where State or local governments have identified uncertainties regarding the constitutional or statutory authority of the national government.

Sec. 3. Federalism Policymaking Criteria. In addition to adhering to the fundamental federalism principles set forth in section 2, agencies shall adhere, to the extent permitted by law, to the following criteria when formulating and implementing policies that have federalism implications:

a. There shall be strict adherence to constitutional principles. Agencies shall closely examine the constitutional and statutory authority supporting any action that would limit the policymaking discretion of the States and shall carefully assess the necessity for such action. To the extent practicable, State and local officials shall be consulted before any such action is implemented. Executive Order 12372 of July 14, 1982 ("Intergovernmental Review of Federal Programs") remains in effect for the programs and activities to which it is applicable.

b. National action limiting the policymaking discretion of the States shall be taken only where there is constitutional and statutory authority for the action and the national activity is appropriate in light of the presence of a problem of national significance. Where there are significant uncertainties as to whether national action is authorized or appropriate, agencies shall consult with appropriate State and local officials to determine whether Federal objectives can be attained by other means.

c. With respect to Federal statutes and regulations administered by the States, the national government shall grant the States the maximum administrative discretion possible. Intrusive Federal oversight of State administration is neither necessary nor desirable.

d. When undertaking to formulate and implement policies that have federalism implications, agencies shall:

L (1) encourage States to develop their own policies to achieve program objectives and to work with appropriate officials in other States;

L (2) where poswsible, defer to the States to establish standards;

L (3) in determining whether to establish uniform national standards, consult with appropriate State and local officials as to the need for national standards and any alternatives that would limit the scope of national standards or otherwise preserve State prerogatives and authority; and

L (4) where national standards are required by Federal statutes, consult with appropriate State and local officials in developing those standards.

ARIZONA, et al., v. UNITED STATES[64]

[Justice Anthony Kennedy]. To address pressing issues related to the large number of aliens within its borders who do not have a lawful right to be in this country, the State of Arizona in 2010 enacted a statute called the Support Our Law Enforcement and Safe Neighborhoods Act.

. . . The law's provisions establish an official state policy of "attrition through enforcement." The question before the Court is whether federal law preempts and renders invalid four separate provisions of the state law.

The Government of the United States has broad, undoubted power over the subject of immigration and the status of aliens. This authority rests, in part, on the National Government's constitutional power to "establish an uniform Rule of Naturalization," and its inherent power as sovereign to control and conduct relations with foreign nations,

The federal power to determine immigration policy is well settled. Immigration policy can affect trade, investment, tourism, and diplomatic relations for the entire Nation, as well as the perceptions and expectations of aliens in this country who seek the full protection of its laws.

It is fundamental that foreign countries concerned about the status, safety, and security of their nationals in the United States must be able to confer and communicate on this subject with one national sovereign, not the 50 separate States.

Federal governance of immigration and alien status is extensive and complex. Congress has specified categories of aliens who may not be admitted to the United States. Unlawful entry and unlawful reentry into the country are federal offenses. Once here, aliens are required to register with the Federal Government and to carry proof of status on their person. Failure to do so is a federal misdemeanor. Federal law also authorizes States to deny noncitizens a range of public benefits; and it imposes sanctions on employers who hire unauthorized workers.

Congress has specified which aliens may be removed from the United States and the procedures for doing so. Aliens may be removed if they were inadmissible at the time of entry, have been convicted of certain crimes, or meet other criteria set by federal law. Removal is a civil, not criminal, matter. A principal feature of the removal system is the broad discretion exercised by immigration officials. . . . Federal officials, as an initial matter, must decide whether it makes sense to pursue removal at all. If removal proceedings commence, aliens may seek asylum and other discretionary relief allowing them to remain in the country or at least to leave without formal removal.

. . . The pervasiveness of federal regulation does not diminish the importance of immigration policy to the States.

Federalism, central to the constitutional design, adopts the principle that both the National and State Governments have elements of sovereignty the other is bound to respect. From the existence of two sovereigns follows the possibility that laws can be in conflict or at cross-purposes. The Supremacy Clause provides a clear rule that federal law "shall be the supreme Law of the Land; and the Judges in every State shall be bound thereby, any Thing in the Constitution or Laws of any State to the Contrary notwithstanding." There is no doubt that Congress may withdraw specified powers from the States by enacting a statute containing an express preemption provision.

State law must also give way to federal law in at least two other circumstances. First, the States are precluded from regulating conduct in a field that Congress, acting within its proper authority, has determined must be regulated by its exclusive governance.

Second, state laws are preempted when they conflict with federal law. This includes cases where "compliance with both federal and state regulations is a physical impossibility," and those instances where the challenged state law "stands as an obstacle to the accomplishment and execution of the full purposes and objectives of Congress

. . . The framework enacted by Congress leads to the conclusion here, as it did in Hines, that the Federal Government has occupied the field of alien registration. The federal statutory directives provide a full set of standards governing alien registration, including the punishment for noncompliance. It was designed as a "'harmonious whole.'" Where Congress occupies an entire field, as it has in the field of alien registration, even complementary state regulation is impermissible. Field preemption reflects a congressional decision to foreclose any state regulation in the area, even if it is parallel to federal standards.

Federal law makes a single sovereign responsible for maintaining a comprehensive and unified system to keep track of aliens within the Nation's borders.

. . . By authorizing state officers to decide whether an alien should be detained for being removable, [Arizona] violates the principle that the removal process is entrusted to the discretion of the Federal Government.

. . . Congress has put in place a system in which state officers may not make warrantless arrests of aliens based on possible removability except in specific, limited circumstances. By nonetheless authorizing state and local officers to engage in these enforcement activities as a general matter, [Arizona] creates an obstacle to the full purposes and objectives of Congress.

The National Government has significant power to regulate immigration. With power comes responsibility, and the sound exercise of national power over immigration depends on the Nation's meeting its responsibility to base its laws on a political will informed by searching, thoughtful, rational civic discourse. Arizona may have understandable frustrations with the problems caused by illegal immigration while that process continues, but the State may not pursue policies that undermine federal law.

[Justice Antonin Scalia, dissenting] The United States is an indivisible "Union of sovereign States." Today's opinion, approving virtually all of the Ninth Circuit's injunction against enforcement of the four challenged provisions of Arizona's law, deprives States of what most would consider the defining characteristic of sovereignty: the power to exclude from the sovereign's territory people who have no right to be there. Neither the

Constitution itself nor even any law passed by Congress supports this result. I dissent.

As a sovereign, Arizona has the inherent power to exclude persons from its territory, subject only to those limitations expressed in the Constitution or constitution-ally imposed by Congress. That power to exclude has long been recognized as inherent in sovereignty. Emer de Vattel's seminal 1758 treatise on the Law of Nations stated: "The sovereign may forbid the entrance of his territory either to foreigners in general, or in particular cases, or to certain persons, or for certain particular pur-poses, according as he may think it advantageous to the state. There is nothing in all this, that does not flow from the rights of domain and sovereignty: every one is obliged to pay respect to the prohibition; and whoever dares violate it, incurs the penalty decreed to render it effectual."

. . . There is no doubt that "before the adoption of the constitution of the United States" each State had the authority to "prevent [itself] from being burdened by an influx of persons" . . . And the Constitution did not strip the States of that authority. To the contrary, two of the Constitution's provisions were designed to enable the States to prevent "the intrusion of obnoxious aliens through other States." . . . The Articles of Confederation had provided that "the free inhabitants of each of these States, paupers, vagabonds and fugitives from justice excepted, shall be entitled to all privileges and immunities of free citizens in the several States." Articles of Confederation, Art. IV. This meant that an unwelcome alien could obtain all the rights of a citizen of one State simply by first becoming an inhabitant of another. To remedy this, the Constitution's Privileges and Immunities Clause provided that "[t]he Citizens of each State shall be entitled to all Privileges and Immunities of Citizens in the several States." But if one State had particularly lax citizenship standards, it might still serve as a gateway for the entry of "obnoxious aliens" into other States. This problem was solved "by authorizing the general government to establish a uniform rule of naturalization throughout the United States." . . . In other words, the naturalization power was given to Congress not to abrogate States' power to exclude those they did not want, but to vindicate it.

. . . In fact, the controversy surrounding the Alien and Sedition Acts involved a debate over whether, under the Constitution, the States had exclusive authority to enact such immigration laws. Criticism of the Sedition Act has become a prominent feature of our First Amendment jurisprudence but one of the Alien Acts also aroused controversy at the time.

The Kentucky and Virginia Resolutions, written in denunciation of these Acts, insisted that the power to exclude unwanted aliens rested solely in the States. Jefferson's Kentucky Resolutions insisted "that alien friends are under the jurisdiction and protection of the laws of the state wherein they are [and] that no power over them has been delegated to the United States, nor

prohibited to the individual states, distinct from their power over citizens."
Madison's Virginia Resolutions likewise contended that the Alien Act purported to give the President "a power nowhere delegated to the federal government." Notably, moreover, the Federalist proponents of the Act defended
it primarily on the ground that "[t]he removal of aliens is the usual preliminary of hostility" and could therefore be justified in exercise of the Federal
Government's war powers.

One would conclude from the foregoing that after the adoption of the Constitution there was some doubt about the power of the Federal Government
to control immigration, but no doubt about the power of the States to do so.
Since the founding era (though not immediately), doubt about the Federal
Government's power has disappeared. Indeed, primary responsibility for
immigration policy has shifted from the States to the Federal Government.
Congress exercised its power "[t]o establish an uniform Rule of Naturalization." But with the fleeting exception of the Alien Act, Congress did not enact
any legislation regulating immigration for the better part of a century.

I accept that as a valid exercise of federal power—not because of the Naturalization Clause (it has no necessary connection to citizenship) but because
it is an inherent attribute of sovereignty no less for the United States than for
the States . . . That is why there was no need to set forth control of immigration as one of the enumerated powers of Congress, although an acknowledgment of that power (as well as of the States' similar power, subject to federal
abridgment) was contained in Art. I, §9, which provided that "[t]he Migration
or Importation of such Persons as any of the States now existing shall think
proper to admit, shall not be prohibited by the Congress prior to the Year one
thousand eight hundred and eight. . ."

In light of the predominance of federal immigration restrictions in modern
times, it is easy to lose sight of the States' traditional role in regulating immigration—and to overlook their sovereign prerogative to do so. I accept as a
given that State regulation is excluded by the Constitution when (1) it has
been prohibited by a valid federal law, or (2) it conflicts with federal regulation—when, for example, it admits those whom federal regulation would
exclude, or excludes those whom federal regulation would admit.

Possibility (1) need not be considered here: there is no federal law prohibiting the States' sovereign power to exclude (assuming federal authority to
enact such a law). The mere existence of federal action in the immigration
area—and the so-called field preemption arising from that action, upon which
the Court's opinion so heavily relies, ante, at 9–11—cannot be regarded as
such a prohibition. We are not talking here about a federal law prohibiting
the States from regulating bubble-gum advertising, or even the construction
of nuclear plants. We are talking about a federal law going to the core of
state sovereignty: the power to exclude. Like elimination of the States' other

inherent sovereign power, immunity from suit, elimination of the States' sovereign power to exclude requires that "Congress . . . unequivocally expres[s] its intent to abrogate." Implicit "field preemption" will not do.

Nor can federal power over illegal immigration be deemed exclusive because of what the Court's opinion solicitously calls "foreign countries['] concern[s] about the status, safety, and security of their nationals in the United States," *ante*, at 3. The Constitution gives all those on our shores the protections of the Bill of Rights—but just as those rights are not expanded for foreign nationals because of their countries' views (some countries, for example, have recently discovered the death penalty to be barbaric), neither are the fundamental sovereign powers of the States abridged to accommodate foreign countries' views. Even in its international relations, the Federal Government must live with the inconvenient fact that it is a Union of independent States, who have their own sovereign powers.

What this case comes down to, then, is whether the Arizona law conflicts with federal immigration law—whether it excludes those whom federal law would admit, or admits those whom federal law would exclude. It does not purport to do so. It applies only to aliens who neither possess a privilege to be present under federal law nor have been removed pursuant to the Federal Government's inherent authority.

The Court opinion's looming specter of inutterable horror—"[i]f §3 of the Arizona statute were valid, every State could give itself independent authority to prosecute fed- eral registration violations,"—seems to me not so horrible and even less looming. But there has come to pass, and is with us today, the specter that Arizona and the States that support it predicted: A Federal Government that does not want to enforce the immigration laws as written, and leaves the States' borders unprotected against immigrants whom those laws would exclude. So the issue is a stark one. Are the sovereign States at the mercy of the Federal Executive's refusal to enforce the Nation's immigration laws?

A good way of answering that question is to ask: Would the States conceivably have entered into the Union if the Constitution itself contained the Court's holding? Today's judgment surely fails that test. At the Constitutional Convention of 1787, the delegates contended with "the jealousy of the states with regard to their sovereignty." . . . Through ratification of the fundamental charter that the Convention produced, the States ceded much of their sovereignty to the Federal Government. But much of it remained jealously guarded—as reflected in the innumerable proposals that never left Independence Hall. Now, imagine a provision—perhaps inserted right after Art. I, §8, cl. 4, the Naturalization Clause—which included among the enumerated powers of Congress "To establish Limitations upon Immigration that will be exclusive and that will be enforced only to the extent the President deems appropriate." The delegates to the Grand Convention would have rushed to the exits.

. . . Arizona has moved to protect its sovereignty—not in contradiction of federal law, but in complete compliance with it. The laws under challenge here do not extend or revise federal immigration restrictions, but merely enforce those restrictions more effectively. If securing its territory in this fashion is not within the power of Arizona, we should cease referring to it as a sovereign State. I dissent.

TENTH AMENDMENT RESOLUTIONS[65]

Arkansas

WHEREAS, the Tenth Amendment to the Constitution of the United States provides that "[t]he powers not delegated to the United States by the Constitution, nor prohibited to it by the States, are reserved to the States respectively, or to the people."; and

WHEREAS, the Tenth Amendment defines the total scope of federal power as being that specifically granted by the Constitution of the United States; and

WHEREAS, the scope of power defined by the Tenth Amendment means that the federal government was created by the states specifically to be an agent of the states; and

WHEREAS, today, in 2009, the states are demonstrably treated as agents of the federal government; and

WHEREAS, the United States Supreme Court has ruled in New York v. United States, 505 U.S. 144 (1992), that Congress may not simply commandeer the legislative and regulatory processes of the states; and

WHEREAS, a number of proposals from previous administrations and some now pending from the present administration and from Congress may further violate the Constitution of the United States,

NOW THEREFORE, BE IT RESOLVED BY THE HOUSE OF REPRESENTATIVES OF THE EIGHTY-SEVENTH GENERAL ASSEMBLY OF THE STATE OF ARKANSAS, THE SENATE CONCURRING THEREIN:

THAT the State of Arkansas hereby claims rights under the Tenth Amendment to the Constitution of the United States over all powers not otherwise enumerated and granted to the federal government by the Constitution of the United States.

BE IT FURTHER RESOLVED that this resolution serve as a request to the federal government, as our agent, to refrain from mandates that are beyond the scope of these constitutionally delegated powers.

New Hampshire

A RESOLUTION affirming States' powers based on the Constitution for the United States and the Constitution of New Hampshire.

Whereas, the Constitution of the State of New Hampshire, Part 1, Article 7 declares that the people of this State have the sole and exclusive right of governing themselves as a free, sovereign, and independent State; and do, and forever hereafter shall, exercise and enjoy every power, jurisdiction, and right, pertaining thereto, which is not, or may not hereafter be, by them expressly delegated to the United States of America in congress assembled; and

Whereas, the Constitution of the State of New Hampshire, Part 2, Article 1 declares that the people inhabiting the territory formerly called the province of New Hampshire, do hereby solemnly and mutually agree with each other, to form themselves into a free, sovereign and independent body-politic, or State, by the name of The State of New Hampshire; and

Whereas, each State acceded to the compact titled The Constitution for the United States of America as a State, and is an integral party, its co-States forming, as to itself, the other party: and

Whereas, the State of New Hampshire when ratifying the Constitution for the United States of America recommended as a change, "First That it be Explicitly declared that all Powers not expressly & particularly Delegated by the aforesaid are reserved to the several States to be, by them Exercised"; and

Whereas, the other States that included recommendations, to wit Massachusetts, New York, North Carolina, Rhode Island, and Virginia, included an identical or similar recommended change; and

Whereas, these recommended changes were incorporated as the Ninth Amendment, "The enumeration in the Constitution, of certain rights, shall not be construed to deny or disparage others retained by the people," and the Tenth Amendment, "The powers not delegated to the United States by the Constitution, nor prohibited by it to the States, are reserved to the States respectively, or to the people," to the Constitution for the United States of America. Therefore, the several States composing the United States of America, are not united on the principle of unlimited submission to their General Government; but that, by a compact under the style and title of a Constitution for the United States of America, and of amendments thereto, they constituted a General Government for special purposes, delegated to that government certain definite powers, reserving, each State to itself, all remaining powers for their own self-government; and

Whereas, the construction applied by the General Government (as is evidenced by sundry of their proceedings) to those parts of the Constitution of the United States which delegate to Congress a power "to lay and collect taxes, duties, imports, and excises, to pay the debts, and provide for the common defense and general welfare of the United States," and "to make all laws which shall be necessary and proper for carrying into execution the powers vested by the Constitution in the government of the United States, or in any department or officer thereof," goes to the destruction of all limits prescribed to their power by the Constitution:

I.   Therefore, words meant by the instrument to be subsidiary only to the execution of limited powers, ought not to be so construed as themselves to give unlimited powers, nor a part to be so taken as to destroy the whole residue of that instrument; and
II. Therefore, whensoever the General Government assumes undelegated powers, its acts are unauthoritative, void, and of no force; and

Whereas, the Constitution of the United States, having delegated to Congress a power to punish treason, counterfeiting the securities and current coin of the United States, piracies, and felonies committed on the high seas, offenses against the law of nations, and slavery, and no other crimes whatsoever:

Therefore, all acts of Congress, the orders of the Executive or orders of the Judiciary of the United States of America which assume to create, define, or punish crimes, other than those so enumerated in the Constitution are altogether void, and of no force; and that the power to create, define, and punish such other crimes is reserved, and, of right, appertains solely and exclusively to the respective States, each within its own territory; and

Whereas, The United States Supreme Court has ruled in New York v. United States, 112 S. Ct. 2408 (1992), that congress may not simply commandeer the legislative and regulatory processes of the States:

Therefore, all compulsory federal legislation that directs States to comply under threat of civil or criminal penalties or sanctions or that requires States to pass legislation or lose federal funding are prohibited; and

Whereas, The Constitution for the United States of America, Article II, Section 2, Clause 2 gives Congress the authority to authorize inferior officers of the government of the United States of America not enumerated in the Constitution by law and for them to be appointed by the manner prescribed by law enacted by the Congress, and that the Constitution gives no such authority to the President:

Therefore, no officer not authorized by the Constitution or by law or exercising a power not authorized by the Constitution, nor their subordinates shall have any authority in, or over the sovereign State of New Hampshire, nor any inhabitant or resident thereof, nor any franchises created under the authority thereof when within the borders of the State of New Hampshire, and

Whereas, the Constitution for the United States of America Article I, Section 1 delegates all legislative power to the Congress, and

Whereas, the Constitution for the United States of America Article II delegates no legislative power to the Executive branch whatsoever. Therefore, any Executive Order that pretends the power to create statutes controlling the States, their inhabitants or their residents is unauthoritive, void and of no force, and

Whereas, the Constitution for the United States of America, Article VI, Section 2 declares "This Constitution, and the Laws of the United States which shall be made in Pursuance thereof; and all Treaties made, or which shall be made, under the Authority of the United States, shall be the supreme Law of the Land; and the Judges in every State shall be bound thereby, any Thing in the Constitution or Laws of any State to the Contrary notwithstanding."; and

Whereas, treaties are ratified by the Senate which being a House of Congress has its jurisdiction limited to the powers enumerated in Article I, Section 8 of the Constitution; and

Whereas, treaties are ratified by the President and the Senate (representing the States) only, but laws are ratified by the House of Representatives (representing the people) and the Senate (representing the States) and the President, no treaty can be lawfully construed to restrict or amend existing law; and

Whereas, treaties are ratified by the President and the Senate (representing the States) only, but the Constitution and its amendments were ratified by the States directly (representing the people), no treaty can be lawfully construed to restrict or amend the Constitution:

Therefore, any treaty which pretends to delegate any powers not delegated to Congress in Article I, Section 8 of the Constitution is altogether void, and of no force; and any order of the Executive or order of the Judiciary which is construed to restrict or amend existing law, or any act of Congress, order of the Executive or order of the Judiciary which is construed to restrict or amend the Constitution for the United States of America based upon compliance with any treaty are altogether void, and of no force; and

Whereas, the government created by this compact was not made the exclusive or final judge of the extent of the powers delegated to itself, since that would have made its discretion, and not the Constitution, the measure of its powers; but that, as in all other cases of compact among powers having no common judge, each party has an equal right to judge for itself, as well of infractions as of the mode and measure of redress:

Therefore, the Legislatures and Legislators of the several States have the right and duty to consider the constitutionality of any legislative act or order promulgated by the government of the United States of America; and to protect their governments, inhabitants, and residents and instruments created under their authority by prohibiting, and if necessary punishing the enforcement any Acts by the Congress of the United States of America, Executive Order of the President of the United States of America or Judicial Order by the Judiciaries of the United States of America which assumes a power not delegated to the government of United States of America by the Constitution for the United States of America; and

Whereas, the Constitution for the United States of America guarantees to every State in this Union a Republican Form of Government, and shall protect each of them against Invasion; and on Application of the Legislature (of a State), or of the Executive (when the Legislature cannot be convened) against domestic Violence. Therefore; there exists a class of Acts by the Congress of the United States, Executive Orders of the President of the United States of America or Judicial Orders by the Judicatories of the United States of America that constitutes a direct challenge to the Constitution for the United States of America by the government of the United States including, but not limited to:

I.   Requiring involuntary servitude or governmental service other than pursuant to, or as an alternative to, incarceration after due process of law.
II. Establishing martial law or a state of emergency within one of the States comprising the United States of America without the consent of the legislature of that State or authority derived from that body.
III. Surrendering any power delegated or not delegated to any incorporation or foreign government; now, therefore, be it.

Resolved by the House of Representatives, the Senate concurring:

That the State of New Hampshire urges its co-States to charge to one if its committees with the duty communicating the preceedings of its Legislature in regard to the government of the United States of America to the corresponding committees of Legislatures of the several States; to assure them that this State continues in the same esteem of their friendship and union which it has manifested from that moment at which a common danger first suggested a common union: that it considers union, for specified national purposes, and particularly to those specified in their federal compact, to be friendly to the peace, happiness, and prosperity of all the States: that faithful to that compact, according to the plain intent and meaning in which it was understood and acceded to by the several parties, it is sincerely anxious for its preservation: that it does also believe, that to take from the States all the powers of self-government and transfer them to a general and consolidated government, without regard to the special delegations and reservations solemnly agreed to in that compact, is not for the peace, happiness, or prosperity of these States;

and that therefore this State is determined, as it doubts not its co-States are, to submit to undelegated, and consequently unlimited powers in no man, or body of men on earth: that in cases of an abuse of the delegated powers, the members of the General Government, being chosen by the people, a change by the people would be the constitutional remedy; but, where powers are assumed which have not been delegated, a nullification of the act is the rightful remedy: that every State has a natural right in cases not within the compact, (casus non foederis), to nullify of their own authority all assumptions of power by others within their limits: that without this right, they would be under the dominion, absolute and unlimited, of whosoever might exercise this right of judgment for them; and

Kentucky

A CONCURRENT RESOLUTION claiming sovereignty over powers not granted to the federal government by the United States Constitution; serving notice to the federal government to cease mandates beyond its authority; and stating Kentucky's position that federal legislation that requires states to comply under threat of loss of federal funding should be prohibited or repealed.

WHEREAS, the Tenth Amendment to the Constitution of the United States provides that "The powers not delegated to the United States by the Constitution, nor prohibited to it by the States, are reserved to the States respectively, or to the people."; and

WHEREAS, the Tenth Amendment defines the total scope of federal power as being that specifically granted by the Constitution of the United States and no more; and

WHEREAS, the scope of power defined by the Tenth Amendment means that the federal government was created by the states specifically to be an agent of the state; and

WHEREAS, today, in 2010, the states are demonstrably treated as agents of the federal government; and

WHEREAS, many federal mandates are directly in violation of the Tenth Amendment to the Constitution of the United States; and

WHEREAS, Article IV, Section 4 of the United States Constitution states that "The United States shall guarantee to every State in this Union a Republican Form of Government . . ." and the Ninth Amendment of the United States Constitution states that "The enumeration in the Constitution, of certain rights, shall not be construed to deny or disparage others retained by the people."; and

WHEREAS, the United States Supreme Court has ruled in New York v. United States, 505 U.S. 144 (1992), that Congress may not simply commandeer the legislative and regulatory processes of the states; and

WHEREAS, a number of proposals from previous administrations and some now pending from the present administration and from Congress may further violate the Constitution of the United States;

NOW, THEREFORE,

Be it resolved by the House of Representatives of the General Assembly of the Commonwealth of Kentucky, the Senate concurring therein:

Section 1. The Commonwealth of Kentucky hereby claims sovereignty under the Tenth Amendment to the Constitution of the United States over all powers not otherwise enumerated and granted to the federal government by the Constitution of the United States.

Section 2. This Resolution serves as notice and demand to the federal government, as our agent, to cease and desist, effective immediately, mandates that are beyond the scope of these constitutionally delegated powers.

Section 3. It is the position of the Commonwealth of Kentucky that all compulsory federal legislation that directs states to comply under threat of civil or criminal penalties or sanctions, or requires states to pass legislation or lose federal funding be prohibited or repealed.

Section 4. The Clerk of the House of Representatives shall distribute a copy of this Resolution to the President of the United States, the President of the United States Senate, the Speaker of the United States House of Representatives, the Speaker of the House and President of the Senate of each state's legislature of the United States of America, and to each member of Kentucky's congressional delegation.

Mississippi

A concurrent resolution reinforcing the fundamental principle and authority of state sovereignty under the tenth amendment to the constitution of the United States over certain powers and discouraging the federal government from imposing certain restrictive mandates.

WHEREAS, the Tenth Amendment to the Constitution of the United States reads: "The powers not delegated to the United States by the Constitution, nor prohibited by it to the States, are reserved to the States respectively, or to the people"; and

WHEREAS, the Tenth Amendment defines the total scope of federal power as being that specifically granted by the Constitution of the United States and no more; and

WHEREAS, Federalism is the constitutional division of powers between the national and state governments and is widely regarded as one of America's most valuable contributions to political science; and

WHEREAS, James Madison, "the Father of the Constitution," said, "The powers delegated to the federal government are few and defined. Those which are to remain in the state governments are numerous and indefinite. The former will be exercised principally on external objects, such as war, peace, negotiation, and foreign commerce. The powers reserved to the several states will extend to all the objects which, in the ordinary course of affairs, concern the lives, liberties, and properties of the people"; and

WHEREAS, Thomas Jefferson emphasized that the states are not "subordinate" to the national government, but rather the two are "coordinate departments of one simple and integral whole. The one is the domestic, the other the foreign branch of the same government"; and

WHEREAS, Alexander Hamilton expressed his hope that "the people will always take care to preserve the constitutional equilibrium between the general and the state governments." He believed that "this balance between the national and state governments forms a double security to the people. If one government encroaches on their rights, they will find a powerful protection in the other. Indeed, they will both be prevented from overpassing their constitutional limits by the certain rivalship which will ever subsist between them"; and

WHEREAS, the scope of power defined by the Tenth Amendment means that the federal government was created by the states specifically to be an agent of the states; and

WHEREAS, today, in 2010, the states are demonstrably treated as agents of the federal government; and

WHEREAS, many federal mandates appear to be in violation of the Tenth Amendment to the Constitution of the United States, and the United States Supreme Court's ruling in New York v. United States, 112 S. Ct. 2408 (1992), stated that Congress may not simply "commandeer the legislative and regulatory processes of the States by directly compelling them to enact and enforce a federal regulatory program"; and

WHEREAS, the Supreme Court in that case went on to express that, "No matter how powerful the federal interest involved, the Constitution simply does not give Congress the authority to require the States to regulate. The Constitution instead gives Congress the authority to regulate matters directly and to pre-empt contrary state regulation. Where a federal interest is sufficiently strong to cause Congress to legislate, it must do so directly; it may not conscript state governments as its agents"; and ST: U.S. Congress; urge to be mindful of state sovereignty enumerated in the 10th Amendment to the U.S. Constitution.

WHEREAS, a number of proposals from previous administrations and some now pending from the present administration and from Congress may further violate the Constitution of the United States; and

WHEREAS, it is incumbent upon the Mississippi Legislature, as an agent for the people of the State of Mississippi, to remind the federal government to act only in ways that will ensure the protection and preservation of constitutional rights granted to each state in the framework of the Constitution of the United States as crafted by our nation's founding fathers, so as not to deny each state the enumerated right of self-governance without an over-reaching arm of federal government mandates and implications:

NOW, THEREFORE, BE IT RESOLVED BY THE HOUSE OF REPRESENTATIVES OF THE STATE OF MISSISSIPPI, THE SENATE CONCURRING THEREIN, That the State of Mississippi hereby reinforces the fundamental principles and authority of state sovereignty under the Tenth Amendment to the Constitution of the United States over all powers not otherwise enumerated and granted to the federal government by the Constitution of the United States and discourage the federal government, as our agent, from imposing certain restrictive mandates that are beyond the scope of these constitutionally delegated powers.

Nebraska

WHEREAS, the Ninth Amendment to the United States

Constitution states that "The enumeration in the Constitution, of certain rights, shall not be construed to deny or disparage others retained by the people;" and

WHEREAS, the Tenth Amendment to the United States Constitution declares that "The powers not delegated to the United States by the Constitution, nor prohibited by it to the States, are reserved to the States respectively, or to the people;" and

WHEREAS, the framers of the United States Constitution envisioned a federal government with "few and defined" delegated powers, whereby state governments retained "numerous and indefinite" powers extending "to all the objects which, in the ordinary course of affairs, concern the lives, liberties, and properties of the people, and the internal order, improvement, and prosperity of the State;" and

WHEREAS, the United States Government has historically and continues to expand its enumerated powers in a manner inconsistent with the Ninth Amendment to the United States Constitution; and

WHEREAS, the United States Government has historically and continues to assert powers not enumerated under Article I, section 8, of the United States Constitution in a manner inconsistent with the Tenth Amendment to the United States Constitution; and

WHEREAS, a balanced federalism is necessary to preserve the inherent rights of the people, from whose consent the just powers of both state and federal governments are derived.

NOW, THEREFORE, BE IT RESOLVED BY THE MEMBERS OF THE ONE HUNDRED FIRST LEGISLATURE OF NEBRASKA, SECOND SESSION:

1. That the Legislature encourages the Congress of the United States to adhere to the principles of federalism in accord with the Ninth and Tenth Amendments to the United States Constitution.

South Carolina

TO AFFIRM THE RIGHTS OF ALL STATES INCLUDING SOUTH CAROLINA BASED ON THE PROVISIONS OF THE NINTH AND TENTH AMENDMENTS TO THE UNITED STATES CONSTITUTION.

Whereas, the Tenth Amendment to the United States Constitution provides that "powers not delegated to the United States by the Constitution, nor prohibited by it to the States, are reserved to the States respectively, or to the people"; and

Whereas, the Tenth Amendment defines the limited scope of federal power as being that specifically granted by the United States Constitution; and

Whereas, the limited scope of authority defined by the Tenth Amendment means that the federal government was created by the states specifically to be an agent of the states; and

Whereas, currently the states are treated as agents of the federal government; and

Whereas, many federal mandates are directly in violation of the Tenth Amendment to the United States Constitution; and

Whereas, the United States Supreme Court has ruled that Congress may not simply commandeer the legislative and regulatory processes of the states; and

Whereas, the State recognizes that as an independent sovereign, the State along with the other states of the union took part in an extensive collective bargaining process through the adoption of the Constitution and the various amendments thereto, and like any other party to any other agreement, the State is bound to uphold the terms and conditions of that agreement. Through this agreement, the states have collectively created the federal government, limiting the scope of its power and authority, as well as ensuring that certain fundamental rights are guaranteed. Also, through this process the states have collectively agreed to limit their own governmental authority by providing that the rights and protections afforded to the people as citizens of the United States are also extended to each person as a citizen of an individual state. Pursuant to that agreement, this State is bound to uphold the principals and protections afforded by all of the constitutional amendments, one of the most notable being the protections afforded by the Fourteenth Amendment which guarantees the privileges and immunities of the United States, due process of law, and equal protection under the law; and

Whereas, pursuant to the Tenth Amendment, by limiting the scope of federal power to only those specifically enumerated in the United States Constitution, the states retain plenary power to govern; and

Whereas, included among all states' plenary power to govern is the broad authority of all state legislatures to appropriate funds for the operation of state agencies and to specify and direct the conditions under which appropriated funds shall be spent; and

Whereas, the General Assembly of the State of South Carolina has exercised its broad authority to appropriate and direct the expenditure of funds by appropriating and directing the expenditure of funds in the Fiscal Year 2009–2010 budget. Now, therefore,

Be it resolved by the Senate, the House of Representatives concurring:

That the General Assembly of the State of South Carolina, by this resolution, claims for the State of South Carolina sovereignty under the Tenth Amendment to the Constitution of the United States over all powers not otherwise enumerated and granted to the federal government by the United States Constitution.

Be it further resolved that all federal governmental agencies, quasi governmental agencies, and their agents and employees operating within the geographic boundaries of the State of South Carolina, and all federal governmental agencies and their agents and employees, whose actions have effect on the inhabitants or lands or waters of the State of South Carolina, shall operate within the confines of the original intent of the Constitution of the United States and abide by the provisions of the Constitution of South Carolina, the South Carolina statutes, or the common law as guaranteed by the Constitution of the United States.

Be it further resolved that this resolution serves as notice and demand to the federal government, as South Carolina's agent, to cease and desist immediately all mandates that are beyond the scope of the federal government's constitutionally delegated powers.

Utah

Be it resolved by the Legislature of the state of Utah, the Governor concurring therein:

WHEREAS, the Tenth Amendment to the Constitution of the United States reads: "The powers not delegated to the United States by the Constitution, nor prohibited by it to the States, are reserved to the States respectively, or to the people";

WHEREAS, the Tenth Amendment defines the total scope of federal power as being that specifically granted to the federal government by the Constitution of the United States and no more;

WHEREAS, the states are often treated as agents of the federal government;

WHEREAS, many federal laws directly contravene the Tenth Amendment;

WHEREAS, it is important that all levels of government work together to serve the citizens of the United States by respecting the constitutional provisions that properly delineate the authority of federal, state, and local governments;

WHEREAS, the Tenth Amendment assures that we, the people of the United States, and each sovereign state in the Union of States, now have, and have always had, rights the federal government may not usurp;

WHEREAS, Article IV, Section 4 of the United States Constitution declares in part, "The United States shall guarantee to every State in this Union a Republican Form of Government," and the Ninth Amendment to the United States Constitution further declares that "The enumeration in the Constitution, of certain rights, shall not be construed to deny or disparage others retained by the people";

WHEREAS, the United States Supreme Court ruled in New York v. United States, 505 U.S. 144 (1992), that Congress may not simply commandeer the legislative and regulatory processes of the states by compelling them to enact and enforce regulatory programs;

WHEREAS, the United States Supreme Court, in Printz v. United States/ Mack v. United States, 521 U.S. 898 (1997), reaffirmed that the Constitution of the United States established a system of "dual sovereignty" that retains "a residuary and inviolable sovereignty" by the states;

WHEREAS, this separation of the two spheres is one of the Constitution's structural protections of liberty; and

WHEREAS, a number of proposals by previous administrations, some now pending proposals by the present administration, and some proposals by Congress may further violate the Tenth Amendment restriction on the scope of federal power:

NOW, THEREFORE, BE IT RESOLVED that the Legislature of the state of Utah, the Governor concurring therein, acknowledge and reaffirm residuary and inviolable sovereignty of the state of Utah under the Tenth Amendment to the Constitution of the United States over all powers not otherwise enumerated and granted to the federal government by the Constitution of the United States.

DONALD J. TRUMP, EXECUTIVE ORDER
ENFORCING STATUTORY PROHIBITIONS ON
FEDERAL CONTROL OF EDUCATION[66]

By the authority vested in me as President by the Constitution and the laws of the United States of America, and in order to restore the proper division of power under the Constitution between the Federal Government and the States and to further the goals of, and to ensure strict compliance with, statutes that prohibit Federal interference with State and local control over education, including section 103 of the Department of Education Organization Act (DEOA) (20 U.S.C. 3403), sections 438 and 447 of the General Education Provisions Act (GEPA), as amended (20 U.S.C. 1232a and 1232j), and sections 8526A, 8527, and 8529 of the Elementary and Secondary Education Act of 1965 (ESEA), as amended by the Every Student Succeeds Act (ESSA) (20 U.S.C. 7906a, 7907, and 7909), it is hereby ordered as follows:

Section 1. Policy. It shall be the policy of the executive branch to protect and preserve State and local control over the curriculum, program of instruction, administration, and personnel of educational institutions, schools, and school systems, consistent with applicable law, including ESEA, as amended by ESSA, and ESEA's restrictions related to the Common Core State Standards developed under the Common Core State Standards Initiative.

Sec. 2. Review of Regulations and Guidance Documents. (a) The Secretary of Education (Secretary) shall review all Department of Education (Department) regulations and guidance documents relating to DEOA, GEPA, and ESEA, as amended by ESSA.

(b) The Secretary shall examine whether these regulations and guidance documents comply with Federal laws that prohibit the Department from exercising any direction, supervision, or control over areas subject to State and local control, including:

i.   the curriculum or program of instruction of any elementary and secondary school and school system;
ii.   school administration and personnel; and
iii. selection and content of library resources, textbooks, and instructional materials.

(c) The Secretary shall, as appropriate and consistent with applicable law, rescind or revise any regulations that are identified pursuant to subsection (b) of this section as inconsistent with statutory prohibitions. The Secretary shall also rescind or revise any guidance documents that are identified pursuant to subsection (b) of this section as inconsistent with statutory prohibitions. The Secretary shall, to the extent consistent with law, publish any proposed regulations and withdraw or modify any guidance documents pursuant to this subsection no later than 300 days after the date of this order.

NOTES

1. Jean Bodin, *Six Books of the Commonwealth,* M. J. Tooley, ed. and trans (Oxford: Blackwell, 1955), 1–16.

2. Thomas Hobbes, *Leviathan,* A. R. Waller, ed. (originally published 1651; Cambridge: Cambridge University Press, 1904), 115–129.

3. Montesquieu, *The Spirit of Laws,* Thomas Nuget, ed., 2 vols, 2nd edition (London: J. Nourse and P. Vaillant, 1752), 1: 175–179.

4. Vattell, *The Law of Nations* (1758; reprinted, Philadelphia: T and J.W. Johnson Law Booksellers, 1853), 1–3.

5. William Blackstone, *Commentaries on the Laws of England,* 4 vols (Oxford: Clarendon Press, 1765), 1: 49–53.

6. Danby Pickering, ed., *The Statutes at Large,* 42 vols (Cambridge: Printed for Benthem, for C. Bathhurst, 1762–1869), 27: 20.

7. Richard Bland, *Inquiry into the Rights of the British Colonies* (Williamsburg, 1766), 20.

8. Stephen Hopkins, *The Rights of the Colonies Examined* (Providence: William Goddard, 1765), 18–20.

9. Alexander Hamilton, *The Farmer Refuted: or a More Impartial and Comprehensive View of the Dispute between Great-Britain and the Colonies* (New York: James Rivington, 1775), 42–43.

10. Henry Cabot Lodge, ed., *The Works of Alexander Hamilton: Federal Edition,* 12 vols (New York: G.P. Putnam and Sons, 1904), 1: 243–248.

11. Meriweather Smith, *Observations on the Fourth and Fifth Articles of the Preliminaries for a Peace* (Richmond: Dixon and Holt, 1783), 4–7. Used by permission from Readex, a division of Newsbank inc and The American Antiquarian Society.

12. Charles Tansill, ed., *Documents Illustrative of the Formation of the Union of the American States* (Washington, D.C.: Government Printing Office, 1927), 953–963.

13. Charles Tansill, ed., *Documents Illustrative of the Formation of the Union of the American States* (Washington, D.C.: Government Printing Office, 1927), 967–978.

14. James Wilson, "State House Speech," *Pennsylvania Packet,* October 10, 1787.

15. Paul L. Ford, ed., *The Federalist: A Commentary on the Constitution of the United States* (New York: Henry Holt and Company, 1898), 54–64.

16. Paul L. Ford, ed., *The Federalist: A Commentary on the Constitution of the United States* (New York: Henry Holt and Company, 1898), 162–168.

17. Paul L. Ford, ed., *The Federalist: A Commentary on the Constitution of the United States* (New York: Henry Holt and Company, 1898), 245–252.

18. Paul L. Ford, ed., *The Federalist: A Commentary on the Constitution of the United States* (New York: Henry Holt and Company, 1898), 294–303.

19. *New York Journal,* October 18, 1787.

20. *New York Journal*, December 27, 1787.

21. Harry Alonzo Cushing, ed., *The Writings of Samuel Adams*, 4 vols (New York: G. P. Putnan's Sons, 1908), 4: 324–325.

22. *The Independent Gazetteer*, August 18, 1789.

23. Jonathan Elliot, ed., *The Debates in the Several State Conventions on the Adoption of the Federal Constitution*, 4 vols (Washington, D.C.: 1836), 3: 21–23; 43–64.

24. Paul L. Ford, ed., *The Writings of Thomas Jefferson*, 12 vols (New York: G. P. Putnam's Sons, 1904), 6: 197–204.

25. Henry Cabot Lodge, ed., *The Works of Alexander Hamilton in Twelve Volumes: Federal Edition* (New York: G.P. Putnam's Sons, 1904), 3: 445–494.

26. *Chisholm v. Georgia 2 U.S. 419 (1793)*.

27. Jonathan Elliot, *The Virginia and Kentucky Resolution of 1798 and '99 with Jefferson's Original Draught Thereof Also, Madison's Report, Calhoun's Address, Resolutions of the Several States in Relation to State Rights with other Documents in Support of The Jeffersonian Doctrines of '98* (Washington, D.C., 1832), 15–19.

28. Jonathan Elliot, *The Virginia and Kentucky Resolution of 1798 and '99 with Jefferson's Original Draught Thereof Also, Madison's Report, Calhoun's Address, Resolutions of the Several States in Relation to State Rights with other Documents in Support of The Jeffersonian Doctrines of '98* (Washington, D.C., 1832), 5–6.

29. Jonathan Elliot, *The Virginia and Kentucky Resolution of 1798 and '99 with Jefferson's Original Draught Thereof Also, Madison's Report, Calhoun's Address, Resolutions of the Several States in Relation to State Rights with other Documents in Support of The Jeffersonian Doctrines of '98* (Washington, D.C., 1832), 21–41.

30. *McCulloch v. Maryland 17 U.S. 316 (1819)*.

31. John Taylor of Caroline, *New Views of the Constitution* (Washington, D.C.: Way and Gideon, 1823), 171–177.

32. *Register of Debates* 21st Congress, 1st Session (Washington, D.C.: Gales and Seaton), 31–41; 43–80.

33. Richard K. Cralle, ed., *The Works of John C. Calhoun: Reports and Public Letters of John C. Calhoun*, 6 vols (New York: D. Appleton and Company, 1870), 6: 59–93.

34. Paul L. Ford, ed., *The Federalist: A Commentary on the Constitution of the United States . . . with Notes, Illustrative Documents . . .* (New York: Henry Holt and Company, 1898), 690–692.

35. Paul L. Ford, ed., *The Federalist: A Commentary on the Constitution of the United States . . . with Notes, Illustrative Documents . . .* (New York: Henry Holt and Company, 1898).

36. James D. Richardson, ed., *Compilations of the Messages and Papers of the Presidents*, 11 vols (Washington, D.C.: Government Printing Office, 1897, 1904), 2: 483–493.

37. James D. Richardson, ed., *Compilations of the Messages and Papers of the Presidents*, 11 vols (Washington, D.C.: Government Print Office, 1897, 1904), 2: 576–591.

38. *A Disquisition on Government and a Discourse on the Constitution and Government of the United States*, Richard K. Cralle, ed. (Columbia: A.S. Johnston, 1851), 111–131.

39. Joseph Story, *Commentaries on the Constitution*, 3 vols (Boston: Hillard, Gray, and Company, 1833), 3: 752–755.

40. Abel Upshur, *A Brief Enquiry into the True Nature and Character of Our Federal Government* (originally published 1840; Philadelphia: John Cambell, 1863), 84–87.

41. *Luther v. Borden 48 U.S. 1 (1849)*.

42. Albert Bushnell Hart and Edward Channing, eds., *American History Leaflets: Colonial and Constitutional*, 1–18 vols (New York: A Lovell and Co., 1892), 12: 3–21.

43. James D. Richardson, ed., *Compilations of the Messages and Papers of the Presidents*, 11 vols (Washington, D.C.: Government Print Office, 1897, 1904), 6: 20–31.

44. F.B. Carpenter and John Herbert Clifford, eds., *The Works of Abraham Lincoln,* 6 volumes, Speeches and Presidential Addresses, 1859–1865 (New York: C.S. Hammond, 1908), 5: 183.

45. The Congressional Globe, *37th Congress, 2nd Session* (Washington, D.C.: Congressional Globe Office, 1862), 736–737.

46. James D. Richardson, ed., *Compilations of the Messages and Papers of the Presidents*, 11 vols (Washington, D.C.: Government Printing Office, 1897, 1904), 2498–2511.

47. *Texas v. White 74 U.S. 400 (1873)*.

48. Woodrow Wilson, "The States and the Federal Government," *The North American Review* 187 (May 1908): 684–701.

49. Albert Beveridge, *The Meaning of the Times and Other Speeches* (Indianapolis: The Bobbs-Merrill Company, 1908), 1–20.

50. Theodore Roosevelt, *New Nationalism* (New York: The Outlook Company, 1910), 11–32.

51. *Platforms of the Two Great Parties from 1856–1920* (La Crosse, WI: Arthur Bentley, 1922), 182–196.

52. George Henry Payne, *The Birth of a New Party: Or Progressive Democracy* (New York: J. L. Nichols & Co, 1912), 303–320.

53. Herbert Croly, *The Promise of American Life* (New York: The MacMillan Company, 1911), 21–36.

54. *Missouri v. Holland 252 U.S. 416 (1920)*.

55. Samuel Rosenman, *Public Papers of the Presidents of the United States: Franklin D. Roosevelt*, 13 vols (New York: Random House, 1938–1948), 11–17.

56. Samuel Rosenman, *Public Papers of the Presidents: Franklin D. Roosevelt*, 13 vols (New York: Random House, 1938–1948), 4: 421–423.

57. *Public Papers of the Presidents: Lyndon B. Johnson*, 10 vols (Washington, D.C.: Office of the Federal Register, 1965–1970), 1: 704–707.

58. *Public Papers of the Presidents: Richard M. Nixon*, 6 vols (Washington, D.C.: Government Printing Office, 1971–1975), 1: 639–645.

59. https://www.reaganlibrary.archives.gov/archives/speeches/1981/12081a.htm accessed December 3, 2016.

60. https://www.reaganlibrary.archives.gov/archives/speeches/1981/73081d.htm accessed December 3, 2016.

61. *New York v. U.S. 505 U.S. 144 (1992).*

62. *Printz v. US 521 U.S. 898 (1997).*

63. https://www.gpo.gov/fdsys/pkg/FR-1999-08-10/pdf/99-20729.pdf#page=1 accessed March 3, 2017.

64. 567 US___.

65. 10th Amendment Resolutions a collection can be found at http://tenthame ndmentcenter.com/nullification/10th-amendment-resolutions/ accessed November 2, 2016.

66. https://www.whitehouse.gov/the-press-office/2017/04/26/presidential-executi ve-order-enforcing-statutory-prohibitions-federal accessed July 15, 2017.

Part II

Civil Liberties

Editors' Note: Civil liberties are generally known as those protections guaranteed by the government to it citizens. It can range from protections held by individuals or to a more general class of citizens. They are sometimes thought of as a shield that is used against unwanted and unwarranted government action. The artifacts that follow span a time frame starting in 1833 to the present day. It is clear that the majority of these documents are in the modern era. This is not without cause. While the notion of civil liberties has roots in the founding era discussions of our political system, the interplay of these liberties and federalism has more recently accelerated.

The first four documents establish the pre-modern boundaries of the protections afforded to citizens from federal government intrusion. The delineation of specific protections is quite limited as these documents reflect a general attitude of federalism. That is, the protection of civil liberties was seen as more of a responsibility of the state governments than the federal government. These boundaries gave states wide latitude as to how they could treat their respective citizens. The variability in citizen protections between states was the most evident on the distinguishing characteristic of race. Beginning with the Platform of the Dixiecrats (1948) document and stretching to the Katzenbach v. McClung case of 1964, the effort to reverse the pervasive Jim Crow laws and culture captured the center of discussion concerning federalism. In less than 20 years, the previous 100 plus years of the debate of the applicability of federal protections toward citizens was rewritten. Each of the landmark court cases presented in this section demonstrate the continued refinement of Federalism's edge in terms of separating state from their ability to legislate discrimination.

The clarity that was created through the Civil Rights Era struggles continued to sink deeper into issues beyond race. Beginning with the Griswold case, federal protections of civil liberties began to take shape on issues such as marriage, sexual identity, and the rights an individual has over their own body. What will likely come in the near future are clarifications on how federalism relates to all aspects of one's life, whether it involves the upbringing of children to the very decision to end one's own life.

BARRON v. BALTIMORE[1]

. . . The plaintiff in error contends that it comes within that clause in the 5th amendment to the constitution, which inhibits the taking of private property for public use, without just compensation. He insists that this amendment, being in favor of the liberty of the citizen, ought to be so constructed as to restrain the legislative power of the State, as well as that of the United States. If this position be untrue, the court can take no jurisdiction of the cause.

The question thus presented is, we think, of great importance, but not of much difficulty.

The constitution was ordained and established by the people of the United States for themselves, for their own government and not for the government of the individual States. Each State established a constitution for itself, and, in that constitution, provided such limitations and restrictions on the powers of its particular government as its judgment dictated. The people of the United States framed such a government for the United States as they supposed best adapted to their situation, and best calculated to promote their interests. The powers they conferred on this government were to be exercised by itself; and the limitations on power, if expressed in general terms, are naturally, and, we think, necessarily applicable to the government created by the instrument. They are limitations of power granted in the instrument itself; not of distinct governments, framed by different persons and for different purposes.

If these propositions be correct, the 5th amendment must be understood as restraining the power of the general government, not as applicable to the States. In their several constitutions they have imposed such restrictions on their governments as their own wisdom suggested; such as they deemed most proper for themselves. It is a subject on which they judge exclusively, and with which others interfere no further than they are supposed to have a common interest. . .

Had the people of the several States, or any of them, required changes in their constitutions; had they required additional safeguards to liberty from the apprehended encroachments of their particular governments; the remedy was in their own hands, and would have been applied by themselves. A convention would have been assembled by the discontented State, and the required improvements would have been made by itself. The unwieldy and cumbrous machinery of procuring a recommendation from two thirds of congress, and the assent of three fourths of their Sister States, could never have occurred to any human being as a mode of doing that which might be effected by the State itself. Had the framers of these amendments intended them to be limitations on the powers of the state governments, they would have imitated the framers of the original constitution, and have expressed that intention. Had congress engaged in the extraordinary occupation of improving the constitutions of several States by affording the people additional protection from the exercise of power by their own governments in matters which concerned themselves alone, they would have declared this purpose in plain and intelligible language.

But it is universally understood, it is a part of the history of the day, that the great revolution which established the constitution of the United States, was not effected without immense opposition. Serious fears were extensively entertained that those powers which the patriot statesmen, who then watched over the interests of our country, deemed essential to union, and to the attainment of those invaluable objects for which union was sought, might be exercised in a manner dangerous to liberty. In almost every convention by which the constitution was adopted, amendments to guard against the abuse of power were recommended. These amendments demanded security against the apprehended encroachments of the general government, not against those of the local governments.

In compliance with a sentiment thus generally expressed to quiet fears thus extensively entertained, amendments were proposed by the required majority in congress, and adopted by the States. These amendments contain no expression indicating an intention to apply them to the state governments. This court cannot so apply them.

We are of opinion that the provision in the 5th amendment to the constitution, declaring that private property shall not be taken for public use without just compensation, is intended solely as a limitation on the exercise of power by the government of the United States, and is not applicable to the legislation of the States. We are therefore of opinion, that there is no repugnancy between the several acts of the general assembly of Maryland, given in evidence by the defendants at the trial of this case, in the court of the State, and the constitution of the United States. This court, therefore, has no jurisdiction of the cause; and it is dismissed.

CIVIL RIGHTS ACT OF 1866[2]

That all persons born in the United States and not subject to any foreign power, excluding Indians not taxed, are hereby declared to be citizens of the

United States; and such citizens, of every race and color, without regard to any previous condition of slavery or involuntary servitude, except as a punishment for crime whereof the party shall have been duly convicted, shall have the same right, in every State and Territory in the United States, to make and enforce contracts, to sue, be parties, and give evidence, to inherit, purchase, lease, sell, hold, and convey real and personal property, and to full and equal benefit of all laws and proceedings for the security of person and property, as is enjoyed by white citizens, and shall be subject to like punishment, pains, and penalties, and to none other, any law, statute, ordinance, regulation, or custom, to the contrary notwithstanding.

Sec. 2. *And be it further enacted,* That any person who, under color of any law, statute, ordinance, regulation, or custom, shall subject, or cause to be subjected, any inhabitant of any State or Territory to the deprivation of any right secured or protected by this act, or to different punishment, pains, or penalties on account of such person having at any time been held in a condition of slavery or involuntary servitude, except as a punishment for crime whereof the party shall have been duly convicted, or by reason of his color or race, than is prescribed for the punishment of white persons, shall be deemed guilty of a misdemeanor, and, on conviction, shall be punished by fine not exceeding one thousand dollars, or imprisonment not exceeding one year, or both, in the discretion of the court.

Sec. 3. *And be it further enacted,* That the district courts of the United States, within their respective districts, shall have, exclusively of the courts of the several States, cognizance of all crimes and offences committed against the provisions of this act, and also, concurrently with the circuit courts of the United States, of all causes, civil and criminal, affecting persons who are denied or cannot enforce in the courts or judicial tribunals of the State or locality where they may be any of the rights secured to them by the first section of this act; and if any suit or prosecution, civil or criminal, has been or shall be commenced in any State court, against any such person, for any cause whatsoever, or against any officer, civil or military, or other person, for any arrest or imprisonment, trespasses, or wrongs done or committed by virtue or under color of authority derived from this act or the act establishing a Bureau for the relief of Freedmen and Refugees, and all acts amendatory thereof, or for refusing to do any act upon the ground that it would be inconsistent with this act, such defendant shall have the right to remove such cause for trial to the proper district or circuit court in the manner prescribed by the "Act relating to habeas corpus and regulating judicial proceedings in certain cases," approved March three, eighteen hundred and sixty-three, and all acts amendatory thereof. The jurisdiction in civil and criminal matters hereby conferred on the district and circuit courts of the United States shall be exercised and enforced in conformity with the laws of the United States, so far as such laws are suitable to carry the same into effect; but in all cases where such laws are not adapted to the object, or are deficient in the provisions necessary to furnish suitable remedies and punish offences against law, the common law, as modified and changed by the constitution and statutes of the State wherein the court having jurisdiction of the cause, civil or criminal, is held, so far as the same is not inconsistent with the Constitution and laws of the United States, shall be extended to and govern said courts in the trial and disposition of such cause, and, if of a criminal nature, in the infliction of punishment on the party found guilty.

Sec. 5. *And be it further enacted*, That it shall be the duty of all marshals and deputy marshals to obey and execute all warrants and precepts issued under the provisions of this act, when to them directed; and should any marshal or deputy marshal refuse to receive such warrant or other process when tendered, or to use all proper means diligently to execute the same, he shall, on conviction thereof, be fined in the sum of one thousand dollars, to the use of the person upon whom the accused is alleged to have committed the offense. And the better to enable the said commissioners to execute their duties faithfully and efficiently, in conformity with the Constitution of the United States and the requirements of this act, they are hereby authorized and empowered, within their counties respectively, to appoint, in writing, under their hands, any one or more suitable persons, from time to time, to execute all such warrants and other process as may be issued by them in the lawful performance of their respective duties; and the persons so appointed to execute any warrant or process as aforesaid shall have authority to summon and call to their aid the bystanders or posse comitatus of the proper county, or such portion of the land or naval forces of the United States, or of the militia, as may be necessary to the performance of the duty with which they are charged, and to insure a faithful observance of the clause of the Constitution which prohibits slavery, in conformity with the provisions of this act; and said warrants shall run and be executed by said officers anywhere in the State or Territory within which they are issued.

Sec. 8. *And be it further enacted*, That whenever the President of the United States shall have reason to believe that offences have been or are likely to be committed against the provisions of this act within any judicial district, it shall be lawful for him, in his discretion, to direct the judge, marshal, and district attorney of such district to attend at such place within the district, and for such time as he may designate, for the purpose of the more speedy arrest and trial of persons charged with a violation of this act; and it shall be the duty of every judge or other officer, when any such requisition shall be received by him, to attend at the place and for the time therein designated.

Sec. 9. *And be it further enacted*, That it shall be lawful for the President of the United States, or such person as he may empower for that purpose, to employ such part of the land or naval forces of the United States, or of the militia, as shall be necessary to prevent the violation and enforce the due execution of this act.

Sec. 10. *And be it further enacted*, That upon all questions of law arising in any cause under the provisions of this act a final appeal may be taken to the Supreme Court of the United States.

ANDREW JOHNSON, VETO OF THE CIVIL RIGHTS ACT[3]

. . . By the first section of the bill, all persons born in the United States, and not subject to any foreign power, excluding Indians not taxed, are declared to be citizens of the United States. . . . It does not purport to declare or confer any other right of citizenship than Federal citizenship; it does not propose to give these classes of persons any status as citizens of States, except that which may result from their status as citizens of the United States. The power to confer the right of State citizenship is just as exclusively with the several States, as the power to confer the right of Federal citizenship is with Congress. The right of Federal citizenship, thus to be conferred in the several excepted ratios before mentioned, is now, for the first time, proposed to be given by law. If, as is claimed by many, all persons who are native born, already are, by virtue of the Constitution, citizens of the United States, the passage of the pending bill cannot be necessary to make them such. If, on the other hand, such persons are not citizens, as may be assumed from the proposed legislation to make them such, the grave question presents itself whether, where eleven of the thirty-six States are unrepresented in Congress at the time, it is sound policy to make our entire colored population, and all other excepted classes, citizens of the United States. Four millions of them have just emerged from slavery into freedom. Can it be reasonably supposed that they possess the requisite qualifications to entitle them to all the privileges and immunities of citizenship of the United States? Have the people of the several States expressed such a conviction? It may also be asked, whether it is necessary that they should be declared citizens in order that they may be secured in the enjoyment of the civil rights proposed to be conferred by the bill. Those rights are, by Federals as well as by State laws, secured to all domiciled aliens and foreigners, even before the completion of the process of naturalization; and it may safely be assumed that the same enactments are sufficient to give like protection and benefits to those for whom this bill provides special legislation. Besides the policy of the Government, from its origin to the present time, seems to have been that persons who are strangers to and unfamiliar with our institutions and laws, should pass through a certain probation; at the end of which, before attaining the coveted prize, they must give evidence of their fitness to receive and to exercise the rights of citizens as contemplated by the Constitution of the United States. The bill in effect proposes a discrimination against large numbers of intelligent, worthy and patriotic foreigners, and in favor of the negro, to whom, after long years of bondage, the avenues to freedom and intelligence have just now been suddenly opened. He must of necessity, from his previous unfortunate condition of servitude, be less informed as to the nature and character of our institutions than he who, coming from abroad, has to some extent, at least, familiarized himself with the principles of a Government to which he voluntarily entrusts life, liberty, and the pursuit of happiness. Yet it is now proposed by a single legislative enactment to confer the rights of citizens upon all persons of African descent, born within the excluded limits of the United States, while persons of foreign birth, who make our land their home, must undergo a probation of five years, and can only then become citizens upon proof that they are of good moral character, attached to the principles of the Constitution of the United States, and well disposed to the good order and happiness of the same. The first section of the bill also contains an enumeration of the rights to be enjoyed by those classes so made citizens in every State and Territory of the United States. These rights are, to make and enforce contracts, to sue, be parties and give evidence, to inherit, purchase, lease, sell, hold, or convey real and personal property, and to have full and equal benefit of all laws and proceedings for the security of persons and property as is enjoyed by white citizens. So, too, they are made subject to the same punishments, pains, and penalties common with white citizens, and to none others. Thus a perfect equality of the white and colored races is attempted to be fixed by a Federal law in every State of the Union, over the vast field of State jurisdiction covered by these enumerated rights. In no one of them can any State exercise any power of discrimination between different races. In the exercise of State policy over matters exclusively affecting the people of each State, it has frequently been thought expedient to discriminate between the two races. By the statutes of some of the States, North as well as South, it is enacted, for instance, that no white person shall intermarry with a negro or mulatto. Chancellor Kent says, speaking of the blacks, that marriages between them and the whites are forbidden in some in some of the States where slavery does not exist, and they are prohibited in all the slaveholding States by law; and when not absolutely contrary to law, they are revolting, and regarded as an offence against public decorum. I do not say that this bill repeals State laws, on the subject of marriage between the two races, for as the whites are forbidden to intermarry with the blacks, the blacks can only make such contracts as the whites themselves are allowed to make, and therefore cannot, under this bill, enter into the marriage contract with the whites. I take this discrimination, however, as an instance of the State policy as to discrimination, and to inquire whether, if Congress can abrogate all State laws of discrimination between the two races, in the matter of real estate, of suits, and of contracts generally, Congress may not also repeal the State laws as to the contract of marriage between the races? Hitherto, every subject embraced in the enumeration of rights contained in the bill has been considered as exclusively belonging to the States; they all relate to the internal policy and economy of the respective States. They are matters which, in each State, concern the domestic condition of its people, varying in each according to its peculiar circumstances and the safety and well-being of its own citizens. I do not mean to say that upon all these subjects there are not Federal restraints; as, for instance, in the State power of legislation over contracts, there is a Federal limitation that no State shall pass a law impairing the obligations of contracts; and, as to crimes, that no State shall pass an *ex-post-facto* law; and, as to money, that no State shall make any thing but gold and silver as legal tender. But where can we find a Federal prohibition against the power of any State to discriminate, as do most of them, between aliens and citizens, between artificial persons called corporations, and naturalized persons, in the right to hold real estate? If it be granted that Congress can repeal all State laws discriminating between the two races on the subject of suffrage and office? If Congress shall declare by law who shall hold lands, who shall testify, who shall have capacity to make a contract in a State, that Congress can also declare by law, without regard to race or color, shall have the right to act as a juror or as a judge, to hold any office, and finally to vote, in every State and Territory of the United States. As respects the Territory of the United States, they come within the power of Congress, for as to them the law-making power is the Federal power; but as to the States, no similar provision exists, vesting in Congress the power to make such rules and regulations for them.

The object of the second section of the bill is to afford discriminating protection to colored persons in the full enjoyment of all the rights secured to them by the preceding section. It declares that "any person who, under color of any law, statute, ordinance, regulation, or custom, shall subject or cause to be subjected any inhabitant of any State or Territory to the deprivation of any rights secured or protected by this act, or to different punishment, pains, or penalties on account of such person having at any time been held in a condition of slavery or involuntary servitude, except as a punishment of crime, whereof the party shall have been duly convicted, or by reason of his color or race, than is prescribed for the punishment of white persons, shall be deemed guilty of a misdemeanor, and on conviction shall be punished by fine not exceeding one thousand dollars, or imprisonment not exceeding one year, or both, in the discretion of the court." This section seems to be designed to apply to some existing or future law of a State or Territory, which may conflict with the provisions of the bill now under consideration. It provides for counteracting such forbidden legislation, by imposing fine and imprisonment upon the legislators who may pass such conflicting laws, or upon the officers or agents who shall put or attempt to put them into execution. It means an official offence, not a common crime, committed against law upon the person or property of the black race. Such an act may deprive the black man of his property, but not of his right to hold property. It means a deprivation of the right itself, either by the State Judiciary or the State Legislature. It is, therefore, assumed that, under this section, members of a State Legislature who should vote for laws conflicting with the provisions of the bill, that judges of the State courts who should render judgments in antagonism with its terms, and that marshals and sheriffs who should as ministerial officers execute processes sanctioned by State laws and issued by State judges in execution of their judgments, could be brought before other tribunals and there subjected to fine and imprisonment, for the performance of the duties which such State laws might impose. The legislation thus proposed invades the judicial power of the State. It says to every State court or judge: If you decide that this act is unconstitutional; if you hold that over such a subject-matter the said law is paramount, under color of a State law refuse the exercise of the right to the negro; your error of judgment, however conscientious, shall subject you to fine and imprisonment. I do not apprehend that the conflicting legislation which the bill seems to contemplate is so likely to occur, as to render it necessary at this time to adopt a measure of such constitutionality. In the next place, this provision of the bill seems to be unnecessary, as adequate judicial remedies could be adopted to secure the desired end without invading the immunities of legislators, always important to be preserved in the interest of public liberty, notwithstanding the independence of the judiciary, always essential to the preservation of individual rights, and without impairing the efficiency of ministerial officers, always necessary for the maintenance of public peace and order. The remedy proposed by this section seems to be in this respect not only anomalous but unconstitutional, for the Constitution guarantees nothing with certainty if it does not insure to the several States the right of making index ruling laws in regard to all matters arising within their jurisdiction, subject only to the restriction, in cases of conflict with the Constitution and constitutional laws of the United States—the latter to be held as the supreme law of the land.

The third section gives the district courts of the United States exclusive cognizance of all crimes and offences committed against the provisions of this act, and concurrent jurisdiction with the circuit courts of the United States, of all civil and criminal cases affecting persons that are denied, or cannot enforce in the courts or judicial tribunals of the State or locality where they may be, any of the rights secured to them by the first section. The construction which I have given to the second section is strengthened by this third section, for it makes clear what kind of denial, or deprivation of rights secured by the first section, was in contemplation. It is a denial or deprivation of such rights in the courts or tribunals of the State. It stands, therefore, clear of doubt that the offence and the penalties provided in the second section are intended for the State judge who, in the clear exercise of his functions as a judge, not acting ministerially but judicially, shall decide contrary to this Federal law. In other words, when a State judge, acting upon a question involving a conflict between a State law and a Federal law, and bound, according to his own judgment and responsibility to give an impartial decision between the two, comes to the conclusion that the State law is valid and the Federal law is invalid, he must not follow the dictates of his own judgment, at the peril of fine and imprisonment. The legislative department of the Government of the United States thus takes from the judicial department of the States the sacred and exclusive duty of judicial decision, and converts the State judge into a mere ministerial officer, bound to decide according to the will of Congress. It is clear that in States which deny to persons, whose rights are secured by the first section of the bill, any one of those rights, all criminal and civil cases affecting them will, by the provisions of the third section, come under the executive cognizance of the Federal tribunals. It follows that if in any State, which denies to a colored person any one of all these rights, that person should commit a crime against the laws of a State—murder, arson, rape, or any other crime—all protection and punishment, through the courts of the State, are taken away, and he can only be tried and punished in the Federal courts. How is the criminal to be tried, if the offence is provided for and punished by Federal law? That law, and not the State law, is to govern. It was only when the offence does not happen to be within the province of Federal law that the Federal courts are to try and punish him under any other law. The resort is to be had to the common law, as modified and changed by State legislation, so far as the same is not inconsistent with the Constitution and laws of the United States. So that over this vast domain of criminal jurisprudence, provided by each State for the protection of its citizens and for the punishment of all persons who violate its criminal laws, Federal law, wherever it can be made to apply, displaces State law. The question naturally arises, from what source Congress derives the power to transfer to Federal tribunals certain classes of cases embraced in this section. The Constitution expressly declares that the judicial power of the United States "shall extend to all cases in law and equity, arising under this Constitution, the laws of the

United States, and treaties made, or which shall be made, under their authority; to all cases affecting ambassadors or other public ministers and consuls; to all cases of admiralty and maritime jurisdiction; to controversies to which the United States shall be a party; to controversies between two or more States; between a State and citizens of another State; between citizens of different States; between citizens of the same State claiming land under grants of different States; and between a State, or the citizens thereof, and foreign States, citizens, or subjects."

Here the judicial power of the United States is expressly set forth and defined; and the act of September 24, 1789, establishing the judicial courts of the United States, in conferring upon the Federal courts jurisdiction over cases originating in State tribunals, is careful to confine them to the classes enumerated in the above recited clause of the Constitution. This section of the bill undoubtedly comprehends cases and authorizes the exercise of powers that are not, by the Constitution, within the jurisdiction of the courts of the United States. To transfer them to these courts would be an exercise of authority well calculated to excite distrust and alarm on the part of all the States, for the bill applies alike to all of them, as well as to those who have not been engaged in rebellion. It may be assumed that this authority is incident to the power granted to Congress by the Constitution as recently amended, to enforce, by appropriate legislation, the article declaring that neither slavery nor involuntary servitude, except as a punishment for crime, whereof the party shall have been duly convicted, shall exist within the United States, or any place subject to their jurisdiction. It cannot, however, be justly claimed that, with a view to the enforcement of this article of the Constitution, there is at present any necessity for the exercise of all the powers which this bill confers. Slavery has been abolished, and at present nowhere exists within the jurisdiction of the United States. Nor has there been, nor is it likely there will be any attempts to revive it by the people of the States. If, however, any such attempt shall be made, it will then become the duty of the General Government to exercise any and all incidental powers necessary and proper to maintain inviolate this great law of freedom. The fourth section of the bill provides that officers and agents of the Freedmen's Bureau shall be empowered to make arrests, and also that other officers shall be specially commissioned for that purpose by the President of the United States. It also authorizes the Circuit Courts of the United States and the Superior Courts of the Territories to appoint, without limitation, commissioners, who are to be charged with the performance of quasi judicial duties. The fifth section empowers the commissioners so to be selected by the court, to appoint, in writing, one or more suitable persons from time to time to execute warrants and processes desirable by the bill. These numerous official agents are made to constitute a sort of police in addition to the military, and are authorized to summon a *posse commitatus*, and even to call to their aid such portion of the land and naval forces of the United States, or of the militia, "as may be necessary to the performance of the duty with which they are charged." This extraordinary power is to be conferred upon agents irresponsible to the Government and to the people, to whose number the discretion of the commissioners is the only limit, and in whose hands such authority might be made a terrible engine of wrong, oppression, and fraud. The general statutes regulating the land and naval forces of the United States, the militia, and the execution of the laws are believed to be adequate for any emergency which can occur in time of peace. If it should prove otherwise, Congress can at any time amend those laws in such a manner as, while subserving the public welfare, not to jeopardize the rights, interests, and liberties of the people.

. . . I do not propose to consider the policy of this bill. To me the details of the bill are fraught with evil. The white race and black race of the South have hitherto lived together under the relation of master and slave—capital owning labor. Now that relation is changed; and as to ownership, capital and labor are divorced. They stand now, each master of itself. In this new relation, one being necessary to the other, there will be a new adjustment, which both are deeply interested in making harmonious. Each has equal power in settling the terms; and, if left to the laws that regulate capital and labor, it is confidently believed that they will satisfactorily work out the problem. Capital, it is true, has more intelligence; but labor is never ignorant as not to understand its own interests, not to know its own value, and not to see that capital must pay that value. This bill frustrates this adjustment. It intervenes between capital and labor, and attempts to settle questions of political economy through the agency of numerous officials, whose interest it will be to foment discord between the two races; for as the breach widens, their employment will continue; and when it is closed, their occupation will terminate. In all our history, in all our experience as a people living under Federal and State law, no such system as that contemplated by the details of this bill has ever before been proposed or adopted. They establish for the security of the colored race safeguards which go indefinitely beyond any that the General Government has ever provided for the white race. In fact, the distinction of race and color is by the bill made to operate in favor of the colored against the white race. They interfere with the municipal legislation of the States; with relations existing exclusively between a State and its citizens, or between inhabitants of the same State; an absorption and assumption of power by the General Government which, if acquiesced in, must sap and destroy our federative system of limited power, and break down the barriers which preserve the rights of the States. It is another step, or rather stride, towards centralization and the concentration of all legislative powers in the National Government. The tendency of the bill must be to resuscitate the spirit of rebellion, and to arrest the progress of those influences which are more closely drawing around the States the bonds of union and peace.

14TH AMENDMENT (RATIFIED, 1868)

Section 1. All persons born or naturalized in the United States, and subject to the jurisdiction thereof, are citizens of the United States and of the State wherein they reside. No State shall make or enforce any law which shall abridge the privileges or immunities of citizens of the United States; nor shall any State deprive any person of life, liberty, or property, without due process of law; nor deny to any person within its jurisdiction the equal protection of the laws.

Section 2. Representatives shall be apportioned among the several States according to their respective numbers, counting the whole number of persons in each State, excluding Indians not taxed. But when the right to vote at any election for the choice of electors for President and Vice President of the United States, Representatives in Congress, the Executive and Judicial officers of a State, or the members of the Legislature thereof, is denied to any of the male inhabitants of such State, being twenty-one years of age, and citizens of the United States, or in any way abridged, except for participation in rebellion, or other crime, the basis of representation therein shall be reduced in the proportion which the number of such male citizens shall bear to the whole number of male citizens twenty-one years of age in such State.

Section 3. No person shall be a Senator or Representative in Congress, or elector of President and Vice President, or hold any office, civil or military, under the United States, or under any State, who, having previously taken an oath, as a member of Congress, or as an officer of the United States, or as a member of any State legislature, or as an executive or judicial officer of any State, to support the Constitution of the United States, shall have engaged in insurrection or rebellion against the same, or given aid or comfort to the enemies thereof. But Congress may, by a vote of two-thirds of each House, remove such disability.

Section 4. The validity of the public debt of the United States, authorized by law, including debts incurred for payment of pensions and bounties for services in suppressing insurrection or rebellion, shall not be questioned. But neither the United States nor any State shall assume or pay any debt or obligation incurred in aid of insurrection or rebellion against the United States, or any claim for the loss or emancipation of any slave; but all such debts, obligations and claims shall be held illegal and void.

Section 5. The Congress shall have power to enforce, by appropriate legislation, the provisions of this article.

PLATFORM OF THE STATES RIGHTS
DEMOCRATIC PARTY (DIXIECRATS) 1948

We believe that the Constitution of the United States is the greatest charter of human liberty ever conceived by the mind of man.

We oppose all efforts to invade or destroy the rights guaranteed by it to every citizen of this republic.

We stand for social and economic justice, which, we believe can be guaranteed to all citizens only by a strict adherence to our Constitution and the avoidance of any invasion or destruction of the constitutional rights of the states and individuals. We oppose the totalitarian, centralized bureaucratic government and the police nation called for by the platforms adopted by the Democratic and Republican Conventions.

We stand for the segregation of the races and the racial integrity of each race; the constitutional right to choose one's associates; to accept private employment without governmental interference, and to earn one's living in any lawful way. We oppose the elimination of segregation, the repeal of miscegenation statutes, the control of private employment by Federal bureaucrats called for by the misnamed civil rights program. We favor home-rule, local self-government and a minimum interference with individual rights.

We oppose and condemn the action of the Democratic Convention in sponsoring a civil rights program calling for the elimination of segregation, social equality by Federal fiat, regulations of private employment practices, voting, and local law enforcement.

We affirm that the effective enforcement of such a program would be utterly destructive of the social, economic and political life of the Southern people, and of other localities in which there may be differences in race, creed or national origin in appreciable numbers.

We stand for the check and balances provided by the three departments of our government. We oppose the usurpation of legislative functions by the executive and judicial departments. We unreservedly condemn the effort to establish in the United States a police nation that would destroy the last vestige of liberty enjoyed by a citizen.

We demand that there be returned to the people to whom of right they belong, those powers needed for the preservation of human rights and the discharge of our responsibility as democrats for human welfare. We oppose a denial of those by political parties, a barter or sale of those rights by a political convention, as well as any invasion or violation of those rights by the Federal Government. We call upon all Democrats and upon all other loyal Americans who are opposed to totalitarianism at home and abroad to unite with us in ignominiously defeating Harry S. Truman, Thomas E. Dewey and every other candidate for public office who would establish a Police Nation in the United States of America.

SOUTHERN MANIFESTO[4]

Declaration of Constitutional Principles

The unwarranted decision of the Supreme Court in the public school cases is now bearing the fruit always produced when men substitute naked power for established law.

The Founding Fathers gave us a Constitution of checks and balances because they realized the inescapable lesson of history that no man or group of men can be safely entrusted with unlimited power. They framed this Constitution with its provisions for change by amendment in order to secure the fundamentals of government against the dangers of temporary popular passion or the personal predilections of public officeholders.

We regard the decisions of the Supreme Court in the school cases as a clear abuse of judicial power. It climaxes a trend in the Federal Judiciary undertaking to legislate, in derogation of the authority of Congress, and to encroach upon the reserved rights of the States and the people.

The original Constitution does not mention education. Neither does the 14th Amendment nor any other amendment. The debates preceding the submission of the 14th Amendment clearly show that there was no intent that it should affect the system of education maintained by the States.

The very Congress which proposed the amendment subsequently provided for segregated schools in the District of Columbia.

When the amendment was adopted in 1868, there were 37 States of the Union . . . .

Every one of the 26 States that had any substantial racial differences among its people, either approved the operation of segregated schools already in existence or subsequently established such schools by action of the same law-making body which considered the 14th Amendment.

As admitted by the Supreme Court in the public school case (*Brown v. Board of Education*), the doctrine of separate but equal schools "apparently originated in *Roberts v. City of Boston* (1849), upholding school segregation against attack as being violative of a State constitutional guarantee of equality." This constitutional doctrine began in the North, not in the South, and it was followed not only in Massachusetts, but in Connecticut, New York, Illinois, Indiana, Michigan, Minnesota, New Jersey, Ohio, Pennsylvania and other northern states until they, exercising their rights as states through the constitutional processes of local self-government, changed their school systems.

In the case of *Plessy v. Ferguson* in 1896 the Supreme Court expressly declared that under the 14th Amendment no person was denied any of his rights if the States provided separate but equal facilities. This decision has been followed in many other cases. It is notable that the Supreme Court, speaking through Chief Justice Taft, a former President of the United States, unanimously declared in 1927 in *Lum v. Rice* that the "separate but equal" principle is "within the discretion of the State in regulating its public schools and does not conflict with the 14th Amendment."

This interpretation, restated time and again, became a part of the life of the people of many of the States and confirmed their habits, traditions, and way of life. It is founded on elemental humanity and commonsense, for parents should not be deprived by Government of the right to direct the lives and education of their own children.

Though there has been no constitutional amendment or act of Congress changing this established legal principle almost a century old, the Supreme Court of the United States, with no legal basis for such action, undertook to exercise their naked judicial power and substituted their personal political and social ideas for the established law of the land.

This unwarranted exercise of power by the Court, contrary to the Constitution, is creating chaos and confusion in the States principally affected. It is destroying the amicable relations between the white and Negro races that have been created through 90 years of patient effort by the good people of both races. It has planted hatred and suspicion where there has been heretofore friendship and understanding.

Without regard to the consent of the governed, outside mediators are threatening immediate and revolutionary changes in our public schools systems. If done, this is certain to destroy the system of public education in some of the States.

With the gravest concern for the explosive and dangerous condition created by this decision and inflamed by outside meddlers:

We reaffirm our reliance on the Constitution as the fundamental law of the land.

We decry the Supreme Court's encroachment on the rights reserved to the States and to the people, contrary to established law, and to the Constitution.

We commend the motives of those States which have declared the intention to resist forced integration by any lawful means.

We appeal to the States and people who are not directly affected by these decisions to consider the constitutional principles involved against the time when they too, on issues vital to them may be the victims of judicial encroachment.

Even though we constitute a minority in the present Congress, we have full faith that a majority of the American people believe in the dual system of government which has enabled us to achieve our greatness and will in time demand that the reserved rights of the States and of the people be made secure against judicial usurpation.

We pledge ourselves to use all lawful means to bring about a reversal of this decision which is contrary to the Constitution and to prevent the use of force in its implementation.

In this trying period, as we all seek to right this wrong, we appeal to our people not to be provoked by the agitators and troublemakers invading our States and to scrupulously refrain from disorder and lawless acts.

BROWN v. BOARD OF EDUCATION OF TOPEKA 2[5]

[CHIEF JUSTICE WARREN] These cases were decided on May 17, 1954. The opinions of that date, declaring the fundamental principle that racial discrimination in public education is unconstitutional, are incorporated herein by reference. All provisions of federal, state, or local law requiring or permitting such discrimination must yield to this principle. There remains for consideration the manner in which relief is to be accorded.

Because these cases arose under different local conditions and their disposition will involve a variety of local problems, we requested further argument on the question of relief. In view of the nationwide importance of the decision, we invited the Attorney General of the United States and the Attorneys General of all states requiring or permitting racial discrimination in public education to present their views on that question. The parties, the United States, and the States of Florida, North Carolina, Arkansas, Oklahoma, Maryland, and Texas filed briefs and participated in the oral argument.

These presentations were informative and helpful to the Court in its consideration of the complexities arising from the transition to a system of public education freed of racial discrimination. The presentations also demonstrated that substantial steps to eliminate racial discrimination in public schools have already been taken, not only in some of the communities in which these cases arose, but in some of the states appearing as *amici curiae*, and in other states as well. Substantial progress has been made in the District of Columbia and in the communities in Kansas and Delaware involved in this litigation. The defendants in the cases coming to us from South Carolina and Virginia are awaiting the decision of this Court concerning relief.

Full implementation of these constitutional principles may require solution of varied local school problems. School authorities have the primary responsibility for elucidating, assessing, and solving these problems; courts will have to consider whether the action of school authorities constitutes good faith implementation of the governing constitutional principles. Because of their proximity to local conditions and the possible need for further hearings, the courts which originally heard these cases can best perform this judicial appraisal. Accordingly, we believe it appropriate to remand the cases to those courts.

In fashioning and effectuating the decrees, the courts will be guided by equitable principles. Traditionally, equity has been characterized by a practical flexibility in shaping its remedies and by a facility for adjusting and reconciling public and private needs. These cases call for the exercise of these traditional attributes of equity power. At stake is the personal interest of the plaintiffs in admission to public schools as soon as practicable on a nondiscriminatory basis. To effectuate this interest may call for elimination of a variety of obstacles in making the transition to school systems operated in accordance with the constitutional principles set forth in our May 17, 1954, decision. Courts of equity may properly take into account the public interest in the elimination of such obstacles in a systematic and effective manner. But it should go without saying that the vitality of these constitutional principles cannot be allowed to yield simply because of disagreement with them.

While giving weight to these public and private considerations, the courts will require that the defendants make a prompt and reasonable start toward full compliance with our May 17, 1954, ruling. Once such a start has been made, the courts may find that additional time is necessary to carry out the ruling in an effective manner. The burden rests upon the defendants to establish that such time is necessary in the public interest and is consistent with good faith compliance at the earliest practicable date. To that end, the courts may consider problems related to administration, arising from the physical condition of the school plant, the school transportation system, personnel, revision of school districts and attendance areas into compact units to achieve a system of determining admission to the public schools on a nonracial basis, and revision of local laws and regulations which may be necessary in solving the foregoing problems. They will also consider the adequacy of any plans the defendants may propose to meet these problems and to effectuate a transition to a racially nondiscriminatory school system. During this period of transition, the courts will retain jurisdiction of these cases.

EISENHOWER, "REMARKS ON LITTLE ROCK"[6]

Good Evening, My Fellow Citizens: For a few minutes this evening I want to speak to you about the serious situation that has arisen in Little Rock. To make this talk I have come to the President's office in the White House.

I could have spoken from Rhode Island, where I have been staying recently, but I felt that, in speaking from the house of Lincoln, of Jackson and of Wilson, my words would better convey both the sadness I feel in the action I was compelled today to take and the firmness with which I intend to pursue this course until the orders of the Federal Court at Little Rock can be executed without unlawful interference.

In that city, under the leadership of demagogic extremists, disorderly mobs have deliberately prevented the carrying out of proper orders from a Federal Court. Local authorities have not eliminated that violent opposition and, under the law, I yesterday issued a Proclamation calling upon the mob to disperse.

This morning the mob again gathered in front of the Central High School of Little Rock, obviously for the purpose of again preventing the carrying out of the Court's order relating to the admission of Negro children to that school.

Whenever normal agencies prove inadequate to the task and it becomes necessary for the Executive Branch of the Federal Government to use its powers and authority to uphold Federal Courts, the President's responsibility is inescapable. In accordance with that responsibility, I have today issued an Executive Order directing the use of troops under Federal authority to aid in the execution of Federal law at Little Rock, Arkansas. This became necessary when my Proclamation of yesterday was not observed, and the obstruction of justice still continues.

It is important that the reasons for my action be understood by all our citizens. As you know, the Supreme Court of the United States has decided that separate public educational facilities for the races are inherently unequal and therefore compulsory school segregation laws are unconstitutional.

Our personal opinions about the decision have no bearing on the matter of enforcement; the responsibility and authority of the Supreme Court to interpret the Constitution are very clear. Local Federal Courts were instructed by the Supreme Court to issue such orders and decrees as might be necessary to achieve admission to public schools without regard to race—and with all deliberate speed.

During the past several years, many communities in our Southern States have instituted public school plans for gradual progress in the enrollment and attendance of school children of all races in order to bring themselves into compliance with the law of the land. They thus demonstrated to the world that we are a nation in which laws, not men, are supreme.

I regret to say that this truth—the cornerstone of our liberties—was not observed in this instance.

It was my hope that this localized situation would be brought under control by city and State authorities. If the use of local police powers had been sufficient, our traditional method of leaving the problems in those hands would have been pursued. But when large gatherings of obstructionists made it impossible for the decrees of the Court to be carried out, both the law and the national interest demanded that the President take action.

. . . Proper and sensible observance of the law then demanded the respectful obedience which the nation has a right to expect from all its people. This, unfortunately, has not been the case at Little Rock. Certain misguided persons, many of them imported into Little Rock by agitators, have insisted upon defying the law and have sought to bring it into disrepute. The orders of the court have thus been frustrated.

The very basis of our individual rights and freedoms rests upon the certainty that the President and the Executive Branch of Government will support and insure the carrying out of the decisions of the Federal Courts, even, when necessary with all the means at the President's command.

Unless the President did so, anarchy would result.

There would be no security for any except that which each one of us could provide for himself.

The interest of the nation in the proper fulfillment of the law's requirements cannot yield to opposition and demonstrations by some few persons.

Mob rule cannot be allowed to override the decisions of our courts.

Now, let me make it very clear that Federal troops are not being used to relieve local and state authorities of their primary duty to preserve the peace and order of the community. Nor are the troops there for the purpose of taking over the responsibility of the School Board and the other responsible local officials in running Central High School. The running of our school system and the maintenance of peace and order in each of our States are strictly local affairs and the Federal Government does not interfere except in a very few special cases and when requested by one of the several States. In the present case the troops are there, pursuant to law, solely for the purpose of preventing interference with the orders of the Court.

The proper use of the powers of the Executive Branch to enforce the orders of a Federal Court is limited to extraordinary and compelling circumstances. Manifestly, such an extreme situation has been created in Little Rock. This challenge must be met and with such measures as will preserve to the people as a whole their lawfully-protected rights in a climate permitting their free and fair exercise. The overwhelming majority of our people in every section of the country are united in their respect for observance of the law—even in those cases where they may disagree with that law.

They deplore the call of extremists to violence.

The decision of the Supreme Court concerning school integration, of course, affects the South more seriously than it does other sections of the country. In that region I have many warm friends, some of them in the city of Little Rock. I have deemed it a great personal privilege to spend in our

Southland tours of duty while in the military service and enjoyable recreational periods since that time.

So from intimate personal knowledge, I know that the overwhelming majority of the people in the South—including those of Arkansas and of Little Rock—are of good will, united in their efforts to preserve and respect the law even when they disagree with it.

They do not sympathize with mob rule. They, like the rest of our nation, have proved in two great wars their readiness to sacrifice for America.

A foundation of our American way of life is our national respect for law.

In the South, as elsewhere, citizens are keenly aware of the tremendous disservice that has been done to the people of Arkansas in the eyes of the nation, and that has been done to the nation in the eyes of the world.

At a time when we face grave situations abroad because of the hatred that Communism bears toward a system of government based on human rights, it would be difficult to exaggerate the harm that is being done to the prestige and influence, and indeed to the safety, of our nation and the world.

Our enemies are gloating over this incident and using it everywhere to misrepresent our whole nation. We are portrayed as a violator of those standards of conduct which the peoples of the world united to proclaim in the Charter of the United Nations. There they affirmed "faith in fundamental human rights" and "in the dignity and worth of the human person" and they did so "without distinction as to race, sex, language or religion."

And so, with deep confidence, I call upon the citizens of the State of Arkansas to assist in bringing to an immediate end all interference with the law and its processes. If resistance to the Federal Court orders ceases at once, the further presence of Federal troops will be unnecessary and the City of Little Rock will return to its normal habits of peace and order and a blot upon the fair name and high honor of our nation in the world will be removed.

Thus will be restored the image of America and of all its parts as one nation, indivisible, with liberty and justice for all.

COOPER v. AARON[7]

[Chief Justice] As this case reaches us, it raises questions of the highest importance to the maintenance of our federal system of government. It necessarily involves a claim by the Governor and Legislature of a State that there is no duty on state officials to obey federal court orders resting on this Court's considered interpretation of the United States Constitution. Specifically, it involves actions by the Governor and Legislature of Arkansas upon the premise that they are not bound by our holding in *Brown v. Board of Education*, [t]hat holding was that the Fourteenth Amendment forbids States to use their governmental powers to bar children on racial grounds from attending schools where there is state participation through any arrangement, management, funds or property. We are urged to uphold a suspension of the Little Rock School Board's plan to do away with segregated public schools in Little Rock until state laws and efforts to upset and nullify our holding in *Brown v. Board of Education* have been further challenged and tested in the courts. We reject these contentions.

. . . the District Courts were directed to require "a prompt and reasonable start toward full compliance," and to take such action as was necessary to bring about the end of racial segregation in the public schools "with all deliberate speed" . . . State authorities were thus duty bound to devote every effort toward initiating desegregation and bringing about the elimination of racial discrimination in the public school system.

. . . On September 2, 1957, the day before these Negro students were to enter Central High, the school authorities were met with drastic opposing action on the part of the Governor of Arkansas, who dispatched units of the Arkansas National Guard to the Central High School grounds and placed the school "off limits" to colored students. As found by the District Court in subsequent proceedings, the Governor's action had not been requested by the school authorities, and was entirely unheralded.

On the morning of the next day, September 4, 1957, the Negro children attempted to enter the high school, but, as the District Court later found, units of the Arkansas National Guard, "acting pursuant to the Governor's order, stood shoulder to shoulder at the school grounds and thereby forcibly prevented the 9 Negro students . . . from entering," as they continued to do every school day during the following three weeks.

. . . the actions of legislators and executive officials of the State of Arkansas, taken in their official capacities, which reflect their own determination to resist this Court's decision in the *Brown* case and which have brought about violent resistance to that decision in Arkansas. In its petition for certiorari filed in this Court, the School Board itself describes the situation in this language: "The legislative, executive, and judicial departments of the state government opposed the desegregation of Little Rock schools by enacting laws, calling out troops, making statements villifying federal law and federal courts, and failing to utilize state law enforcement agencies and judicial processes to maintain public peace."

. . . The constitutional rights of respondents are not to be sacrificed or yielded to the violence and disorder which have followed upon the actions of the Governor and Legislature.

Thus, law and order are not here to be preserved by depriving the Negro children of their constitutional rights. The record before us clearly establishes that the growth of the Board's difficulties to a magnitude beyond its unaided power to control is the product of state action. Those difficulties, as counsel for the Board forthrightly conceded on the oral argument in this Court, can also be brought under control by state action.

The controlling legal principles are plain. The command of the Fourteenth Amendment is that no "State" shall deny to any person within its jurisdiction the equal protection of the laws.

"A State acts by its legislative, its executive, or its judicial authorities. It can act in no other way. The constitutional provision, therefore, must mean that no agency of the State, or of the officers or agents by whom its powers are exerted, shall deny to any person within its jurisdiction the equal protection of the laws. Whoever, by virtue of public position under a State government, . . . denies or takes away the equal protection of the laws violates the constitutional inhibition; and, as he acts in the name and for the State, and is clothed with the State's power, his act is that of the State. This must be so, or the constitutional prohibition has no meaning."

Thus, the prohibitions of the Fourteenth Amendment extend to all action of the State denying equal protection of the laws; whatever the agency of the State taking the action, or whatever the guise in which it is taken[.] In short, the constitutional rights of children not to be discriminated against in school admission on grounds of race or color declared by this Court in the *Brown* case can neither be nullified openly and directly by state legislators or state executive or judicial officers nor nullified indirectly by them through evasive schemes for segregation whether attempted "ingeniously or ingenuously."

What has been said, in the light of the facts developed, is enough to dispose of the case. However, we should answer the premise of the actions of the Governor and Legislature that they are not bound by our holding in the *Brown* case. It is necessary only to recall some basic constitutional propositions which are settled doctrine.

Article VI of the Constitution makes the Constitution the "supreme Law of the Land." In 1803, Chief Justice Marshall, speaking for a unanimous Court, referring to the Constitution as "the fundamental and paramount law of the nation," declared in the notable case of *Marbury v. Madison*, that "It is emphatically the province and duty of the judicial department to say what the law is." This decision declared the basic principle that the federal judiciary is supreme in the exposition of the law of the Constitution, and that principle has ever since been respected by this Court and the Country as a permanent and indispensable feature of our constitutional system. It follows that the interpretation of the Fourteenth Amendment enunciated by this Court in the *Brown* case is the supreme law of the land, and Art. VI of the Constitution makes it of binding effect on the States "any Thing in the Constitution or Laws of any State to the Contrary notwithstanding." Every state legislator and executive and judicial officer is solemnly committed by oath taken pursuant to Art. VI, cl. 3 "to support this Constitution." Chief Justice Taney, speaking for a unanimous Court in 1859, said that this requirement reflected the framers' "anxiety to preserve it [the Constitution] in full force, in all its powers, and to guard against resistance to or evasion of its authority, on the part of a State. . . ."

No state legislator or executive or judicial officer can war against the Constitution without violating his undertaking to support it. Chief Justice Marshall spoke for a unanimous Court in saying that: "If the legislatures of the several states may at will, annul the judgments of the courts of the United States, and destroy the rights acquired under those judgments, the constitution itself becomes a solemn mockery . . . ."

A Governor who asserts a power to nullify a federal court order is similarly restrained. If he had such power, said Chief Justice Hughes, in 1932, also for a unanimous Court, "it is manifest that the fiat of a state Governor, and not the Constitution of the United States, would be the supreme law of the land; that the restrictions of the Federal Constitution upon the exercise of state power would be but impotent phrases . . . ."

It is, of course, quite true that the responsibility for public education is primarily the concern of the States, but it is equally true that such responsibilities, like all other state activity, must be exercised consistently with federal constitutional requirements as they apply to state action. The Constitution created a government dedicated to equal justice under law. The Fourteenth Amendment embodied and emphasized that ideal. State support of segregated schools through any arrangement, management, funds, or property cannot be squared with the Amendment's command that no State shall deny to any person within its jurisdiction the equal protection of the laws. The right of a student not to be segregated on racial grounds in schools so maintained is indeed so fundamental and pervasive that it is embraced in the concept of due process of law. The basic decision in *Brown* . . . The principles announced in that decision and the obedience of the States to them, according to the command of the Constitution, are indispensable for the protection of the freedoms guaranteed by our fundamental charter for all of us. Our constitutional ideal of equal justice under law is thus made a living truth.

GEORGE WALLACE, "SEGREGATION NOW, SEGREGATION FOREVER"[8]

Today I have stood, where once Jefferson Davis stood, and took an oath to my people. It is very appropriate then that from this Cradle of the Confederacy, this very Heart of the Great Anglo-Saxon Southland, that today we sound the drum for freedom as have our generations of forebears before us done, time and time again through history. Let us rise to the call of freedom-loving blood that is in us and send our answer to the tyranny that clanks its chains upon the South. In the name of the greatest people that have ever trod this earth, I draw the line in the dust and toss the gauntlet before the feet of tyranny . . . and I say . . . segregation today . . . segregation tomorrow . . . segregation forever.

. . . Let us send this message back to Washington by our representatives who are with us today—that from this day we are standing up, and the heel of tyranny does not fit the neck of an upright man . . . that we intend to take the offensive and carry our fight for freedom across the nation, wielding the balance of power we know we possess in the Southland . . . that WE, not the insipid bloc of voters of some sections . . . will determine in the next election who shall sit in the White House of these United States . . . That from this day, from this hour . . . from this minute . . . we give the word of a race of honor that we will tolerate their boot in our face no longer . . . and let those certain judges put that in their opium pipes of power and smoke it for what it is worth.

Hear me, Southerners! You sons and daughters who have moved north and west throughout this nation . . . we call on you from your native soil to join with us in national support and vote . . . and we know . . . wherever you are . . . away from the hearths of the Southland . . . that you will respond, for though you may live in the farthest reaches of this vast country . . . your heart has never left Dixieland.

And you native sons and daughters of old New England's rock-ribbed patriotism . . . and you sturdy natives of the great Mid-West . . . and you descendants of the far West flaming spirit of pioneer freedom . . . we invite you to come and be with us . . . for you are of the Southern spirit . . . and the Southern philosophy . . . you are Southerners too and brothers with us in our fight.

. . . And while the manufacturing industries of free enterprise have been coming to our state in increasing numbers, attracted by our bountiful natural resources, our growing numbers of skilled workers and our favorable conditions, their present rate of settlement here can be increased from the trickle they now represent to a stream of enterprise and endeavor, capital and expansion that can join us in our work of development and enrichment of the educational futures of our children, the opportunities of our citizens and the fulfillment of our talents as God has given them to us. To realize our ambitions and to bring to fruition our dreams, we as Alabamians must take cognizance of the world about us. We must re-define our heritage, re-school our thoughts in the lessons our forefathers knew so well, first hand, in order to function and to grow and to prosper. We can no longer hide our head in the sand and tell ourselves that the ideology of our free fathers is not being

attacked and is not being threatened by another idea . . . for it is. We are
faced with an idea that if a centralized government assume enough authority,
enough power over its people, that it can provide a utopian life . . that if given
the power to dictate, to forbid, to require, to demand, to distribute, to edict
and to judge what is best and enforce that will produce only "good" . . . and
it shall be our father . . . and our God. . . .

We find we have replaced faith with fear . . . and though we may give lip
service to the Almighty . . in reality, government has become our god. It is,
therefore, a basically ungodly government and its appeal to the pseudo-intel-
lectual and the politician is to change their status from servant of the people to
master of the people . . . to play at being God . . . without faith in God . . . and
without the wisdom of God. It is a system that is the very opposite of Christ
for it feeds and encourages everything degenerate and base in our people as
it assumes the responsibilities that we ourselves should assume. Its pseudo-
liberal spokesmen and some Harvard advocates have never examined the
logic of its substitution of what it calls "human rights" for individual rights,
for its propaganda play on words has appeal for the unthinking. Its logic is
totally material and irresponsible as it runs the full gamut of human desires
. . . including the theory that everyone has voting rights without the spiritual
responsibility of preserving freedom. Our founding fathers recognized those
rights . . . but only within the framework of those spiritual responsibilities.
But the strong, simple faith and sane reasoning of our founding fathers
has long since been forgotten as the so-called "progressives" tell us that
our Constitution was written for "horse and buggy" days . . . so were the
Ten Commandments.

. . . This nation was never meant to be a unit of one . . . but a united of the
many . . . that is the exact reason our freedom loving forefathers established
the states, so as to divide the rights and powers among the states, insuring that
no central power could gain master government control.

In united effort we were meant to live under this government . . . whether
Baptist, Methodist, Presbyterian, Church of Christ, or whatever one's denomination or religious belief . . . each respecting the others right to a separate
denomination . . . each, by working to develop his own, enriching the total of
all our lives through united effort. And so it was meant in our political lives
. . . whether Republican, Democrat, Prohibition, or whatever political party
. . . each striving from his separate political station . . . respecting the rights
of others to be separate and work from within their political framework . . .
and each separate political station making its contribution to our lives . . .

And so it was meant in our racial lives . . . each race, within its own framework has the freedom to teach . . . to instruct . . . to develop . . . to ask for
and receive deserved help from others of separate racial stations. This is the
great freedom of our American founding fathers . . . but if we amalgamate

into the one unit as advocated by the communist philosophers . . . then the enrichment of our lives . . . the freedom for our development . . . is gone forever. We become, therefore, a mongrel unit of one under a single all powerful government . . . and we stand for everything . . . and for nothing.

The true brotherhood of America, of respecting the separateness of others . . . and uniting in effort . . . has been so twisted and distorted from its original concept that there is a small wonder that communism is winning the world.

We invite the negro citizens of Alabama to work with us from his separate racial station . . . as we will work with him . . . to develop, to grow in individual freedom and enrichment. We want jobs and a good future for BOTH races . . . the tubercular and the infirm. This is the basic heritage of my religion, if which I make full practice . . . for we are all the handiwork of God.

But we warn those, of any group, who would follow the false doctrine of communistic amalgamation that we will not surrender our system of government . . . our freedom of race and religion . . . that freedom was won at a hard price and if it requires a hard price to retain it . . . we are able . . . and quite willing to pay it.

The liberals' theory that poverty, discrimination and lack of opportunity is the cause of communism is a false theory . . . if it were true the South would have been the biggest single communist bloc in the western hemisphere long ago . . . for after the great War Between the States, our people faced a desolate land of burned universities, destroyed crops and homes, with manpower depleted and crippled, and even the mule, which was required to work the land, was so scarce that whole communities shared one animal to make the spring plowing. There were no government handouts, no Marshall Plan aid, no coddling to make sure that our people would not suffer; instead the South was set upon by the vulturous carpetbagger and federal troops, all loyal Southerners were denied the vote at the point of bayonet, so that the infamous, illegal 14th Amendment might be passed. There was no money, no food and no hope of either. But our grandfathers bent their knee only in church and bowed their head only to God . . . We remind all within hearing of this Southland that a Southerner, Peyton Randolph, presided over the Continental Congress in our nation's beginning . . . that a Southerner, Thomas Jefferson, wrote the Declaration of Independence, that a Southerner, George Washington, is the Father of our country . . . that a Southerner, James Madison, authored our Constitution, that a Southerner, George Mason, authored the Bill of Rights and it was a Southerner who said, "Give me liberty . . . or give me death," Patrick Henry. Southerners played a most magnificent part in erecting this great divinely inspired system of freedom . . . and as God is our witnesses, Southerners will save it.

Let us, as Alabamians, grasp the hand of destiny and walk out of the shadow of fear . . . and fill our divine destination. Let us not simply defend

. . . but let us assume the leadership of the fight and carry our leadership across this nation. God has placed us here in this crisis . . . let is not fail in this . . . our most historical moment.

HEART OF ATLANTA MOTEL, INC. v. UNITED STATES[9]

. . . Title II of the Civil Rights Act of 1964 is a valid exercise of Congress' power under the Commerce Clause as applied to a place of public accommodation serving interstate travelers.

The case comes here on admissions and stipulated facts. Appellant owns and operates the Heart of Atlanta Motel, which has 216 rooms available to transient guests. . . . Appellant solicits patronage from outside the State of Georgia through various national advertising media, including magazines of national circulation; it maintains over 50 billboards and highway signs within the State, soliciting patronage for the motel; it accepts convention trade from outside Georgia and approximately 75% of its registered guests are from out of State. Prior to passage of the Act, the motel had followed a practice of refusing to rent rooms to Negroes, and it alleged that it intended to continue to do so . . .

The appellant contends that Congress, in passing this Act, exceeded its power to regulate commerce under Art. I,§ 8, cl. 3, of the Constitution of the United States; that the Act violates the Fifth Amendment because appellant is deprived of the right to choose its customers . . . resulting in a taking of its liberty and property without due process of law . . . without just compensation . . .

. . . The sole question posed is, therefore, the constitutionality of the Civil Rights Act of 1964 as applied to these facts. The legislative history of the Act indicates that Congress based the Act on § 5 and the Equal Protection Clause of the Fourteenth Amendment, as well as its power to regulate interstate commerce under Art. I, § 8, cl. 3, of the Constitution.

The Senate Commerce Committee made it quite clear that the fundamental object of Title II was to vindicate "the deprivation of personal dignity that surely accompanies denials of equal access to public establishments."

. . . Our study of the legislative record, made in the light of prior cases, has brought us to the conclusion that Congress possessed ample power in this regard, and we have therefore not considered the other grounds relied upon. . . .

While the Act, as adopted, carried no congressional findings, the record of its passage through each house is replete with evidence of the burdens that discrimination by race or color places upon interstate commerce.

. . . In short, the determinative test of the exercise of power by the Congress under the Commerce Clause is simply whether the activity sought to be regulated is "commerce which concerns more States than one" and has a real and substantial relation to the national interest. . . . In framing Title II of this Act, Congress was also dealing with what it considered a moral problem. But that fact does not detract from the overwhelming evidence of the disruptive effect that racial discrimination has had on commercial intercourse. . . .

Nor does the Act deprive appellant of liberty or property under the Fifth Amendment. The commerce power invoked here by the Congress is a specific and plenary one authorized by the Constitution itself. The only questions are: (1) whether Congress had a rational basis for finding that racial discrimination by motels affected commerce, and (2) if it had such a basis, whether the means it selected to eliminate that evil are reasonable and appropriate.

. . . As we have pointed out, 32 States now have such provisions and no case has been cited to us where the attack on a state statute has been successful, either in federal or state courts. . . . As a result, the constitutionality of such state statutes stands unquestioned . . .

We find no merit in the remainder of appellant's contentions, including that of "involuntary servitude." As we have seen, 32 States prohibit racial discrimination in public accommodations. These laws but codify the common law innkeeper rule, which long predated the Thirteenth Amendment. It is difficult to believe that the Amendment was intended to abrogate this principle . . .

We therefore conclude that the action of the Congress in the adoption of the Act as applied here to a motel which concededly serves interstate travelers is within the power granted it by the Commerce Clause of the Constitution, as interpreted by this Court for 140 years. It may be argued that Congress could have pursued other methods to eliminate the obstructions it found in interstate commerce caused by racial discrimination. But this is a matter of policy that rests entirely with the Congress, not with the courts. How obstructions in commerce may be removed—what means are to be employed—is within the sound and exclusive discretion of the Congress. It is subject only to one caveat—that the means chosen by it must be reasonably adapted to the end permitted by the Constitution. We cannot say that its choice here was not so adapted. The Constitution requires no more.

KATZENBACH v. McCLUNG[10]

. . . Ollie's Barbecue is a family owned restaurant in Birmingham, Alabama, specializing in barbecued meats and homemade pies, with a seating capacity of 220 customers. It is located on a state highway 11 blocks from an interstate one and a somewhat greater distance from railroad and bus stations.

The restaurant caters to a family and white-collar trade with a take-out service for Negroes. It employs 36 persons, two-thirds of whom are Negroes.

In the 12 months preceding the passage of the Act, the restaurant purchased locally approximately $150,000 worth of food, $69,683 or 46% of which was meat that it bought from a local supplier who had procured it from outside the State. The District Court expressly found that a substantial portion of the food served in the restaurant had moved in interstate commerce. The restaurant has refused to serve Negroes in its dining accommodations since its original opening in 1927, and, since July 2, 1964, it has been operating in violation of the Act.

. . . On the merits, the District Court held that the Act could not be applied under the Fourteenth Amendment because it was conceded that the State of Alabama was not involved in the refusal of the restaurant to serve Negroes. It was also admitted that the Thirteenth Amendment was authority neither for validating nor for invalidating the Act. . . . There must be, it said, a close and substantial relation between local activities and interstate commerce which requires control of the former in the protection of the latter. The court concluded, however, that the Congress, rather than finding facts sufficient to meet this rule, had legislated a conclusive presumption that a restaurant affects interstate commerce if it serves or offers to serve interstate travelers or if a substantial portion of the food which it serves has moved in commerce. This, the court held, it could not do, because there was no demonstrable connection between food purchased in interstate commerce and sold in a restaurant and the conclusion of Congress that discrimination in the restaurant would affect that commerce.

. . . There, we outlined the overall purpose and operational plan of Title II, and found it a valid exercise of the power to regulate interstate commerce insofar as it requires hotels and motels to serve transients without regard to their race or color. In this case, we consider its application to restaurants which serve food a substantial portion of which has moved in commerce.

. . . Section 201(a) of Title II commands that all persons shall be entitled to the full and equal enjoyment of the goods and services of any place of public accommodation without discrimination or segregation on the ground of race, color, religion, or national origin, and § 201(b) defines establishments as places of public accommodation if their operations affect commerce or segregation by them is supported by state action. Sections 201(b)(2) and (c) place any "restaurant . . . principally engaged in selling food for consumption on the premises" under the Act "if . . . it serves or offers to serve interstate travelers or a substantial portion of the food which it serves . . . has moved in commerce."

. . . As we noted in *Heart of Atlanta Motel*, both Houses of Congress conducted prolonged hearings on the Act. And, as we said there, while no formal findings were made, which, of course, are not necessary, it is well that we make mention of the testimony at these hearings the better to understand the problem before Congress and determine whether the Act is a reasonable and appropriate means toward its solution. The record is replete with testimony of the burdens placed on interstate commerce by racial discrimination in restaurants. . . . This diminutive spending springing from a refusal to serve Negroes and their total loss as customers has, regardless of the absence of direct evidence, a close connection to interstate commerce. The fewer customers a restaurant enjoys, the less food it sells, and consequently the less it buys.

. . . Moreover, there was an impressive array of testimony that discrimination in restaurants had a direct and highly restrictive effect upon interstate travel by Negroes. This resulted, it was said, because discriminatory practices prevent Negroes from buying prepared food served on the premises while on a trip, except in isolated and unkempt restaurants and under most unsatisfactory and often unpleasant conditions. This obviously discourages travel and obstructs interstate commerce, for one can hardly travel without eating.

. . . This Court has held time and again that this power extends to activities of retail establishments, including restaurants, which directly or indirectly burden or obstruct interstate commerce. We have detailed the cases in *Heart of Atlanta Motel*, and will not repeat them here.

Nor are the cases holding that interstate commerce ends when goods come to rest in the State of destination apposite here. That line of cases has been applied with reference to state taxation or regulation, but not in the field of federal regulation.

. . . Here, as there, Congress has determined for itself that refusals of service to Negroes have imposed burdens both upon the interstate flow of food and upon the movement of products generally. Of course, the mere fact that Congress has said when particular activity shall be deemed to affect commerce does not preclude further examination by this Court. But where we find that the legislators, in light of the facts and testimony before them, have a rational basis for finding a chosen regulatory scheme necessary to the protection of commerce, our investigation is at an end. . . .

Insofar as the sections of the Act here relevant are concerned, §§ 201(b) (2) and (c), Congress prohibited discrimination only in those establishments having a close tie to interstate commerce, *i.e.*, those, like the McClungs', serving food that has come from out of the State. We think, in so doing, that Congress acted well within its power to protect and foster commerce in extending the coverage of Title II only to those restaurants offering to serve interstate travelers or serving food, a substantial portion of which has moved in interstate commerce.

. . . The power of Congress in this field is broad and sweeping; where it keeps within its sphere and violates no express constitutional limitation it has been the rule of this Court, going back almost to the founding days of the Republic, not to interfere. The Civil Rights Act of 1964, as here applied, we find to be plainly appropriate in the resolution of what the Congress found to be a national commercial problem of the first magnitude. We find it in no violation of any express limitations of the Constitution and we therefore declare it valid.

GRISWOLD v. CONNECTICUT[11]

[MR. JUSTICE DOUGLAS delivered the opinion of the Court] Appellant Griswold is Executive Director of the Planned Parenthood League of Connecticut. Appellant Buxton is a licensed physician and a professor at the Yale Medical School who served as Medical Director for the League at its Center in New Haven—a center open and operating from November 1 to November 10, 1961, when appellants were arrested.

They gave information, instruction, and medical advice to *married persons* as to the means of preventing conception. They examined the wife and prescribed the best contraceptive device or material for her use. Fees were usually charged, although some couples were serviced free.

. . . we are met with a wide range of questions that implicate the Due Process Clause of the Fourteenth Amendment . . . We do not sit as a superlegislature to determine the wisdom, need, and propriety of laws that touch economic problems, business affairs, or social conditions. This law, however, operates directly on an intimate relation of husband and wife and their physician's role in one aspect of that relation.

The association of people is not mentioned in the Constitution nor in the Bill of Rights. The right to educate a child in a school of the parents' choice—whether public or private or parochial—is also not mentioned. Nor is the right to study any particular subject or any foreign language. Yet the First Amendment has been construed to include certain of those rights. In other words, the State may not, consistently with the spirit of the First Amendment, contract the spectrum of available knowledge. The right of freedom of speech and press includes not only the right to utter or to print, but the right to distribute, the right to receive, the right to read and freedom of inquiry, freedom of thought, and freedom to teach—indeed, the freedom of the entire university community. Without those peripheral rights, the specific rights would be less secure.

[S]pecific guarantees in the Bill of Rights have penumbras, formed by emanations from those guarantees that help give them life and substance. Various guarantees create zones of privacy. The right of association contained in the penumbra of the First Amendment is one, as we have seen.

The Third Amendment, in its prohibition against the quartering of soldiers "in any house" in time of peace without the consent of the owner, is another facet of that privacy. The Fourth Amendment explicitly affirms the "right of the people to be secure in their persons, houses, papers, and effects, against unreasonable searches and seizures." The Fifth Amendment, in its Self-Incrimination Clause, enables the citizen to create a zone of privacy which government may not force him to surrender to his detriment. The Ninth Amendment provides: "The enumeration in the Constitution, of certain rights, shall not be construed to deny or disparage others retained by the people."

. . . The present case, then, concerns a relationship lying within the zone of privacy created by several fundamental constitutional guarantees. And it concerns a law which, in forbidding the use of contraceptives, rather than regulating their manufacture or sale, seeks to achieve its goals by means having a maximum destructive impact upon that relationship. Such a law cannot stand in light of the familiar principle, so often applied by this Court, that a "governmental purpose to control or prevent activities constitutionally subject to state regulation may not be achieved by means which sweep unnecessarily broadly and thereby invade the area of protected freedoms."

Would we allow the police to search the sacred precincts of marital bedrooms for telltale signs of the use of contraceptives? The very idea is repulsive to the notions of privacy surrounding the marriage relationship.

We deal with a right of privacy older than the Bill of Rights—older than our political parties, older than our school system. Marriage is a coming together for better or for worse, hopefully enduring, and intimate to the degree of being sacred. It is an association that promotes a way of life, not causes; a harmony in living, not political faiths; a bilateral loyalty, not commercial or social projects. Yet it is an association for as noble a purpose as any involved in our prior decisions.

LOVING v. VIRGINIA[12]

[MR. CHIEF JUSTICE WARREN delivered the opinion of the Court] This case presents a constitutional question never addressed by this Court: whether a statutory scheme adopted by the State of Virginia to prevent marriages between persons solely on the basis of racial classifications violates the Equal Protection and Due Process Clauses of the Fourteenth Amendment. For reasons which seem to us to reflect the central meaning of those constitutional commands, we conclude that these statutes cannot stand consistently with the Fourteenth Amendment.

. . . The State argues that statements in the Thirty-ninth Congress about the time of the passage of the Fourteenth Amendment indicate that the Framers did not intend the Amendment to make unconstitutional state miscegenation laws. Many of the statements alluded to by the State concern the debates over the Freedmen's Bureau Bill, which President Johnson vetoed, and the Civil Rights Act of 1866, 14 Stat. 27, enacted over his veto. While these statements have some relevance to the intention of Congress in submitting the Fourteenth Amendment, it must be understood that they pertained to the passage of specific statutes, and not to the broader, organic purpose of a constitutional amendment. As for the various statements directly concerning the Fourteenth Amendment, we have said in connection with a related problem that, although these historical sources "cast some light" they are not sufficient to resolve the problem; "[a]t best, they are inconclusive. The most avid proponents of the post-War Amendments undoubtedly intended them to remove all legal distinctions among 'all persons born or naturalized in the United States.' Their opponents, just as certainly, were antagonistic to both the letter and the spirit of the Amendments, and wished them to have the most limited effect."

. . . There is patently no legitimate overriding purpose independent of invidious racial discrimination which justifies this classification. The fact that Virginia prohibits only interracial marriages involving white persons demonstrates that the racial classifications must stand on their own justification, as measures designed to maintain White Supremacy. We have consistently denied the constitutionality of measures which restrict the rights of citizens on account of race. There can be no doubt that restricting the freedom to marry solely because of racial classifications violates the central meaning of the Equal Protection Clause.

These statutes also deprive the Lovings of liberty without due process of law in violation of the Due Process Clause of the Fourteenth Amendment. The freedom to marry has long been recognized as one of the vital personal rights essential to the orderly pursuit of happiness by free men.

Marriage is one of the "basic civil rights of man," fundamental to our very existence and survival . . . To deny this fundamental freedom on so unsupportable a basis as the racial classifications embodied in these statutes, classifications so directly subversive of the principle of equality at the heart of the Fourteenth Amendment, is surely to deprive all the State's citizens of liberty without due process of law. The Fourteenth Amendment requires that the freedom of choice to marry not be restricted by invidious racial discriminations. Under our Constitution, the freedom to marry, or not marry, a person of another race resides with the individual, and cannot be infringed by the State.

ROE v. WADE[13]

. . . The Texas statutes that concern us here . . . make it a crime to "procure an abortion," as therein defined, or to attempt one, except with respect to "an abortion procured or attempted by medical advice for the purpose of saving the life of the mother." Similar statutes are in existence in a majority of the States.

Roe alleged that . . . that she was unable to get a "legal" abortion in Texas because her life did not appear to be threatened by the continuation of her pregnancy . . .

. . . On the merits, the District Court held that the "fundamental right of single women and married persons to choose whether to have children is protected by the Ninth Amendment, through the Fourteenth Amendment," and that the Texas criminal abortion statutes were void on their face because they were both unconstitutionally vague and constituted an overbroad infringement of the plaintiffs' Ninth Amendment rights. . . .

The principal thrust of appellant's attack on the Texas statutes is that they improperly invade a right, said to be possessed by the pregnant woman, to choose to terminate her pregnancy. Appellant would discover this right in the concept of personal "liberty" embodied in the Fourteenth Amendment's Due Process Clause; or in personal, marital, familial, and sexual privacy said to be protected by the Bill of Rights or its penumbras, *see Griswold v. Connecticut.*

It perhaps is not generally appreciated that the restrictive criminal abortion laws in effect in a majority of States today are of relatively recent vintage. Those laws, generally proscribing abortion or its attempt at any time during pregnancy except when necessary to preserve the pregnant woman's life, are not of ancient or even of common law origin. Instead, they derive from statutory changes effected, for the most part, in the latter half of the 19th century. . . . We are also told, however, that abortion was practiced in Greek times as well as in the Roman Era, . . . that "it was resorted to without scruple." . . . Greek and Roman law afforded little protection to the unborn.

. . . Most Greek thinkers, on the other hand, commended abortion, at least prior to viability. *See* Plato, Republic, V, 461; Aristotle, Politics, VII, 1335b 25 . . . The absence of a common law crime for pre-quickening abortion appears to have developed from a confluence of earlier philosophical, theological, and civil and canon law concepts of when life begins.

. . . In this country, the law in effect in all but a few States until mid-19th century was the preexisting English common law.

The State has a legitimate interest in seeing to it that abortion, like any other medical procedure, is performed under circumstances that insure maximum safety for the patient.

. . . the State retains a definite interest in protecting the woman's own health and safety when an abortion is proposed at a late stage of pregnancy. . . .

The Constitution does not explicitly mention any right of privacy . . . the Court has recognized that a right of personal privacy, or a guarantee of certain areas or zones of privacy, does exist under the Constitution. In varying contexts, the Court or individual Justices have, indeed, found at least the roots of that right in the First Amendment, . . . in the Fourth and Fifth Amendments, . . . in the penumbras of the Bill of Rights, . . . in the Ninth Amendment, . . . or in the concept of liberty guaranteed by the first section of the Fourteenth Amendment . . . These decisions make it clear that only personal rights that can be deemed "fundamental" or "implicit in the concept of ordered liberty," *Palko v. Connecticut*, . . .

This right of privacy, whether it be founded in the Fourteenth Amendment's concept of personal liberty and restrictions upon state action, as we feel it is, or, as the District Court determined, in the Ninth Amendment's reservation of rights to the people, is broad enough to encompass a woman's decision whether or not to terminate her pregnancy. The detriment that the State would impose upon the pregnant woman by denying this choice altogether is apparent. . . . The Court's decisions recognizing a right of privacy also acknowledge that some state regulation in areas protected by that right is appropriate. . . .

As noted above, a State may properly assert important interests in safeguarding health, in maintaining medical standards, and in protecting potential life. At some point in pregnancy, these respective interests become sufficiently compelling to sustain . . .

Although the results are divided, most of these courts have agreed that the right of privacy, however based, is broad enough to cover the abortion decision; that the right, nonetheless, is not absolute, and is subject to some limitations; and that, at some point, the state interests as to protection of health, medical standards, and prenatal life, become dominant. . . .

Where certain "fundamental rights" are involved, the Court has held that regulation limiting these rights may be justified only by a "compelling state interest," . . . and that legislative enactments must be narrowly drawn to express only the legitimate state interests at stake. . . .

. . . The appellee and certain *amici* argue that the fetus is a "person" within the language and meaning of the Fourteenth Amendment . . . . The Constitution does not define "person" in so many words. . . . the use of the word is such that it has application only post-natally. . . .

All this, together with our observation, *supra*, that, throughout the major portion of the 19th century, prevailing legal abortion practices were far freer than they are today, persuades us that the word "person," as used in the Fourteenth Amendment, does not include the unborn. . . .

. . . We need not resolve the difficult question of when life begins. When those trained in the respective disciplines of medicine, philosophy, and theology are unable to arrive at any consensus, the judiciary, at this point in the development of man's knowledge, is not in a position to speculate as to the answer.

. . . As we have noted, the common law found greater significance in quickening. Physician and their scientific colleagues have regarded that event with less interest and have tended to focus either upon conception, upon live birth, or upon the interim point at which the fetus becomes "viable," that is, potentially able to live outside the mother's womb, albeit with artificial aid. Viability is usually placed at about seven months (28 weeks) but may occur earlier, even at 24 weeks.

. . . With respect to the State's important and legitimate interest in the health of the mother, the "compelling" point, in the light of present medical knowledge, is at approximately the end of the first trimester. . . . It follows that, from and after this point, a State may regulate the abortion procedure to the extent that the regulation reasonably relates to the preservation and protection of maternal health. . . . With respect to the State's important and legitimate interest in potential life, the "compelling" point is at viability. . . . A state criminal abortion statute of the current Texas type, that excepts from criminality only a lifesaving procedure on behalf of the mother, without regard to pregnancy stage and without recognition of the other interests involved, is violative of the Due Process Clause of the Fourteenth Amendment.

. . . The decision leaves the State free to place increasing restrictions on abortion as the period of pregnancy lengthens, so long as those restrictions are tailored to the recognized state interests.

[MR. JUSTICE REHNQUIST, dissenting] . . . I would reach a conclusion opposite to that reached by the Court. I have difficulty in concluding, as the Court does, that the right of "privacy" is involved in this case.

. . . The decision here to break pregnancy into three distinct terms and to outline the permissible restrictions the State may impose in each one, for example, partakes more of judicial legislation than it does of a determination of the intent of the drafters of the Fourteenth Amendment.

The fact that a majority of the States reflecting, after all, the majority sentiment in those States, have had restrictions on abortions for at least a century is a strong indication, it seems to me, that the asserted right to an abortion is not "so rooted in the traditions and conscience of our people as to be ranked as fundamental," *Snyder v. Massachusetts.*

PLANNED PARENTHOOD OF SOUTHEASTERN PENNSYLVANIA et al. v CASEY[14]

. . . The Act requires that a woman seeking an abortion give her informed consent prior to the abortion procedure, and specifies that she be provided with certain information at least 24 hours before the abortion is performed. . . . For a minor to obtain an abortion, the Act requires the informed consent of one of her parents, but provides for a judicial bypass option if the minor does not wish to or cannot obtain a parent's consent. . . . Another provision of the Act requires that, unless certain exceptions apply, a married woman seeking an abortion must sign a statement indicating that she has notified her husband of her intended abortion . . .

Roe's essential holding, . . . is a recognition of the right of the woman to choose to have an abortion before viability and . . . . [b]efore viability, the State's interests are not strong enough to support a prohibition of abortion or the imposition of a substantial obstacle to the woman's effective right to elect the procedure. . . . a confirmation of the State's power to restrict abortions after fetal viability, if the law contains exceptions for pregnancies which endanger the woman's life or health . . . the State has legitimate interests from the outset of the pregnancy in protecting the health of the woman and the life of the fetus that may become a child. . . .

Neither the Bill of Rights nor the specific practices of States at the time of the adoption of the Fourteenth Amendment marks the outer limits of the substantive sphere of liberty which the Fourteenth Amendment protects. . . . Our precedents "have respected the private realm of family life which the state cannot enter." *Prince v. Massachusetts*, . . . These matters, involving the most intimate and personal choices a person may make in a lifetime, choices central to personal dignity and autonomy, are central to the liberty protected by the Fourteenth Amendment. At the heart of liberty is the right to define one's own concept of existence, of meaning, of the universe, and of the mystery of human life. Beliefs about these matters could not define the attributes of personhood were they formed under compulsion of the State.

Although *Roe* has engendered opposition, it has in no sense proven "unworkable," . . . representing as it does a simple limitation beyond which a state law is unenforceable.

. . . The ability of women to participate equally in the economic and social life of the Nation has been facilitated by their ability to control their reproductive lives. . . .

While the outer limits of this aspect of [protected liberty] have not been marked by the Court, it is clear that among the decisions that an individual may make without unjustified government interference are personal decisions "relating to marriage, procreation, contraception, family relationships, and child rearing and education." . . .

We have seen how time has overtaken some of *Roe*'s factual assumptions: advances in maternal health care allow for abortions safe to the mother later in pregnancy than was true in 1973, . . . and advances in neonatal care have advanced viability to a point somewhat earlier. . . .

We conclude, however, that the urgent claims of the woman to retain the ultimate control over her destiny and her body, claims implicit in the meaning of liberty, require us to perform that function. Liberty must not be extinguished for want of a line that is clear. . . . We conclude the line should be drawn at viability, so that before that time the woman has a right to choose to terminate her pregnancy. We adhere to this principle for two reasons. First, as we have said, is the doctrine of *stare decisis*

The second reason is that the concept of viability . . . is the time at which there is a realistic possibility of maintaining and nourishing a life outside the womb, so that the independent existence of the second life can in reason and all fairness be the object of state protection that now overrides the rights of the woman.

. . . Those cases decided that any regulation touching upon the abortion decision must survive strict scrutiny, to be sustained only if drawn in narrow terms to further a compelling state interest. . . . The trimester framework no doubt was erected to ensure that the woman's right to choose not become so subordinate to the State's interest in promoting fetal life that her choice exists in theory but not in fact. We do not agree, however, that the trimester approach is necessary to accomplish this objective.

Only where state regulation imposes an undue burden on a woman's ability to make this decision does the power of the State reach into the heart of the liberty protected by the Due Process Clause. . . . Not all burdens on the right to decide whether to terminate a pregnancy will be undue. In our view, the undue burden standard is the appropriate means of reconciling the State's interest with the woman's constitutionally protected liberty.

. . . And a statute which, while furthering the interest in potential life or some other valid state interest, has the effect of placing a substantial obstacle in the path of a woman's choice cannot be considered a permissible means of serving its legitimate ends.

[CHIEF JUSTICE REHNQUIST, with whom JUSTICE WHITE, JUSTICE SCALIA, and JUSTICE THOMAS join, concurring in the judgment in part and dissenting in part: . . . We believe that *Roe* was wrongly decided, and that it can and should be overruled consistently with our traditional approach to *stare decisis* in constitutional cases. . . .

. . . Although they reject the trimester framework that formed the underpinning of *Roe*, JUSTICES O'CONNOR, KENNEDY, and SOUTER adopt a revised undue burden standard to analyze the challenged regulations. We conclude, however, that such an outcome is an unjustified constitutional compromise . . . One cannot ignore the fact that a woman is not isolated in her pregnancy, and that the decision to abort necessarily involves the destruction of a fetus . . . Nor do the historical traditions of the American people support the view that the right to terminate one's pregnancy is "fundamental."

. . . the "undue burden" standard, which is created largely out of whole cloth by the authors of the joint opinion. It is a standard which even today does not command the support of a majority of this Court . . . the standard will do nothing to prevent "judges from roaming at large in the constitutional field" guided only by their personal views.

OBERGEFELL v. HODGES[15]

[Justice Anthony Kennedy] The centrality of marriage to the human condition makes it unsurprising that the institution has existed for millennia and across civilizations. Since the dawn of history, marriage has transformed strangers into relatives, binding families and societies together . . . There are untold references to the beauty of marriage in religious and philosophical texts spanning time, cultures, and faiths, as well as in art and literature in all their forms. It is fair and necessary to say these references were based on the understanding that marriage is a union between two persons of the opposite sex.

. . . Indeed, changed understandings of marriage are characteristic of a Nation where new dimensions of freedom become apparent to new generations, often through perspectives that begin in pleas or protests and then are considered in the political sphere and the judicial process.

. . . In the late 20th century, following substantial cultural and political developments, same-sex couples began to lead more open and public lives and to establish families. This development was followed by a quite extensive discussion of the issue in both governmental and private sectors and by a shift in public attitudes toward greater tolerance. As a result, questions about the rights of gays and lesbians soon reached the courts, where the issue could be discussed in the formal discourse of the law.

. . . Under the Due Process Clause of the Fourteenth Amendment, no State shall "deprive any person of life, liberty, or property, without due process of law." The fundamental liberties protected by this Clause include most of the rights enumerated in the Bill of Rights . . . In addition these liberties extend to certain personal choices central to individual dignity and autonomy, including intimate choices that define personal identity and beliefs.

. . . The identification and protection of fundamental rights is an enduring part of the judicial duty to interpret the Constitution. That responsibility, however, "has not been reduced to any formula." Rather, it requires courts to exercise reasoned judgment in identifying interests of the person so fundamental that the State must accord them its respect. That process is guided by many of the same considerations relevant to analysis of other constitutional provisions that set forth broad principles rather than specific requirements. History and tradition guide and discipline this inquiry but do not set its outer boundaries . . . That method respects our history and learns from it without allowing the past alone to rule the present.

The nature of injustice is that we may not always see it in our own times. The generations that wrote and ratified the Bill of Rights and the Fourteenth Amendment did not presume to know the extent of freedom in all of its dimensions, and so they entrusted to future generations a charter protecting the right of all persons to enjoy liberty as we learn its meaning. When new insight reveals discord between the Constitution's central protections and a received legal stricture, a claim to liberty must be addressed.

. . . Applying these established tenets, the Court has long held the right to marry is protected by the Constitution. . . . Over time and in other contexts, the Court has reiterated that the right to marry is fundamental under the Due Process Clause.

. . . Choices about marriage shape an individual's destiny. . . . The nature of marriage is that, through its enduring bond, two persons together can find other freedoms, such as expression, intimacy, and spirituality. This is true for all persons, whatever their sexual orientation . . . There is dignity in the bond between two men or two women who seek to marry and in their autonomy to make such profound choices.

A second principle in this Court's jurisprudence is that the right to marry is fundamental because it supports a two-person union unlike any other in its importance to the committed individuals . . . "Marriage is a coming together for better or for worse, hopefully enduring, and intimate to the degree of being sacred. It is an association that promotes a way of life, not causes; a harmony in living, not political faiths; a bilateral loyalty, not commercial or social projects. Yet it is an association for as noble a purpose as any involved in our prior decisions.

. . . A third basis for protecting the right to marry is that it safeguards children and families and thus draws meaning from related rights of childrearing, procreation, and education . . . Under the laws of the several States, some of marriage's protections for children and families are material. But marriage also confers more profound benefits. By giving recognition and legal structure to their parents' relationship, marriage allows children "to understand the integrity and closeness of their own family and its concord with other families in their community and in their daily lives."

. . . Excluding same-sex couples from marriage thus conflicts with a central premise of the right to marry. Without the recognition, stability, and predictability marriage offers, their children suffer the stigma of knowing their families are somehow lesser. They also suffer the significant material costs of being raised by unmarried parents, relegated through no fault of their own to a more difficult and uncertain family life. The marriage laws at issue here thus harm and humiliate the children of same-sex couples.

That is not to say the right to marry is less meaningful for those who do not or cannot have children. An ability, desire, or promise to procreate is not and has not been a prerequisite for a valid marriage in any State. In light of precedent protecting the right of a married couple not to procreate, it cannot be said the Court or the States have conditioned the right to marry on the capacity or commitment to procreate. The constitutional marriage right has many aspects, of which childbearing is only one.

. . . For that reason, just as a couple vows to support each other, so does society pledge to support the couple, offering symbolic recognition and material benefits to protect and nourish the union. Indeed, while the States are in general free to vary the benefits they confer on all married couples, they have throughout our history made marriage the basis for an expanding list of governmental rights, benefits, and responsibilities. These aspects of marital status include: taxation; inheritance and property rights; rules of intestate succession; spousal privilege in the law of evidence; hospital access; medical decision making authority; adoption rights; the rights and benefits of survivors; birth and death certificates; professional ethics rules; campaign finance restrictions; workers' compensation benefits; health insurance; and child custody, support, and visitation rules.

. . . The right of same-sex couples to marry that is part of the liberty promised by the Fourteenth Amendment is derived, too, from that Amendment's guarantee of the equal protection of the laws. The Due Process Clause and the Equal Protection Clause are connected in a profound way, though they set forth independent principles. Rights implicit in liberty and rights secured by equal protection may rest on different precepts and are not always coextensive, yet in some instances each may be instructive as to the meaning and reach of the other. In any particular case one Clause may be thought to capture the essence of the right in a more accurate and comprehensive way, even as the two Clauses may converge in the identification and definition of the right.

. . . Indeed, in interpreting the Equal Protection Clause, the Court has recognized that new insights and societal understandings can reveal unjustified inequality within our most fundamental institutions that once passed unnoticed and unchallenged. . . . [P]recedents show the Equal Protection Clause can help to identify and correct inequalities in the institution of marriage, vindicating precepts of liberty and equality under the Constitution.

This dynamic also applies to same-sex marriage. It is now clear that the challenged laws burden the liberty of same-sex couples, and it must be further acknowledged that they abridge central precepts of equality. Here the marriage laws enforced by the respondents are in essence unequal: same-sex couples are denied all the benefits afforded to opposite-sex couples and are barred from exercising a fundamental right. Especially against a long history of disapproval of their relationships, this denial to same-sex couples of the right to marry works a grave and continuing harm. The imposition of this disability on gays and lesbians serves to disrespect and subordinate them. And the Equal Protection Clause, like the Due Process Clause, prohibits this unjustified infringement of the fundamental right to marry.

These considerations lead to the conclusion that the right to marry is a fundamental right inherent in the liberty of the person, and under the Due Process and Equal Protection Clauses of the Fourteenth Amendment couples of the same-sex may not be deprived of that right and that liberty. The Court now holds that same-sex couples may exercise the fundamental right to marry. No longer may this liberty be denied to them . . . the State laws challenged by Petitioners in these cases are now held invalid to the extent they exclude same-sex couples from civil marriage on the same terms and conditions as opposite-sex couples.

[Justice Thomas, with whom Justice Scalia joins, dissent].The Court's decision today is at odds not only with the Constitution, but with the principles upon which our Nation was built. Since well before 1787, liberty has been understood as freedom from government action, not entitlement to government benefits. The Framers created our Constitution to preserve that understanding of liberty. Yet the majority invokes our Constitution in the name of a "liberty" that the Framers would not have recognized, to the detriment of the liberty they sought to protect. Along the way, it rejects the idea—captured in our Declaration of Independence—that human dignity is innate and suggests instead that it comes from the Government. This distortion of our Constitution not only ignores the text, it inverts the relationship between the individual and the state in our Republic. I cannot agree with it.

The majority's decision today will require States to issue marriage licenses to same-sex couples and to recognize same-sex marriages entered in other States largely based on a constitutional provision guaranteeing "due process" before a person is deprived of his "life, liberty, or property" . . . It distorts the constitutional text, which guarantees only whatever "process" is "due" before a person is deprived of life, liberty, and property . . . Worse, it invites judges to do exactly what the majority has done here—"'roa[m] at large in the constitutional field' guided only by their personal views" as to the "'fundamental rights'" protected by that document.

By straying from the text of the Constitution, substantive due process exalts judges at the expense of the People from whom they derive their authority. Petitioners argue that by enshrining the traditional definition of marriage in their State Constitutions through voter-approved amendments, the States have put the issue "beyond the reach of the normal democratic process." But the result petitioners seek is far less democratic. They ask nine judges on this Court to enshrine their definition of marriage in the Federal Constitution and thus put it beyond the reach of the normal democratic process for the entire Nation. That a "bare majority" of this Court is able to grant this wish, wiping out with a stroke of the keyboard the results of the political process in over 30 States, based on a provision that guarantees only "due process" is but further evidence of the danger of substantive due process.

As used in the Due Process Clauses, "liberty" most likely refers to "the power of loco-motion, of changing situation, or removing one's person to whatsoever place one's own inclination may direct; without imprisonment or restraint, unless by due course of law." 1 W. Blackstone, Commentaries on the Laws of England 130 (1769) (Blackstone). That definition is drawn from the historical roots of the Clauses and is consistent with our Constitution's text and structure.

. . . Petitioners cannot claim, under the most plausible definition of "liberty," that they have been imprisoned or physically restrained by the States for participating in same-sex relationships. To the contrary, they have been able to cohabitate and raise their children in peace. They have been able to hold civil marriage ceremonies in States that recognize same-sex marriages and private religious ceremonies in all States. They have been able to travel freely around the country, making their homes where they please. Far from being incarcerated or physically restrained, petitioners have been left alone to order their lives as they see fit.

Nor, under the broader definition, can they claim that the States have restricted their ability to go about their daily lives as they would be able to absent governmental restrictions. Petitioners do not ask this Court to order the States to stop restricting their ability to enter same-sex relationships, to engage in intimate behavior, to make vows to their partners in public ceremonies, to engage in religious wedding ceremonies, to hold themselves out as married, or to raise children. The States have imposed no such restrictions. Nor have the States prevented petitioners from approximating a number of incidents of marriage through private legal means, such as wills, trusts, and powers of attorney.

Instead, the States have refused to grant them governmental entitlements. Petitioners claim that as a matter of "liberty," they are entitled to access privileges and benefits that exist solely *because of* the government. They want, for example, to receive the State's *imprimatur* on their marriages—on state issued marriage licenses, death certificates, or other official forms. And they want to receive various monetary benefits, including reduced inheritance taxes upon the death of a spouse, compensation if a spouse dies as a result of a work-related injury, or loss of consortium damages in tort suits. But receiving governmental recognition and benefits has nothing to do with any understanding of "liberty" that the Framers would have recognized.

NOTES

1. *Barron v. Mayor & City Council of Baltimore, 32 U.S. 7 Pet. 243 243 (1833).*

2. *The Public Statues of the United States,* 18 vols (Boston: Little, Brown, and Co, 1847–1873 and Washington, D.C.: Government Printing Office, 1878–1936), 14: 27–30.

3. James D. Richardson, ed., *Compilations of the Messages and Papers of the Presidents,* 11 vols (Washington, D.C.: Government Printing Office, 1897, 1904), 6: 405–413.

4. Congressional Record, 84th Congress Second Session. *Vol. 102, part 4* (March 12, 1956) (Washington, D.C.: Governmental Printing Office, 1956), 4459–4460.

5. *Brown v. Board of Education of Topeka, 347 U.S. 483 (1957).*

6. *Public Papers of the Presidents: Dwight D. Eisenhowser, 1957* (Washington, D.C.: Government Printing Office, 1958), 689-694

7. *Cooper v. Aaron, 358 U.S. 1 (1958).*

8. http://digital.archives.alabama.gov/cdm/singleitem/collection/voices/id/2952/rec/5 accessed March 23, 2017.

9. *Heart of Atlanta Motel, Inc. v. United States, 379 U.S. 241 (1964).*

10. *Katzenbach v. McClung, 379 U.S. 294 (1964).*

11. *Griswold v. Connecticut, 381 U.S. 479 (1965).*

12. *Loving v. Virginia, 388 U.S. 1 (1967).*

13. *Roe v. Wade, 410 U.S. 113 (1973).*

14. *Planned Parenthood of Southeastern Pa. v. Casey 505 U.S. 833 (1992).*

15. *Obergefell v. Hodges 576 US ___ (2015).*

Part III

Commerce Clause

Editors' Note: The Commerce Clause is easy to identify. It is found in Article 1, Section 8, Clause 3 of the United States Constitution. The operative language states the federal government has the right "to regulate commerce with foreign nations, and among the several states, and with the Indian tribes." While the clause is easy to identify, its exact interpretation demonstrates an evolving nature.

A defining characteristic of the federal regime that was established with the Constitution was its positioning in commerce. Under previous political arrangements, this power never fell on a sole U.S. actor. Under the colonial system, the Crown dictated the larger boundaries and orientation of commerce in the Americas. With the War of Independence came a rejection of this centralization of commerce power. This era of decentralization was short lived as commerce power was gathered together with the ratification of the Constitution and centralized under the purview of Congress. The Commerce Clause developed into one of the strongest powers wielded by the federal government. It, however, was not always this straightforward.

In keeping with a punctuated equilibrium model, the development of the Commerce Clause is rather stable until a critical event or juncture occurs on the political landscape. Many of the developments of this aspect of federalism arise out of growth and complexity of the economy. The first document, the Supreme Court case of Gibbons v. Ogden, *sets the tone for the expanse of the Commerce Clause for well over 100 years. The author of this case, Chief Justice John Marshall, lays out in simple terms the federal preeminence in commerce that occurs outside and between state boundaries. Justice Marshall derives his opinion from his understanding of what the Founding Fathers intended for the field of play in commerce. His understanding placed the federal government in the driver's seat if you will. This overall impression would fluctuate someone over the next 100 years, however the peak of Commerce Clause power is reached with the case of* Wickard v Filburn. *On its face, the authority of an individual property and business owner to grow crops for their own consumption would not seem to create a situation ripe for the application of the Commerce Clause. The situation surrounding the case, however, was not so simple. The case occurs during World War II and in a context of a nation, and its industrial and farming might, fully engulfed in contributing to the arsenals of democracy. With this case, the net effect of wheat production on a handful of acres was not too small or protected from the reach of the federal government.*

If the ebb and flow of federalism is seen as a pendulum, as far as commerce was concerned there was no more swing, no more movement for 50 years. The Commerce Clause became one of the primary tools utilized by the government to legislate. At the turn of the last century, the Congressional use of the Commerce Clause was knocked back on its heels with the Lopez *and* Morrison *cases. The waters were quickly muddied with the* Gonzales v. Raich *case which allowed federal law to overrule state law. The coming years will likely reap a series of cases that more finely delineate the boundaries of federal commerce powers.*

GIBBONS v. OGDEN (1824)[1]

. . . [T]he enlightened patriots who framed our Constitution, and the people who adopted it, must be understood to have employed words in their natural sense, . . . "Congress shall have power to regulate commerce with foreign nations, and among the several States, and with the Indian tribes."

. . . Commerce, undoubtedly, is traffic, but it is something more: it is intercourse. It describes the commercial intercourse between nations, and parts of nations, in all its branches, and is regulated by prescribing rules for carrying on that intercourse. . . .

. . . The power over commerce, including navigation, was one of the primary objects for which the people of America adopted their government, and must have been contemplated in forming it. . . . The subject to which the power is next applied is to commerce "among the several States." The word "among" means intermingled with. . . . Commerce among the States cannot stop at the external boundary line of each State, but may be introduced into the interior. . . .

But, in regulating commerce with foreign nations, the power of Congress does not stop at the jurisdictional lines of the several States. It would be a very useless power if it could not pass those lines. . . .

It is the power to regulate, that is, to prescribe the rule by which commerce is to be governed. This power, like all others vested in Congress, is complete in itself, may be exercised to its utmost extent, and acknowledges no limitations other than are prescribed in the Constitution

. . . It is obvious that the government of the Union, in the exercise of its express powers—that, for example, of regulating commerce with foreign nations and among the States—may use means that may also be employed by a State in the exercise of its acknowledged powers—that, for example, of regulating commerce within the State.

The acknowledged power of a State to regulate its police, its domestic trade, and to govern its own citizens may enable it to legislate on this subject to a considerable extent, and the adoption of its system by Congress, and the application of it to the whole subject of commerce, does not seem to the Court to imply a right in the States so to apply it of their own authority. . . .

In one case and the other, the acts of New York must yield to the law of Congress, . . . [as] the framers of our Constitution foresaw this state of things, and provided for it by declaring the supremacy not only of itself, but of the laws made in pursuance of it. . . .

UNITED STATES v. E. C. KNIGHT CO. (1895)[2]

. . . "The object in purchasing the Philadelphia refineries was to obtain a greater influence or more perfect control over the business of refining and selling sugar in this country."

. . . The bill charged that the contracts under which these purchases were made constituted combinations in restraint of trade, and that in entering into them, the defendants combined and conspired to restrain the trade and commerce in refined sugar among the several states and with foreign nations, contrary to the Act of Congress of July 2, 1890.

. . . Commerce succeeds to manufacture, and is not a part of it. The power to regulate commerce is the power to prescribe the rule by which commerce shall be governed, and is a power independent of the power to suppress monopoly.

. . . The regulation of commerce applies to the subjects of commerce, and not to matters of internal police. Contracts to buy, sell, or exchange goods to be transported among the several states, the transportation and its instrumentalities, and articles bought, sold, or exchanged for the purposes of such transit among the states or put in the way of transit, may be regulated; but this is because they form part of interstate trade or commerce. The fact that an article is manufactured for export to another state does not, of itself, make it an article of interstate commerce, and the intent of the manufacturer does not determine the time when the article or product passes from the control of the state and belongs to commerce.

. . . Manufacture is transformation—the fashioning of raw materials into a change of form for use. The functions of commerce are different. The buying and selling, and the transportation incidental thereto, constitute commerce, and the regulation of commerce in the constitutional sense embraces the regulation at least of such transportation. . .

Contracts, combinations, or conspiracies to control domestic enterprise in manufacture, agriculture, mining, production in all its forms, or to raise or lower prices or wages might unquestionably tend to restrain external as well as domestic trade, but the restraint would be an indirect result, however inevitable, and whatever its extent, and such result would not necessarily determine the object of the contract, combination, or conspiracy.

. . . There was nothing in the proofs to indicate any intention to put a restraint upon trade or commerce, and the fact, as we have seen, that trade or commerce might be indirectly affected was not enough to entitle complainants to a decree. . . . [T]o grant the relief prayed, and dismissed the bill, and we are of opinion that the circuit court of appeals did not err in affirming that decree.

HAMMER v. DAGENHART (1918)[3]

. . . The controlling question for decision is: is it within the authority of Congress in regulating commerce among the States to prohibit the transportation in interstate commerce of manufactured goods, the product of a factory in which . . . children under the age of fourteen have been employed or permitted to work . . .

. . . The thing intended to be accomplished by this statute is the denial of the facilities of interstate commerce to those manufacturers in the States who employ children within the prohibited ages. The act, in its effect, does not regulate transportation among the States, but aims to standardize the ages at which children may be employed in mining and manufacturing within the States. . . . The making of goods and the mining of coal are not commerce, nor does the fact that these things are to be afterwards shipped or used in interstate commerce make their production a part thereof. . . . If it were otherwise, all manufacture intended for interstate shipment would be brought under federal control to the practical exclusion of the authority of the States. . . . In other words, that the unfair competition thus engendered may be controlled by closing the channels of interstate commerce to manufacturers in those States where the local laws do not meet what Congress deems to be the more just standard of other States.

. . . The Commerce Clause was not intended to give to Congress a general authority to equalize such conditions. . . . The grant of authority over a purely federal matter was not intended to destroy the local power always existing and carefully reserved to the States in the Tenth Amendment to the Constitution.

That there should be limitations upon the right to employ children in mines and factories in the interest of their own and the public welfare, all will admit. . . . The power of the States to regulate their purely internal affairs by such laws as seem wise to the local authority is inherent, and has never been surrendered to the general government.

To sustain this statute would not be, in our judgment, a recognition of the lawful exertion of congressional authority over interstate commerce, but would sanction an invasion by the federal power of the control of a matter purely local in its character, and over which no authority has been delegated to Congress in conferring the power to regulate commerce among the States.

. . . In our view, the necessary effect of this act is, by means of a prohibition against the movement in interstate commerce of ordinary commercial commodities, to regulate the hours of labor of children in factories and mines within the States, a purely state authority. Thus, the act in a two-fold sense is repugnant to the Constitution. It not only transcends the authority delegated to Congress over commerce, but also exerts a power as to a purely local matter to which the federal authority does not extend.

A. L. A. SCHECHTER POULTRY CORP.
v. UNITED STATES (1935)[4]

. . . The "Live Poultry Code" was promulgated under the National Industrial Recovery Act. . . . [It] authorizes the President to approve "codes of fair competition." . . . Such codes "shall not permit monopolies or monopolistic practices." . . . The Code fixes the number of hours for workdays.

. . . Congress cannot delegate legislative power to the President to exercise an unfettered discretion to make whatever laws he thinks may be needed or advisable for the rehabilitation and expansion of trade or industry. . . . In view of the scope of that broad declaration, . . . the discretion of the President in approving or prescribing codes . . . is virtually unfettered. We think that the code-making authority this conferred is an unconstitutional delegation of legislative power.

. . . The undisputed facts thus afford no warrant for the argument that the poultry handled by defendants at their slaughterhouse markets was in a "*current*" or "*flow*" of interstate commerce, and was thus subject to congressional regulation. The mere fact that there may be a constant flow of commodities into a State does not mean that the flow continues after the property has arrived, and has become commingled with the mass of property within the State, and is there held solely for local disposition and use. So far as the poultry here in question is concerned, the flow in interstate commerce had ceased. . . . Hence, decisions which deal with a stream of interstate commerce—where goods come to rest within a State temporarily and are later to go forward in interstate commerce—and with the regulations of transactions involved in that practical continuity of movement, are not applicable here.

. . . In determining how far the federal government may go in controlling intrastate transactions upon the ground that they "affect" interstate commerce, there is a necessary and well established distinction between direct and indirect effects. The precise line can be drawn only as individual cases arise, but the distinction is clear in principle. . . . But where the effect of intrastate transactions upon interstate commerce is merely indirect, such transactions remain within the domain of state power.

. . . The persons employed in slaughtering and selling in local trade are not employed in interstate commerce. Their hours and wages have no direct relation to interstate commerce.

It is not the province of the Court to consider the economic advantages or disadvantage of such a centralized system. It is sufficient to say that the Federal Constitution does not provide for it.

On both the grounds we have discussed, the attempted delegation of legislative power, and the attempted regulation of intrastate transaction which affect interstate commerce only indirectly, we hold he code provisions here in question to be invalid and that the judgment of conviction must be reversed.

NLRB v. JONES & LAUGHLIN STEEL CORP., 301 U.S. 1 (1937)[5]

In a proceeding under the National Labor Relations Act of 1935, . . . [t]he unfair labor practices charged were that the corporation was discriminating against members of the union with regard to hire and tenure of employment, and was coercing and intimidating its employees in order to interfere with their self-organization.

. . . The authority of the federal government may not be pushed to such an extreme as to destroy the distinction, which the commerce clause itself establishes, between commerce "among the several States" and the internal concerns of a State. That distinction between what is national and what is local in the activities of commerce is vital to the maintenance of our federal system.

Fully recognizing the legality of collective action on the part of employees in order to safeguard their proper interests, we said that Congress was not required to ignore this right, but could safeguard it.

. . . Undoubtedly the scope of this power must be considered in the light of our dual system of government, and may not be extended so as to embrace effects upon interstate commerce so indirect and remote that to embrace them, in view of our complex society, would effectually obliterate the distinction between what is national and what is local and create a completely centralized government

. . . The close and intimate effect which brings the subject within the reach of federal power may be due to activities in relation to productive industry although the industry, when separately viewed, is local. This has been abundantly illustrated in the application of the federal Anti-Trust Act.

When industries organize themselves on a national scale, making their relation to interstate commerce the dominant factor in their activities, how can it be maintained that their industrial labor relations constitute a forbidden field into which Congress may not enter when it is necessary to protect interstate commerce from the paralyzing consequences of industrial war? . . . Instead of being beyond the pale, we think that it presents in a most striking way the close and intimate relation which a manufacturing industry may have to interstate commerce, and we have no doubt that Congress had constitutional authority to safeguard the right of respondent's employees to self-organization and freedom in the choice of representatives for collective bargaining.

Our conclusion is that the order of the Board was within its competency, and that the Act is valid as here applied. The judgment of the Circuit Court of Appeals is reversed, and the cause is remanded for further proceedings in conformity with this opinion.

UNITED STATES v. DARBY (1941)[6]

. . . [Does] Congress has constitutional power to prohibit the shipment in interstate commerce of lumber manufactured by employees whose wages are less than a prescribed minimum or whose weekly hours of labor at that wage are greater than a prescribed maximum, and, second, whether it has power to prohibit the employment of workmen in the production of goods "for interstate commerce" at other than prescribed wages and hours. . . .

While manufacture is not, of itself, interstate commerce, the shipment of manufactured goods interstate is such commerce, and the prohibition of such shipment by Congress is indubitably a regulation of the commerce.

. . . The motive and purpose of the present regulation are plainly to make effective the Congressional conception of public policy that interstate commerce should not be made the instrument of competition in the distribution of goods produced under substandard labor conditions, which competition is injurious to the commerce and to the states from and to which the commerce flows.

. . . Whatever their motive and purpose, regulations of commerce which do not infringe some constitutional prohibition are within the plenary power conferred on Congress by the Commerce Clause. Subject only to that limitation, presently to be considered, we conclude that the prohibition of the shipment interstate of goods produced under the forbidden substandard labor conditions is within the constitutional authority of Congress.

. . . [I]n *Hammer v. Dagenhart*, . . . [t]he reasoning and conclusion of the Court's opinion there cannot be reconciled with the conclusion which we have reached . . .

. . . There remains the question whether such restriction on the production of goods for commerce is a permissible exercise of the commerce power. The power of Congress over interstate commerce is not confined to the regulation of commerce among the states. It extends to those activities intrastate which so affect interstate commerce or the exercise of the power of Congress over . . .

. . . In the absence of Congressional legislation on the subject, state laws which are not regulations of the commerce itself or its instrumentalities are not forbidden, even though they affect interstate commerce. But it does not follow that Congress may not, by appropriate legislation, regulate intrastate activities where they have a substantial effect on interstate commerce.

. . . A familiar like exercise of power is the regulation of intrastate transactions which are so commingled with or related to interstate commerce that all must be regulated if the interstate commerce is to be effectively controlled.

. . . Our conclusion is unaffected by the Tenth Amendment. The amendment states but a truism that all is retained which has not been surrendered. There is nothing in the history of its adoption to suggest that it was more than declaratory of the relationship between the national and state governments as it had been established by the Constitution before the amendment, or that its purpose was other than to allay fears that the new national government might seek to exercise powers not granted, and that the states might not be able to exercise fully their reserved powers.

WICKARD v. FILBURN (1942)[7]

. . . The appellee filed his complaint against the Secretary of Agriculture of the United States, . . . [and] sought to enjoin enforcement against himself of the marketing penalty imposed by . . . the Agricultural Adjustment Act of 1938, upon that part of his 1941 wheat crop which was available for marketing in excess of the marketing quota established for his farm. He also sought a declaratory judgment that the wheat marketing quota provisions of the Act were unconstitutional because not sustainable under the Commerce Clause or consistent with the Due Process Clause of the Fifth Amendment.

The appellee for many years past has owned and operated a small farm . . . [where it] . . . has been his practice to raise a small acreage of winter wheat . . . to sell a portion of the crop; to feed part to poultry and livestock on the farm, some of which is sold; to use some in making flour for home consumption, and to keep the rest for the following seeding. . . . the Agricultural Adjustment Act of 1938 . . . established for the appellee's 1941 crop a wheat acreage allotment of 11.1 acres . . . [h]e sowed, however, 23 acres . . .

The general scheme of the Agricultural Adjustment Act of 1938 as related to wheat is to control the volume moving in interstate and foreign commerce in order to avoid surpluses and shortages and the consequent abnormally low or high wheat prices and obstructions to commerce.

. . . Appellee says that this is a regulation of production and consumption of wheat. Such activities are, he urges, beyond the reach of . . . the Commerce Clause, since they are local in character. . . . [T]he Government argues that the statute regulates neither production nor consumption, but only marketing, and . . . is sustainable as a "necessary and proper" implementation of the power of Congress over interstate commerce.

. . . But even if appellee's activity be local, and though it may not be regarded as commerce, it may still, whatever its nature, be reached by Congress if it exerts a substantial economic effect on interstate commerce. . . . The effect of consumption of home-grown wheat on interstate commerce is due to the fact that it constitutes the most variable factor in the disappearance of the wheat crop. . . . That appellee's own contribution to the demand for wheat may be trivial by itself is not enough to remove him from the scope of federal regulation where, as here, his contribution, taken together with that of many others similarly situated, is far from trivial.

. . . Home-grown wheat in this sense competes with wheat in commerce. . . . Control of total supply, upon which the whole statutory plan is based, depends upon control of individual supply.

U.S. v. LOPEZ (1995)[8]

. . . We start with first principles. The Constitution creates a Federal Government of enumerated powers. As James Madison wrote: "The powers delegated by the proposed Constitution to the federal government are few and defined. Those which are to remain in the State governments are numerous and indefinite." This constitutionally mandated division of authority "was adopted by the Framers to ensure protection of our fundamental liberties." "Just as the separation and independence of the coordinate branches of the Federal Government serve to prevent the accumulation of excessive power in anyone branch, a healthy balance of power between the States and the Federal Government will reduce the risk of tyranny and abuse from either front."

The commerce power "is the power to regulate; that is, to prescribe the rule by which commerce is to be governed. This power, like all others vested in congress, is complete in itself, may be exercised to its utmost extent, and acknowledges no limitations, other than are prescribed in the constitution."

. . . Under our federal system, the "'States possess primary authority for defining and enforcing the criminal law.'" . . . When Congress criminalizes conduct already denounced as criminal by the States, it effects a "'change in the sensitive relation between federal and state criminal jurisdiction.

. . . In recognizing this fact we preserve one of the few principles that has been consistent since the Clause was adopted. The regulation and punishment of intrastate violence that is not directed at the instrumentalities, channels, or goods involved in interstate commerce has always been the province of the States.

UNITED STATES v. MORRISON (2000)[9]

In these cases we consider the constitutionality of . . . [Violence Against Women Act of 1994] which provides a federal civil remedy for the victims of gender-motivated violence.

. . . this Court has always recognized a limit on the commerce power inherent in "our dual system of government." . . . First, Congress may regulate the use of the channels of interstate commerce. Second, Congress is empowered to regulate and protect the instrumentalities of interstate commerce. . . . Finally, Congress' commerce authority includes the power to regulate those activities having a substantial relation to interstate commerce . . .

. . . But a fair reading of *Lopez* shows that the noneconomic, criminal nature of the conduct at issue was central to our decision in that case.

. . . Gender-motivated crimes of violence are not, in any sense of the phrase, economic activity. While we need not adopt a categorical rule against aggregating the effects of any noneconomic activity in order to decide these cases. . . . the existence of congressional findings is not sufficient, by itself, to sustain the constitutionality of Commerce Clause legislation.

. . . If accepted, petitioners' reasoning would allow Congress to regulate any crime as long as the nationwide, aggregated impact of that crime has substantial effects on employment, production, transit, or consumption. Indeed, if Congress may regulate gender motivated violence, it would be able to regulate murder or any other type of violence since gender-motivated violence, as a subset of all violent crime, is certain to have lesser economic impacts than the larger class of which it is a part.

. . . We accordingly reject the argument that Congress may regulate non-economic, violent criminal conduct based solely on that conduct's aggregate effect on interstate commerce

. . . The regulation and punishment of intrastate violence that is not directed at the instrumentalities, channels, or goods involved in interstate commerce has always been the province of the States. . . . With its careful enumeration of federal powers and explicit statement that all powers not granted to the Federal Government are reserved, the Constitution cannot realistically be interpreted as granting the Federal Government an unlimited license to regulate.

Affirmed.

GONZALES v. RAICH (2005)[10]

. . . The question presented in this case is whether the power vested in Congress . . . includes the power to prohibit the local cultivation and use of marijuana in compliance with California law. . . . Respondents . . . [are] seeking injunctive and declaratory relief prohibiting the enforcement of the federal Controlled Substances Act (CSA).

. . . The question before us, however, is not whether it is wise to enforce the statute in these circumstances; rather, it is whether Congress' power to regulate interstate markets for medicinal substances encompasses the portions of those markets that are supplied with drugs produced and consumed locally.

. . . The main objectives of the CSA were to conquer drug abuse and to control the legitimate and illegitimate traffic in controlled substances. Congress was particularly concerned with the need to prevent the diversion of drugs from legitimate to illicit channels.

. . . Like the farmer in *Wickard*, respondents are cultivating, for home consumption, a fungible commodity for which there is an established, albeit illegal, interstate market. . . . Here too, Congress had a rational basis for concluding that leaving home-consumed marijuana outside federal control would similarly affect price and market conditions.

. . . The parallel concern . . . is the likelihood that the high demand in the interstate market will draw such marijuana into that market. . . . [T]he diversion of homegrown marijuana tends to frustrate the federal interest in eliminating commercial transactions in the interstate market in their entirety.

In both cases, the regulation is squarely within Congress' commerce power because production of the commodity meant for home consumption, be it wheat or marijuana, has a substantial effect on supply and demand in the national market for that commodity.

. . . we have never required Congress to make particularized findings in order to legislate

. . . Given the enforcement difficulties that attend distinguishing between marijuana cultivated locally and marijuana grown elsewhere, . . . we have no difficulty concluding that Congress had a rational basis for believing that failure to regulate the intrastate manufacture and possession of marijuana would leave a gaping hole in the CSA.

. . . The Supremacy Clause unambiguously provides that if there is any conflict between federal and state law, federal law shall prevail.

. . . Under the present state of the law, however, the judgment of the Court of Appeals must be vacated.

NOTES

1. *Gibbons v. Ogden, 22 U.S. 9 Wheat. 1 1 (1824).*
2. *United States v. E. C. Knight Co., 156 U.S. 1 (1895).*
3. *Hammer v. Dagenhart, 247 U.S. 251 (1918).*
4. *A. L. A. Schechter Poultry Corp. v. United States, 295 U.S. 495 (1935).*
5. *NLRB v. Jones & Laughlin Steel Corp., 301 U.S. 1 (1937).*
6. *United States v. Darby, 312 U.S. 100 (1941).*
7. *Wickard v. Filburn, 317 U.S. 111 (1942).*
8. *United States v. Lopez 514 U.S. 549 (1995).*
9. *United States v. Morrison 529 U.S. 598 (2000).*
10. *Gonzales v. Raich 545 U.S. 1 (2005).*

Part IV

Incorporation Cases

Editors' Note: Arguably the most diverse substantive section of artifacts in this collection, falls under the heading of Incorporation. The documents run the gamut from free speech and protections against double jeopardy, to a right to armed self-defense and the protections of private property. While these documents are not strongly united in a particular substantive theme, they are threaded together in terms of their application, and intended target—citizenship. The central question pertains to what, if any, protections are granted to individual citizens via the U.S. Constitution. The extremes of the two schools of thought that govern this topic paint the picture that either none of the elements of the Bill of Rights apply to state governments, or all of these fundamental rights constrain both the federal and state governments.

A cursory view of the documents that follow illustrate the fact that, that like other notions in this volume, there is not a gradual rise having the upper hand in the balance of federalism. Its history is marked by relative calm that is punctuated by crisis which in turn brings change. The word incorporation is not found in the Constitution, nor was it explicitly used by the Founders to describe a process that was to come in the future. Over time, what did develop was more of a debate of whether the Bill of Rights reflected such fundamental elements of citizenship, that they were nonnegotiable regardless if it were state or national governments threatening infringement. This perspective is categorized as total incorporation. On the other hand, the doctrine of selective incorporation more closely reflects the actions of the Supreme Court in the modern era. That is, rights and protections from the Constitution are recognized as held by citizens in more of a step-wise fashion. Take for instance the case of Mcdonald v. Chicago. *Prior to this case, the Second Amendment protections of the "right of the people to keep and bear arms" only applied to the federal government. State governments could, and did,*

255

enact legislation that contravened the words and spirit of these protections. This case brought the last of the major Bill of Rights protections to bear against state governments. Notable exceptions that are still not incorporated are some of the various jury rights found in the Fifth, Sixth, and Seventh Amendments, and the no quartering of troops provision found in the Third Amendment. As most amendments are now viewed as inclusive of both state and federal governments, the ongoing debate of incorporation is likely drawing to a close.

PREAMBLE TO THE BILL OF RIGHTS 1791

The Conventions of a number of the States having at the time of their adopting the Constitution, expressed a desire, in order to prevent misconstruction or abuse of its powers, that further declaratory and restrictive clauses should be added: And as extending the ground of public confidence in the Government, will best insure the beneficent ends of its institution

FIRST AMENDMENT

Gitlow v. People (1925)[1]

. . . The first charged that the defendant had advocated, advised and taught the duty, necessity and propriety of overthrowing and overturning organized government by force, violence and unlawful means, by certain writings therein set forth entitled "The Left Wing Manifesto . . .

There was no evidence of any effect resulting from the publication and circulation of the Manifesto.

. . . the intent, purpose and fair meaning of the Manifesto; that its words must be taken in their ordinary meaning, . . . that a mere statement that unlawful acts might accomplish such a purpose would be insufficient, unless there was a teaching, advising and advocacy of employing such unlawful acts for the purpose of overthrowing government . . .

. . . Manifesto . . . contemplate[d] the overthrow and destruction of the governments of the United States and of all the States, not by the free action of the majority of the people through the ballot box . . . but by immediately organizing the industrial proletariat into militant Socialist unions and at the earliest opportunity through mass strike and force and violence . . .

The Court of Appeals held that the Manifesto "advocated the overthrow of this government by violence, or by unlawful means." . . . it was said: . . . As we read this manifesto, we feel entirely clear that the jury were justified in rejecting the view that it was a mere academic and harmless discussion of the advantages of communism. . . . It is true that there is no advocacy in specific terms of the use of . . . force or violence . . .

. . . The sole contention here is, essentially, that as there was no evidence of any concrete result flowing from the publication of the Manifesto . . ., the statute as construed and applied by the trial court penalizes the mere utterance, as such, of "doctrine" having no quality of incitement, without regard . . . to the likelihood of unlawful sequences . . .

. . . The Manifesto, plainly . . . advocates and urges in fervent language mass action which shall progressively foment industrial disturbances and, through political mass strikes and revolutionary mass action, overthrow and destroy organized parliamentary government.

. . . For present purposes, we may and do assume that freedom of speech and of the press which are protected by the First Amendment from abridgment by Congress are among the fundamental personal rights and "liberties" protected by the due process clause of the Fourteenth Amendment from impairment by the States.

. . . It is a fundamental principle, long established, that the freedom of speech and of the press which is secured by the Constitution does not confer an absolute right to speak or publish, without responsibility, whatever one may choose, or an unrestricted and unbridled license that gives immunity for every possible use of language and prevents the punishment of those who abuse this freedom.

. . . That a State in the exercise of its police power may punish those who abuse this freedom by utterances inimical to the public welfare, tending to corrupt public morals, incite to crime, or disturb the public peace, is not open to question. . . .

. . . That utterances inciting to the overthrow of organized government by unlawful means present a sufficient danger of substantive evil to bring their punishment within the range of legislative discretion is clear. Such utterances, by their very nature, involve danger to the public peace and to the security of the State. . . . A single revolutionary spark may kindle a fire that, smouldering for a time, may burst into a sweeping and destructive conflagration. . . .

We cannot hold that the present statute is an arbitrary or unreasonable exercise of the police power of the State unwarrantably infringing the freedom of speech or press, and we must and do sustain its constitutionality.

. . . And finding, for the reasons stated, that the statute is not, in itself, unconstitutional, and that it has not been applied in the present case in derogation of any constitutional right, the judgment of the Court of Appeals is affirmed.

Near v. Minnesota (1931)[2]

. . . the County Attorney of Hennepin County brought this action to enjoin the publication of what was described as a "malicious, scandalous and defamatory newspaper, magazine and periodical" . . . There is no question but that the articles made serious accusations against the public officers named and others in connection with the prevalence of crimes and the failure to expose and punish them.

. . . It is no longer open to doubt that the liberty of the press, and of speech, is within the liberty safeguarded by the due process clause of the Fourteenth Amendment from invasion by state action. It was found impossible to conclude that this essential personal liberty of the citizen was left unprotected by the general guaranty of fundamental rights of person and property. . . . Liberty of speech, and of the press, is also not an absolute right, and the State may punish its abuse.

. . . It is apparent that, under the statute, the publication is to be regarded as defamatory if it injures reputation, . . . The object of the statute is not punishment, in the ordinary sense, but suppression of the offending newspaper or periodical.

. . . unless the owner or publisher is able and disposed to bring competent evidence to satisfy the judge that the charges are true and are published with good motives and for justifiable ends, his newspaper or periodical is suppressed and further publication is made punishable as a contempt. This is of the essence of censorship.

. . . In determining the extent of the constitutional protection, it has been generally, if not universally, considered that it is the chief purpose of the guaranty to prevent previous restraints upon publication.

. . . The fact that, for approximately one hundred and fifty years, there has been almost an entire absence of attempts to impose previous restraints upon publications relating to the malfeasance of public officers is significant of the deep-seated conviction that such restraints would violate constitutional right. . . . The general principle that the constitutional guaranty of the liberty of the press gives immunity from previous restraints has been approved in many decisions under the provisions of state constitutions. . . . For these reasons we hold the statute, . . . to be an infringement of the liberty of the press guaranteed by the Fourteenth Amendment.

[JUSTICE BUTLER, dissenting]. . . This Court should not reverse the judgment below upon the ground that, in some other case, the statute may be applied in a way that is repugnant to the freedom of the press protected by the Fourteenth Amendment.

The Act was passed in the exertion of the State's power of police, and this court is, by well established rule, required to assume, until the contrary is clearly made to appear, that there exists in Minnesota a state of affairs that justifies this measure for the preservation of the peace and good order of the State.

It is of the greatest importance that the States shall be untrammeled and free to employ all just and appropriate measures to prevent abuses of the liberty of the press.

DeJonge v. Oregon (1937)[3]

. . . The charge is that appellant assisted in the conduct of a meeting which was called under the auspices of the Communist Party, an organization advocating criminal syndicalism. The defense was . . . that, while it was held under the auspices of the Communist Party, neither criminal syndicalism nor any unlawful conduct was taught or advocated at the meeting, either by appellant or by others.

. . . His sole offense as charged, and for which he was convicted and sentenced to imprisonment for seven years, was that he had assisted in the conduct of a public meeting, albeit otherwise lawful, which was held under the auspices of the Communist Party . . . However innocuous the object of the meeting, however lawful the subjects and tenor of the addresses, however reasonable and timely the discussion, all those assisting in the conduct of the meeting would be subject to imprisonment as felons if the meeting were held by the Communist Party. . . .

While the States are entitled to protect themselves from the abuse of the privileges of our institutions through an attempted substitution of force and violence in the place of peaceful political action in order to effect revolutionary changes in government, none of our decisions goes to the length of sustaining such a curtailment of the right of free speech and assembly as the Oregon statute demands in its present application . . . The right of peaceable assembly is a right cognate to those of free speech and free press, and is equally fundamental.

. . . The First Amendment of the Federal Constitution expressly guarantees that right against abridgment by Congress. But explicit mention there does not argue exclusion elsewhere. For the right is one that cannot be denied without violating those fundamental principles of liberty and justice which lie at the base of all civil and political institutions—principles which the Fourteenth Amendment embodies in the general terms of its due process clause. . . .

. . . We hold that the Oregon statute, as applied to the particular charge as defined by the state court, is repugnant to the due process clause of the Fourteenth Amendment.

Everson v. Board of Education (1947)[4]

A New Jersey statute authorizes its local school districts to make rules and contracts for the transportation of children to and from schools . . . this money was for the payment of transportation of some children in the community to Catholic parochial schools. These church schools give their students, in addition to secular education, regular religious instruction conforming to the religious tenets and modes of worship of the Catholic Faith. . . .

. . . It is much too late to argue that legislation intended to facilitate the opportunity of children to get a secular education serves no public purpose.

. . . Prior to the adoption of the Fourteenth Amendment, the First Amendment did not apply as a restraint against the states . . . The "establishment of religion" clause of the First Amendment means at least this: neither a state nor the Federal Government can set up a church. Neither can pass laws which aid one religion, aid all religions, or prefer one religion over another.

. . . New Jersey cannot hamper its citizens in the free exercise of their own religion. Consequently, it cannot exclude individual Catholics, Lutherans, Mohammedans, Baptists, Jews, Methodists, Nonbelievers, Presbyterians, or the members of any other faith, *because of their faith, or lack of it,* from receiving the benefits of public welfare legislation . . . in protecting the citizens of New Jersey against state-established churches, to be sure that we do not inadvertently prohibit New Jersey from extending its general state law benefits to all its citizens without regard to their religious belief.

Measured by these standards, we cannot say that the First Amendment prohibits New Jersey from spending tax-raised funds to pay the bus fares of parochial school pupils as a part of a general program . . . Moreover, state-paid policemen, detailed to protect children going to and from church schools from the very real hazards of traffic, would serve much the same purpose and accomplish much the same result as state provisions intended to guarantee free transportation of a kind which the state deems to be best for the school children's welfare.

. . . the First Amendment . . . requires the state to be a neutral in its relations with groups of religious believers and nonbelievers; it does not require the state to be their adversary. State power is no more to be used so as to handicap religions than it is to favor them.

. . . The First Amendment has erected a wall between church and state. That wall must be kept high and impregnable. We could not approve the slightest breach. New Jersey has not breached it here.

[JUSTICE JACKSON, dissenting] . . . before these school authorities draw a check to reimburse for a student's fare, they must ask just that question, and, if the school is a Catholic one, they may render aid because it is such, while if it is of any other faith or is run for profit, the help must be withheld

. . . it cannot make public business of religious worship or instruction, or of attendance at religious institutions of any character.

Religious teaching cannot be a private affair when the state seeks to impose regulations which infringe on it indirectly, and a public affair when it comes to taxing citizens of one faith to aid another, or those of no faith to aid all.

Edwards v. South Carolina (1963)[5]

. . . The petitioners, 187 in number, were convicted in a magistrate's court in Columbia, South Carolina, of the common law crime of breach of the peace. . . . We granted certiorari, . . . to consider the claim that these convictions cannot be squared with the Fourteenth Amendment of the United States Constitution.

There was no substantial conflict in the trial evidence . . . Late in the morning of March 2, 1961, the petitioners, high school and college students of the Negro race, met at the Zion Baptist Church in Columbia. From there, at about noon, they walked in separate groups of about 15 to the South Carolina State House grounds, an area of two city blocks open to the general public. Their purpose was "to submit a protest to the citizens of South Carolina, along with the Legislative Bodies of South Carolina, our feelings and our dissatisfaction with the present condition of discriminatory actions against Negroes in general, and to let them know that we were dissatisfied, and that we would like for the laws which prohibited Negro privileges in this State to be removed."

. . . and no evidence at all of any threatening remarks, hostile gestures, or offensive language on the part of any member of the crowd . . . There was no obstruction of pedestrian or vehicular traffic within the State House grounds.

In the situation and under the circumstances thus described, the police authorities advised the petitioners that they would be arrested if they did not disperse within 15 minutes . . . Instead of dispersing, the petitioners engaged in . . . loudly singing "The Star Spangled Banner" and other patriotic and religious songs, while stamping their feet and clapping their hands. After 15 minutes had passed, the police arrested the petitioners and marched them off to jail.

. . . the Supreme Court of South Carolina said that . . . "In general terms, a breach of the peace is a violation of public order, a disturbance of the public tranquility, by any act or conduct inciting to violence . . . Nor is actual personal violence an essential element in the offense" . . .

It has long been established that these First Amendment freedoms are protected by the Fourteenth Amendment from invasion by the States . . . The circumstances in this case reflect an exercise of these basic constitutional rights in their most pristine and classic form . . .

These petitioners were convicted of an offense so generalized as to be, in the words of the South Carolina Supreme Court, "not susceptible of exact definition." And they were convicted upon evidence which showed no more than that the opinions which they were peaceably expressing were sufficiently opposed to the views of the majority of the community to attract a crowd and necessitate police protection.

The Fourteenth Amendment does not permit a State to make criminal the peaceful expression of unpopular views.

. . . "The maintenance of the opportunity for free political discussion to the end that government may be responsive to the will of the people and that changes may be obtained by lawful means, an opportunity essential to the security of the Republic, is a fundamental principle of our constitutional system. A statute which, upon its face and as authoritatively construed, is so vague and indefinite as to permit the punishment of the fair use of this opportunity is repugnant to the guaranty of liberty contained in the Fourteenth Amendment."

For these reasons, we conclude that these criminal convictions cannot stand.

[JUSTICE CLARK, dissenting] . . . The priceless character of First Amendment freedoms cannot be gainsaid, but it does not follow that they are absolutes immune from necessary state action reasonably designed for the protection of society . . . For that reason, it is our duty to consider the context in which the arrests here were made. Certainly the city officials would be constitutionally prohibited from refusing petitioners access to the State House grounds merely because they disagreed with their views.

It was only after the large crowd had gathered, among which the City Manager and Chief of Police recognized potential troublemakers, and which, together with the students, had become massed on and around the "horse-shoe" so closely that vehicular and pedestrian traffic was materially impeded, . . . that any action against the petitioners was taken . . . The question thus seems to me whether a State is constitutionally prohibited from enforcing laws to prevent breach of the peace in a situation where city officials in good faith believe, and the record shows, that disorder and violence are imminent, merely because the activities constituting that breach contain claimed elements of constitutionally protected speech and assembly. To me, the answer under our cases is clearly in the negative.

SECOND AMENDMENT

Joseph Story, *Commentaries on the Constitution (1833)*[6]

The next amendment is: "A well regulated militia being necessary to the security of a free state, the right of the people to keep and bear arms shall not be infringed."

The importance of this article will scarcely be doubted by any persons, who have duly reflected upon the subject. The militia is the natural defense of a free country against sudden foreign invasions, domestic insurrections, and domestic usurpations of power by rulers. It is against sound policy for a free people to keep up large military establishments and standing armies in time of peace, both from the enormous expenses, with which they are attended, and the facile means, which they afford to ambitious and unprincipled rulers, to subvert the government, or trample upon the rights of the people. The right of the citizens to keep and bear arms has justly been considered, as the palladium of the liberties of a republic; since it offers a strong moral check against the usurpation and arbitrary power of rulers; and will generally, even if these are successful in the first instance, enable the people to resist and triumph over them. And yet, though this truth would seem so clear, and the importance of a well regulated militia would seem so undeniable, it cannot be disguised, that among the American people there is a growing indifference to any system of militia discipline, and a strong disposition, from a sense of its burthens, to be rid of all regulations. How it is practicable to keep the people duly armed without some organization, it is difficult to see. There is certainly no small danger, that indifference may lead to disgust, and disgust to contempt; and thus gradually undermine all the protection intended by this clause of our national bill of rights.

United States v. Cruikshank, (1875)[7]

. . . We have in our political system a government of the United States and a government of each of the several States. Each one of these governments is distinct from the others, and each has citizens of its own who owe it allegiance and whose rights, within its jurisdiction, it must protect. The same person may be at the same time a citizen of the United States and a citizen of a State, but his rights of citizenship under one of these governments will be different from those he has under the other . . .

The people of the United States resident within any State are subject to two governments—one State and the other National—but there need be no conflict between the two. . . . They are established for different purposes, and have separate jurisdictions. . . . True, it may sometimes happen that a person is amenable to both jurisdictions for one and the same act . . . It is the natural consequence of a citizenship which owes allegiance to two sovereignties and claims protection from both.

The Government of the United States is one of delegated powers alone. Its authority is defined and limited by the Constitution. All powers not granted to it by that instrument are reserved to the States or the people . . .

The right of the people peaceably to assemble for lawful purposes existed long before the adoption of the Constitution of the United States. In fact, it is, and always has been, one of the attributes of citizenship under a free government. It "derives its source," to use the language of Chief Justice Marshall in *Gibbons v. Ogden, . . .* "from those laws whose authority is acknowledged by civilized man throughout the world." It is found wherever civilization exists. It was not, therefore, a right granted to the people by the Constitution.

Only such existing rights were committed by the people to the protection of Congress as came within the general scope of the authority granted to the national government.

The first amendment . . . was not intended to limit the powers of the State governments in respect to their own citizens, but to operate upon the National Government alone. . . .

The particular amendment now under consideration assumes the existence of the right of the people to assemble for lawful purposes, and protects it against encroachment by Congress. The right was not created by the amendment; neither was its continuance guaranteed, except as against congressional interference. For their protection in its enjoyment, therefore, the people must look to the States.

The right of the people peaceably to assemble for the purpose of petitioning Congress for a redress of grievances, or for any thing else connected with the powers or the duties of the national government, is an attribute of national citizenship, and, as such, under the protection of, and guaranteed by, the United States. The very idea of a government republican in form implies a right on the part of its citizens to meet peaceably for consultation in respect to public affairs and to petition for a redress of grievances. If it had been alleged in these counts that the object of the defendants was to prevent a meeting for such a purpose, the case would have been within the statute, and within the scope of the sovereignty of the United States. Such, however, is not the case. The offence, as stated in the indictment, will be made out, if it be shown that the object of the conspiracy was to prevent a meeting for any lawful purpose whatever.

The second and tenth counts are equally defective. The right there specified is that of "bearing arms for a lawful purpose." This is not a right granted by the Constitution. Neither is it in any manner dependent upon that instrument for its existence. The second amendment declares that it shall not be infringed, but this, as has been seen, means no more than that it shall not be infringed by Congress. This is one of the amendments that has no other effect than to restrict the powers of the national government, . . .

The very highest duty of the States, when they entered into the Union under the Constitution, was to protect all persons within their boundaries in the enjoyment of these "unalienable rights with which they were endowed by their Creator." Sovereignty, for this purpose, rests alone with the States. . . .

The Fourteenth Amendment prohibits a State from depriving any person of life, liberty, or property without due process of law, but this adds nothing to the rights of one citizen as against another. It simply furnishes an additional guaranty against any encroachment by the States upon the fundamental rights which belong to every citizen as a member of society.

The fourth and twelfth counts charge the intent to have been to prevent and hinder the citizens named, who were of African descent and persons of color, in "the free exercise and enjoyment of their several right and privilege to the full and equal benefit of all laws and proceedings, then and there, before that time, enacted or ordained by the said State of Louisiana and by the United States, and then and there, at that time, being in force in the said State and District of Louisiana aforesaid, for the security of their respective persons and property, then and there, at that time enjoyed at and within said State and District of Louisiana by white persons, being citizens of said State of Louisiana and the United States, for the protection of the persons and property of said white citizens."

There is no allegation that this was done because of the race or color of the persons conspired against. When stripped of its verbiage, the case as presented amounts to nothing more than that the defendants conspired to prevent certain citizens of the United States, being within the State of Louisiana, from enjoying the equal protection of the laws of the State and of the United States.

The Fourteenth Amendment prohibits a State from denying to any person within its jurisdiction the equal protection of the laws; but this provision does not, any more than the one which precedes it, and which we have just considered, add anything to the rights which one citizen has under the Constitution against another. The equality of the rights of citizens is a principle of republicanism. Every republican government is in duty bound to protect all its citizens in the enjoyment of this principle, if within its power. That duty was originally assumed by the States, and it still remains there. The only obligation resting upon the United States is to see that the States do not deny the right. This the amendment guarantees, but no more. The power of the national government is limited to the enforcement of this guaranty.

The sixth and fourteenth counts state the intent of the defendants to have been to hinder and prevent the citizens named, being of African descent, and colored, . . . [the] right and privilege to vote. . . . In *Minor v. Happersett*, . . . we decided that the Constitution of the United States has not conferred the right of suffrage upon anyone, and that the United States have no voters of their own creation in the States. . . . From this, it appears that the right of suffrage is not a necessary attribute of national citizenship, but that exemption from discrimination in the exercise of that right on account of race, &c., is. The right to vote in the States comes from the States, but the right of exemption from the prohibited discrimination comes from the United States. . . .

Inasmuch, therefore, as it does not appear in these counts that the intent of the defendants was to prevent these parties from exercising their right to vote.

Presser v. Illinois (1886)[8]

. . . We think it clear that the sections under consideration, which only forbid bodies of men to associate together as military organizations, or to drill or parade with arms in cities and towns unless authorized by law, do not infringe the right of the people to keep and bear arms. But a conclusive answer to the contention that this amendment prohibits the legislation in question lies in the fact that the amendment is a limitation only upon the power of Congress and the national government, and not upon that of the state. . . .

It is undoubtedly true that all citizens capable of bearing arms constitute the reserved military force or reserve militia of the United States as well as of the states, and, . . . the states cannot, . . . prohibit the people from keeping and bearing arms so as to deprive the United States of their rightful resource for maintaining the public security.

. . . The plaintiff in error next insists that the sections of the Military Code of Illinois under which he was indicted are an invasion of that clause of the first section of the Fourteenth Amendment . . . It is only the privileges and immunities of citizens of the United States that the clause relied on was intended to protect. A state may pass laws to regulate the privileges and immunities of its own citizens, provided that in so doing it does not abridge their privileges and immunities as citizens of the United States . . . The only clause in the Constitution which upon any pretense could be said to have any relation whatever to his right to associate with others as a military company is found in the First Amendment.

. . . This is a right which . . . [is] an attribute of national citizenship, and, as such, under the protection of and guaranteed by the United States. But . . . the right peaceably to assemble was not protected by the clause referred to unless the purpose of the assembly was to petition the government for a redress of grievances.

The right voluntarily to associate together as a military company or organization or to drill or parade with arms without and independent of an act of Congress or law of the state authorizing the same is not an attribute of national citizenship . . . state governments, . . . have the power to regulate or prohibit associations and meetings of the people . . . and have also the power to control and regulate the organization, drilling, and parading of military bodies and associations, . . . The exercise of this power by the states is necessary to the public peace, safety, and good order. To deny the power would be to deny the right of the state to disperse assemblages organized for sedition and treason, and the right to suppress armed mobs bent on riot and rapine.

In respect to these points, we have to say that they present no federal question. It is not, therefore, our province to consider or decide them.

Hamilton v. Regents of University of California (1934)[9]

This is an appeal . . . from a judgment of the highest court of California sustaining a state law that requires students at its University to take a course in military science and tactics, the validity of which was by the appellants challenged as repugnant to the Constitution and laws of the United States.

. . . The primary object of there establishing units of the training corps is to qualify students for appointment in the Officers Reserve Corps. . . . These minors . . . petition the United States government to grant exemption from military service to such citizens who are members of the Methodist Episcopal Church as conscientiously believe that participation in war is a denial of their supreme allegiance to Jesus Christ.

. . . because of their religious and conscientious objections, they declined to take the prescribed course, and . . . [were] suspended . . . from the University.

. . . The state court, [at] a rehearing . . . deny[ed] the application, handed down an opinion in which it held that . . . military tactics is expressly required to be included among the subjects which shall be taught at the University, and that it is the duty of the regents to prescribe the nature and extent of the courses to be given.

. . . By their assignment of errors, appellants call upon this Court to decide whether the challenged provisions of the state Constitution, organic act, and regents' order, insofar as they impose compulsory military training, are repugnant to the privileges and immunities clause of the Fourteenth Amendment, the due process clause of that amendment, or the treaty that is generally called the Briand-Kellogg Peace Pact.

. . . We take judicial notice of the long established voluntary cooperation between federal and state authorities in respect of the military instruction given in the land grant colleges.

. . . Undoubtedly every state has authority to train its able-bodied male citizens . . . to serve in the United States Army or in state militia . . . So long as its action is within retained powers and not inconsistent with any exertion of the authority of the national government and transgresses no right safeguarded to the citizen by the Federal Constitution.

. . . The "privileges and immunities" protected are only those that belong to citizens of the United States, as distinguished from citizens of the states . . . The privilege of the native-born conscientious objector to avoid bearing arms comes not from the Constitution, but from the acts of Congress.

. . . Plainly there is no ground for the contention that the regents' order, requiring able-bodied male students under the age of twenty-four as a condition of their enrollment to take the prescribed instruction in military science and tactics, transgresses any constitutional right asserted by these appellants.

United States v. Miller (1939)[10]

. . . feloniously transport in interstate commerce . . . a certain firearm, to-wit, a double barrel 12-gauge Stevens shotgun having a barrel less than 18 inches in length, . . . transporting said firearm in interstate commerce as aforesaid, not having registered . . . under authority of the said Act of Congress known as the National Firearms Act.

A duly interposed demurrer alleged: the National Firearms Act is not a revenue measure, but an attempt to usurp police power reserved to the States, and is therefore unconstitutional.

Also, it offends the inhibition of the Second Amendment to the Constitution . . .

The District Court held that section eleven of the Act violates the Second Amendment. It accordingly sustained the demurrer and quashed the indictment.

In the absence of any evidence tending to show that possession or use of a "shotgun having a barrel of less than eighteen inches in length" at this time has some reasonable relationship to the preservation or efficiency of a well regulated militia, we cannot say that the Second Amendment guarantees the right to keep and bear such an instrument. Certainly it is not within judicial notice that this weapon is any part of the ordinary military equipment, or that its use could contribute to the common defense.

. . . The Militia which the States were expected to maintain and train is set in contrast with Troops which they were forbidden to keep without the consent of Congress. The sentiment of the time strongly disfavored standing armies; the common view was that adequate defense of country and laws could be secured through the Militia—civilians primarily, soldiers on occasion

. . . the Militia comprised . . . "A body of citizens enrolled for military discipline." And . . . these men were expected to appear bearing arms supplied by themselves and of the kind in common use at the time . . . "In all the colonies, as in England, the militia system was based on the principle of the assize of arms. This implied the general obligation of all adult male inhabitants to possess arms, and, with certain exceptions, to cooperate in the work of defense."

. . . Most if not all of the States have adopted provisions touching the right to keep and bear arms. Differences in the language employed in these have naturally led to somewhat variant conclusions concerning the scope of the right guaranteed. But none of them seems to afford any material support for the challenged ruling of the court below.

We are unable to accept the conclusion of the court below, and the challenged judgment must be reversed.

McDonald v. Chicago (2010)[11]

Two years ago, in *District of Columbia* v. *Heller*, . . . (2008), we held that the Second Amendment protects the right to keep and bear arms for the purpose of self-defense, and we struck down a District of Columbia law that banned the possession of handguns in the home. The city of Chicago (City) . . . argue that their laws are constitutional because the Second Amendment has no application to the States . . . Applying the standard that is well established in our case law, we hold that the Second Amendment right is fully applicable to the States.

. . . Chicago enacted its handgun ban to protect its residents "from the loss of property and injury or death from firearms" . . . The Chicago petitioners and their *amici*, however, argue that the handgun ban has left them vulnerable to criminals.

. . . Petitioners' primary submission is that this right is among the "privileges or immunities of citizens of the United States" and that the narrow interpretation of the Privileges or Immunities Clause adopted in the *Slaughter-House Cases, supra*, should now be rejected. As a secondary argument, petitioners contend that the Fourteenth Amendment's Due Process Clause "incorporates" the Second Amendment right.

. . . The *Slaughter-House Cases*, . . . concluded that the Privileges or Immunities Clause protects only those rights "which owe their existence to the Federal government, its National character, its Constitution, or its laws" . . . In drawing a sharp distinction between the rights of federal and state citizenship . . . We therefore decline to disturb the *Slaughter-House* holding.

At the same time, however, this Court's decisions in *Cruikshank*, *Presser*, and *Miller* do not preclude us from considering whether the Due Process Clause of the Fourteenth Amendment makes the Second Amendment right binding on the States.

. . . The Court used different formulations in describing the boundaries of due process . . . In *Snyder v. Massachusetts*, (1934), the Court spoke of rights that are "so rooted in the traditions and conscience of our people as to be ranked as fundamental." And in *Palko*, the Court famously said that due process protects those rights that are "the very essence of a scheme of ordered liberty" and essential to "a fair and enlightened system of justice." . . .

With this framework in mind, we now turn directly to the question whether the Second Amendment right to keep and bear arms is incorporated in the concept of due process. In answering that question, as just explained, we must decide whether the right to keep and bear arms is fundamental to *our* scheme of ordered liberty . . . or as we have said in a related context, whether this right is "deeply rooted in this Nation's history and tradition" . . .

Our decision in *Heller* points unmistakably to the answer. Self-defense is a basic right, recognized by many legal systems from ancient times to the present day, and in *Heller,* we held that individual self-defense is "the *central component*" of the Second Amendment right . . . Explaining that "the need for defense of self, family, and property is most acute" in the home, we found that this right applies to handguns because they are "the most preferred firearm in the nation to 'keep' and use for protection of one's home and family," . . . Thus, we concluded, citizens must be permitted "to use [handguns] for the core lawful purpose of self-defense."

. . . *Heller* makes it clear that this right is "deeply rooted in this Nation's history and tradition" . . . *Heller* explored the right's origins, noting that the 1689 English Bill of Rights explicitly protected a right to keep arms for self-defense, . . . and that by 1765, Blackstone was able to assert that the right to keep and bear arms was "one of the fundamental rights of Englishmen[.]"

Blackstone's assessment was shared by the American colonists. As we noted in *Heller,* King George III's attempt to disarm the colonists in the 1760's and 1770's "provoked polemical reactions by Americans invoking their rights as Englishmen to keep arms" . . . The right to keep and bear arms was considered no less fundamental by those who drafted and ratified the Bill of Rights. "During the 1788 ratification debates, the fear that the federal government would disarm the people in order to impose rule through a standing army or select militia was pervasive in Antifederalist rhetoric" . . . Federalists responded, not by arguing that the right was insufficiently important to warrant protection but by contending that the right was adequately protected by the Constitution's assignment of only limited powers to the Federal Government. . . . Thus, Antifederalists and Federalists alike agreed that the right to bear arms was fundamental to the newly formed system of government . . . But those who were fearful that the new Federal Government would infringe traditional rights such as the right to keep and bear arms insisted on the adoption of the Bill of Rights as a condition for ratification of the Constitution . . . In addition to the four States that had adopted Second Amendment analogues before ratification, nine more States adopted state constitutional provisions protecting an individual right to keep and bear arms between 1789 and 1820 . . . Founding-era legal commentators confirmed the importance of the right to early Americans. St. George Tucker, for example, described the right to keep and bear arms as "the true palladium of liberty" and explained that prohibitions on the right would place liberty "on the brink of destruction." . . .

After the Civil War, . . . armed parties, often consisting of ex-Confederate soldiers serving in the state militias, forcibly took firearms from newly freed slaves.

. . . Union Army commanders took steps to secure the right of all citizens to keep and bear arms, . . . but the 39th Congress concluded that legislative action was necessary. Its efforts to safeguard the right to keep and bear arms demonstrate that the right was still recognized to be fundamental.

The most explicit evidence of Congress' aim appears in §14 of the Freedmen's Bureau Act of 1866, which provided that "the right . . . to have full and equal benefit of all laws and proceedings concerning personal liberty, personal security, . . . *including the constitutional right to bear arms*, shall be secured to and enjoyed by all the citizens . . . without respect to race or color, or previous condition of slavery" . . . thus explicitly guaranteed that "all the citizens," black and white, would have "the constitutional right to bear arms."

The Civil Rights Act of 1866 . . . which was considered at the same time as the Freedmen's Bureau Act, similarly sought to protect the right of all citizens to keep and bear arms . . . The unavoidable conclusion is that the Civil Rights Act, like the Freedmen's Bureau Act, aimed to protect "the constitutional right to bear arms" and not simply to prohibit discrimination.

. . . Today, it is generally accepted that the Fourteenth Amendment was understood to provide a constitutional basis for protecting the rights set out in the Civil Rights Act of 1866. . . .

In debating the Fourteenth Amendment, the 39th Congress referred to the right to keep and bear arms as a fundamental right deserving of protection. Senator Samuel Pomeroy described three "indispensable" "safeguards of liberty under our form of Government." . . . Evidence from the period immediately following the ratification of the Fourteenth Amendment only confirms that the right to keep and bear arms was considered fundamental.

. . . The right to keep and bear arms was also widely protected by state constitutions at the time when the Fourteenth Amendment was ratified . . . A clear majority of the States in 1868, therefore, recognized the right to keep and bear arms as being among the foundational rights necessary to our system of Government.

. . . Municipal respondents, in effect, ask us to treat the right recognized in *Heller* as a second-class right, subject to an entirely different body of rules than the other Bill of Rights guarantees that we have held to be incorporated into the Due Process Clause.

. . . There is nothing new in the argument that, in order to respect federalism and allow useful state experimentation, a federal constitutional right should not be fully binding on the States. . . . Under our precedents, if a Bill of Rights guarantee is fundamental from an American perspective, then, . . . that guarantee is fully binding on the States and thus *limits* (but by no means eliminates) their ability to devise solutions to social problems that suit local needs and values . . .

As evidence that the Fourteenth Amendment has not historically been understood to restrict the authority of the States to regulate firearms . . . It is important to keep in mind that *Heller*, while striking down a law that prohibited the possession of handguns in the home, recognized that the right to keep and bear arms is not "a right to keep and carry any weapon whatsoever in any manner whatsoever and for whatever purpose" . . . We made it clear in *Heller* that our holding did not cast doubt on such longstanding regulatory measures as "prohibitions on the possession of firearms by felons and the mentally ill," "laws forbidding the carrying of firearms in sensitive places such as schools and government buildings, or laws imposing conditions and qualifications on the commercial sale of arms."

In *Heller*, we held that the Second Amendment protects the right to possess a handgun in the home for the purpose of self-defense. Unless considerations of *stare decisis* counsel otherwise, a provision of the Bill of Rights that protects a right that is fundamental from an American perspective applies equally to the Federal Government and the States. . . . We therefore hold that the Due Process Clause of the Fourteenth Amendment incorporates the Second Amendment right recognized in *Heller*. The judgment of the Court of Appeals is reversed, and the case is remanded for further proceedings.

[Justice Thomas, concurring in part and concurring in the judgment] I agree with the Court that the Fourteenth Amendment makes the right to keep and bear arms set forth in the Second Amendment "fully applicable to the States" . . . I write separately because I believe there is a more straightforward path to this conclusion through the Fourteenth Amendment's Privileges or Immunities Clause . . . As a consequence of this Court's marginalization of the Clause, litigants seeking federal protection of fundamental rights turned to the remainder of . . . that section's command that every State guarantee "due process" to any person before depriving him of "life, liberty, or property."

. . . The notion that a constitutional provision that guarantees only "process" before a person is deprived of life, liberty, or property could define the substance of those rights strains credulity for even the most casual user of words. Moreover, this fiction is a particularly dangerous one . . . This Court's substantive due process framework fails to account for both the text of the Fourteenth Amendment and the history that led to its adoption, filling that gap with a jurisprudence devoid of a guiding principle. I believe the original meaning of the Fourteenth Amendment offers a superior alternative.

Thus, the objective of this inquiry is to discern what "ordinary citizens" at the time of ratification would have understood the Privileges or Immunities Clause to mean . . . At the time of Reconstruction, the terms "privileges" and "immunities" had an established meaning as synonyms for "rights." The two words, standing alone or paired together, were used interchangeably with the words "rights," "liberties," and "freedoms," and had been since the time of Blackstone . . . A number of antebellum judicial decisions used the terms in this manner. . . .

The fact that a particular interest was designated as a "privilege" or "immunity," rather than a "right," "liberty," or "freedom," revealed little about its substance. Blackstone, for example, used the terms "privileges" and "immunities" to describe both the inalienable rights of individuals and the positive-law rights of corporations.

The group of rights-bearers to whom the Privileges or Immunities Clause applies is, of course, "citizens." By the time of Reconstruction, it had long been established that both the States and the Federal Government existed to preserve their citizens' inalienable rights, and that these rights were considered "privileges" or "immunities" of citizenship.

This tradition begins with our country's English roots . . . As English subjects, the colonists considered themselves to be vested with the same fundamental rights as other Englishmen. They consistently claimed the rights of English citizenship in their founding documents, repeatedly referring to these rights as "privileges" and "immunities."

. . . Even though the Bill of Rights did not apply to the States, other provisions of the Constitution did limit state interference with individual rights. Article IV, §2, cl. 1 provides that "[t]he Citizens of each State shall be entitled to all Privileges and Immunities of Citizens in the several States." The text of this provision resembles the Privileges or Immunities Clause, and it can be assumed that the public's understanding of the latter was informed by its understanding of the former.

Article IV, §2 was derived from a similar clause in the Articles of Confederation, and reflects the dual citizenship the Constitution provided to all Americans after replacing that "league" of separate sovereign States . . . By virtue of a person's citizenship in a particular State, he was guaranteed whatever rights and liberties that State's constitution and laws made available.

. . . When describing those "fundamental" rights, Justice Washington [in the *Corfield v. Coryell* case] thought it "would perhaps be more tedious than difficult to enumerate" them all, but suggested that they could "be all comprehended under" a broad list of "general heads," such as "[p]rotection by the government," "the enjoyment of life and liberty, with the right to acquire and possess property of every kind," "the benefit of the writ of habeas corpus," and the right of access to "the courts of the state," among others. . . .

This evidence plainly shows that the ratifying public understood the Privileges or Immunities Clause to protect constitutionally enumerated rights, including the right to keep and bear arms . . . in light of the States and Federal Government's shared history of recognizing certain inalienable rights in their citizens, is that the privileges and immunities of state and federal citizenship overlap.

. . . I reject *Slaughter-House* insofar as it precludes any overlap between the privileges and immunities of state and federal citizenship . . . In my view, the record makes plain that the Framers of the Privileges or Immunities Clause and the ratifying-era public understood—just as the Framers of the Second Amendment did—that the right to keep and bear arms was essential to the preservation of liberty. The record makes equally plain that they deemed this right necessary to include in the minimum baseline of federal rights that the Privileges or Immunities Clause established in the wake of the War over slavery . . .

[Justice Stevens, dissenting] . . . substantive due process analysis generally requires us to consider the term "liberty" in the Fourteenth Amendment, and that this inquiry may be informed by but does not depend upon the content of the Bill of Rights . . . Liberty claims that are inseparable from the customs that prevail in a certain region, the idiosyncratic expectations of a certain group, or the personal preferences of their champions, may be valid claims in some sense; but they are not of constitutional stature . . .

. . . our law has long recognized that the home provides a kind of special sanctuary in modern life . . . The State generally has a lesser basis for regulating private as compared to public acts, and firearms kept inside the home generally pose a lesser threat to public welfare as compared to firearms taken outside.

The notion that a right of self-defense *implies* an auxiliary right to own a certain type of firearm presupposes not only controversial judgments about the strength and scope of the (posited) self-defense right, but also controversial assumptions about the likely effects of making that type of firearm more broadly available. It is a very long way from the proposition that the Fourteenth Amendment protects a basic individual right of self-defense to the conclusion that a city may not ban handguns . . . The question we must decide is whether the interest in keeping in the home a firearm of one's choosing—a handgun, for petitioners—is one that is "comprised within the term liberty" in the Fourteenth Amendment.

. . . firearms have a fundamentally ambivalent relationship to liberty. Just as they can help homeowners defend their families and property from intruders, they can help thugs and insurrectionists murder innocent victims. The threat that firearms will be misused is far from hypothetical, for gun crime has devastated many of our communities. . . . Hence, in evaluating an asserted right to be free from particular gun-control regulations, liberty is on both sides of the equation . . . *Your* interest in keeping and bearing a certain firearm may diminish *my* interest in being and feeling safe from armed violence . . . It is at least reasonable for a democratically elected legislature to take such concerns into account in considering what sorts of regulations would best serve the public welfare.

. . . If a legislature's response to dangerous weapons ends up impinging upon the liberty of any individuals in pursuit of the greater good, it invariably does so on the basis of more than the majority's " 'own moral code,' " . . . While specific policies may of course be misguided, gun control is an area in which it "is quite wrong . . . to assume that regulation and liberty occupy mutually exclusive zones—that as one expands, the other must contract."

. . . the United States is an international outlier in the permissiveness of its approach to guns does not suggest that our laws are bad laws. It does suggest that this Court may not need to assume responsibility for making our laws still more permissive.

. . . It was the States, not private persons, on whose immediate behalf the Second Amendment was adopted . . . The Second Amendment, in other words, "is a federalism provision" . . . It is directed at preserving the autonomy of the sovereign States, and its logic therefore "resists" incorporation by a federal court *against* the States. . . .

. . . But the reasons that motivated the Framers to protect the ability of militiamen to keep muskets available for military use when our Nation was in its infancy, or that motivated the Reconstruction Congress to extend full citizenship to the freedmen in the wake of the Civil War, have only a limited bearing on the question that confronts the homeowner in a crime-infested metropolis today.

. . . This history of intrusive regulation is not surprising given that the very text of the Second Amendment calls out for regulation, . . . and the ability to respond to the social ills associated with dangerous weapons goes to the very core of the States' police powers . . . So long as the regulatory measures they have chosen are not "arbitrary, capricious, or unreasonable," we should be allowing them to "try novel social and economic" policies . . . It "is more in keeping . . . with our status as a court in a federal system," under these circumstances, "to avoid imposing a single solution . . . from the top down."

FOURTH AMENDMENT

Mapp v. Ohio (1961)[12]

. . . Appellant stands convicted of knowingly having had in her possession and under her control certain lewd and lascivious books, pictures, and photographs. . . . [T]he Supreme Court of Ohio found that her conviction was valid though "based primarily upon the introduction in evidence of lewd and lascivious books and pictures unlawfully seized during an unlawful search of defendant's home."

. . . Cleveland police officers arrived at appellant's residence in that city pursuant to information that "a person [was] hiding out in the home, who was wanted for questioning in connection with a recent bombing, and that there was a large amount of policy paraphernalia being hidden in the home" . . . When Miss Mapp did not come to the door immediately, at least one of the several doors to the house was forcibly opened . . . and the policemen gained admittance . . . The obscene materials for possession of which she was ultimately convicted were discovered in the course of that widespread search.

At the trial, no search warrant was produced by the prosecution, nor was the failure to produce one explained or accounted for . . . The State says that, even if the search were made without authority, or otherwise unreasonably, it is not prevented from using the unconstitutionally seized evidence at trial, citing *Wolf v. Colorado*, 338 U. S. 25 (1949), in which this Court did indeed hold "that, in a prosecution in a State court for a State crime, the Fourteenth Amendment does not forbid the admission of evidence obtained by an unreasonable search and seizure."

. . . "the Fourth Amendment . . . put the courts of the United States and Federal officials, in the exercise of their power and authority, under limitations and restraints [and] . . . forever secure[d] the people, their persons, houses, papers and effects against all unreasonable searches and seizures under the guise of law . . . and the duty of giving to it force and effect is obligatory upon all entrusted under our Federal system with the enforcement of the laws."

. . . Nevertheless, after declaring that the "security of one's privacy against arbitrary intrusion by the police" is "implicit in the concept of ordered liberty" and, as such, enforceable against the States through the Due Process Clause . . .

Since the Fourth Amendment's right of privacy has been declared enforceable against the States through the Due Process Clause of the Fourteenth, it is enforceable against them by the same sanction of exclusion as is used against the Federal Government. Were it otherwise . . . the assurance against unreasonable federal searches and seizures would be "a form of words," valueless and undeserving of mention in a perpetual charter of inestimable human liberties, so too, without that rule, the freedom from state invasions of privacy would be so ephemeral and so neatly severed from its conceptual nexus with the freedom from all brutish means of coercing evidence as not to merit this Court's high regard as a freedom "implicit in the concept of ordered liberty."

. . . There is no war between the Constitution and common sense. Presently, a federal prosecutor may make no use of evidence illegally seized, but a State's attorney across the street may, although he supposedly is operating under the enforceable prohibitions of the same Amendment. Thus, the State, by admitting evidence unlawfully seized, serves to encourage disobedience to the Federal Constitution which it is bound to uphold. . . .

[JUSTICE HARLAN, whom MR. JUSTICE FRANKFURTER and MR. JUSTICE WHITTAKER join, dissenting] . . . This reasoning ultimately rests on the unsound premise that, because *Wolf* carried into the States, as part of "the concept of ordered liberty" embodied in the Fourteenth Amendment, the principle of "privacy" underlying the Fourth Amendment . . . it must follow that whatever configurations of the Fourth Amendment have been developed in the particularizing federal precedents are likewise to be deemed a part of "ordered liberty," and as such are enforceable against the States. For me, this does not follow at all.

. . . The preservation of a proper balance between state and federal responsibility in the administration of criminal justice demands patience on the part of those who might like to see things move faster among the States in this respect.

. . . I think this Court can increase respect for the Constitution only if it rigidly respects the limitations which the Constitution places upon it, and respects as well the principles inherent in its own processes. In the present case, I think we exceed both, and that our voice becomes only a voice of power, not of reason.

FIFTH AMENDMENT

Chicago, B. & Q. R. Co. v. Chicago (1897)[13]

. . . certain rulings of the state court, which, it is alleged, were in disregard of that part of the Fourteenth Amendment declaring that no State shall deprive any person of his property without due process of law, or deny the equal protection of the laws to any person within its jurisdiction.

The Constitution of Illinois provides that "no person shall be deprived of life, liberty or property, without due process of law." Article 2, § 2. It also provides: "Private property shall not be taken or damaged for public use without just compensation . . . [and] where no compensation is made to such railroad company, the city shall restore such railroad track, right of way or land to its former state, or in a sufficient manner not to have impaired its usefulness."

. . . Due protection of the rights of property has been regarded as a vital principle of republican institutions. "Next in degree to the right of personal liberty," Mr. Broom, in his work on constitutional Law, says, "is that of enjoying private property without undue interference or molestation." (p. 228.) The requirement that the property shall not be taken for public use without just compensation is but "an affirmance of a great doctrine established by the common law for the protection of private property. It is founded in natural equity, and is laid down as a principle of universal law. Indeed, in a free government, almost all other rights would become worthless if the government possessed an uncontrollable power over the private fortune of every citizen."

. . . The legislature may prescribe a form of procedure to be observed in the taking of private property for public use, but it is not due process of law if provision be not made for compensation. Notice to the owner to appear in some judicial tribunal and show cause why his property shall not be taken for public use without compensation would be a mockery of justice. Due process of law, as applied to judicial proceedings instituted for the taking of private property for public use means, therefore, such process as recognizes the right of the owner to be compensated if his property be wrested from him and transferred to the public. The mere form of the proceeding instituted against the owner, even if he be admitted to defend, cannot convert the process used into due process of law, if the necessary result be to deprive him of his property without compensation.

. . . In *Scott v. Toledo* . . . the late Mr. Justice Jackson, while Circuit Judge, had occasion to consider this question. After full consideration, that able judge said:

"Whatever may have been the power of the States on this subject prior to the adoption of the Fourteenth Amendment to the Constitution, it seems clear that, since that amendment went into effect, such limitations and restraints have been placed upon their power in dealing with individual rights that the States cannot now lawfully appropriate private property for the public benefit or to public uses without compensation to the owner . . . The conclusion of the court on this question is that, since the adoption of the Fourteenth Amendment, compensation for private property taken for public uses constitutes an essential element in 'due process of law,' and that, without such compensation, the appropriation of private property to public uses, no matter under what form of procedure it is taken, would violate the provisions of the federal Constitution."

. . . In our opinion, a judgment of a state court, even if it be authorized by statute, whereby private property is taken for the State or under its direction for public use, without compensation made or secured to the owner, is, upon principle and authority, wanting in the due process of law required by the Fourteenth Amendment of the Constitution of the United States, and the affirmance of such judgment by the highest court of the State is a denial by that State of a right secured to the owner by that instrument.

Malloy v. Hogan (1964)[14]

. . . In this case, we are asked to reconsider prior decisions holding that the privilege against self-incrimination is not safeguarded against state action by the Fourteenth Amendment.

. . . The petitioner was asked a number of questions related to events surrounding his arrest and conviction. He refused to answer any question "on the grounds it may tend to incriminate me" . . . [T]he Connecticut Supreme Court of Errors . . . held that the Fifth Amendment's privilege against self-incrimination was not available to a witness in a state proceeding, that the Fourteenth Amendment extended no privilege to him, and that the petitioner had not properly invoked the privilege available under the Connecticut Constitution.

. . . The Court has not hesitated to reexamine past decisions according the Fourteenth Amendment a less central role in the preservation of basic liberties than that which was contemplated by its Framers when they added the Amendment to our constitutional scheme. . . .

We hold today that the Fifth Amendment's exception from compulsory self-incrimination is also protected by the Fourteenth Amendment against abridgment by the States . . . "[i]n criminal trials in the courts of the United States, wherever a question arises whether a confession is incompetent because not voluntary, the issue is controlled by that portion of the Fifth Amendment to the Constitution of the United States commanding that no person 'shall be compelled in any criminal case to be a witness against himself' . . . Under this test, the constitutional inquiry is not whether the conduct of state officers in obtaining the confession was shocking, but whether the confession was "free and voluntary: that is, [it] must not be extracted by any sort of threats or violence, nor obtained by any direct or implied promises, however slight, nor by the exertion of any improper influence."

In other words, the person must not have been compelled to incriminate himself. We have held inadmissible even a confession secured by so mild a whip as the refusal, under certain circumstances, to allow a suspect to call his wife until he confessed.

. . . Governments, state and federal, are thus constitutionally compelled to establish guilt by evidence independently and freely secured, and may not, by coercion, prove a charge against an accused out of his own mouth. Since the Fourteenth Amendment prohibits the States from inducing a person to confess through "sympathy falsely aroused" . . . or other like inducement far short of "compulsion by torture" . . . it follows *a fortiori* that it also forbids the States to resort to imprisonment, as here, to compel him to answer questions that might incriminate him. The Fourteenth Amendment secures against state invasion the same privilege that the Fifth Amendment guarantees against federal infringement—the right of a person to remain silent unless he chooses to speak in the unfettered exercise of his own will, and to suffer no penalty.

. . . The philosophy of each Amendment and of each freedom is complementary to, although not dependent upon, that of the other in its sphere of influence—the very least that, together, they assure in either sphere is that no man is to be convicted on unconstitutional evidence."

. . . What is accorded is a privilege of refusing to incriminate one's self, and the feared prosecution may be by either federal or state authorities . . .

It would be incongruous to have different standards determine the validity
of a claim of privilege based on the same feared prosecution depending on
whether the claim was asserted in a state or federal court. Therefore, the same
standards must determine whether an accused's silence in either a federal or
state proceeding is justified.

[MR. JUSTICE HARLAN, whom MR. JUSTICE CLARK joins, dissent-
ing] . . . While it is true that the Court deals today with only one aspect of state
criminal procedure, and rejects the wholesale "incorporation" of such federal
constitutional requirements, the logical gap between the Court's premises and
its novel constitutional conclusion can, I submit, be bridged only by the additional premise that the Due Process Clause of the Fourteenth Amendment is a
shorthand directive to this Court to pick and choose among the provisions of
the first eight Amendments and apply those chosen, freighted with their entire
accompanying body of federal doctrine, to law enforcement in the States.

I accept and agree with the proposition that continuing reexamination of
the constitutional conception of Fourteenth Amendment "due process" of
law is required, and that development of the community's sense of justice
may, in time, lead to expansion of the protection which due process affords.
In particular, in this case, I agree that principles of justice to which due process gives expression, as reflected in decisions of this Court, prohibit a State,
as the Fifth Amendment prohibits the Federal Government, from imprisoning
a person *solely* because he refuses to give evidence which may incriminate
him under the laws of the State . . . I do not understand, however, how this
process of reexamination, which must refer always to the guiding standard of
due process of law, including, of course, reference to the particular guarantees
of the Bill of Rights, can be short-circuited by the simple device of incorporating into due process, without critical examination, the whole body of law
which surrounds a specific prohibition directed against the Federal Government. The consequence of such an approach to due process as it pertains to
the States is inevitably disregard of all relevant differences which may exist
between state and federal criminal law and its enforcement. The ultimate
result is compelled uniformity, which is inconsistent with the purpose of our
federal system and which is achieved either by encroachment on the States'
sovereign powers or by dilution in federal law enforcement of the specific
protections found in the Bill of Rights.

. . . The Court's undiscriminating approach to the Due Process Clause carries serious implications for the sound working of our federal system in the
field of criminal law.

The Court concludes, almost without discussion. that "the same standards
must determine whether an accused's silence in either a federal or state
proceeding is justified" . . . About all that the Court offers in explanation of
this conclusion is the observation that it would be "incongruous" if different

standards governed the assertion of a privilege to remain silent in state and federal tribunals. Such "incongruity," however, is at the heart of our federal system. The powers and responsibilities of the state and federal governments are not congruent; under our Constitution, they are not intended to be. Why should it be thought, as an *a priori* matter, that limitations on the investigative power of the States are, in all respects, identical with limitations on the investigative power of the Federal Government? This certainly does not follow from the fact that we deal here with constitutional requirements, for the provisions of the Constitution which are construed are different.

As the Court pointed out in *Abbate v. United States* . . . "the States, under our federal system, have the principal responsibility for defining and prosecuting crimes." The Court endangers this allocation of responsibility for the prevention of crime when it applies to the States doctrines developed in the context of federal law enforcement without any attention to the special problems which the States, as a group or particular States, may face. If the power of the States to deal with local crime is unduly restricted, the likely consequence is a shift of responsibility in this area to the Federal Government, with its vastly greater resources. Such a shift, if it occurs, may, in the end, serve to weaken the very liberties which the Fourteenth Amendment safeguards by bringing us closer to the monolithic society which our federalism rejects. Equally dangerous to our liberties is the alternative of watering down protections against the Federal Government embodied in the Bill of Rights so as not unduly to restrict the powers of the States . . . Rather than insisting, almost by rote, that the Connecticut court, in considering the petitioner's claim of privilege, was required to apply the "federal standard," the Court should have fulfilled its responsibility under the Due Process Clause by inquiring whether the proceedings below met the demands of fundamental fairness which due process embodies. Such an approach may not satisfy those who see in the Fourteenth Amendment a set of easily applied "absolutes" which can afford a haven from unsettling doubt. It is, however, truer to the spirit which requires this Court constantly to reexamine fundamental principles and, at the same time, enjoins it from reading its own preferences into the Constitution.

Benton v. Maryland (1969)[15]

. . . because the first jury had found him not guilty of larceny, retrial would violate the constitutional prohibition against subjecting persons to double jeopardy for the same offense.

. . . After consideration of all the questions before us, we find no bar to our decision of the double jeopardy issue. On the merits, we hold that the Double Jeopardy Clause of the Fifth Amendment is applicable to the States through the Fourteenth Amendment, and we reverse petitioner's conviction for larceny.

. . . In 1937, this Court decided the landmark case of *Palko v. Connecticut,* . . . . Palko, although indicted for first-degree murder, had been convicted of murder in the second degree after a jury trial in a Connecticut state court. The State appealed and won a new trial. Palko argued that the Fourteenth Amendment incorporated, as against the States, the Fifth Amendment requirement that no person "be subject for the same offence to be twice put in jeopardy of life or limb." The Court disagreed. Federal double jeopardy standards were not applicable against the States. Only when a kind of jeopardy subjected a defendant to "a hardship so acute and shocking that our polity will not endure it," . . ., did the Fourteenth Amendment apply. The order for a new trial was affirmed. In subsequent appeals from state courts, the Court continued to apply this lesser *Palko* standard . . .

. . . In an increasing number of cases, the Court "has rejected the notion that the Fourteenth Amendment applies to the States only a 'watered-down, subjective version of the individual guarantees of the Bill of Rights . . . "*Malloy v. Hogan* . . . (1964) . . . Only last Term, we found that the right to trial by jury in criminal cases was "fundamental to the American scheme of justice," *Duncan v. Louisiana* . . . (1968), and held that the Sixth Amendment right to a jury trial was applicable to the States through the Fourteenth Amendment . . . For the same reasons, we today find that the double jeopardy prohibition of the Fifth Amendment represents a fundamental ideal in our constitutional heritage, and that it should apply to the States through the Fourteenth Amendment. Insofar as it is inconsistent with this holding, *Palko v. Connecticut* is overruled.

. . . Our recent cases have thoroughly rejected the *Palko* notion that basic constitutional rights can be denied by the States as long as the totality of the circumstances does not disclose a denial of "fundamental fairness." Once it is decided that a particular Bill of Rights guarantee is "fundamental to the American scheme of justice," *Duncan v. Louisiana* . . . the same constitutional standards apply against both the State and Federal Governments . . . The fundamental nature of the guarantee against double jeopardy can hardly be doubted. Its origins can be traced to Greek and Roman times, and it became established in the common law of England long before this Nation's independence . . . As with many other elements of the common law, it was carried into the jurisprudence of this Country through the medium of Blackstone, who codified the doctrine in his Commentaries. "[T]he plea of *autrefois acquit,* or a former acquittal," he wrote, "is grounded on this universal maxim of the common law of England that no man is to be brought into jeopardy of his life more than once for the same offence."

Today, every State incorporates some form of the prohibition in its constitution or common law.

. . . The judgment is vacated, and the case is remanded for further proceedings not inconsistent with this opinion.

[JUSTICE HARLAN, whom MR. JUSTICE STEWART joins, dissenting] . . . I would hold, in accordance with *Palko v. Connecticut* . . . (1937), that the Due Process Clause of the Fourteenth Amendment does not take over the Double Jeopardy Clause of the Fifth, as such. Today *Palko* becomes another casualty in the so-far unchecked march toward "incorporating" much, if not all, of the Federal Bill of Rights into the Due Process Clause. This march began, with a Court majority, in 1961 when *Mapp v. Ohio* . . . was decided and, before the present decision, found its last stopping point in *Duncan v. Louisiana* . . . (1968), decided at the end of last Term. . . . [I]n the *Duncan* case, I undertook to show that the "selective incorporation" doctrine finds no support either in history or in reason.

SIXTH AMENDMENT

In re Oliver (1948)[16]

. . . A Michigan circuit judge summarily sent the petitioner to jail for contempt of court. We must determine whether he was denied the procedural due process guaranteed by the Fourteenth Amendment . . . After petitioner had given certain testimony, the judge-grand jury, still in secret session, told petitioner that neither he nor his advisors believed petitioner's story—that it did not "jell" . . . In carrying out this authority a judge-grand jury is authorized to appoint its own prosecutors, detectives and aides at public expense, all or any of whom may, at the discretion of the justice of the peace or judge, be admitted to the inquiry.

. . . This nation's accepted practice of guaranteeing a public trial to an accused has its roots in our English common law heritage. The exact date of its origin is obscure, but it likely evolved long before the settlement of our land as an accompaniment of the ancient institution of jury trial . . . Today, almost without exception, every state, by constitution, statute, or judicial decision, requires that all criminal trials be open to the public.

The traditional Anglo-American distrust for secret trials has been variously ascribed to the notorious use of this practice by the Spanish Inquisition, to the excesses of the English Court of Star Chamber, and to the French monarchy's abuse of the *lettre de cachet*. All of these institutions obviously symbolized a menace to liberty. In the hands of despotic groups, each of them had become an instrument for the suppression of political and religious heresies in ruthless disregard of the right of an accused to a fair trial. Whatever other benefits the guarantee to an accused that his trial be conducted in public may confer upon our society, the guarantee has always been recognized as a safeguard against any attempt to employ our courts as instruments of persecution . . .

In giving content to the constitutional and statutory commands that an accused be given a public trial, the state and federal courts have differed over what groups of spectators, if any, could properly be excluded from a criminal trial. But, unless in Michigan and in one-man grand jury contempt cases, no court in this country has ever before held, so far as we can find, that an accused can be tried, convicted, and sent to jail when everybody else is denied entrance to the court except the judge and his attaches.

. . . We further hold that failure to afford the petitioner a reasonable opportunity to defend himself against the charge of false and evasive swearing was a denial of due process of law. A person's right to reasonable notice of a charge against him, and an opportunity to be heard in his defense—a right to his day in court—are basic in our system of jurisprudence, and these rights include, as a minimum, a right to examine the witnesses against him, to offer testimony, and to be represented by counsel.

. . . It is "the law of the land" that no man's life, liberty or property be forfeited as a punishment until there has been a charge fairly made and fairly tried in a public tribunal. . . . The petitioner was convicted without that kind of trial.

Gideon v. Wainwright (1963)[17]

. . . Appearing in court without funds and without a lawyer, petitioner asked the court to appoint counsel for him, whereupon the following colloquy took place:

"The COURT: Mr. Gideon, I am sorry, but I cannot appoint Counsel to represent you in this case. . . . the only time the Court can appoint Counsel to represent a Defendant is when that person is charged with a capital offense.

Put to trial before a jury, Gideon conducted his defense about as well as could be expected from a layman . . . The jury returned a verdict of guilty, and . . . petitioner filed in the Florida Supreme Court this habeas corpus petition attacking his conviction and sentence on the ground that the trial court's refusal to appoint counsel for him denied him rights . . . Since 1942, when *Betts v. Brady* . . . was decided by a divided Court, the problem of a defendant's federal constitutional right to counsel in a state court has been a continuing source of controversy and litigation in both state and federal courts.

. . . It was held that a refusal to appoint counsel for an indigent defendant charged with a felony did not necessarily violate the Due Process Clause of the Fourteenth Amendment, which . . . the Court deemed to be the only applicable federal constitutional provision. The Court said: "Asserted denial [of due process] is to be tested by an appraisal of the totality of facts in a given case. That which may, in one setting, constitute a denial of fundamental fairness, shocking to the universal sense of justice, may, in other circumstances, and in the light of other considerations, fall short of such denial."

. . . Upon full reconsideration, we conclude that *Betts v. Brady* should be overruled.

The Sixth Amendment provides, "In all criminal prosecutions, the accused shall enjoy the right . . . to have the Assistance of Counsel for his defense." We have construed this to mean that, in federal courts, counsel must be provided for defendants unable to employ counsel unless the right is competently and intelligently waived. Betts argued that this right is extended to indigent defendants in state courts by the Fourteenth Amendment. In response, the Court stated that, while the Sixth Amendment laid down "no rule for the conduct of the States, the question recurs whether the constraint laid by the Amendment upon the national courts expresses a rule so fundamental and essential to a fair trial, and so, to due process of law, that it is made obligatory upon the States by the Fourteenth Amendment."

. . . We think the Court in *Betts* had ample precedent for acknowledging that those guarantees of the Bill of Rights which are fundamental safeguards of liberty immune from federal abridgment are equally protected against state invasion by the Due Process Clause of the Fourteenth Amendment. This same principle was recognized, explained, and applied in *Powell v. Alabama*, (1932), a case upholding the right of counsel, where the Court held that, despite sweeping language to the contrary in *Hurtado v. California*, (1884), the Fourteenth Amendment "embraced" those "fundamental principles of liberty and justice which lie at the base of all our civil and political institutions,'" even though they had been "specifically dealt with in another part of the federal Constitution.

. . . "We concluded that certain fundamental rights, safeguarded by the first eight amendments against federal action, were also safeguarded against state action by the due process of law clause of the Fourteenth Amendment, and among them the fundamental right of the accused to the aid of counsel in a criminal prosecution." *Grosjean v. American Press Co.,* (1936).

. . . In light of these and many other prior decisions of this Court, it is not surprising that the *Betts* Court, when faced with the contention that "one charged with crime, who is unable to obtain counsel, must be furnished counsel by the State," conceded that "[e]xpressions in the opinions of this court lend color to the argument" . . . The fact is that, in deciding as it did—that "appointment of counsel is not a fundamental right, essential to a fair trial"— the Court in *Betts v. Brady* made an abrupt break with its own well considered precedents. In returning to these old precedents, sounder, we believe, than the new, we but restore constitutional principles established to achieve a fair system of justice. Not only these precedents, but also reason and reflection, require us to recognize that, in our adversary system of criminal justice, any person hauled into court, who is too poor to hire a lawyer, cannot be assured a fair trial unless counsel is provided for him. This seems to us to be an obvious truth. Governments, both state and federal, quite properly spend vast sums of money to establish machinery to try defendants accused of crime . . . The right of one charged with crime to counsel may not be deemed fundamental and essential to fair trials in some countries, but it is in ours. From the very beginning, our state and national constitutions and laws have laid great emphasis on procedural and substantive safeguards designed to assure fair trials before impartial tribunals in which every defendant stands equal before the law. This noble ideal cannot be realized if the poor man charged with crime has to face his accusers without a lawyer to assist him.

Pointer v. Texas (1965)[18]

. . . The question we find necessary to decide in this case is whether the Amendment's guarantee of a defendant's right "to be confronted with the witnesses against him," which has been held to include the right to cross-examine those witnesses, is also made applicable to the States by the Fourteenth Amendment.

. . . It cannot seriously be doubted at this late date that the right of cross-examination is included in the right of an accused in a criminal case to confront the witnesses against him. And probably no one, certainly no one experienced in the trial of lawsuits, would deny the value of cross-examination in exposing falsehood and bringing out the truth in the trial of a criminal case

. . . The fact that this right appears in the Sixth Amendment of our Bill of Rights reflects the belief of the Framers of those liberties and safeguards that confrontation was a fundamental right essential to a fair trial in a criminal prosecution. Moreover, the decisions of this Court and other courts throughout the years have constantly emphasized the necessity for cross-examination as a protection for defendants in criminal cases. This Court, in *Kirby v. United States* . . . referred to the right of confrontation as "[o]ne of the fundamental guarantees of life and liberty," and "a right long deemed so essential for the due protection of life and liberty that it is guarded against legislative and judicial action by provisions in the Constitution of the United States and in the constitutions of most if not of all the States composing the Union."

. . . There are few subjects, perhaps, upon which this Court and other courts have been more nearly unanimous than in their expressions of belief that the right of confrontation and cross-examination is an essential and fundamental requirement for the kind of fair trial which is this country's constitutional goal. Indeed, we have expressly declared that to deprive an accused of the right to cross-examine the witnesses against him is a denial of the Fourteenth Amendment's guarantee of due process of law.

. . . "In the constitutional sense, trial by jury in a criminal case necessarily implies at the very least that the 'evidence developed' against a defendant shall come from the witness stand in a public courtroom where there is full judicial protection of the defendant's right of confrontation, of cross-examination, and of counsel."

. . . We hold that petitioner was entitled to be tried in accordance with the protection of the confrontation guarantee of the Sixth Amendment, and that that guarantee, like the right against compelled self-incrimination, is "to be enforced against the States under the Fourteenth Amendment according to the same standards that protect those personal rights against federal encroachment."

Under this Court's prior decisions, the Sixth Amendment's guarantee of confrontation and cross-examination was unquestionably denied petitioner in this case. As has been pointed out, a major reason underlying the constitutional confrontation rule is to give a defendant charged with crime an opportunity to cross-examine the witnesses against him. . . . Since we hold that the right of an accused to be confronted with the witnesses against him must be determined by the same standards whether the right is denied in a federal or state proceeding, it follows that use of the transcript to convict petitioner denied him a constitutional right, and that his conviction must be reversed.

Parker v. Gladden (1966)[19]

. . . At a hearing on the petition, the trial court found that a court bailiff assigned to shepherd the sequestered jury . . . stated to one of the jurors . . . "Oh that wicked fellow [petitioner], he is guilty."

. . . We believe that the statements of the bailiff to the jurors are controlled by the command of the Sixth Amendment, made applicable to the States through the Due Process Clause of the Fourteenth Amendment. It guarantees that "the accused shall enjoy the right to a . . . trial, by an impartial jury . . . [and] be confronted with the witnesses against him" . . . "the 'evidence developed' against a defendant shall come from the witness stand in a public courtroom where there is full judicial protection of the defendant's right of confrontation, of cross-examination, and of counsel."

Klopfer v. North Carolina (1967)[20]

. . . The question involved in this case is whether a State may indefinitely postpone prosecution on an indictment without stated justification over the objection of an accused who has been discharged from custody.

. . . The consequence of this extraordinary criminal procedure is made apparent by the case before the Court. A defendant indicted for a misdemeanor may be denied an opportunity to exonerate himself in the discretion of the solicitor and held subject to trial, over his objection, throughout the unlimited period in which the solicitor may restore the case to the calendar. During that period, there is no means by which he can obtain a dismissal or have the case restored to the calendar for trial.

. . . Noting that some 18 months had elapsed since the indictment, petitioner, a professor of zoology at Duke University, contended that the pendency of the indictment greatly interfered with his professional activities and with his travel here and abroad . . . deprived him of his right to a speedy trial as required by the Fourteenth Amendment to the United States Constitution . . .

The petitioner is not relieved of the limitations placed upon his liberty by this prosecution merely because its suspension permits him to go "whithersoever he will." The pendency of the indictment may subject him to public scorn and deprive him of employment, and almost certainly will force curtailment of his speech, associations and participation in unpopular causes. By indefinitely prolonging this oppression, as well as the "anxiety and concern accompanying public accusation," the criminal procedure condoned in this case by the Supreme Court of North Carolina clearly denies the petitioner the right to a speedy trial which we hold is guaranteed to him by the Sixth Amendment of the Constitution of the United States.

While there has been a difference of opinion as to what provisions of this Amendment to the Constitution apply to the States through the Fourteenth Amendment, that question has been settled . . . We hold that petitioner was entitled to be tried in accordance with the protection of the confrontation guarantee of the Sixth Amendment, and that that guarantee, like the right against compelled self-incrimination, is "to be enforced against the States under the Fourteenth Amendment according to the same standards that protect those personal rights against federal encroachment" . . . We hold here that the right to a speedy trial is as fundamental as any of the rights secured by the Sixth Amendment. That right has its roots at the very foundation of our English law heritage. Its first articulation in modern jurisprudence appears to have been made in Magna Carta (1215), wherein it was written, "We will sell to no man, we will not deny or defer to any man either justice or right"; but evidence of recognition of the right to speedy justice in even earlier times is found in the Assize of Clarendon (1166). By the late thirteenth century, justices, armed with commissions of gaol delivery and/or oyer and terminer were visiting the countryside three times a year. These justices, Sir Edward Coke wrote in Part II of his Institutes, "have not suffered the prisoner to be long detained, but, at their next coming, have given the prisoner full and speedy justice, . . . without detaining him long in prison."

To Coke, prolonged detention without trial would have been contrary to the law and custom of England; but he also believed that the delay in trial, by itself, would be an improper denial of justice. . . . Coke's Institutes were read in the American Colonies by virtually every student of the law. Indeed, Thomas Jefferson wrote that, at the time he studied law (1762–1767), "*Coke Lyttleton* was the universal elementary book of law students." And . . . when George Mason drafted the first of the colonial bills of rights, he set forth a principle of Magna Carta, using phraseology similar to that of Coke's explication: "[I]n all capital or criminal prosecutions," the Virginia Declaration of Rights of 1776 provided, "a man hath a right . . . to a speedy trial." That this right was considered fundamental at this early period in our history is evidenced by its guarantee in the constitutions of several of the States of the new nation, as well as by its prominent position in the Sixth Amendment. Today, each of the 50 States guarantees the right to a speedy trial to its citizens. The history of the right to a speedy trial and its reception in this country clearly establish that it is one of the most basic rights preserved by our Constitution.

For the reasons stated above, the judgment must be reversed and remanded for proceedings not inconsistent with the opinion of the Court.

Washington v. Texas (1967)[21]

. . . We granted certiorari in this case to determine whether the right of a defendant in a criminal case under the Sixth Amendment to have compulsory process for obtaining witnesses in his favor is applicable to the States through the Fourteenth Amendment, and whether that right was violated by a state procedural statute providing that persons charged as principals, accomplices, or accessories in the same crime cannot be introduced as witnesses for each other.

. . . Two Texas statutes provided at the time of the trial in this case that persons charged or convicted as co-participants in the same crime could not testify for one another, although there was no bar to their testifying for the State.

We have not previously been called upon to decide whether the right of an accused to have compulsory process for obtaining witnesses in his favor, guaranteed in federal trials by the Sixth Amendment, is so fundamental and essential to a fair trial that it is incorporated in the Due Process Clause of the Fourteenth Amendment . . . We have held that due process requires that the accused have the assistance of counsel for his defense, that he be confronted with the witnesses against him, and that he have the right to a speedy and public trial.

The right of an accused to have compulsory process for obtaining witnesses in his favor stands on no lesser footing than the other Sixth Amendment rights that we have previously held applicable to the States. This Court had occasion in *In re Oliver,* (1948), to describe what it regarded as the most basic ingredients of due process of law. It observed that:

"A person's right to reasonable notice of a charge against him, and an opportunity to be heard in his defense—a right to his day in court—are basic in our system of jurisprudence, and these rights include, as a minimum, a right to examine the witnesses against him, to offer testimony, and to be represented by counsel."

The right to offer the testimony of witnesses, and to compel their attendance, if necessary, is in plain terms the right to present a defense, the right to present the defendant's version of the facts as well as the prosecution's to the jury, so it may decide where the truth lies. Just as an accused has the right to confront the prosecution's witnesses for the purpose of challenging their testimony, he has the right to present his own witnesses to establish a defense. This right is a fundamental element of due process of law.

. . . Joseph Story, in his famous Commentaries on the Constitution of the United States, observed that the right to compulsory process was included in the Bill of Rights in reaction to the notorious common law rule that, in cases of treason or felony, the accused was not allowed to introduce witnesses in his defense at all. Although the absolute prohibition of witnesses for the defense had been abolished in England by statute before 1787, the Framers of the Constitution felt it necessary specifically to provide that defendants in criminal cases should be provided the means of obtaining witnesses so that their own evidence, as well as the prosecution's, might be evaluated by the jury.

. . . The federal courts followed the common law restrictions for a time, despite the Sixth Amendment . . . The holding in *United States v. Reid* was not satisfactory to later generations, however, and, in 1918, this Court expressly overruled it, refusing to be bound by "the dead hand of the common law rule of 1789,"

. . . The rule disqualifying an alleged accomplice from testifying on behalf of the defendant cannot even be defended on the ground that it rationally sets apart a group of persons who are particularly likely to commit perjury. . . .

. . . We hold that the petitioner in this case was denied his right to have compulsory process for obtaining witnesses in his favor because the State arbitrarily denied him the right to put on the stand a witness who was physically and mentally capable of testifying to events that he had personally observed, and whose testimony would have been relevant and material to the defense. The Framers of the Constitution did not intend to commit the futile act of giving to a defendant the right to secure the attendance of witnesses whose testimony he had no right to use.

SEVENTH AMENDMENT

Minneapolis & St. Louis R. Co. v. Bombolis (1916)[22]

. . . By the Constitution and laws of Minnesota in civil causes, after a case has been under submission to a jury for a period of twelve hours without a unanimous verdict, five sixths of the jury are authorized to reach a verdict, which is entitled to the legal effect of a unanimous verdict at common law.

It has been so long and so conclusively settled that the Seventh Amendment exacts a trial by jury according to the course of the common law—that is, by a unanimous verdict . . . that it is not now open in the slightest to question that, if the requirements of that Amendment applied to the action of the State of Minnesota in adopting the statute concerning a less than unanimous verdict, or controlled the state court in enforcing that statute in the trial which is under review, both the statute and the action of the court were void because of repugnancy to the Constitution of the United States.

. . . Two propositions as to the operation and effect of the Seventh Amendment are as conclusively determined as is that concerning the nature and character of the jury required by that Amendment, where applicable. (a) That the first ten Amendments, including, of course, the Seventh, are not concerned with state action, and deal only with federal action . . . And, as a necessary corollary, (b) that the Seventh Amendment applies only to proceedings in courts of the United States, and does not in any manner whatever govern or regulate trials by jury in state courts, or the standards which must be applied concerning the same . . . So completely and conclusively have both of these principles been settled, so expressly have they been recognized without dissent or question almost from the beginning in the accepted interpretation of the Constitution, in the enactment of laws by Congress and proceedings in the federal courts, and by state constitutions and state enactments and proceedings in the state courts, that it is true to say that to concede that they are open to contention would be to grant that nothing whatever had been settled as to the power of state and federal governments or the authority of state and federal courts and their mode of procedure from the beginning.

. . . that the right to jury trial which the Seventh Amendment secures is a substantial one in that it exacts a substantial compliance with the common law standard as to what constitutes a jury.

. . . Moreover, the proposition is in conflict with an essential principle upon which our dual constitutional system of government rests—that is, that

lawful rights of the citizen, whether arising from a legitimate exercise of state
or national power, unless excepted by express constitutional limitation or
by valid legislation to that effect, are concurrently subject to be enforced in
the courts of the state or nation when such rights come within in the general
scope of the jurisdiction conferred upon such courts by the authority, state or
nation, creating them. . . . the unity of the governments, national and state,
and the common fealty of all courts, both state and national, to both state and
national Constitutions, and the duty resting upon them, when it was within
the scope of their authority, to protect and enforce rights lawfully created,
without reference to the particular government from whose exercise of lawful
power the right arose.

EIGHTH AMENDMENT

Robinson v. California (1962)[23]

. . . A California statute makes it a criminal offense for a person to "be
addicted to the use of narcotics." This appeal draws into question the constitutionality of that provision of the state law, as construed by the California
courts in the present case.

. . . "There can be no question of the authority of the state in the exercise
of its police power to regulate the administration, sale, prescription and use of
dangerous and habit forming drugs . . . The right to exercise this power is so
manifest in the interest of the public health and welfare that it is unnecessary
to enter upon a discussion of it beyond saying that it is too firmly established
to be successfully called in question."

Such regulation, it can be assumed, could take a variety of valid forms . . .
This statute . . . is not one which punishes a person for the use of narcotics,
for their purchase, sale or possession, or for antisocial or disorderly behavior
resulting from their administration. It is not a law which even purports to provide or require medical treatment. Rather, we deal with a statute which makes
the "status" of narcotic addiction a criminal offense, for which the offender
may be prosecuted "at any time before he reforms." California has said that a
person can be continuously guilty of this offense, whether or not he has ever
used or possessed any narcotics within the State, and whether or not he has
been guilty of any antisocial behavior there.

It is unlikely that any State at this moment in history would attempt to
make it a criminal offense for a person to be mentally ill, or a leper, or to be
afflicted with a venereal disease . . . But, in the light of contemporary human
knowledge, a law which made a criminal offense of such a disease would
doubtless be universally thought to be an infliction of cruel and unusual punishment in violation of the Eighth and Fourteenth Amendments. . . .

We cannot but consider the statute before us as of the same category. In this Court, counsel for the State recognized that narcotic addiction is an illness. Indeed, it is apparently an illness which may be contracted innocently or involuntarily. We hold that a state law which imprisons a person thus afflicted as a criminal, even though he has never touched any narcotic drug within the State or been guilty of any irregular behavior there, inflicts a cruel and unusual punishment in violation of the Fourteenth Amendment. To be sure, imprisonment for ninety days is not, in the abstract, a punishment which is either cruel or unusual. But the question cannot be considered in the abstract. Even one day in prison would be a cruel and unusual punishment for the "crime" of having a common cold.

We are not unmindful that the vicious evils of the narcotics traffic have occasioned the grave concern of government. There are, as we have said, countless fronts on which those evils may be legitimately attacked. We deal in this case only with an individual provision of a particularized local law as it has so far been interpreted by the California courts.

[JUSTICE WHITE, dissenting] . . . I am not at all ready to place the use of narcotics beyond the reach of the States' criminal laws. I do not consider appellant's conviction to be a punishment for having an illness or for simply being in some status or condition, but rather a conviction for the regular, repeated or habitual use of narcotics immediately prior to his arrest and in violation of the California law.

. . . In my opinion, on this record, it was within the power of the State of California to confine him by criminal proceedings for the use of narcotics or for regular use amounting to habitual use.

. . . The Fourteenth Amendment is today held to bar any prosecution for addiction regardless of the degree or frequency of use, and the Court's opinion bristles with indications of further consequences. If it is "cruel and unusual punishment" to convict appellant for addiction, it is difficult to understand why it would be any less offensive to the Fourteenth Amendment to convict him for use on the same evidence of use which proved he was an addict . . . At the very least, it has effectively removed California's power to deal effectively with the recurring case under the statute where there is ample evidence of use but no evidence of the precise location of use. Beyond this, it has cast serious doubt upon the power of any State to forbid the use of narcotics under threat of criminal punishment.

. . . Finally, I deem this application of "cruel and unusual punishment" so novel that I suspect the Court was hard put to find a way to ascribe to the Framers of the Constitution the result reached today rather than to its own notions of ordered liberty. If this case involved economic regulation, the present Court's allergy to substantive due process would surely save the statute and prevent the Court from imposing its own philosophical predilections upon state legislatures or Congress. I fail to see why the Court deems it more appropriate to write into the Constitution its own abstract notions of how best to handle the narcotics problem, for it obviously cannot match either the States or Congress in expert understanding.

Schilb v. Kuebel (1971)[24]

. . . In order to gain his liberty pending trial . . . Schilb deposited $75 in cash with the clerk of the court . . . At his ensuing trial . . . was convicted of traffic obstruction. When he paid his fine, the amount Schilb had deposited was returned to him decreased, however, by $7.50 retained as "bail bond costs" by the court clerk pursuant to the statute. The amount so retained was 1% of the specified bail and 10% of the amount actually deposited.

Schilb, by this purported state class action against the court clerk, the county, and the county treasurer, attacks the statutory 1% charge on Fourteenth Amendment due process and equal protection ground . . . Bail, of course, is basic to our system of law . . . and the Eighth Amendment's proscription of excessive bail has been assumed to have application to the States through the Fourteenth Amendment . . . But we are not at all concerned here with any fundamental right to bail or with any Eighth Amendment-Fourteenth Amendment question of bail excessiveness. Our concern, instead, is with the 1% cost retention provision. This smacks of administrative detail and of procedure, and is hardly to be classified as a "fundamental" right or as based upon any suspect criterion. The applicable measure, therefore, must be the traditional one: is the distinction drawn by the statutes invidious and without rational basis? . . .

With this background, we turn to the appellants' primary argument. It is threefold: (1) that the 1% retention charge . . . is imposed on only one segment of the class gaining pretrial release; (2) that it is imposed on the poor and nonaffluent, and not on the rich and affluent; (3) that its imposition with respect to an accused found innocent amounts to a court cost assessed against the not-guilty person.

We are compelled to note preliminarily that the attack on the Illinois bail statutes, in a very distinct sense, is paradoxical. The benefits of the new system, as compared with the old, are conceded. And the appellants recognize that, under the pre-1964 system, Schilb's particular bail bond cost would have been 10% of his bail, or $75; that this premium price for his pretrial freedom, once paid, was irretrievable; and that, if he could not have raised the $75, he would have been consigned to jail until his trial. Thus, under the old system, the cost of Schilb's pretrial freedom was $75, but under the new it was only $7.50. While acknowledging this obvious benefit of the statutory reform, Schilb and his co-appellants decry the classification the statutes make and

present the usual argument that the legislation must be struck down because it does not reform enough.

. . . "The Equal Protection Clause requires more of a state law than non-discriminatory application within the class it establishes. It also imposes a requirement of some rationality in the nature of the class singled out. To be sure, the constitutional demand is not a demand that a statute necessarily apply equally to all persons. 'The Constitution does not require things which are different in fact . . . to be treated in law as though they were the same.' Hence, legislation may impose special burdens upon defined classes in order to achieve permissible ends. But the Equal Protection Clause does require that, in defining a class subject to legislation, the distinctions that are drawn have 'some relevance to the purpose for which the classification is made.'"

. . . The poor man-affluent man argument centers, of course, in *Griffin v. Illinois,* . . . (1956), and in the many later cases that "reaffirm allegiance to the basic command that justice be applied equally to all persons."

In no way do we withdraw today from the *Griffin* principle . . . The situation, therefore, wholly apart from the fact that appellant Schilb himself has not pleaded indigency, is not one where we may assume that the Illinois plan works to deny relief to the poor man merely because of his poverty.

. . . We refrain from nullifying this Illinois statute that, with its companion sections, has brought reform and needed relief to the State's bail system.

[MR. JUSTICE BRENNAN delivered the opinion of the Court] In this case, we are asked to reconsider prior decisions holding that the privilege against self-incrimination is not safeguarded against state action by the Fourteenth Amendment.[25]

. . . The petitioner was arrested during a gambling raid in 1959 by Hartford, Connecticut, police. He pleaded guilty to the crime of pool selling, a misdemeanor, and was sentenced to one year in jail and fined $500. The sentence was ordered to be suspended after 90 days, at which time he was to be placed on probation for two years. About 16 months after his guilty plea, petitioner was ordered to testify before a referee appointed by the Superior Court of Hartford County to conduct an inquiry into alleged gambling and other criminal activities in the county. The petitioner was asked a number of questions related to events surrounding his arrest and conviction. He refused to answer any question "on the grounds it may tend to incriminate me." The Superior Court adjudged him in contempt, and committed him to prison until he was willing to answer the questions. Petitioner's application for a writ of habeas corpus was denied by the Superior Court, and the Connecticut Supreme Court of Errors affirmed . . . The latter court held that the Fifth Amendment's privilege against self-incrimination was not available to a witness in a state proceeding, that the Fourteenth Amendment extended no privilege to him, and that the petitioner had not properly invoked the privilege available under the Connecticut Constitution. We granted certiorari . . . We reverse. We hold that the Fourteenth Amendment guaranteed the petitioner the protection of the Fifth Amendment's privilege against self-incrimination and that, under the applicable federal standard, the Connecticut Supreme Court of Errors erred in holding that the privilege was not properly invoked.

. . . The extent to which the Fourteenth Amendment prevents state invasion of rights enumerated in the first eight Amendments has been considered in numerous cases in this Court since the Amendment's adoption in 1868. Although many Justices have deemed the Amendment to incorporate all eight of the Amendments . . . the view which has thus far prevailed dates from the decision in 1897 in *Chicago, B. & Q. R. Co. v. Chicago,* . . . which held that the Due Process Clause requires the States to pay just compensation for private property taken for public use. . . . It was on the authority of that decision that the Court said in 1908, in *Twining v. New Jersey, supra,* that "it is possible that some of the personal rights safeguarded by the first eight Amendments against National action may also be safeguarded against state action because a denial of them would be a denial of due process of law."

. . . The Court has not hesitated to reexamine past decisions according the Fourteenth Amendment a less central role in the preservation of basic liberties than that which was contemplated by its Framers when they added the Amendment to our constitutional scheme. . . .

Court held that, in the light of later decisions . . . it was taken as settled that ". . . the Fourth Amendment's right of privacy has been declared enforceable against the States through the Due Process Clause of the Fourteenth."

We hold today that the Fifth Amendment's exception from compulsory self-incrimination is also protected by the Fourteenth Amendment against abridgment by the States . . . We discuss first the decisions which forbid the use of coerced confessions in state criminal prosecutions . . . "[i]n criminal trials in the courts of the United States, wherever a question arises whether a confession is incompetent because not voluntary, the issue is controlled by that portion of the Fifth Amendment to the Constitution of the United States commanding that no person 'shall be compelled in any criminal case to be a witness against himself.'"

. . . Under this test, the constitutional inquiry is not whether the conduct of state officers in obtaining the confession was shocking, but whether the confession was "free and voluntary: that is, [it] must not be extracted by any sort of threats or violence, nor obtained by any direct or implied promises, however slight, nor by the exertion of any improper influence."

In other words, the person must not have been compelled to incriminate himself. We have held inadmissible even a confession secured by so mild a whip as the refusal, under certain circumstances, to allow a suspect to call

his wife until he confessed . . . The marked shift to the federal standard in state cases began with *Lisenba v. California* . . . where the Court spoke of the accused's "free choice to admit, to deny or to refuse to answer" . . . The shift reflects recognition that the American system of criminal prosecution is accusatorial, not inquisitorial, and that the Fifth Amendment privilege is its essential mainstay.

Governments, state and federal, are thus constitutionally compelled to establish guilt by evidence independently and freely secured, and may not, by coercion, prove a charge against an accused out of his own mouth. Since the Fourteenth Amendment prohibits the States from inducing a person to confess through "sympathy falsely aroused" . . . or other like inducement far short of "compulsion by torture," . . . it follows *a fortiori* that it also forbids the States to resort to imprisonment, as here, to compel him to answer questions that might incriminate him. The Fourteenth Amendment secures against state invasion the same privilege that the Fifth Amendment guarantees against federal infringement—the right of a person to remain silent unless he chooses to speak in the unfettered exercise of his own will, and to suffer no penalty, as held in *Twining,* for such silence.

This conclusion is fortified by our recent decision in *Mapp v. Ohio,* . . . which had held "that, . . . as to the Federal Government, the Fourth and Fifth Amendments, and, as to the States, the freedom from unconscionable invasions of privacy and the freedom from convictions based upon coerced confessions, do enjoy an 'intimate relation' in their perpetuation of 'principles of humanity and civil liberty [secured] . . . only after years of struggle[.]'

The philosophy of each Amendment and of each freedom is complementary to, although not dependent upon, that of the other in its sphere of influence—the very least that, together, they assure in either sphere is that no man is to be convicted on unconstitutional evidence." . . .

The respondent Sheriff concedes in his brief that, under our decisions, particularly those involving coerced confessions, "the accusatorial system has become a fundamental part of the fabric of our society and, hence, is enforceable against the States." . . . The State urges, however, that the availability of the federal privilege to a witness in a state inquiry is to be determined according to a less stringent standard than is applicable in a federal proceeding. We disagree. . . . In the coerced confession cases, involving the policies of the privilege itself, there has been no suggestion that a confession might be considered coerced if used in a federal, but not a state, tribunal. The Court thus has rejected the notion that the Fourteenth Amendment applies to the States only a "watered-down, subjective version of the individual guarantees of the Bill of Rights" . . . What is accorded is a privilege of refusing to incriminate one's self, and the feared prosecution may be by either federal or state authorities . . . It would be incongruous to have different standards

determine the validity of a claim of privilege based on the same feared prosecution depending on whether the claim was asserted in a state or federal
court. Therefore, the same standards must determine whether an accused's
silence in either a federal or state proceeding is justified.

. . . The conclusions of the Court of Errors, tested by the federal standard,
fail to take sufficient account of the setting in which the questions were asked.
The interrogation was part of a wide-ranging inquiry into crime, including
gambling, in Hartford. It was admitted on behalf of the State at oral argument—and indeed it is obvious from the questions themselves—that the
State desired to elicit from the petitioner the identity of the person who ran
the pool-selling operation in connection with which he had been arrested in
1959. It was apparent that petitioner might apprehend that, if this person were
still engaged in unlawful activity, disclosure of his name might furnish a link
in a chain of evidence sufficient to connect the petitioner with a more recent
crime for which he might still be prosecuted. . . .

[MR. JUSTICE HARLAN, whom MR. JUSTICE CLARK joins, dis-
senting] Connecticut has adjudged this petitioner in contempt for refusing
to answer questions in a state inquiry. The courts of the State, whose laws
embody a privilege against self-incrimination, refused to recognize the petitioner's claim of privilege, finding that the questions asked him were not
incriminatory. This Court now holds the contempt adjudication unconstitutional because, it is decided: (1) the Fourteenth Amendment makes the Fifth
Amendment privilege against self-incrimination applicable to the States; (2)
the federal standard justifying a claim of this privilege likewise applies to
the States, and (3) judged by that standard the petitioner's claim of privilege
should have been upheld.

. . . While it is true that the Court deals today with only one aspect of state
criminal procedure, and rejects the wholesale "incorporation" of such federal
constitutional requirements, the logical gap between the Court's premises and
its novel constitutional conclusion can, I submit, be bridged only by the additional premise that the Due Process Clause of the Fourteenth Amendment is a
shorthand directive to this Court to pick and choose among the provisions of
the first eight Amendments and apply those chosen, freighted with their entire
accompanying body of federal doctrine, to law enforcement in the States.

I accept and agree with the proposition that continuing reexamination of
the constitutional conception of Fourteenth Amendment "due process" of
law is required, and that development of the community's sense of justice
may, in time, lead to expansion of the protection which due process affords.
In particular, in this case, I agree that principles of justice to which due process gives expression, as reflected in decisions of this Court, prohibit a State,
as the Fifth Amendment prohibits the Federal Government, from imprisoning
a person *solely* because he refuses to give evidence which may incriminate

him under the laws of the State . . . I do not understand, however, how this process of reexamination, which must refer always to the guiding standard of due process of law, including, of course, reference to the particular guarantees of the Bill of Rights, can be short-circuited by the simple device of incorporating into due process, without critical examination, the whole body of law which surrounds a specific prohibition directed against the Federal Government. The consequence of such an approach to due process as it pertains to the States is inevitably disregard of all relevant differences which may exist between state and federal criminal law and its enforcement. The ultimate result is compelled uniformity, which is inconsistent with the purpose of our federal system and which is achieved either by encroachment on the States' sovereign powers or by dilution in federal law enforcement of the specific protections found in the Bill of Rights.

. . . The Court's undiscriminating approach to the Due Process Clause carries serious implications for the sound working of our federal system in the field of criminal law.

The Court concludes, almost without discussion that "the same standards must determine whether an accused's silence in either a federal or state proceeding is justified." About all that the Court offers in explanation of this conclusion is the observation that it would be "incongruous" if different standards governed the assertion of a privilege to remain silent in state and federal tribunals. Such "incongruity," however, is at the heart of our federal system. The powers and responsibilities of the state and federal governments are not congruent; under our Constitution, they are not intended to be. Why should it be thought, as an *a priori* matter, that limitations on the investigative power of the States are, in all respects, identical with limitations on the investigative power of the Federal Government? This certainly does not follow from the fact that we deal here with constitutional requirements, for the provisions of the Constitution which are construed are different.

As the Court pointed out in *Abbate v. United States* . . . "the States, under our federal system, have the principal responsibility for defining and prosecuting crimes." The Court endangers this allocation of responsibility for the prevention of crime when it applies to the States doctrines developed in the context of federal law enforcement without any attention to the special problems which the States, as a group or particular States, may face. If the power of the States to deal with local crime is unduly restricted, the likely consequence is a shift of responsibility in this area to the Federal Government, with its vastly greater resources. Such a shift, if it occurs, may, in the end, serve to weaken the very liberties which the Fourteenth Amendment safeguards by bringing us closer to the monolithic society which our federalism rejects. Equally dangerous to our liberties is the alternative of watering down protections against the Federal Government embodied in the Bill of Rights so as not

unduly to restrict the powers of the States . . . Rather than insisting, almost
by rote, that the Connecticut court, in considering the petitioner's claim of
privilege, was required to apply the "federal standard," the Court should have
fulfilled its responsibility under the Due Process Clause by inquiring whether
the proceedings below met the demands of fundamental fairness which due
process embodies. Such an approach may not satisfy those who see in the
Fourteenth Amendment a set of easily applied "absolutes" which can afford a
haven from unsettling doubt. It is, however, truer to the spirit which requires
this Court constantly to reexamine fundamental principles and, at the same
time, enjoins it from reading its own preferences into the Constitution.

NOTES

1. *Gitlow v. People of New York, 268 U.S. 652 (1925).*
2. *Near v. Minnesota, 283 U.S. 697 (1931).*
3. *DeJonge v. Oregon, 299 U.S. 353 (1937).*
4. *Everson v. Board of Education, 330 U.S. 1 (1947).*
5. *Edwards v. South Carolina, 372 U.S. 229 (1963).*
6. Joseph Story, *Commentaries on the Constitution,* 3 vols (Boston: Hillard, Gray, and Company, 1833), 3: 746–748.
7. *United States v. Cruikshank, 92 U.S. 542 (1875).*
8. *Presser v. Illinois, 116 U.S. 252 (1886).*
9. *Hamilton v. Regents of University of California, 293 U.S. 245 (1934).*
10. *United States v. Miller, 307 U.S. 174 (1939).*
11. *McDonald v. Chicago 561 U.S. 742 (2010).*
12. *Mapp v. Ohio, 367 U.S. 643 (1961).*
13. *Chicago, B. & Q. R. Co. v. Chicago, 166 U.S. 226 (1897).*
14. *Malloy v. Hogan, 378 U.S. 1 (1964).*
15. *Benton v. Maryland, 395 U.S. 784 (1969).*
16. *In re Oliver, 333 U.S. 257 (1948).*
17. *Gideon v. Wainwright, 372 U.S. 335 (1963).*
18. *Pointer v. Texas, 380 U.S. 400 (1965).*
19. *Parker v. Gladden, 385 U.S. 363 (1966).*
20. *Klopfer v. North Carolina, 386 U.S. 213 (1967).*
21. *Washington v. Texas, 388 U.S. 14 (1967).*
22. *Minneapolis & St. Louis R. Co. v. Bombolis, 241 U.S. 211 (1916).*
23. *Robinson v. California, 370 U.S. 660 (1962).*
24. *Schilb v. Kuebel, 404 U.S. 357 (1971).*
25. *Malloy v. Hogan, 378 U.S. 1 (1964).*

Index

About the Editors

Aaron N. Coleman is Associate Professor of History and Chair of the History and Political Science Department at the University of the Cumberlands. Aaron received his PhD in early American history from the University of Kentucky. He is the author of *The American Revolution, State Sovereignty, and the American Constitutional Settlement, 1765–1800* (Lexington Books, 2016). Aaron lives in Williamsburg, KY, with his wife, Dr. Emily Coleman, and their two children.

Christopher S. Leskiw is Professor of Political Science and Vice President for Academic Affairs at the University of the Cumberlands. He received his PhD in International Politics from Vanderbilt University. He resides in Williamsburg, KY, with his wife and two boys.